Oleg Sych

ASP.NET
Dynamic Data

UNLEASHED

SAMS | 800 East 96th Street, Indianapolis, Indiana 46240 USA

ASP.NET Dynamic Data Unleashed

Copyright © 2012 by Pearson Education, Inc.

ISBN-13: 978-0-6723-3565-5

ISBN-10: 0-672-33565-4

Library of Congress Cataloging-in-Publication Data is on file.

Printed in the United States of America

First Printing: May 2012

Trademarks

Warning and Disclaimer

Bulk Sales

Pearson offers excellent discounts on this book when ordered in quantity for bulk purchases or special sales. For more information, please contact:

U.S. Corporate and Government Sales
1-800-382-3419
corpsales@pearsontechgroup.com

For sales outside of the U.S., please contact:

International Sales
+1-317-581-3793
international@pearsontechgroup.com

Editor-in-Chief
Greg Wiegand

Executive Editor
Neil Rowe

Development Editor
Mark Renfrow

Managing Editor
Kristy Hart

Project Editor
Anne Goebel

Copy Editor
Christal White,
Language Logistics,
LLC

Indexer
Christine Karpeles

Proofreader
Sarah Kearns

Technical Editors
Scott Hunter
David Ebbo

Publishing Coordinator
Cindy Teeters

Cover Designer
Gary Adair

Senior Compositor
Gloria Schurick

Contents at a Glance

Table of Contents

About the Author

Oleg Sych has been working as a professional software engineer since 1993, building distributed enterprise applications since 2000, and leading development teams since 2002. Between 2009 and 2011, Oleg received several MVP awards from Microsoft in C# and Visual Studio ALM categories. His professional interests include agile software architecture and development process. In his spare time, Oleg is trying to learn how to ski, play tennis, and raise teenage boys.

Dedication

To Tanyusha, Gleb, and Nickita. I am nothing without you.

Acknowledgments

This book would not be possible without help from Brook Farling, Scott Hunter, David Ebbo, Neil Rowe, and Sven Aelterman. Thank you!

We Want to Hear from You!

As the reader of this book, *you* are our most important critic and commentator. We value your opinion and want to know what we're doing right, what we could do better, what areas you'd like to see us publish in, and any other words of wisdom you're willing to pass our way.

You can email or write me directly to let me know what you did or didn't like about this book—as well as what we can do to make our books stronger.

Please note that I cannot help you with technical problems related to the topic of this book, and that due to the high volume of mail I receive, I might not be able to reply to every message.

When you write, please be sure to include this book's title and author as well as your name and phone or email address. I will carefully review your comments and share them with the author and editors who worked on the book.

Email: feedback@samspublishing.com

Mail: Neil Rowe
         Executive Editor
         Sams Publishing
         800 East 96th Street
         Indianapolis, IN 46240 USA

Reader Services

Visit our website and register this book at informit.com/register for convenient access to any updates, downloads, or errata that might be available for this book.

Preface

Most of the web applications that exist today work with data. From a simple guest book page on a personal website, to a large product catalog of an online retailer, to customer relationship management (CRM) and enterprise resource planning (ERP) systems—applications help people work with data. Working with data means dealing with *CRUD*. Every database application must allow users to Create, Read (or Retrieve), Update, and Delete records. A product catalog will not be functional unless users can add new products to the catalog, search for and retrieve existing products, update product information, and delete discontinued products from the catalog. Of course, a product catalog rarely exists by itself; it is usually a part of a larger e-commerce system, which has to support all CRUD operations not only for products, but also for customers, suppliers, shipping companies, orders, and more.

Implementing each type of CRUD operation requires some form of *presentation, business,* and *data access logic.* Implementing them in your applications usually requires a lot of repetition. Data access logic for products is similar to data access logic for customers, as well as suppliers and shipping companies. You write SQL or .NET code (or both) to insert, select, update, and delete database records. Presentation logic for products is also similar to presentation logic for customers, suppliers, and shipping companies. You create ASP.NET pages with text boxes, drop-down lists, validation controls, links, and buttons. What truly distinguishes the different types of entities is their purpose—the business logic they represent. The *Product* entity has attributes such as description, price, picture, and rules that define how to validate product names, what to do when a new product is added to the catalog, or when an existing product is discontinued. The *Customer* entity has different attributes—first name, last name, credit card numbers—and rules that define what to do when a customer changes his billing address or requests to close his account.

Understanding the business logic, a developer can usually figure out how to implement the required data access and presentation logic. The resulting application might not look very pretty, but it will perform its business function. The ASP.NET framework provided all building blocks required for implementing database applications, and although it made web developers a lot more productive, it offered little assistance with the repetitive coding of CRUD operations and made it easy for them to fall into the trap of code reuse by copy and paste. It is unfortunate that a typical ASP.NET application has numerous web pages full of validators and code-behind files where data access code is intermixed with business logic.

There are many techniques for reducing code duplication. In ASP.NET, user controls are an excellent way to extract common presentation logic and reuse it in multiple pages. Patterns, such as Domain Model and Active Record (Fowler, 2002), can be used to encapsulate business and data access logic in application code. Some developers also choose to use stored procedures and implement this logic in database code instead. Separation of the business and data access code from the presentation code allows you to reuse it in multiple web pages without duplication. However, implementing business and data access layers requires more forethought, expertise, and commitment from developers. To be effective, these techniques must be introduced in the application architecture early. Retrofitting them to an existing application requires a lot of refactoring (Fowler, et al., 1999) and can be very costly. It is not unusual for such a refactoring effort to be longer than the initial application implementation itself.

For .NET developers, introduction of LINQ in version 3.5 was a major leap forward. LINQ to SQL and Entity Framework combined the simplicity of *Language-Integrated Queries* with the sophistication of *Metadata Mapping* (Fowler, 2002), making the Domain Model pattern available for mainstream .NET projects. In ASP.NET, both Dynamic Data and MVC can take advantage of the metadata exposed by the LINQ-based frameworks and generate controls or entire pages in ASP.NET applications based on the domain model. Together, these frameworks give web developers powerful, robust, and easy-to-use tools and guidance for implementing data access, business, and presentation logic while reducing code duplication and improving code reuse.

ASP.NET WebForms (with Dynamic Data extensions) and MVC are complementary frameworks that offer unique advantages for different types of web applications. Dynamic Data is a great fit for applications with a large number of similar data-oriented screens, while MVC works better for a small number of unique screens. Most real-world web application projects can benefit from both. Early in the project, Dynamic Data gives you a working user interface, which you can use to discuss the domain model with the business users. As you contine to evolve our understanding of the domain and change the model, Dynamic Data will automatically regenerate the user interface at run time, without forcing you to create and maintain custom web pages. When the domain model is more stable, you can decide which pages have unique requirements and have to be customized. In the end, you may end up replacing some of the web pages with MVC views built on top of the same underlying business and data access logic. The resulting web application can be a mix of a large number of web pages generated by Dynamic Data for maintaining reference data and a small number of unique, public-facing pages implemented in MVC.

The initial version of ASP.NET Dynamic Data, released as part of the .NET Framework 3.5 Service Pack 1, suffered from some short-term limitations and a lingering problem of perception. The fully-featured version, released with the .NET Framework 4, received very little publicity from Microsoft and the developer community focused its attention on the MVC framework instead. This is unfortunate because according to Microsoft's research at the time of this writing, 80% of existing ASP.NET applications are built with WebForms and could take advantage of the productivity improvements Dynamic Data extensions offer without requiring a rewrite in MVC.

This book is meant to correct some of the perceptions, fill the information gap, and help you see Dynamic Data for what it is—a useful tool in the ASP.NET developer's toolbox. The first part offers an in-depth look at the Dynamic Data building blocks, shows how they can be used individually to make routine WebForms programming tasks easier, and explains how the components fit together to make dynamic generation of entire pages and websites possible. The second part explains how to solve real-world problems—implementing business logic while keeping it separate from the presentation, extending Dynamic Data components and metadata to make them even more powerful, and much more. I hope you find it useful.

Oleg Sych
February 2012
Oldsmar, Florida

PART I

Dynamic Data Fundamentals

IN THIS PART

Getting Started

Dynamic Data is an extension of the ASP.NET WebForms framework. It includes a number of new controls for rendering common UI elements dynamically, including data entry fields, forms, lists, and search criteria. These controls complement the standard ASP.NET controls—GridView, FormView, DetailsView, and ListView and serve as building blocks for creating new or improving existing web pages.

Dynamic controls are not a black box. They rely on templates included in the Web projects and can be customized by developers. At run time, the dynamic controls rely on *metadata* to locate and render the templates appropriate for a particular model element. For example, when rendering a data entry control for a foreign key column, Dynamic Data chooses a template with a drop-down list. However, when rendering control for a string column, it chooses a template with a text box.

Dynamic Data supports a number of existing LINQ-based data models, including LINQ to SQL and Entity Framework. In addition to the powerful and easy-to-use data access functionality, these frameworks also provide rich metadata APIs that get you detailed information about tables in the data model, including their names, attributes, data types, and relationships. Because these APIs are different, Dynamic Data provides its own metadata API that hides the inconsistencies and exposes information most relevant to user interface development. This approach helps to keep the user interface code largely independent from the underlying data access framework. With the exception of the many-to-many field template, unique to the Entity Framework, most of the dynamic templates work equally well with both LINQ to SQL and Entity Framework, allowing developers to reuse the templates between different web applications or change the data access framework without rewriting the presentation logic.

In addition to the data entry controls, Dynamic Data also takes advantage of the URL routing to generate entire websites based on the metadata exposed by the data model and the page templates defined by the developer. Out of the box, Dynamic Data web applications already support common operations such as creating a new entity, displaying a list of entities based on search criteria, or changing or deleting an existing entity. These pages are fully functional and integrated in the application; they can handle different column types and include validation and error handling logic.

Dynamic Data is backward compatible with non-LINQ-based data access frameworks, such as the traditional ADO.NET with DataSets, as well as custom business objects. With very little effort, developers can extend existing WebForms applications to take advantage of the rich field templating capabilities. Unfortunately, page templating and dynamic search capabilities are currently supported only with LINQ-based frameworks and discussion of Dynamic Data without them would not be complete.

NOTE

Although it shares many common elements with the ASP.NET MVC framework, including LINQ-based data models and data annotation attributes, Dynamic Data has several distinct advantages. It works with existing WebForms applications and does not require web developers to introduce a completely new presentation framework. Unlike MVC, it supports dynamic rendering of UI elements not only at the field level, but also at the entity and page levels, which can significantly reduce the amount of code developers have to write and maintain. Moreover, Dynamic Data's ability to generate complex LINQ queries at runtime, based on the search criteria entered by the user, has no direct equivalent in MVC.

Dynamic Data is ideal for implementing maintenance and administration pages in web applications as it supports most of the functionality they require out of the box. However, the biggest advantage Dynamic Data offers is a higher degree of code reuse. The resulting consistency of user interface across different screens and entities is especially important in customer-facing pages of web applications.

Creating a New Dynamic Data Application

Visual Studio 2010 includes two different flavors of project templates for Dynamic Data:

▶   ASP.NET Dynamic Data Entities

▶   ASP.NET Dynamic Data LINQ to SQL

Figure 1.1 shows how these templates appear in the New Web Site dialog of Visual Studio. These project templates are nearly identical, and you should choose one based on the data access technology you want to use. If your project, like the sample project accompanying this book, uses Entity Framework, choose the *ASP.NET Dynamic Data Entities* project flavor.

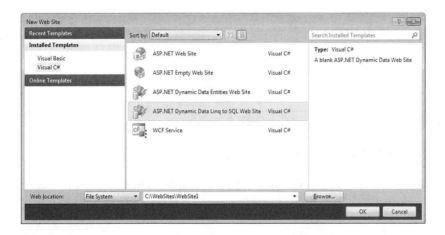

FIGURE 1.1   Dynamic Data website templates.

You can choose either Visual Basic or Visual C# flavors of the Dynamic Data project templates depending on your language preference. Aside from Visual Basic being slightly more verbose than C# when it comes to defining lambda expressions, both languages work equally well.

In Visual Studio, you also have a choice of creating either a *Web Application* project or a *Web Site*. A Web *Site* is simply a folder that contains page (.aspx), control (.ascx), and code-behind files. This type of Visual Studio project is appropriate for web applications where content is stored primarily in the page files, as it enables developers to change and deploy one page at a time. A Web *Application* project, on the other hand, is more appropriate for applications where content is stored primarily in a database and the page files contain only the logic required to retrieve and display it.

Although Dynamic Data offers both Web Site and Web Application project templates, its intent fits closer with the Web Application project model. Figure 1.2 shows the Dynamic Data project templates in the New Project dialog of Visual Studio. The sample project accompanying this book is based on the *ASP.NET Dynamic Data Entities Web Application* project template.

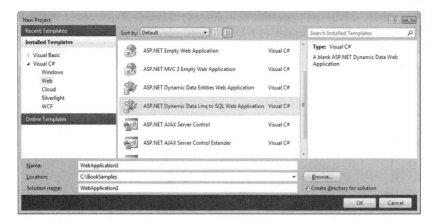

FIGURE 1.2 Dynamic Data Web Application project templates.

Figure 1.3 shows an example of a new Dynamic Data web application project, which as you can see, is similar to a regular Web Application project; it includes a default master page (Site.master), a cascading style sheet (Site.css), and a landing page (Default.aspx). However, it is not quite ready to run.

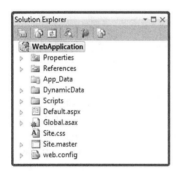

FIGURE 1.3 Dynamic Data Web Application project.

Creating a Data Model

Your first task after creating a new Dynamic Data project is to create a data model. Because the sample project in this book is based on Entity Framework, you would choose the *ADO.NET Entity Data Model* template from the Data folder in the Add New Item dialog (see Figure 1.4).

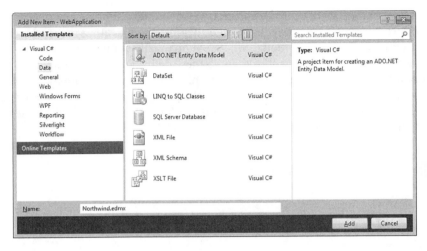

FIGURE 1.4 Data model templates.

The data model includes some or all tables in a single database, so when naming the data model file, it is a good idea to use the name of the database it will represent. In this book, Northwind sample database is used, and the entity data model file is *Northwind.edmx*.

NOTE

The Northwind sample database for SQL Server is available for download from Microsoft at the following address:

http://www.microsoft.com/downloads/en/details.aspx?FamilyID=06616212-0356-46a0-8da2-eebc53a68034

Originally developed for SQL Server 2000, it works with versions 2005 and 2008.

The installation program, SQL2000SampleDb.msi, extracts the database files and scripts in the "C:\SQL Server 2000 Sample Databases" directory on your computer. You can create the Northwind database by running the following commands in the Command Prompt window:

```
c:
cd "SQL Server 2000 Sample Databases"
sqlcmd -S .\sqlexpress -E -i instnwnd.sql
```

Note that in this example, -S .\sqlexpress refers to a local installation of the Express edition of SQL Server. If you have a default installation of the Developer or another edition on your computer, you need to change this parameter to . or specify the actual name your SQL Server.

When a new entity data model is added to the project, Visual Studio automatically opens the Entity Data Model Wizard that guides you through the process of creating the model. You can choose to create an empty data model, where you manually define new entities, specify their properties and associations, and then map these definitions to the storage definitions imported from a database later. However, in this example, you choose the option to generate the model from the database. After prompting you to enter the connection string, the wizard displays the page shown in Figure 1.5 for you to select the database tables, views, and stored procedures to be included in the model.

FIGURE 1.5 Entity Data Model Wizard.

In this example, you want to include all database tables in the model. The resulting Northwind entity data model, after some cleanup to improve readability, is shown in Figure 1.6.

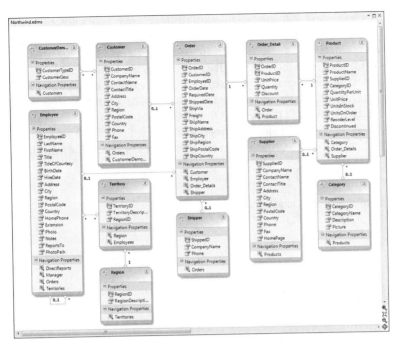

FIGURE 1.6 Northwind data model.

Entity Framework allows you to write strongly typed database queries using C# and Visual Basic code as opposed to traditional T-SQL statements embedded in string constants or literals. Consider an ASP.NET page in Listing 1.1 that displays database records in a GridView control.

LISTING 1.1 Entity Framework Sample (Markup)

```
<%@ Page Language="C#"
  MasterPageFile="~/Site.master" CodeBehind="SamplePage.aspx.cs"
  Inherits="WebApplication.Samples.Ch01.AdoNet.SamplePage" %>

<asp:Content ContentPlaceHolderID="main" runat="server">
  <asp:GridView ID="gridView" runat="server" />
</asp:Content>
```

Aside from relying on Site.master, the default master page provided by the Dynamic Data project template, this page is very simple and has only one GridView control.

In the code-behind shown in Listing 1.2, the NorthwindEntities class is generated by Visual Studio based on the information in the Northwind.edmx in this project. This class encapsulates the database connection and allows you to use LINQ (language-integrated query) to select records from the Customers table. LINQ resembles the traditional SQL syntax to which many database developers are accustomed. It is usually a little more compact, but more importantly, it is safer and easier to maintain. The Entity Framework automatically generates parameterized SQL queries, eliminating SQL injection vulnerabilities, and allows the compiler to check the query correctness and find typos in table and column names that would otherwise go unnoticed until the query is executed at run time.

The resulting web page is shown in Figure 1.7.

LISTING 1.2 Entity Framework Sample (Code-Behind)

```
using System;
using System.Linq;
using DataModel;

namespace WebApplication.Samples.Ch01.EntityFramework
{
  public partial class SamplePage : System.Web.UI.Page
  {
    protected void Page_Load(object sender, EventArgs e)
    {
      using (NorthwindEntities context = new NorthwindEntities())
      {
        var query = from c in context.Customers
                    select c;

        this.gridView.DataSource = query.ToList();
        this.gridView.DataBind();
      }
    }
  }
}
```

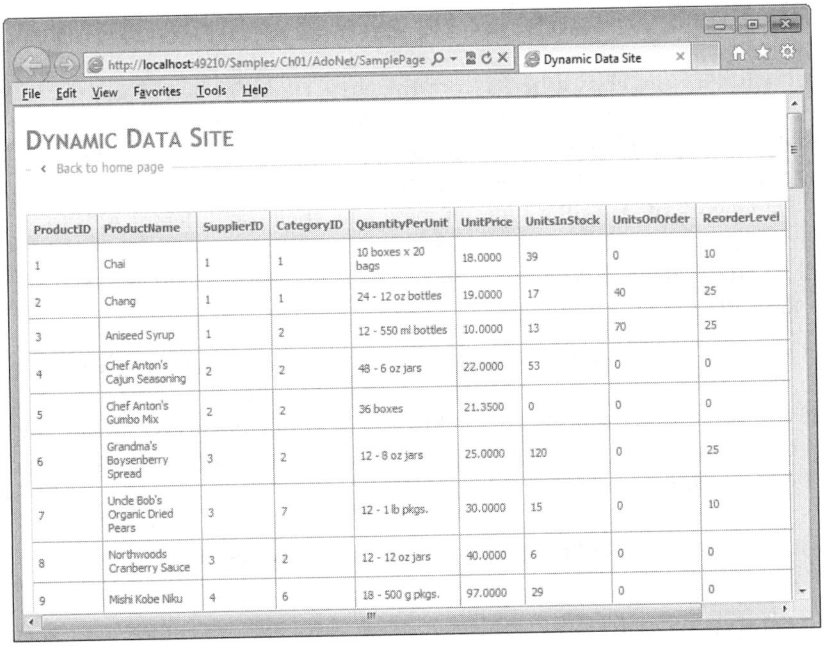

FIGURE 1.7 GridView with customer records from the Northwind Database.

ASP.NET also provides a *data source control* designed to work with Entity Framework. Data source controls encapsulate the database operations needed by typical CRUD screens and allow you to implement them declaratively, using markup instead of code. By changing the previous example to use the `EntityDataSource`, you eliminate the code-behind file while keeping functionality of the page intact.

LISTING 1.3 EntityDataSource Sample (Markup)

```
<%@ Page Language="C#" MasterPageFile="~/Site.master" %>

<asp:Content ContentPlaceHolderID="main" runat="server">
  <asp:GridView ID="gridView" DataSourceID="dataSource" runat="server" />
  <asp:EntityDataSource ID="dataSource" runat="server"
    ConnectionString="name=NorthwindEntities"
    DefaultContainerName="NorthwindEntities" EntitySetName="Customers" />
</asp:Content>
```

The page in Listing 1.3 has an `EntityDataSource` control configured to access the Customers table from the NorthwindEntities data model. The `GridView` control is now data-bound declaratively, using the `DataSourceID` attribute, which contains the ID of the `EntityDataSource` control.

Metadata in Entity Framework and Dynamic Data

The generated NorthwindEntities class inherits from the `ObjectContext` base class provided by Entity Framework. This class, as well as its LINQ to SQL counterpart, `DataContext`, provides access to rich metadata describing all tables in the data model, including their names, columns, data types, associations, and more. Although both LINQ to SQL and Entity Framework offer similar types of metadata, they use different APIs to represent it. Dynamic Data encapsulates these differences, provides a single metadata API that works for both of these frameworks, and extends it with presentation metadata, such as display labels and validation error messages.

Rich metadata API enables Dynamic Data web applications to generate user interface elements such as data entry fields, forms, and entire pages at runtime, all based on the definitions derived from the database and extended by the developer. However, before the web application can access this metadata, the data context class needs to be registered in the application Global.asax file as in Listing 1.4.

LISTING 1.4   Registering Data Model with Dynamic Data in Global.asax.cs

```csharp
using System;
using System.Data.Entity;
using System.Web.DynamicData;
using DataModel;

namespace WebApplication
{
  public class Global : System.Web.HttpApplication
  {
    public static readonly MetaModel DefaultModel = new MetaModel();

    void Application_Start(object sender, EventArgs e)
    {
      DefaultModel.RegisterContext(typeof(NorthwindEntities));
    }
  }
}
```

Field Templates and Dynamic Controls

Dynamic Data field templates take advantage of the metadata and make it easier to implement data entry controls and validation logic for individual fields or columns in tables exposed by the data model. Listing 1.5 shows an example of a simple edit page implemented using field templates.

LISTING 1.5   DynamicControl and Field Template Sample (Markup)

```
<%@ Page Language="C#"
  MasterPageFile="~/Site.master" CodeBehind="SamplePage.aspx.cs"
  Inherits="WebApplication.Samples.Ch01.FieldTemplate.SamplePage" %>

<asp:Content ContentPlaceHolderID="main" runat="server">
  <asp:ValidationSummary runat="server" />
  <asp:FormView ID="formView" runat="server" DataSourceID="dataSource"
    DataKeyNames="ProductID" DefaultMode="Edit">
    <EditItemTemplate>
      Product Name:
      <asp:DynamicControl DataField="ProductName" Mode="Edit" runat="server" />
      <br />
      Units in Stock:
      <asp:DynamicControl DataField="UnitsInStock" Mode="Edit" runat="server" />
      <br />
      <asp:LinkButton Text="Update" CommandName="Update" runat="server" />
    </EditItemTemplate>
  </asp:FormView>
  <asp:EntityDataSource ID="dataSource" runat="server"
    ConnectionString="name=NorthwindEntities" EnableUpdate="true"
    DefaultContainerName="NorthwindEntities" EntitySetName="Products" />
</asp:Content>
```

DynamicControl is a new ASP.NET control provided by Dynamic Data. Based on the MetaTable associated with its FormView, as well as its own DataField and Mode properties, this control selects an appropriate *field template* from the *FieldTemplates* folder of the Dynamic Data project shown in Figure 1.8. For the ProductName and UnitsInStock fields in this example, the dynamic controls will select the Text_Edit.ascx and Integer_Edit.ascx templates, respectively.

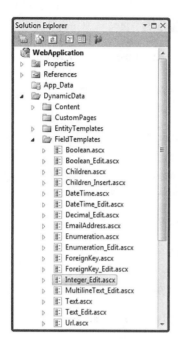

FIGURE 1.8   Dynamic Data field templates.

The last bit of magic this page needs is a Page_Init event handler in the code-behind to associate a MetaTable object describing the Products table with the FormView control, as shown in Listing 1.6.

LISTING 1.6   DynamicControl and Field Template Sample (Code-Behind)

```
using System;
using System.Web.DynamicData;

namespace WebApplication.Samples.Ch01.FieldTemplate
{
  public partial class SamplePage : System.Web.UI.Page
  {
    protected void Page_Init(object sender, EventArgs e)
    {
      MetaTable table = Global.DefaultModel.GetTable(this.dataSource.EntitySetName);
      this.formView.SetMetaTable(table);
    }
  }
}
```

The resulting web page rendered at runtime is shown in Figure 1.9.

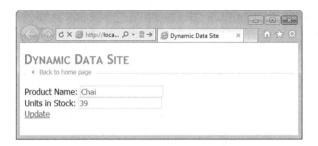

FIGURE 1.9   Data entry form with field templates.

Field templates are nothing more than a special type of user controls, which should be familiar to most WebForms developers. Listing 1.7 shows the `Integer_Edit` field template after a minor cleanup to improve readability.

LISTING 1.7   Integer_Edit Field Template (Markup)

```
<%@ Control Language="C#" CodeBehind="Integer_Edit.ascx.cs"
  Inherits="WebApplication.DynamicData.FieldTemplates.Integer_EditField" %>

<asp:TextBox ID="textBox" runat="server" Text="<%# FieldValueEditString %>" />

<asp:RequiredFieldValidator runat="server" ID="requiredFieldValidator"
  ControlToValidate="textBox" Enabled="false" />
<asp:CompareValidator runat="server" ID="compareValidator"
  ControlToValidate="textBox" Operator="DataTypeCheck" Type="Integer" />
<asp:RegularExpressionValidator runat="server" ID="regularExpressionValidator"
  ControlToValidate="textBox" Enabled="false" />
<asp:RangeValidator runat="server" ID="rangeValidator"
  ControlToValidate="textBox" Type="Integer" Enabled="false"
  EnableClientScript="true" MinimumValue="0" MaximumValue="100" />
<asp:DynamicValidator runat="server" ID="dynamicValidator"
  ControlToValidate="textBox" Display="Static" />
```

As you can see, it has a TextBox control for entering the field value and a CompareValidator to prevent users from typing alphabetic symbols. This is similar to the markup you would normally write by hand to validate the UnitsInStock values. However, in the field template, all controls are initialized in the code-behind shown in Listing 1.8 based on the metadata information describing the column.

LISTING 1.8   Integer_Edit Field Template (Code-behind)

```
using System;
using System.Collections.Specialized;
using System.Web.DynamicData;
using System.Web.UI;

namespace WebApplication.DynamicData.FieldTemplates
{
  public partial class Integer_EditField : FieldTemplateUserControl
  {
    public override Control DataControl
    {
      get { return this.textBox; }
    }

    protected void Page_Load(object sender, EventArgs e)
    {
      this.textBox.ToolTip = this.Column.Description;

      this.SetUpValidator(this.requiredFieldValidator);
      this.SetUpValidator(this.compareValidator);
      this.SetUpValidator(this.regularExpressionValidator);
      this.SetUpValidator(this.rangeValidator);
      this.SetUpValidator(this.dynamicValidator);
    }

    protected override void ExtractValues(IOrderedDictionary dictionary)
    {
      dictionary[this.Column.Name] = this.ConvertEditedValue(this.textBox.Text);
    }
  }
}
```

Field templates are incredibly flexible. This particular template, Integer_Edit, can be reused for other integer columns in the Product table, such as UnitsOnOrder and ReorderLevel, as well as integer columns in all other tables in the data model. The field template will even configure the RangeValidator based on the range of values appropriate for a data type of the particular column, such as Int16 or Int32. All you need to do is place a DynamicControl on your page and specify its DataField and Mode properties.

Data Annotations

The data entry page created using dynamic controls has one significant difference compared to a page that uses traditional text boxes and validators. Notice the error message shown in Figure 1.10 includes the actual column name, *UnitsInStock*, as opposed to something like "Units in Stock" that you might expect to see in a user-friendly application. This is because the `DynamicControl` cannot infer the display name from the original column name. In this particular case, you could use capitalization of letters to split the column name into individual words, but in general, Dynamic Data cannot rely on this being the case. Your column names could use underscores, abbreviations, acronyms, or numbers that would be impossible for the framework to convert to readable English, let alone other languages you might need to support in your application.

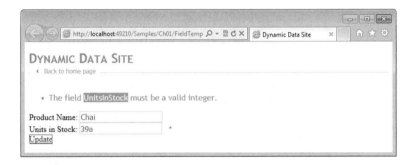

FIGURE 1.10 Dynamic data entry page with validation errors.

In traditional ASP.NET code, you would have specified the error message in page markup, using the `ErrorMessage` attribute of the `CompareValidator` control. However, in the Dynamic Data example, the `CompareValidator` resides in the `Integer_Edit` field template that can be reused for all integer columns in the data model. You cannot simply hard-code the "Units in Stock" error message there because it would make error messages for all other columns wrong. Instead, you need to extend the data model and specify a human-readable display name for the UnitsInStock column that will be used in labels and error messages presented to users.

At this time, neither Entity Framework nor LINQ to SQL allow you to specify display names for columns in the graphical designer. Instead, you need to use data annotations and extend the model in code. *Data annotations* are .NET attributes defined in the `System.Component.DataAnnotations` namespace. They can be applied to entity classes and their properties to extend table and column metadata information used by Dynamic Data. Listing 1.9 shows an example of using the `DisplayAttribute` to specify a human-readable display name for the UnitsInStock column of the Product table.

LISTING 1.9   Extending Product Metadata Using Data Annotations

```
using System;
using System.ComponentModel.DataAnnotations;

namespace DataModel
{
  [MetadataType(typeof(Product.Metadata))]
  partial class Product
  {
    public abstract class Metadata
    {
      [Display(Name = "Units in Stock")]
      public object UnitsInStock { get; set; }
    }
  }
}
```

Notice that the Product class is declared with the `partial` keyword. This effectively extends the definition of the Product entity class generated by the Entity Framework designer, making everything in this code snippet a part of the generated Product class. This is necessary because you cannot place the `DisplayAttribute` directly on the generated UnitsInStock property. Any changes made in the generated code by hand will be lost the next time the code is regenerated. Instead, you define a separate class (called *Metadata* in this example) and use the `MetadataTypeAttribute` to associate it with the entity class, Product. Any data annotation attributes placed on the properties of the Metadata class will have the same effect as if they were placed on the actual properties of the Product class, such as the UnitsInStock in this example. After making these changes, the error message displayed by the `Integer_Edit` field template when the user enters alphabetic symbols in the UnitsInStock field will include the human-readable display name.

Entity Templates

Metadata used by Dynamic Data includes not only information about individual columns, but also the information about entire tables. If you need to build a data entry page that includes all fields of the Products table, you can replace all individual `DynamicControl` instances with a single `DynamicEntity` control.

LISTING 1.10   DynamicEntity and Entity Template Sample (Markup)

```
<%@ Page Language="C#"
  MasterPageFile="~/Site.master" CodeBehind="SamplePage.aspx.cs"
  Inherits="WebApplication.Samples.Ch01.EntityTemplate.SamplePage" %>

<asp:Content runat="server" ContentPlaceHolderID="main">
```

```
<asp:ValidationSummary runat="server" />
<asp:FormView ID="formView" runat="server" DataSourceID="dataSource"
   DataKeyNames="ProductID" DefaultMode="Edit">
  <EditItemTemplate>
    <asp:DynamicEntity Mode="Edit" runat="server" />
    <tr><td>
      <asp:LinkButton Text="Update" CommandName="Update" runat="server" />
    </td></tr>
  </EditItemTemplate>
</asp:FormView>
<asp:EntityDataSource ID="dataSource" runat="server"
   ConnectionString="name=NorthwindEntities" EnableUpdate="true"
   DefaultContainerName="NorthwindEntities" EntitySetName="Products" />
</asp:Content>
```

DynamicEntity is another control provided by Dynamic Data. Based on the table associated with the FormView control to which it belongs as well as its own Mode property, the control will choose and load an appropriate entity template. With the Products table in this example, the resulting web page will look similar to the one shown in Figure 1.11.

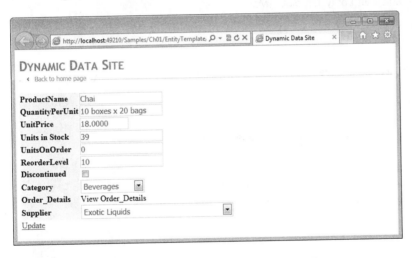

FIGURE 1.11   Dynamic Data entry page with entity template.

Out of the box, Dynamic Data project templates offer three default entity templates that implement a simple, single-column, top-down form layout. These entity templates (see Figure 1.12) are used for all types of entities by default unless the developer provides a custom template for a particular entity.

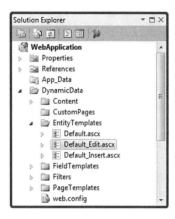

FIGURE 1.12   Entity templates in Dynamic Data project.

As you might expect, entity templates are also a special type of ASP.NET user control. Entity templates are located in the `DynamicData/EntityTemplates` folder of the web project. Listing 1.11 shows code from the Default_Edit entity template.

LISTING 1.11   Default_Edit Entity Template (Markup)

```
<%@ Control Language="C#" CodeBehind="Default_Edit.ascx.cs"
  Inherits="WebApplication.DynamicData.EntityTemplates.Default_EditEntityTemplate"%>

<asp:EntityTemplate runat="server" ID="entityTemplate">
  <itemtemplate>
    <tr class="td">
      <td class="DDLightHeader">
        <asp:Label runat="server" OnInit="Label_Init" />
      </td>
      <td>
        <asp:DynamicControl runat="server" Mode="Edit"
          OnInit="DynamicControl_Init" />
      </td>
    </tr>
  </itemtemplate>
</asp:EntityTemplate>
```

Inside of this user control, you have an `EntityTemplate` control, similar to the `Repeater` control in ASP.NET WebForms. Its purpose is to provide a markup template with a `Label` and a `DynamicControl` that will be rendered for each column in the table. Listing 1.12 shows the code-behind file where all this happens.

LISTING 1.12 Default_Edit Entity Template (Code-Behind)

```csharp
using System;
using System.Web.DynamicData;
using System.Web.UI;
using System.Web.UI.WebControls;

namespace WebApplication.DynamicData.EntityTemplates
{
  public partial class Default_EditEntityTemplate : EntityTemplateUserControl
  {
    private MetaColumn currentColumn;

    protected override void OnLoad(EventArgs e)
    {
      IEnumerable<MetaColumn> scaffoldColumns = this.Table.GetScaffoldColumns(
        this.Mode, this.ContainerType);
      foreach (MetaColumn column in scaffoldColumns)
      {
        this.currentColumn = column;
        Control namingContainer = new DefaultEntityTemplate._NamingContainer();
        this.entityTemplate.ItemTemplate.InstantiateIn(namingContainer);
        this.entityTemplate.Controls.Add(namingContainer);
      }
    }

    protected void Label_Init(object sender, EventArgs e)
    {
      ((Label)sender).Text = this.currentColumn.DisplayName;
    }

    protected void DynamicControl_Init(object sender, EventArgs e)
    {
      ((DynamicControl)sender).DataField = this.currentColumn.Name;
    }
  }
}
```

As you can see, the control overrides the OnLoad method, retrieves the list of metadata columns from the table and instantiates the EntityTemplate inside the foreach loop for every column. The Label_Init event handler initializes label's text with the display name of the column and the DynamicControl_Init event handler initializes the dynamic control with the name of the column itself. The rest is done by the DynamicControl instances, which load and render the appropriate field templates based on the column metadata.

Some visual aspects of entity templates, such as display names of the columns and their order, can be controlled using metadata attributes. However, the overall layout of the default template is fundamentally a single column of labels on the left and the data entry controls on the right. When this layout is insufficient, you can create custom entity templates to fit your requirements.

Grid Columns and Dynamic Fields

So far, only data entry forms have been discussed, where a single record or entity is displayed at a time. However, Dynamic Data offers great productivity enhancements for list type pages that display multiple records.

LISTING 1.13   GridView and DynamicField Sample (Markup)

```
<%@ Page Language="C#"
  MasterPageFile="~/Site.master" CodeBehind="SamplePage.aspx.cs"
  Inherits="WebApplication.Samples.Ch01.DynamicField.SamplePage" %>

<asp:Content ContentPlaceHolderID="main" runat="server">
  <asp:ValidationSummary runat="server"/>
  <asp:GridView ID="gridView" runat="server" DataSourceID="dataSource"
    DataKeyNames="ProductID" AutoGenerateEditButton="true"
    AllowPaging="true" AutoGenerateColumns="false" >
    <columns>
      <asp:DynamicField DataField="ProductName" />
      <asp:DynamicField DataField="UnitsInStock" />
    </columns>
  </asp:GridView>
  <asp:EntityDataSource ID="dataSource" runat="server"
    ConnectionString="name=NorthwindEntities" EnableUpdate="true"
    DefaultContainerName="NorthwindEntities" EntitySetName="Products" />
</asp:Content>
```

DynamicField is a data control field that can be used with both GridView and DetailsView controls, allowing them to take advantage of the rich field templating functionality offered by Dynamic Data. Figure 1.13 shows how this page looks at runtime.

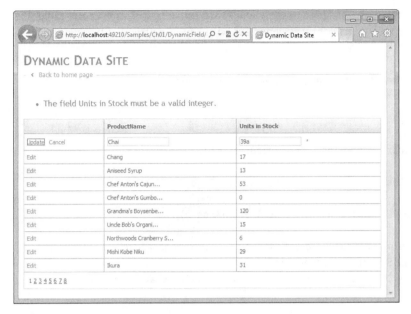

FIGURE 1.13   GridView page with dynamic field columns.

Similar to DynamicControl, DynamicField uses column metadata to automatically select and load an appropriate field template. In other words, pages built with FormView, DetailsView, and GridView controls can reuse the same set of field templates.

Like the DynamicEntity control, which allows you to build a data entry form that includes all columns of a particular table, Dynamic Data offers a similar capability for grid columns. In Listing 1.14, the explicit definitions of fields for ProductName and UnitsInStock have been removed. Instead, the AutoGenerateColumns property of the GridView control is set to true.

LISTING 1.14   DefaultAutoFieldGenerator Sample (Markup)

```
<%@ Page Language="C#"
  MasterPageFile="~/Site.master" CodeBehind="SamplePage.aspx.cs"
  Inherits="WebApplication.Samples.Ch01.FieldGenerator.SamplePage" %>

<asp:Content ContentPlaceHolderID="main" runat="server">
  <asp:ValidationSummary ID="ValidationSummary1" runat="server"/>
  <asp:GridView ID="gridView" runat="server" DataSourceID="dataSource"
    DataKeyNames="ProductID" AutoGenerateEditButton="true"
    AllowPaging="true" AutoGenerateColumns="true"/>
  <asp:EntityDataSource ID="dataSource" runat="server"
    ConnectionString="name=NorthwindEntities" EnableUpdate="true"
    DefaultContainerName="NorthwindEntities" EntitySetName="Products" />
</asp:Content>
```

By default, the GridView control generates a BoundField for every column in the table. Instead, you want to replace its columns generator with the one provided by Dynamic Data as shown in Listing 1.15.

LISTING 1.15   DefaultAutoFieldGenerator Sample (Code-Behind)

```
using System;
using System.Web.DynamicData;

namespace WebApplication.Samples.Ch01.FieldGenerator
{
  public partial class SamplePage : System.Web.UI.Page
  {
    protected void Page_Init(object sender, EventArgs e)
    {
      MetaTable table = Global.DefaultModel.GetTable(this.dataSource.EntitySetName);
      this.gridView.SetMetaTable(table);
      this.gridView.ColumnsGenerator = new DefaultAutoFieldGenerator(table);
    }
  }
}
```

Note that DefaultAutoFieldGenerator class, despite of its somewhat misleading name, is actually provided by Dynamic Data. Based on columns of the specified MetaTable, it generates DynamicField instances for a GridView or DetailsView control that use it. Figure 1.14 shows the resulting page based on this code. Notice that the UnitsInStock column is using the Integer_Edit field template.

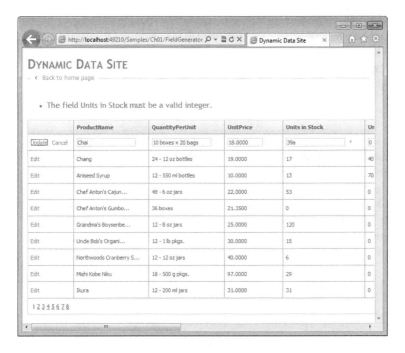

FIGURE 1.14   GridView with Dynamic Field Generator.

Filter Templates

In a real-world application, the number of products would probably exceed the mere eight pages in the Northwind sample. Thus, no application would be complete without some form of search functionality. Consider Listing 1.16, where the grid page has been extended from the previous example with a `DynamicFilter` and a `QueryExtender` control.

LISTING 1.16   QueryExtender and DynamicFilter Sample (Markup)

```
<%@ Page Language="C#"
  MasterPageFile="~/Site.master" CodeBehind="SamplePage.aspx.cs"
  Inherits="WebApplication.Samples.Ch01.DynamicFilter.SamplePage" %>

<asp:Content ContentPlaceHolderID="main" runat="server">
  Filter by Category:
  <asp:DynamicFilter ID="categoryFilter" DataField="Category" runat="server" />
  <asp:ValidationSummary runat="server"/>
  <asp:GridView ID="gridView" runat="server" DataSourceID="dataSource"
    DataKeyNames="ProductID" AutoGenerateEditButton="true"
    AllowPaging="true" AutoGenerateColumns="true"/>
  <asp:EntityDataSource ID="dataSource" runat="server"
```

```
  ConnectionString="name=NorthwindEntities" EnableUpdate="true"
  DefaultContainerName="NorthwindEntities" EntitySetName="Products" />
<asp:QueryExtender runat="server" TargetControlID="dataSource">
  <asp:DynamicFilterExpression ControlID="categoryFilter" />
</asp:QueryExtender>
</asp:Content>
```

QueryExtender is a special nonvisual control. Using the TargetControlID property, it is associated with a LINQ-based data source control, such as the EntityDataSource in this example or LinqDataSource provided by LINQ to SQL. At run time, the QueryExtender can modify the LINQ query constructed by the data source control before it is converted to SQL and sent to the database server for execution. QueryExtender uses one or more *data source expressions*. In this example, there is a DynamicFilterExpression associated with a DynamicFilter control at the top of the page. Before going too much deeper, look at Figure 1.15, which shows the resulting page at run time.

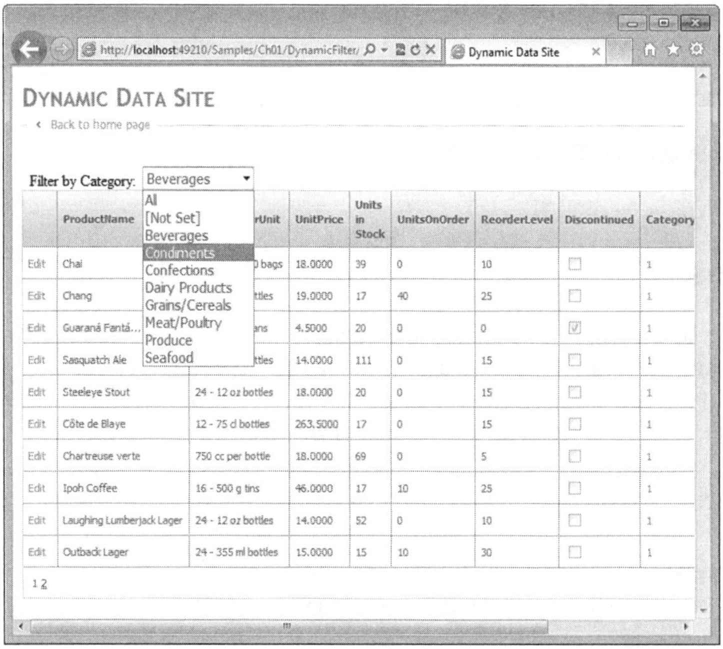

FIGURE 1.15   QueryExtender and DynamicFilter Sample.

DynamicFilter is a special control provided by Dynamic Data. Based on the column name specified in its DataField property and the metadata information, it selects and renders an appropriate *filter template* where the user can specify search criteria for this column. Figure 1.16 shows the filter templates available in Dynamic Data projects out of the box.

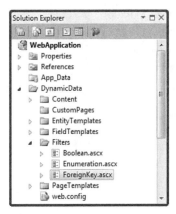

FIGURE 1.16   Filter templates in a Dynamic Data project.

It comes as no surprise that filter templates are also a special kind of ASP.NET user controls located in the `DynamicData/Filters` folder of the web application project. In this example, there is a filter based on the Category column of the Products table. This column is a foreign key pointing to the Categories table of the Northwind database. The default filter provided by Dynamic Data for a foreign key column is a drop-down list that displays all records from the table it references. The markup from ForeignKey.ascx is shown in Listing 1.17.

LISTING 1.17   ForeignKey Filter Template (Markup)

```
<%@ Control Language="C#" CodeBehind="ForeignKey.ascx.cs"
  Inherits="WebApplication.DynamicData.Filters.ForeignKeyFilter" %>

<asp:DropDownList runat="server" ID="dropDownList" AutoPostBack="True"
  OnSelectedIndexChanged="DropDownList_SelectedIndexChanged">
  <asp:ListItem Text="All" Value="" />
</asp:DropDownList>
```

This looks deceptively simple, and as you would expect, the heavy lifting is done in code, by dynamically loading the list of database records to populate the drop-down list and constructing a lambda expression that represents an additional where clause for the LINQ query. You will not be looking at the code-behind of the filter templates just yet. Filtering functionality is by far the most complex code in Dynamic Data; the detailed discussion of this topic is found in Chapter 5, "Filter Templates."

The `QueryExtender` control supports multiple filter expressions. If you need to allow users to search products by Supplier, you can simply add a new `DynamicFilter` control to the form and a new `DynamicFilterExpression` to the `QueryExtender`. However, if you need to have dynamic filters for *all* supported columns in the table, you can do it more quickly with the help of the `QueryableFilterRepeater` control, as shown in Listing 1.18.

LISTING 1.18   QueryExtender and QueryableFilterRepeater Sample (Markup)

```
<%@ Page Language="C#"
  MasterPageFile="~/Site.master" CodeBehind="SamplePage.aspx.cs"
  Inherits="WebApplication.Samples.Ch01.FilterRepeater.SamplePage" %>

<asp:Content ContentPlaceHolderID="main" runat="server">
  <asp:QueryableFilterRepeater runat="server" ID="filterRepeater">
    <ItemTemplate>
      <%# Eval("DisplayName") %>:
      <asp:DynamicFilter ID="DynamicFilter" runat="server" />
      <br />
    </ItemTemplate>
  </asp:QueryableFilterRepeater>
  <asp:ValidationSummary runat="server"/>
  <asp:GridView ID="gridView" runat="server" DataSourceID="dataSource"
    DataKeyNames="ProductID" AutoGenerateEditButton="true"
    AllowPaging="true" AutoGenerateColumns="true"/>
  <asp:EntityDataSource ID="dataSource" runat="server"
    ConnectionString="name=NorthwindEntities" EnableUpdate="true"
    DefaultContainerName="NorthwindEntities" EntitySetName="Products" />
  <asp:QueryExtender runat="server" TargetControlID="dataSource">
    <asp:DynamicFilterExpression ControlID="filterRepeater" />
  </asp:QueryExtender>
</asp:Content>
```

QueryableFilterRepeater is another control provided by Dynamic Data. It is somewhat similar to the EntityTemplate control used in entity templates. The QueryableFilterRepeater control instantiates its ItemTemplate for every column in the MetaTable that has an appropriate filter template. This example uses a data binding expression, <%# Eval("DisplayName") %>, to render the display name of the column and a DynamicFilter to render the appropriate filter template. Instead of creating dynamic filter expressions for the individual dynamic filter controls, the QueryExtender is configured with a single expression pointing to the filter repeater itself. Figure 1.17 shows the resulting page.

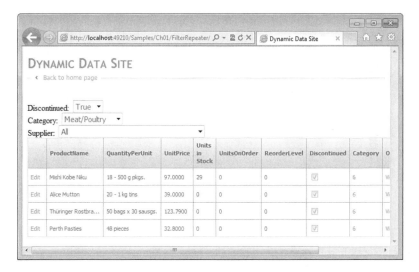

FIGURE 1.17   QueryExtender and QueryableFilterRepeater Sample.

You might be disappointed to see that only three filters were generated for the entire Products table that contains almost a dozen of different columns. That is because Dynamic Data project template offers only three filter templates out of the box—Boolean, Enumeration, and ForeignKey. However, as you will see in Chapter 5, it is straightforward to create your own filter templates for other data types.

Page Templates and URL Routing

By now, you have been introduced to the major building blocks Dynamic Data offers for creating CRUD pages. Field and entity templates are used to build pages for inserting, editing, and displaying a single record. Filter templates and the field generator are used to build list pages that allow search and display of multiple records. If you look back at the code samples, you might notice that the only thing tying them to a particular table is the configuration of the EntityDataSource control in page markup. By simply changing the page to initialize the EntitySetName property of the EntityDataSource programmatically, perhaps based on a URL parameter, you could reuse a single page for any number of different tables. This is precisely what the Dynamic Data page templates do.

Out of the box, Dynamic Data project template offers five page templates, which are shown in Figure 1.18.

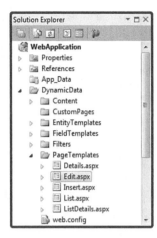

FIGURE 1.18   Page templates in a Dynamic Data project.

Page templates rely on URL routing to determine the table they need to display and require additional setup. Listing 1.19 shows how this is done in the Global.asax file of the web application.

LISTING 1.19   Registering Dynamic Data URL Route in Global.asax.cs

```csharp
using System;
using System.Web.DynamicData;
using System.Web.Routing;
using DataModel;

namespace WebApplication
{
  public class Global : System.Web.HttpApplication
  {
    public static readonly MetaModel DefaultModel = new MetaModel();

    void Application_Start(object sender, EventArgs e)
    {
      var modelConfiguration = new ContextConfiguration();
      modelConfiguration.ScaffoldAllTables = true;
      DefaultModel.RegisterContext(typeof(NorthwindEntities), modelConfiguration);
      RouteTable.Routes.Add(new DynamicDataRoute("{table}/{action}.aspx"));
    }
  }
}
```

In particular, you need to create a `DynamicDataRoute` and register it in the global `RouteTable`. The route object defines a special URL format where the traditional `QueryString` parameters become a part of the virtual path. In this example, the route defines a {table} parameter, so instead of a URL like

```
http://server/DynamicData/PageTemplates/Edit.aspx?table=Products
```

you could simply type

```
http://server/Products/Edit.aspx.
```

Another parameter in this route is {action}. Action usually matches the name of one of the available page templates, such as the built-in List, Details, Edit, and Insert.

In Listing 1.19, you might have also noticed that in this code the NorthwindEntities data model is registered with a `ContextConfiguration` object. The `ContextConfiguration` allows you to provide additional information to Dynamic Data regarding the data model, such as specify that all tables should be *scaffolded* by default. Scaffolding a table means making it visible to the user in the UI generated by Dynamic Data. Usually, you scaffold only those few tables you want your user to be able to view and edit directly. However, in this example, all of them are scaffolded to illustrate the use of page templates.

Figure 1.19 shows the default home page provided for web applications by the Dynamic Data project template.

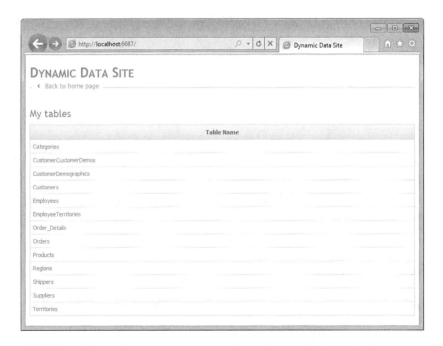

FIGURE 1.19   Default home page of a Dynamic Data Web Application.

This page, Default.aspx, uses `GridView` and `DynamicHyperLink` controls to display the list of all visible tables in the data model. Clicking a table link on the Default.aspx page opens a web page similar to that shown in Figure 1.20. Notice the URL in the address bar of the web browser:

```
http://localhost/Products/List.aspx.
```

As discussed previously, this is a *virtual* URL. There is no physical Products folder in this sample project. Instead, ASP.NET used the `DynamicDataRoute` configured in the Global.asax to pass the HTTP request to the List.aspx in the `DynamicData/PageTemplates` folder.

FIGURE 1.20   Web page produced by the List page template.

The List page template is similar to the web pages built from scratch earlier in this chapter. It also includes a `EntityDataSource` and a `GridView` controls but configures them slightly differently, as shown here:

```
protected MetaTable table;

protected void Page_Init(object sender, EventArgs e)
{
  this.table = DynamicDataRouteHandler.GetRequestMetaTable(this.Context);
  this.gridView.SetMetaTable(this.table,
    this.table.GetColumnValuesFromRoute(this.Context));
  this.dataSource.EntityTypeFilter = this.table.EntityType.Name;
}
```

Notice the call to the `GetRequestMetaTable` method of the `DynamicDataRouteHandler` class. This method extracts the table name from the URL and finds the matching table in the default `MetaModel`. Having obtained the required `MetaTable`, this code associates it with the `GridView` control and configures the `EntityDataSource`.

NOTE

Setting the `EntityTypeFilter` property as opposed to the `EntitySetName` property of the EntityDataSource control allows this code to work correctly not only with the simple, table-per-type mapping that has been used thus far in the Northwind sample. It also supports the more advanced table mappings offered by the Entity Framework, which are discussed in Chapter 2, "Entity Framework."

The List page template also uses the `DynamicHyperLink` control in a databound `GridView`:

```
<asp:TemplateField>
  <ItemTemplate>
    <asp:DynamicHyperLink runat="server" Action="Edit" Text="Edit" /> 
    <asp:LinkButton runat="server" CommandName="Delete" Text="Delete" /> 
    <asp:DynamicHyperLink runat="server" Text="Details" />
  </ItemTemplate>
</asp:TemplateField>
```

When bound to a single entity object, the `DynamicHyperLink` generates a URL with additional parameters. `Action` property of the `DynamicHyperLink` class specifies the name of the page template, Edit in this example. When bound to a Product with the primary key column (ProductID) equal to one, this control generates a URL that looks like `http://localhost/Products/Edit.aspx?ProductID=1`. Figure 1.21 shows the web page displayed by this link.

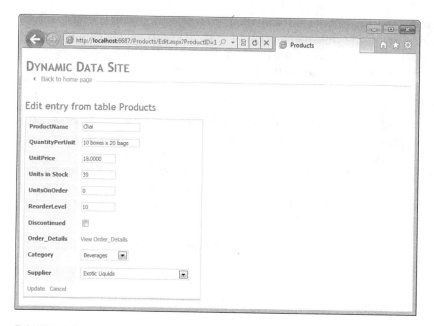

FIGURE 1.21   Web page produced by the Edit page template.

Another page template, Edit.aspx, generates this page. Similar to the List.aspx page template, it extracts table name from the request URL and configures its EntityDataSource control. Although there are some additional controls that have not been discussed, this template is very similar to the page created from scratch in the *Entity Templates* section of this chapter.

The Insert and Details page templates are similar to the Edit template and provide user interface for creating a new record or displaying an existing record in read-only mode respectively.

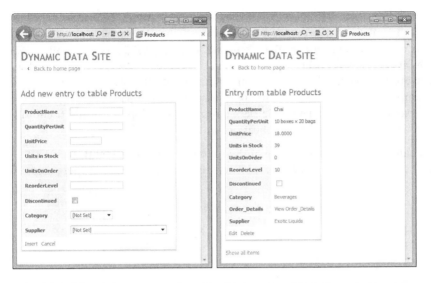

FIGURE 1.22   Web pages produced by the Insert and Details page templates.

Summary

Dynamic Data is an extension of the ASP.NET WebForms framework that consists of three major building blocks: metadata, templates, and controls.

The *metadata* API relies on a LINQ-based data access framework, such as Entity Framework or LINQ to SQL, and provides a common programming interface focused on the business and presentation logic. When the information offered by the underlying data access framework is insufficient, the metadata API relies on Data Annotations, the .NET attributes defined in the `System.ComponentModel.DataAnnotations` namespace, to provide information about display names of columns and tables, order, and visibility of the individual columns and more.

The Dynamic Data *templates* implement individual user interface fragments of the web application. *Field* templates are ASP.NET user controls that encapsulate user interface necessary for a single field value. *Entity* templates are ASP.NET user controls that rely on multiple field templates to implement user interface for an entire database record in a form layout. *Filter* templates are ASP.NET user controls that implement logic required to enter search criteria and generate a LINQ query based on a single column. *Page* templates are ASP.NET pages that use entity templates and implement the supporting logic for navigation and CRUD operations. Dynamic Data projects provide a number of different templates out of the box and enable developers to create new templates to fit their specific project needs.

The Dynamic Data *controls* use the metadata information to automatically load and display appropriate templates. `DynamicControl` can be used with the `FormView` and `ListView` controls to load an appropriate field template. `DynamicField` serves a similar purpose; however, it is designed for use with the `GridView` and `DetailsView` controls. The `DynamicEntity` control automatically loads an appropriate entity template, and the `DynamicFilter` control automatically loads an appropriate filter template. Although these controls are used extensively in the Dynamic Data templates, developers can use them in regular pages and controls of WebForms applications as well.

This chapter has barely scratched the surface of the functionality offered by the ASP.NET Dynamic Data. The remaining chapters of Part I offer a closer look at each of these areas.

CHAPTER 2

Entity Framework

Although it is possible to build ASP.NET Dynamic Data applications with plain ADO.NET data access components, some of its features, such as foreign key templates and filtering, require a modern, LINQ-enabled data access framework such as LINQ to SQL or Entity Framework.

LINQ to SQL was introduced in Visual Studio 2008 and .NET Framework 3.5 as a database-specific implementation of LINQ—Language Integrated Query functionality in C# and Visual Basic. LINQ allows developers to use SQL-like queries directly in the application code as opposed to calling stored procedures or passing SQL statements as strings for execution to a database server. LINQ to SQL was quickly followed by the ADO.NET Entity Framework, released with .NET Framework 3.5 Service Pack 1. LINQ to SQL was designed for simplicity and close integration with Microsoft SQL Server; the Entity Framework was designed for maximum flexibility and multiple database platforms.

Although LINQ-based data access code is much simpler than the traditional code based on ADO.NET, it represents a significant paradigm shift compared to the approach .NET and database developers have been trained to use for over a decade. The ways you retrieve and manipulate data and the way you submit changes and implement business logic are very different with LINQ-based data access frameworks, and using some of the old tricks and habits can lead you in the direction where you are fighting the framework instead of letting it help you.

Because the ASP.NET Dynamic Data relies heavily on LINQ, developers need to have a working knowledge of the underlying data access framework to understand how its web controls work and how to customize them effectively. In this chapter, you are given an overview of the ADO.NET Entity Framework from a pure data access prospective, avoiding the specifics related to ASP.NET web applications in general or Dynamic Data in particular. If you are already familiar with Entity Framework or LINQ to SQL, you can probably skip this chapter.

Understanding Entity Model

The ADO.NET Entity Framework is an Object-relational mapping (ORM) framework developed by Microsoft as part of the .NET Framework. It allows developers to define entities, properties, and associations and map them to the underlying database tables and columns. In version 4.0, you typically create the entities and mappings using the Entity Designer in Visual Studio, which generates the application classes that can be used to query the database with LINQ and manipulate database records in a form of .NET objects.

Creating Entity Model

To get started, you first need to add a new Entity Framework data model to your project (in this chapter, we work with a simple Console Application project template). Select the ADO.NET Entity Data Model item from the Data template category in the Add New Item dialog of Visual Studio, as shown in Figure 2.1.

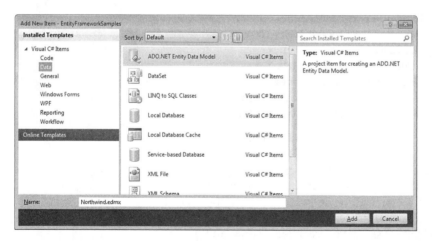

FIGURE 2.1 Adding ADO.NET Entity Data Model to a project.

After entering the file name and clicking Add, you see the Entity Data Model Wizard shown in Figure 2.2, which prompts you to either generate the model from an existing database or create an empty one. If the database already exists, choose the option to generate the model. You can choose the option to create an empty model if you are lucky enough to be working on a "green field" project for which the database does not yet exist and you want to rely on the Entity Framework to generate the database for you. In this discussion, assume the first scenario and generate the model from the Northwind sample database.

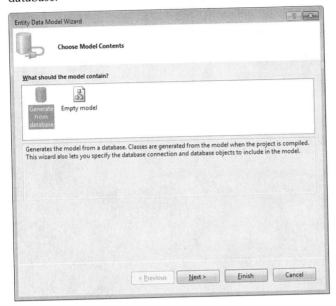

FIGURE 2.2 Choosing to generate model from database.

After clicking Next on the Choose Model Contents page of the Entity Data Model Wizard, your next step is to choose a connection that will be used to access the database, as shown in Figure 2.3. If you already defined a connection to the Northwind database in Visual Studio's Server Explorer, you can choose it from the list of available connections. Otherwise, create a new connection that points to your Northwind sample database.

Notice that the entity connection string includes information about the underlying database provider that will be used to connect to the database. Entity Framework relies on the ADO.NET providers for low-level database connectivity, and you can see the familiar connection information, such as Data Source and Initial Catalog, as part of the "provider connection string."

Just like with traditional ADO.NET applications, you have the option of storing the Entity Framework connection string in the application configuration file. This is usually a good idea: It avoids specifying the database server name and other connection information explicitly in application code. The Entity Framework does not relieve you from the duty of protecting database credentials. In this example, we are using integrated security and do not need to worry about a username and password in plain text in the configuration file. If you choose to specify database credentials, you need to secure the configuration file appropriately, such as by encrypting the connection string section.

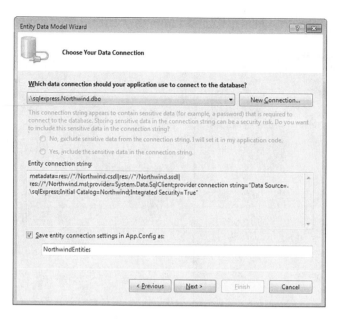

FIGURE 2.3 Choosing Data Connection.

When you have configured the connection and clicked Next on the Choose Your Data Connection page of the Entity Data Model Wizard, you are prompted to select the database objects to include in the model as shown in Figure 2.4. You can choose any number of existing Tables, Views, and Stored Procedures the wizard detects in the database. For now, choose a single table, Products, and click Finish.

Usually you want to accept default values for the remaining options on this page. The option to *Pluralize or singularize generated object names* instructs the wizard to automatically determine appropriate entity names based on the table names. For databases, such as Northwind, where table names are in plural form (Products), the generated entity name will be singular (Product). This is desirable because in .NET applications, names of classes that represent a single object are usually in singular form, helping to distinguish them from collections that can have multiple items.

The option to *Include foreign key columns in the model* determines whether columns like SupplierID of the Products table will be available in the application code. This is particularly useful for web applications that have to be stateless and cannot preserve entity objects between requests. The first version of Entity Framework released in .NET 3.5 SP1 did not support this option, and it exists today only for backward compatibility, allowing you to turn it off. Keep this option on unless you are working with a model created using previous versions of the framework.

The *Model Namespace* setting refers to an internal namespace used by the model itself. It has nothing to do with the namespace of your application classes, and you can safely ignore it, leaving the default value suggested by the tool.

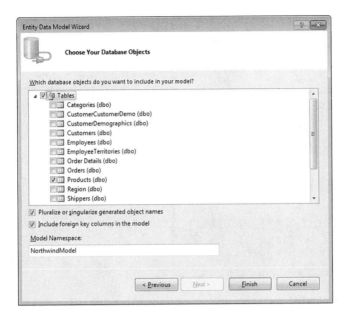

FIGURE 2.4 Choosing database objects.

When you click Finish, the Entity Data Model Wizard creates a new EDMX file, adds it to the project, and opens it in an Entity Designer window shown in Figure 2.5.

The diagrams used by the Entity Framework should be familiar to most database developers because they closely resemble database and UML diagrams. The newly created entity, Product, is displayed as a rectangle with a list of scalar properties derived from the columns of the Products table.

The Entity Designer relies on the Properties window of Visual Studio to display and allow you to modify various elements of the model, such as the names of the entity types, their access/visibility, properties, and so on. Explore the new entity model by selecting the entity and its property items in the Entity Designer and observing the information available in the Property Window. Notice that in addition to the names, data types, and other attributes, the Entity Designer also allows you to specify a short Summary and/or a Long Description for every item in the model, making it a reasonably good place to store developer-focused documentation of the data model—even though this information is not available in Dynamic Data applications by default.

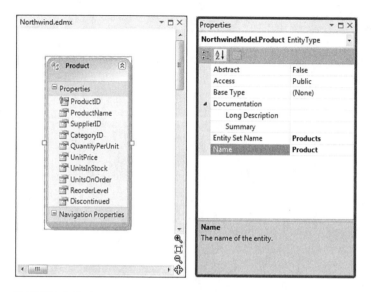

FIGURE 2.5 Entity Designer and Properties windows.

The Entity Designer automatically creates a C# file (or Visual Basic file, depending on the type of project you are using) that Solution Explorer hides under the EDMX file. This file contains classes generated from the entity data model, such as the Product entity in this example. After a major cleanup to improve readability, it can be boiled down to the following pseudo-code:

```
public partial class Product : EntityObject
{
   public int ProductID { get; set; }
   public string ProductName { get; set; }
   public int? SupplierID { get; set; }
   public int? CategoryID { get; set; }
   public string QuantityPerUnit { get; set; }
   public decimal? UnitPrice { get; set; }
   public short? UnitsInStock { get; set; }
   public short? UnitsOnOrder { get; set; }
   public short? ReorderLevel { get; set; }
   public bool Discontinued { get; set; }
}
```

Notice that the Product class closely resembles the Products table it represents. It has properties, such as `ProductID` and `ProductName`, with names and types closely matching those of the database columns. However, unlike the Products table, the `Product` class encapsulates a single row and not the entire table.

ObjectContext and Simple Queries

Another class automatically generated by the Entity Designer is the `ObjectContext` called `NorthwindEntities`, shown here in pseudo-code form:

```
public partial class NorthwindEntities : ObjectContext
{
  public ObjectSet<Product> Products { get; }
}
```

An `ObjectContext` encapsulates a database connection, allows you to query the database using LINQ (Language Integrated Query), and manipulate data rows using entity classes instead of the general-purpose `DataRow` objects used with classic ADO.NET. Here is how we can retrieve a list of products for which the number of units in stock dropped below the reorder level:

```
using (NorthwindEntities context = new NorthwindEntities())
{
  var query = from p in context.Products
              where p.UnitsInStock < p.ReorderLevel
              select p;

  foreach (Product p in query)
    Console.WriteLine(p.ProductName);
}
```

The `Products` property of the `NorthwindEntities` class encapsulates the Products database table. It returns an `ObjectSet` of `Product` instances, which can be used in LINQ queries such as the one in the example just displayed.

Associations

The entity model can also define associations between entities. In the database, relationships are represented as foreign keys, such as the one from the SupplierID column of the Products table referencing the SupplierID column of the Suppliers table. To take advantage of this capability of the Entity Framework, you need to add the Suppliers table to the entity model. The easiest way to do this with an existing database is by using the Update Wizard. Simply right-click the surface of the Entity Designer and choose Update Model from Database.... This brings up an Update Wizard dialog, similar to the one shown in Figure 2.6.

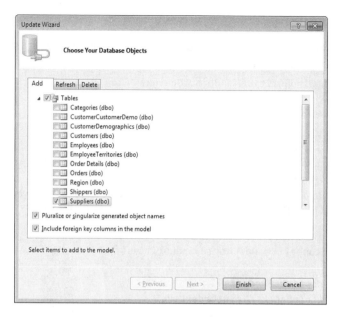

FIGURE 2.6 Adding database objects to the model.

The Update Wizard is very similar to the Entity Data Model Wizard you used to create the model initially. It uses the connection string stored in the application configuration file to retrieve the list of database tables, views, and stored procedures that exist in the target database but have not been added to the entity model yet. Any tables that were previously included in the model are refreshed automatically, meaning that database schema changes are merged in the model. For this example, add the Suppliers table and click the Finish button.

> **NOTE**
>
> Note that the Update Wizard uses the pluralization and foreign key column options you selected when creating the model. Avoid changing these options; it results in inconsistently named entity classes and object set properties.

When the Update Wizard finishes updating the model, you see the new entity types, Supplier in this case, displayed in the Entity Designer along with the association (shown as a dotted line) that was created based on the SupplierID foreign key, similar to what is shown in Figure 2.7.

The Entity Framework supports several different types of associations. What we have in this case is a one-to-many association between Supplier and Product entities. In other words, for each Supplier instance there might be zero or more Product instances as indicated by the * symbol on the design surface. The SupplierID property is nullable, so a Product does not have to have a Supplier specified, which is indicated by the 0..1 multiplicity in the model. If the SupplierID column did not allow null values, making a

Supplier required for each Product, the multiplicity on the Supplier end of the association would have been 1 instead.

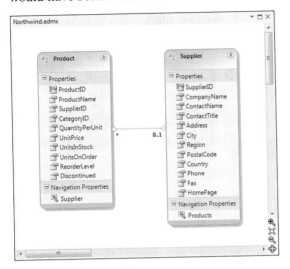

FIGURE 2.7 Association between entities.

In addition to the associations, the Update Wizard also adds *navigation* properties to the entities such as the `Supplier` property in the Product entity. Unlike the underlying *scalar* property `SupplierID`, which only stores a key value, the `Supplier` property returns an instance of the Supplier entity it represents. On the opposite end of this association, the Supplier class has a Products navigation property that returns an `EntityCollection` of Product instances associated with a particular Supplier. Here is how the generated code looks if you take a look at the `NorthwindEntities.Designer.cs`:

```
public partial class Product : EntityObject
{
  // ...
  public int? SupplierID { get; set; }
  public Supplier Supplier { get; set; }
  // ...
}

public partial class Supplier : EntityObject
{
  public int SupplierID { get; set; }
  public EntityCollection<Product> Products { get; set; }
  // ...
}
```

Querying Across Associations

LINQ supports queries that take advantage of associations defined in the model. Here is how you could write a query that returns all Products where the Supplier is located in London:

```
var query = from p in context.Products
            where p.Supplier.City == "London"
            select p;
```

Notice how the Supplier navigation property of the Product entity allows you to filter based on the City property of the Supplier entity. This query could be rewritten to more closely resemble a *traditional* SQL query, as follows:

```
var query = from p in context.Products
            from s in context.Suppliers
            where p.SupplierID == s.SupplierID
              && s.City == "London"
            select p;
```

Although the first version of the query might look strange to someone used to working with SQL statements, it is simply a more elegant and concise way of expressing a join query in LINQ.

Modifying and Saving Entities

To create new and modify existing rows in a database table with the Entity Framework, you need to manipulate the entity instances. In the example that follows, the code retrieves a specific Product instance, updates its UnitsInStock property value, and then submits changes to the database by calling the SaveChanges method of the ObjectContext:

```
using (NorthwindEntities context = new NorthwindEntities())
{
  var query = from p in context.Products
              where p.ProductName == "Outback Lager"
              select p;
  Product outbackLager = query.First();
  outbackLager.UnitsInStock += outbackLager.UnitsOnOrder;
  context.SaveChanges();
}
```

The SaveChanges method uses information in the entity model, the primary key definitions in particular, to generate an appropriate UPDATE SQL statement necessary to modify the UnitsInStock field value of the row in the Products table.

To insert a new row into a database table, you need to create a new entity instance and add it to the context as shown next. For newly added entities, the object context automatically generates INSERT SQL statements.

```
using (NorthwindEntities context = new NorthwindEntities())
{
   Product p = new Product() { ProductName = "Mukuzani" };
   context.Products.AddObject(p);
   context.SaveChanges();
}
```

LINQ to Entities

Language Integrated Query functionality is not unique to the Entity Framework. It is a general purpose feature of the C# and Visual Basic programming languages that takes advantage of the .NET classes in the System.Linq namespace that define the various query expressions and operations. Entity Framework implements a LINQ flavor, called LINQ to Entities, that allows translating .NET queries into the underlying SQL queries for Microsoft SQL Server and other database engines.

Query Execution

LINQ queries are objects that implement an IQueryable<T> interface and store the query compiled in a form of a LINQ expression:

```
IQueryable<Product> query = from p in context.Products
                            where p.Supplier.City == "London"
                            select p;
Console.WriteLine(query.Expression);
```

The query is not executed until it is actually accessed by enumeration, as in this example:

```
foreach (Product p in query)
   Console.WriteLine(p.ProductName);
```

or with one of the LINQ extension methods, such as First.

```
Product product = query.First();
```

The query object itself does not store the entities retrieved from the database. This is important mainly for performance reasons—every time you access the query by enumerating entities it returns or call one of the LINQ extension methods, a new SQL query is sent to the database engine. If you need to access the query results multiple times, it would be much faster to store the entities the query returns in a list and access the list, which does not trigger the query execution:

```
List<Product> products = query.ToList();
foreach (Product p in products)
  Console.WriteLine(p.ProductName);
```

Object Identity

A crucial difference exists between Entity Framework and classic ADO.NET in the way they handle rows retrieved from the database. Where ADO.NET treats the rows as *values*, Entity Framework treats them as *objects*, so if a particular table row is returned by two different queries, they return the same .NET object. The following code illustrates this example by retrieving the same Product by ProductName and by ProductID:

```
Product chai1 = (from p in context.Products
                 where p.ProductName == "Chai"
                 select p).First();
Product chai2 = (from p in context.Products
                 where p.ProductID == 1
                 select p).First();
if (object.ReferenceEquals(chai1, chai2))
  Console.WriteLine("chai1 and chai2 are the same object");
```

This behavior is different from the classic ADO.NET where you would get two different DataRow objects that held the same field values. To implement this functionality, the ObjectContext keeps track of all objects materialized from the data returned by queries, and if a new query returns data for which an object already exists in the context, that object is used and the newly returned data is discarded. Although this might seem counterintuitive from the database point of view (if the Chai product record changed between two queries, isn't it logical to see the new values?), this is actually consistent with a behavior you would intuitively expect from a .NET object. Consider the following example:

```
Product chai = (from p in context.Products
                where p.ProductName == "Chai"
                select p).First();
chai.UnitsInStock += 50;
List<Product> allProducts = (from p in context.Products
                             select p).ToList();
Console.WriteLine(chai.UnitsInStock);
```

Here, the code modifies the number of units in stock for the Chai product object and then executes another query that happens to retrieve it again. Because the code holds a reference to the Chai in a local variable, you would not expect an "unrelated" operation to change its UnitsInStock property; the Entity Framework implements this behavior.

Lazy and Eager Loading

By default in version 4 of Entity Framework, a newly created entity model has the Lazy Loading option enabled. This allows you to traverse the navigation properties and query-related entities without actually writing any queries at all.

```
var query = from p in context.Products
            select p;
foreach (Product p in query)
   Console.WriteLine(p.ProductName + " " + p.Supplier.CompanyName);
```

In the preceding example, there is only one explicit query, which returns all products. However, when enumerating the Product objects it returns, the code also prints out the name of the Supplier for each product. The simple act of referencing the Supplier property of a Product instance causes the related Supplier entity to be loaded from the database by the ObjectContext.

Code that takes advantage of lazy loading is very clean and works great when loading of related entities is infrequent. However, a separate query is sent to the database engine every time the Supplier property is referenced. Even though the individual queries can be small and return little data, in a loop, it might be faster to retrieve all Suppliers along with their Products in a single query. This is called *eager loading*. Entity Framework allows you to do it by calling the Include method and specifying the name of the navigation property that needs to be eager-loaded.

```
var query = from p in context.Products.Include("Supplier")
            select p;
foreach (Product p in query)
   Console.WriteLine(p.ProductName + " " + p.Supplier.CompanyName);
```

This version of the code only executes a single database query at the beginning of the foreach loop. The query retrieves both Product and their associated Supplier entities from the database. No additional requests are sent to the database when the Supplier's company name is printed out in the loop.

Projections

When a query returns entities, it needs to retrieve values of all of its properties from the database. It is an equivalent of SELECT * SQL statement. When you are only interested in a particular set of columns, you can significantly reduce the amount of data returned and improve performance with the help of projections, or in common terms, by "selecting" only those columns you are interested in. The following code sample only needs the CompanyName and City values of the Supplier entity, so instead of returning an entire entity, it returns instances of an anonymous type that includes just the required properties.

```
var query = from s in context.Suppliers
            select new { s.CompanyName, s.City };
foreach (var item in query)
  Console.WriteLine(item.CompanyName + " " + item.City );
```

An anonymous type is declared in-place, with property names inferred from the names of the Supplier properties that provide the values. It serves as a Data Transfer Object (DTO) that holds Supplier property values in place of the actual Supplier instances. This particular code could be also rewritten to use an explicitly defined DTO class, like so:

```
class SupplierProjection
{
  public string CompanyName;
  public string City;
}

var query = from s in context.Suppliers
            select new SupplierProjection
            {
              CompanyName = s.CompanyName,
              City = s.City
            };
```

As you can see, the version based on the anonymous type is much more concise and closely resembles the SQL syntax. However, visibility of anonymous types is limited to the methods where they are defined. You need to declare the projection classes explicitly if you need to pass the DTOs to another function for further processing.

NOTE

Projection objects are not entity instances. They do not participate in the identity management process of the ObjectContext and cannot be used to change the underlying database records.

Sorting

The orderby LINQ keyword can be used to sort query results. Here is how you could sort the list of Products in the order of UnitPrice, from highest to lowest:

```
var query = from p in context.Products
            orderby p.UnitPrice descending
            select p;
```

By default, orderby acts like its counterpart in SQL: Sorting is performed in ascending order. To reverse the sort order for a property, use the descending LINQ keyword after the property name. LINQ also includes the ascending keyword, but like its counterpart in SQL, is rarely used because it is the default.

Multiple properties can be specified as well, separated by comas. If the descending keyword is used with multiple columns specified in the orderby list, it applies only to the property on its immediate left, such as the UnitsOnOrder in the next example:

```
var query = from p in context.Products
            orderby p.UnitsInStock, p.UnitsOnOrder descending
            select p;
```

Grouping

The group..by LINQ operator can be used to group query results by one or more property values. For example, we could get a list of Products grouped by their Suppliers with the LINQ query shown here:

```
var query = from p in context.Products
            group p by p.SupplierID into g
            select new{
               Supplier = g.FirstOrDefault().Supplier,
               Products = g
            };
foreach (var group in query)
{
   Console.WriteLine("Supplier: " + group.Supplier.CompanyName);
   foreach (var product in group.Products)
      Console.WriteLine("\t" + product.ProductName);
}
```

The group by operator returns an object that implements the IGrouping<TKey, TElement> interface, where TKey is the type of the property used for grouping, such as the SupplierID in our example, and TElement is the type of entity whose instances are being grouped, which in our example is the Product entity. An IGrouping<TKey, TElement> object is also an IEnumerable<TElement>, so you can access all elements in a group simply by enumerating it. Although it would be possible to have the query return the IGrouping objects directly, it is common to have it return an anonymous type that makes the results easier to understand. In this example, the code "selects" an anonymous type where Supplier property contains a Supplier instance and the Products property contains all of the Product instances offered by that supplier.

Joins

Although LINQ makes many queries that normally require a join in SQL possible with simple traversal of the entity relationships, it also supports joins where the explicit relationships might not exist in the data model. For example, although we have address information for Customers and Suppliers defined in the Northwind data model, there is no explicit relationship connecting them. To cross-reference customers and suppliers located in the same city, we would need to perform a join, as shown here:

```
var query = from c in context.Customers
            join s in context.Suppliers on c.City equals s.City
            select new {
                c.City,
                Customer = c.CompanyName,
                Supplier = s.CompanyName
            };
foreach (var item in query)
  Console.WriteLine(item.City + " " + item.Customer + " " +
    item.Supplier);
```

The example just displayed uses the join keyword, which mimics the JOIN operator introduced by the SQL-92 standard. You can also use syntax that resembles the "old-style" joins as well:

```
var query = from c in context.Customers
            from s in context.Suppliers
            where c.City == s.City
            select new {
                c.City,
                Customer = c.CompanyName,
                Supplier = s.CompanyName
            };
```

Composing Queries

An additional benefit of having LINQ queries compiled in LINQ expressions is that they can be further modified before execution. This is often beneficial when constructing a query based on options specified by the user.

```
string city = "London";
bool sortByContactName = true;

var query = from c in context.Customers select c;

if (city != null)
  query = from c in query where c.City == city select c;

if (sortByContactName)
  query = from c in query orderby c.ContactName select c;
else
  query = from c in query orderby c.CompanyName select c;

foreach(Customer c in query)
  Console.WriteLine(c.CompanyName + " " + c.ContactName);
```

In this example, the query returns `Customer` objects dynamically, based on the values of two variables. The values are hard-coded here for simplicity, but in a real application they would be entered by a user.

LINQ allows any `IQueryable` to appear in the `from` part of another query, and this code takes advantage of this to augment the original query with additional operators. Notice that the original query simply returns all customers. If the city parameter is specified, the code adds a `where` clause to filter customers based on the specified value and replaces the original query. You can also sort the query results based on the value of the `sortByContactName` variable—by `ContactName` if it is `true` or by `CompanyName` if it is `false`.

Because of the delayed execution, the final query is sent to the database only once, when the `foreach` statement enumerates it after all of the query modifications have been made. Composing LINQ queries in this fashion allows you to create the most specific query required for your scenario and helps to ensure its correctness, thanks to the thorough validation performed by the C# compiler.

> **NOTE**
>
> It is also possible to create LINQ queries dynamically, from strings that contain property names and operators. Chapter 5, "Filter Templates," provides a detailed discussion on this topic.

SQL Translation

The Entity Framework translates LINQ queries into actual SQL statements based on the information in the data model and sends them for execution to the database server. Because LINQ query syntax is significantly different from SQL syntax, you might find it helpful to see the actual SQL statements your Entity Framework application executes.

The easiest and least obtrusive way to do this with Microsoft SQL Server is by using the SQL Server Profiler, which is as part of the Management Tools—Complete feature you can select during SQL client installation. Alternatively, you can change your application code to do it as well.

```
var query = from c in context.Customers
            where c.City == "London"
            orderby c.CompanyName
            select c;
ObjectQuery objectQuery = (ObjectQuery)query;
Console.WriteLine(objectQuery.ToTraceString());
```

The `IQueryable` objects produced by the C# compiler when compiling LINQ to Entities queries are actually of the type `ObjectQuery`. This class is provided by the Entity Framework and offers a `ToTraceString` method that can be used to get the actual SQL statement to which the LINQ query will be translated. The LINQ query in the example just shown is translated into the SQL statement shown next. Although slightly more verbose than a typical hand-written SQL would be, it is recognizable and easy enough to read:

```
SELECT
[Extent1].[CustomerID] AS [CustomerID],
[Extent1].[CompanyName] AS [CompanyName],
[Extent1].[ContactName] AS [ContactName],
[Extent1].[ContactTitle] AS [ContactTitle],
[Extent1].[Address] AS [Address],
[Extent1].[City] AS [City],
[Extent1].[Region] AS [Region],
[Extent1].[PostalCode] AS [PostalCode],
[Extent1].[Country] AS [Country],
[Extent1].[Phone] AS [Phone],
[Extent1].[Fax] AS [Fax]
FROM [dbo].[Customers] AS [Extent1]
WHERE N'London' = [Extent1].[City]
ORDER BY [Extent1].[CompanyName] ASC
```

Notice that the literal 'London' is embedded in this SQL statement only because it was hard-coded in the original LINQ query. If the value comes from a method parameter or a variable, which is normally the case when executing queries in response to user input, the Entity Framework generates parameterized SQL statements.

```
string city = "London";
var query = from c in context.Customers
            where c.City == city
            select c;
```

The modified LINQ query just shown translates into the following SQL statement where the city is no longer embedded in the query itself and instead passed as a parameter:

```
SELECT
[Extent1].[CustomerID] AS [CustomerID],
[Extent1].[CompanyName] AS [CompanyName],
[Extent1].[ContactName] AS [ContactName],
[Extent1].[ContactTitle] AS [ContactTitle],
[Extent1].[Address] AS [Address],
[Extent1].[City] AS [City],
[Extent1].[Region] AS [Region],
[Extent1].[PostalCode] AS [PostalCode],
[Extent1].[Country] AS [Country],
[Extent1].[Phone] AS [Phone],
[Extent1].[Fax] AS [Fax]
FROM [dbo].[Customers] AS [Extent1]
WHERE [Extent1].[City] = @p__linq__0
```

Generation of the parameterized SQL is important for two reasons. On one hand, it improves application performance as database servers can reuse the same execution plan with different parameter values. If the parameter values were embedded in the SQL text, each parameter value would make a unique new query for which the server would have to recalculate and cache the execution plan, consuming additional CPU and RAM resources. On the other hand, parameterized SQL statements are immune to SQL injection attacks, very common in applications that generate dynamic SQL statements as strings. Here is an example that illustrates the problem:

```
string city = "'; drop database Northwind; select '";
string sql = string.Format(
   "select * from Customers where City = '{0}'", city);
Console.WriteLine(sql);
```

Imagine that in the code snippet just shown the value of the city variable is supplied by the user and the application uses it to create a query that returns only the customers in the specified city. With this naïve implementation, a malicious user could enter a specially constructed string that modifies the original SQL statement the developer intended to execute and injects one or more unexpected SQL statements, allowing him to destroy data or get access to restricted information. Following is the SQL statement this code generates. Notice that instead of an innocent SELECT statement, we have a DROP DATABASE injected in an otherwise valid SQL batch:

```
select * from Customers where City = '';
drop database Northwind;
select ''
```

However, in the SQL statement generated by the Entity Framework, the city value is passed to the database server as a *parameter*, making it impossible to modify the original SQL statement and inject a malicious payload. Even if the value was hard-coded in the application like in the first example in this section, the automatic encoding of literal values performed by the Entity Framework would still prevent the injection.

Compiled Queries

It takes a certain amount of CPU and time resources for Entity Framework to translate the LINQ queries into their equivalent SQL statements before they can be executed. When a particular query is executed repeatedly, you can improve application performance by precompiling it, as shown in the following example:

```
static Func<NorthwindEntities, string, IQueryable<Customer>>
customersByCity =
  CompiledQuery.Compile<NorthwindEntities, string, IQueryable<Customer>>(
    (context, city) =>
      from c in context.Customers
      where c.City == city
      select c
  );
```

In this code snippet, a familiar LINQ query is compiled with the help of the `Compile` method of the `CompiledQuery` class and stored in a static field called `customersByCity`. The compiled query itself is a lambda expression, which takes an object context as its first parameter, a city as its second, and returns an `IQueryable` of Customer. Typically, a compiled query like this is stored in a static field of a class that performs the data access and can benefit from compiled queries.

The data access code based on compiled queries is similar to the traditional LINQ queries in that it still needs to create an `ObjectContext`, like NorthwindEntities in this ongoing example. However, instead of using LINQ queries directly, it calls the `Invoke` method of one or more of the compiled query objects as shown here:

```
using (NorthwindEntities context = new NorthwindEntities())
{
  var customers = customersByCity.Invoke(context, "London");
  foreach (Customer c in customers)
    Console.WriteLine(c.ContactName);
}
```

The work required to translate the compiled LINQ query into SQL statement is performed the first time the compiled query is executed. So the program will still take the performance hit the first time the compiled query is executed in an `AppDomain`; however, all subsequent executions of the compiled query will take advantage of the information cached by the Entity Framework the first time and run faster.

Query composition defeats the caching logic the Entity Framework uses and negates the benefits of query compilation. To keep the benefits of query compilation, you need to compile the *entire* query and avoid modifying it in any way. As an example, consider the code that follows, which adds an `orderby` clause to the same compiled query used in the previous sample:

```
var customers = customersByCity.Invoke(context, "London");
customers = from c in customers
            orderby c.ContactName
            select c;
foreach (Customer c in customers)
  Console.WriteLine(c.ContactName);
```

The actual LINQ query executed in this sample is different from the compiled query and cannot take advantage of the Entity Framework caching logic.

To avoid doing this by accident, you can change the compiled query to return an `IEnumerable` instead of an `IQueryable`.

```
static Func<NorthwindEntities, string, IEnumerable<Customer>>
  customersByCity =
  CompiledQuery.Compile<NorthwindEntities, string, IEnumerable<Customer>>(
    (context, city) =>
      from c in context.Customers
```

```
        where c.City == city
        select c
);
```

Having a compiled query return an `IEnumerable` forces any composition done with a compiled query to be done in the application memory after the original query has already been executed instead of modifying the original compiled query before sending it to the database server. If the amount of data returned by the query is small, this approach can yield better performance. On the other hand, if the query returns a large volume of data and requires a lot of post-processing, it might be faster to take a hit on query preparation but let the database server do the heavy lifting instead. You need to measure actual performance to make a good implementation choice.

Extension Methods

C# and Visual Basic syntax covers only a subset of the query operators supported by the Entity Framework. To take full advantage of its querying capabilities, you might need to use one or more of the LINQ extension methods defined in the static class Queryable from the `System.Linq` namespace. Here is a typical LINQ query, which should look familiar by now:

```
var customers = from c in context.Customers
                where c.City == "London"
                select c;
```

.NET CLR has no special IL instructions for LINQ keywords. Instead, the compiler converts the LINQ syntax into lambda expressions and calls to LINQ extension methods. Here is how this code can be rewritten using extension methods explicitly:

```
var customers = context.Customers
                    .Where(c => c.City == "London")
                    .Select(c => c);
```

Notice how instead of the `where` keyword, it's the `Where` extension method. `c => c.City == "London"` is a lambda expression that takes c, an instance of the Customer class, as a parameter and returns a Boolean value that indicates whether a particular customer matches the filter criteria. `Where` is an extension method defined in the Queryable class for the `IQueryable` interface. In other words, `Queryable.Where` takes an `IQueryable` interface as its first parameter and, in essence, extends the `IQueryable` interface by adding a `Where` method to it, hence the term "extension method."

```
public static IQueryable<TSource> Where<TSource>(
    this IQueryable<TSource> source,
    Expression<Func<TSource, bool>> predicate)
```

You can think of lambda expressions as a kind of shorthand version of anonymous delegates—a compact way of declaring small functions. However, when used with `IQueryable`, lambda expressions are not compiled directly into IL instructions. Instead, they are parsed into Expression objects and passed to the Entity Framework, which translates them to SQL statements and sends them to database engine for execution.

Where is only one of the many LINQ extension methods available for use with Entity Framework. This list includes methods like Average, Min, Max, Sum, and Count, which have similar names and work like the aggregate functions in SQL. Other methods, such as Any and Contains, also have direct counterparts in SQL with very different names. Any is LINQ's equivalent of the EXISTS operator, and Contains is an equivalent of the IN operator in SQL. Yet some methods have no direct counterparts in SQL at all, such as the All method, which returns true if all elements of a sequence match the specified criteria.

Table 2.1 provides a summary of the LINQ extension methods. Take a minute to review the list to get an idea of what is available. However, a complete discussion of LINQ operators and extension methods deserves much more time and pages than can be allotted here.

TABLE 2.1 LINQ Extension Methods

Method	Description
Aggregate	Applies an accumulator function over a sequence.
All	Determines whether all the elements of a sequence satisfy a condition.
Any	Determines whether a sequence contains any elements that satisfy a condition.
Average	Computes the average of a sequence of numeric values.
Cast	Converts the elements of a sequence to the specified type.
Concat	Concatenates two sequences.
Contains	Determines whether a sequence contains a specified element.
Count	Returns the number of elements in a sequence.
DefaultIfEmpty	Returns the elements of the specified sequence or a default value in a singleton collection if the sequence is empty.
Distinct	Returns distinct elements from a sequence.
ElementAt	Returns the element at a specified index in a sequence.
ElementAtOrDefault	Returns the element at a specified index in a sequence or a default value if the index is out of range.
Except	Returns elements from the first sequence except those that are also in the second sequence.
First	Returns the first element of a sequence.
FirstOrDefault	Returns the first element of a sequence or a default value if the sequence contains no elements.
GroupBy	Groups the elements of a sequence.
Intersect	Returns elements from the first sequence that are also in the second sequence.
Join	Performs an inner join of two sequences.
Last	Returns the last element in a sequence.

Method	Description
LastOrDefault	Returns the last element in a sequence or a default value if the sequence contains no elements.
LongCount	Returns the number of elements in a sequence as an Int64 value.
Max	Returns a maximum value in a sequence of numbers.
Min	Returns a minimum value in a sequence of numbers.
OrderBy	Sorts the elements of a sequence in ascending order.
OrderByDescending	Sorts the elements of a sequence in descending order.
Reverse	Inverts the order of the elements in a sequence.
Select	Projects each element of a sequence into a new form.
SelectMany	Combines multiple sequences into one and projects each element into a new form.
SequenceEqual	Determines whether two sequences contain equal elements.
Single	Returns the only element of a sequence and throws an exception if there is not exactly one element in the sequence.
SingleOrDefault	Returns the only element of a sequence or a default value if the sequence is empty; this method throws an exception if there is more than one element in the sequence.
Skip	Bypasses a specified number of elements in a sequence and then returns the remaining elements.
SkipWhile	Bypasses elements in a sequence as long as a specified condition is true and then returns the remaining elements.
Sum	Computes the sum of a sequence of numeric values.
Take	Returns a specified number of elements from the start of a sequence.
TakeWhile	Returns elements from a sequence as long as a specified condition is true.
ThenBy	Performs a subsequent ordering of the elements in a sequence in ascending order.
ThenByDescending	Performs a subsequent ordering of the elements in a sequence in descending order
Union	Returns distinct elements from two input sequences.
Where	Returns elements from a sequence that match the specified filter criteria.
Zip	Merges each element of the first sequence with an element that has the same index in the second sequence.

A wealth of reference information about LINQ is available on MSDN. The following page is a great starting point when you are looking for a quick example of a particular extension method or operator:

```
http://msdn.microsoft.com/en-us/vcsharp/aa336746.aspx
```

The following provides a complete reference of all LINQ extension methods available, giving you a comprehensive, but more difficult-to-navigate, list:

```
http://msdn.microsoft.com/en-us/library/system.linq.queryable.aspx
```

Entity Lifecycle

As you already know, in addition to its formidable querying capabilities, the Entity Framework also helps you implement typical data access scenarios, such as creating a new entity, finding an existing entity, and modifying or deleting it. To do this, the ObjectContext keeps track of all entities throughout their lifecycles—from creation to modification to deletion.

Tracking Changes

When a new entity instance is added to an ObjectContext, the context records its state as Added. The following code shows how to examine entity state changes:

```
Product p = new Product() { ProductName = "Mukuzani" };
context.Products.AddObject(p);
Console.WriteLine(context.ObjectStateManager.GetObjectStateEntry(p).State);
context.SaveChanges();
Console.WriteLine(context.ObjectStateManager.GetObjectStateEntry(p).State);
```

The ObjectStateManager property of the ObjectContext class returns the actual object, keeping track of all new entities that have been added to the context or existing entities retrieved from the database. In this code, we use its GetObjectStateEntry method to retrieve an ObjectStateEntry object that represents the newly added Product entity:

```
[Flags]
public enum EntityState
{
   Detached = 1,
   Unchanged = 2,
   Added = 4,
   Deleted = 8,
   Modified = 16
}
```

The State property of the ObjectStateEntry returns an EntityState enumeration value, which for newly created objects has the value Added until we call the SaveChanges method of the ObjectContext, at which point the new entity is submitted to the database and the entity state becomes Unchanged.

In the next example, when an existing Product entity is retrieved from the database, its state is initially Unchanged. Then, as soon as the Category property is assigned, it becomes Modified. After the SaveChanges method is called and the changes are submitted to the database, the entity state becomes Unchanged again:

```
Product product = context.Products.First(p => p.ProductName=="Mukuzani");
product.Category = context.Categories.First(c => c.CategoryName==
    "Beverages");
context.SaveChanges();
```

In the next scenario, an existing Product entity is deleted, and its state changes from Unchanged to Deleted as soon as the DeleteObject method of the Products entity set is called. At this point, the entity has been marked for deletion but not deleted yet in the database. When the SaveChanges method of the context is called, the row storing the entity is "physically" deleted from the Products table. The deleted Product entity is also removed from the ObjectContext, and trying to get its ObjectStateEntry will result in an InvalidOperationException:

```
Product product = context.Products.First(p => p.ProductName == "Mukuzani");
context.Products.DeleteObject(product);
context.SaveChanges();
```

Optimistic Concurrency Control

Most enterprise database applications require access by multiple simultaneous users. When many people have access to the same data records, there is always a chance of two people trying to modify the same record.

The following code illustrates this scenario by creating two different instances of the NorthwindEntities context, retrieving two different copies of the same Product entity, making different changes to it and trying to save the changes. Obviously, you wouldn't write code like this in a real-world application—context1 and context2 simply illustrate the actions performed by two different users running your application on two different computers:

```
using (NorthwindEntities context1 = new NorthwindEntities())
using (NorthwindEntities context2 = new NorthwindEntities())
{
    Product product1 = context1.Products.First(p => p.ProductName == "Chai");
    Product product2 = context2.Products.First(p => p.ProductName == "Chai");

    product1.UnitsInStock = 50;
    product2.UnitsInStock = 20;

    context1.SaveChanges();
    context2.SaveChanges();
}
```

When you run this code, you might notice that the second user (represented by `context2`) submits the changes last and the changes made by the first user are lost.

To prevent data loss, database applications have traditionally relied on record locking. When a user starts editing a particular record, the application would lock it, preventing others from modifying it at the same time. This approach works better when the number of users is small and the number of records is large, thus reducing the chance of contention. However, physical locking can prevent other users not only from changing but also from reading the locked records. This can lead to significant performance degradation and is generally considered a bad practice.

The Entity Framework has built-in support for an alternative strategy, called *Optimistic Concurrency Control*. When saving modified entities, the `ObjectContext` generates UPDATE statements with a WHERE clause that ensures that changes are made only if the entity has not changed since the last time it was retrieved from the database. In other words, the framework assumes that chances of contention are low and, optimistically, allows you to modify the entity without locking the record. If somebody else modified the same record in the meantime, you simply get an exception when calling the `SaveChanges` method.

To take advantage of the optimistic concurrency support, first you need to modify the definitions of the properties in the Entity Designer to set their Concurrency Mode values to `Fixed`, as shown in Figure 2.8. You need to do this for all properties you want the Entity Framework to check for modifications before saving the entity.

FIGURE 2.8 Setting Property Concurrency Mode.

When the model has been modified, calling the `SaveChanges` for `context1` in the previous code example generates the following SQL statement:

```
exec sp_executesql N'update [dbo].[Products]
set [UnitsInStock] = @0
where (([ProductID] = @1) and ([UnitsInStock] = @2))
',N'@0 smallint,@1 int,@2 smallint',@0=50,@1=1,@2=20
```

It is a dynamic, parameterized update statement that sets the UnitsInStock column to its new value, 50 (specified as the @0 parameter), but only if its current value (specified as the @2 parameter) is still the same as the original value 20 saved when the Product entity was retrieved from the database. If the current value of the UnitsInStock column does not match the original value, no records are updated, and the SaveChanges method of the ObjectContext class throws the OptimisticConcurrencyException.

> **NOTE**
>
> If you are using Microsoft SQL Server, you can take advantage of the ROWVERSION (formerly known as TIMESTAMP) column type, designed specifically for optimistic concurrency control. When any changes are made to a row, the server automatically updates its ROWVERSION column value. If your entity has a property mapped to a ROWVERSION column, it is the only one whose Concurrency Mode needs to be set to Fixed. Otherwise, you will want to set it for *all* entity properties and avoid partial data loss.

What does your application need to do when it encounters an OptimisticConcurrencyException? Usually you simply want to let the current user know that somebody else has already changed the record he is trying to modify, let him take note of the changes he was trying to make, and refresh the record to see the other users' modifications. The following code illustrates this scenario from the pure data access point of view:

```
Product product = context.Products.First(p => p.ProductName == "Chai");
product.UnitsInStock = 50;
try
{
  context.SaveChanges();
}
catch (OptimisticConcurrencyException e)
{
  context.Refresh(RefreshMode.StoreWins,
    e.StateEntries.Select(s => s.Entity));
}
```

Notice how after catching an OptimisticConcurrencyException, the code calls the Refresh method of the ObjectContext. This method takes a RefreshMode enumeration, which determines whose changes will be preserved and an IEnumerable of entity objects that need to be refreshed. The RefreshMode.StoreWins value means that changes made by the other users will be preserved. You can also pass the ClientWins value, which would ignore changes of other users and keep the modifications made by the current user. The exception object itself provides a list of entities that failed to save—it is retrieved with the help of the StateEntries property, which returns a collection of the familiar ObjectStateEntry objects, providing access to their entities.

In a web application, however, it is often sufficient to handle the optimistic concurrency errors by simply displaying them to the user and asking him to either refresh the current or go back to the previous page, which automatically discards the changes he made and reloads the latest version of the entity from the database.

Transactions

Transactions help applications to make sure that any changes leave the database in a consistent state. If multiple changes are made as part of a single transaction, the database server ensures that either all of them complete successfully or any incomplete changes are rolled back to the state before the transaction began. By default, database servers, and Microsoft SQL Server in particular, execute each SQL statement in a separate transaction. Although this behavior is sufficient to ensure that any single request leaves the database in a consistent state, when multiple records need to be modified, a transaction that spans multiple requests is required.

As an example, let's consider a scenario of adding a new product to the Northwind database. Perhaps this is done by an automated inventory import process, reading data from a spreadsheet or a flat file. The file contains a list of products along with their categories, and the process needs to link each new product to an existing category or create a new category if it doesn't already exist. Here is how to implement it using Entity Framework (the actual values are hard-coded here as an illustration, of course):

```
Category wines = context.Categories.First(c => c.CategoryName == "Wines");
if (wines == null)
{
  wines = new Category() { CategoryName = "Wines" };
  context.Categories.AddObject(wines);
}

Product p = new Product() { ProductName = "Mukuzani", Category = wines };
context.Products.AddObject(p);

context.SaveChanges();
```

Notice that it is possible for this code to create two entities, one for a new Product and one for a new Category. Both of these entities are submitted to the database when the SaveChanges method of the ObjectContext is called. However, if for any reason a new Product cannot be saved (perhaps there is already another product with this name in our database), you don't want to have an orphaned Category without any Products in it. To implement this requirement, you can submit both the new Category and the new Product as part of a single transaction so that if the new Product cannot be inserted, the new Category is removed as well.

```
using (TransactionScope transaction = new TransactionScope())
using (NorthwindEntities context = new NorthwindEntities())
{
```

```
      Category wines = context.Categories
        .FirstOrDefault(c => c.CategoryName == "Wines");
      if (wines == null)
      {
        wines = new Category() { CategoryName = "Wines" };
        context.Categories.AddObject(wines);
      }

      Product p = new Product() { ProductName = "Mukuzani", Category = wines };
      context.Products.AddObject(p);

      context.SaveChanges();
      transaction.Complete();
  }
```

In this new version of the code, the `TransactionScope` class from the `System.Transactions` assembly and namespace is being used. By creating a new instance of this class, you start a database transaction (think of it as of the `BEGIN TRANSACTION` statement in SQL for now) and by calling the `Complete` method, you are committing it (`COMMIT TRANSACTION`). The `TransactionScope` class implements the `IDisposable` interface so that when a transaction scope instance is disposed and the `Complete` method has not been called, the transaction is automatically rolled back. By placing the `TransactionScope` instance inside of the `using` statement you guarantee that if any exceptions are thrown while you are manipulating the `Category` and `Product` instances and the `Complete` method doesn't get called, the entire transaction will be rolled back (`ROLLBACK TRANSACTION`) before control leaves this code.

`TransactionScope` instances can be hierarchical. If your method creates a transaction scope and calls another method that creates its own, by default this second transaction scope becomes a part of the first one, and any changes performed within it are executed as part of the same database transaction. `TransactionScope` also supports distributed transactions that span multiple databases or servers. Simply place all relevant code inside of a single `TransactionScope`, and it will automatically escalate the transaction from a single server to the Microsoft Distributed Transaction Coordinator (DTC) to perform a two-phase commit.

Read-Only ObjectContext

Preserving object identity and keeping track of changes are great features when you are writing code that needs to not only retrieve data from the database, but also make changes. However, it requires the `ObjectContext` to check every database row against the internal dictionary of previously materialized objects and store both original and current values of all entity properties. This comes at the cost of additional CPU resources required to perform the lookup and increased memory consumption to store the additional property values. The tradeoff is usually well justified in a typical rich-client application that retrieves and manipulates a relatively small number of entities at a time. However, web applications and applications working with large numbers of entities in batch mode can increase performance by disabling the change tracking and identity management as shown here:

```
context.Products.MergeOption = MergeOption.NoTracking;

var chaiQuery = from p in context.Products
                where p.ProductName == "Chai"
                select p;
```

The MergeOption property is defined in the ObjectQuery<T> base class and thus can be specified for the Products ObjectSet. It affects all entities returned by the query, which in this case includes only Product entities. The NoTracking value instructs the ObjectContext to bypass the identity and property value tracking for the query results, which can be illustrated by running the following code:

```
Product chai1 = chaiQuery.First();
Product chai2 = chaiQuery.First();
if (!object.ReferenceEquals(chai1, chai2))
    Console.WriteLine("chai1 and chai2 are different objects");
```

When running this code, notice that chai1 and chai2, initialized by two different executions of the same query, are actually two different objects. Had you not modified the MergeOption for this query, the object context would have detected that the Chai entity had already been retrieved and returned the same entity for both query executions.

Entity Model in Depth

The Entity Model consists of three different sections, each describing a separate aspect of the model. This is best illustrated by opening a newly created EDMX file in a text editor. When stripped of actual content, it looks similar to this:

```xml
<?xml version="1.0" encoding="utf-8"?>
<Edmx Version="2.0" xmlns="http://schemas.microsoft.com/ado/2008/10/edmx">
  <Runtime>
    <StorageModels/>
    <ConceptualModels/>
    <Mappings/>
  </Runtime>
</Edmx>
```

> **NOTE**
>
> The EDMX files contain plain XML and work well with most modern source control systems. However, unless you are working on a trivial project with just a handful of tables and only one developer, eventually you will need to look at the EDMX in its raw XML form instead of relying on the Entity Designer. If you have multiple developers on your team, at some point you will need to merge the changes made by different developers at the same time, and even if you are the only developer working with the EDMX, it is always a good idea to review changes made by the Update Wizard in a large model before checking them in. For these reasons, it is important for developers to be familiar with the entity model XML schema, which is why some of its concepts are introduced here.

The *storage model* describes the database schema as it was captured by the Entity Designer last time when the Update Wizard was used to update model from the database. It includes definitions of tables and their foreign key relationships, as well as views and stored procedures. You can examine the storage model with the help of the Model Browser, a tool window you can open by right-clicking the surface of the Entity Designer and selecting Model Browser from the context menu. Figure 2.9 shows an example of the storage model definition of the Products table.

FIGURE 2.9 Storage model.

The raw XML definition of the Products table looks similar to what's shown next. The `Property` elements define the individual columns, and Key element includes `PropertyRef` elements for all columns in the primary key:

```
<EntityType Name="Products">
  <Key>
    <PropertyRef Name="ProductID" />
  </Key>
  <Property Name="ProductID" Type="int" Nullable="false"
    StoreGeneratedPattern="Identity" />
  <Property Name="ProductName" Type="nvarchar" Nullable="false"
    MaxLength="40" />
  <Property Name="SupplierID" Type="int" />
  <Property Name="CategoryID" Type="int" />
  <Property Name="QuantityPerUnit" Type="nvarchar" MaxLength="20" />
  <Property Name="UnitPrice" Type="money" />
  <Property Name="UnitsInStock" Type="smallint" />
  <Property Name="UnitsOnOrder" Type="smallint" />
  <Property Name="ReorderLevel" Type="smallint" />
  <Property Name="Discontinued" Type="bit" Nullable="false" />
</EntityType>
```

The *conceptual model* describes the entities from the application standpoint. You can also examine the conceptual model using the Model Browser. It displays the conceptual model at the top of the tree view (Figure 2.10 shows an example of the conceptual model generated from the Northwind sample database). However, the Entity Designer, which presents the conceptual model in a UML-like diagram, might be a better option for working with the conceptual model, especially when the number of entities is not large.

FIGURE 2.10 Conceptual model.

Usually the entities in the conceptual model are closely related to the tables and views in the storage model. However, entity types are higher-level constructs and do not necessarily match the database tables they represent. In particular, the Product entity has a singular name, but the Products table name is plural. It also has navigation properties that allow you to traverse entity relationships without having to immediately resort to joins in LINQ queries.

Following is the raw XML definition of the Product entity. Notice that the XML element names, EntityType, Key, and Property, are similar to those used in the storage model definition. The NavigationProperty element, on the other hand, is used only in the conceptual model:

```
<EntityType Name="Product">
  <Key>
    <PropertyRef Name="ProductID" />
  </Key>
  <Property Name="ProductID" Type="Int32" Nullable="false"
    annotation:StoreGeneratedPattern="Identity" />
  <Property Name="ProductName" Type="String" Nullable="false"
    MaxLength="40" Unicode="true" FixedLength="false" />
  <Property Name="SupplierID" Type="Int32" />
  <Property Name="CategoryID" Type="Int32" />
  <Property Name="QuantityPerUnit" Type="String" MaxLength="20"
    Unicode="true" FixedLength="false" />
  <Property Name="UnitPrice" Type="Decimal" Precision="19" Scale="4" />
  <Property Name="UnitsInStock" Type="Int16" />
  <Property Name="UnitsOnOrder" Type="Int16" />
  <Property Name="ReorderLevel" Type="Int16" />
  <Property Name="Discontinued" Type="Boolean" Nullable="false" />
  <NavigationProperty Name="Supplier" FromRole="Product" ToRole="Supplier"
    Relationship="NorthwindModel.FK_Products_Suppliers" />
  <NavigationProperty Name="Category" FromRole="Product" ToRole="Category"
    Relationship="NorthwindModel.FK_Products_Categories" />
  <NavigationProperty Name="Order_Details"
    FromRole="Product" ToRole="Order_Detail"
    Relationship="NorthwindModel.FK_Order_Details_Products" />
</EntityType>
```

Some database tables, such as the EmployeeTerritories in the Northwind sample database, might not have corresponding entity types at all. The many-to-many association between the Employees and the Territories tables requires a third table, sometimes called a "junction table," to implement in a relational database system. However, in the conceptual entity model, the many-to-many association between the Employee and Territory entities can be supported directly by their Territories and Employees navigation properties.

The *mapping model* connects the storage and conceptual models and allows for some degree of differences between them. The Mapping Details tool window shows the mapping information for the entity, currently selected in the Entity Designer or the Model Browser window. Figure 2.11 shows an example of the mapping for the Product entity.

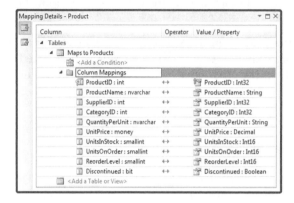

FIGURE 2.11 Mapping model.

The Mapping Details window shows the database table to which the currently selected entity type is mapped, followed by a list of column mappings, with database columns listed on the left side and the entity properties shown on the right. In this example, the entire entity model is reverse-engineered from an existing Northwind sample database, so the storage and conceptual models are nearly identical, making the mapping very straightforward. However, if you want to customize the conceptual model, you can configure the entity mapping manually.

The underlying XML representation of the mapping model fairly closely matches what the Mapping Details window displays. Following is the mapping of the Product entity type to the Products table of the Northwind database:

```
<EntityTypeMapping TypeName="NorthwindModel.Product">
  <MappingFragment StoreEntitySet="Products">
    <ScalarProperty Name="ProductID" ColumnName="ProductID" />
    <ScalarProperty Name="ProductName" ColumnName="ProductName" />
    <ScalarProperty Name="SupplierID" ColumnName="SupplierID" />
    <ScalarProperty Name="CategoryID" ColumnName="CategoryID" />
    <ScalarProperty Name="QuantityPerUnit" ColumnName="QuantityPerUnit" />
    <ScalarProperty Name="UnitPrice" ColumnName="UnitPrice" />
    <ScalarProperty Name="UnitsInStock" ColumnName="UnitsInStock" />
    <ScalarProperty Name="UnitsOnOrder" ColumnName="UnitsOnOrder" />
    <ScalarProperty Name="ReorderLevel" ColumnName="ReorderLevel" />
    <ScalarProperty Name="Discontinued" ColumnName="Discontinued" />
  </MappingFragment>
</EntityTypeMapping>
```

Mapping Entity Type to Multiple Tables

A fairly common problem in database applications is the mismatch between the shape of database tables and entity types. For example, a common database optimization technique is to separate frequently accessed columns from rarely accessed ones by placing them in two separate tables. The idea is to reduce the amount of data that has to be read from disk during table or index scan operations. This scenario can be illustrated by splitting the Customers table from the Northwind database in two—Customer and CustomerAddress:

```
create table split.Customer(
  CustomerID nchar(5) not null primary key,
  CompanyName nvarchar(40),
  ContactName nvarchar(30) not null,
  ContactTitle nvarchar(30)
);

create table split.CustomerAddress(
  CustomerID nchar(5) not null primary key,
  Address nvarchar(60),
  City nvarchar(15),
  Region nvarchar(15),
  PostalCode nvarchar(10),
  Country nvarchar(15),
  Phone nvarchar(24),
  Fax nvarchar(24)
);
```

Even though the Customer information is now split in two tables, definition of the Customer entity in the conceptual model does not have to change—it continues to have both contact and address properties. You can map it to two tables instead of one; Figure 2.12 shows how this looks in the Mapping Details window of the Entity Designer. When the entity mapping has been modified, you can continue working with it in the application code as if it were still mapped to a single table:

```
var query = from c in context.Customers
            select c;
foreach (Customer c in query)
  Console.WriteLine(c.ContactName + " " + c.Address);
```

Under the hood, the Entity Framework automatically generates the SQL join queries required to retrieve the customer information from what is now two tables, allowing you to keep a holistic view of the Customer entity in the application code.

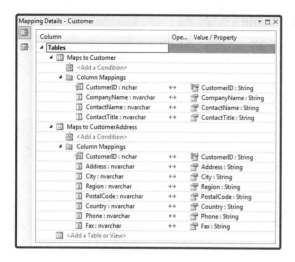

FIGURE 2.12 Entity type mapped to two separate tables.

Entity Type Inheritance

You can also use class inheritance to model your entities. For example, suppose you need a conceptual model that supports distinguishing visitors of your website from the actual customers who have already placed one or more orders. In this model, User entity type describes all users of an application. Another entity type, Customer, inherits from it and represents customers, a specialized type of users. Figure 2.13 shows how this model looks in the entity designer.

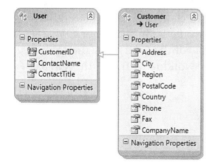

FIGURE 2.13 Entity type inheritance.

This conceptual model can be mapped to the same two tables created earlier, Customer and CustomerAddress. The User entity type is mapped to the Customer table, and the Customer entity type is mapped to the CustomerAddress table. Here is the mapping definition in raw XML form:

```
<EntitySetMapping Name="Users">
  <EntityTypeMapping TypeName="IsTypeOf(NorthwindModel2.User)">
    <MappingFragment StoreEntitySet="Customer">
      <ScalarProperty Name="ContactTitle" ColumnName="ContactTitle" />
      <ScalarProperty Name="ContactName" ColumnName="ContactName" />
      <ScalarProperty Name="CustomerID" ColumnName="CustomerID" />
    </MappingFragment>
  </EntityTypeMapping>
  <EntityTypeMapping TypeName="IsTypeOf(NorthwindModel2.Customer)">
    <MappingFragment StoreEntitySet="CustomerAddress">
      <ScalarProperty Name="Fax" ColumnName="Fax" />
      <ScalarProperty Name="Phone" ColumnName="Phone" />
      <ScalarProperty Name="Country" ColumnName="Country" />
      <ScalarProperty Name="PostalCode" ColumnName="PostalCode" />
      <ScalarProperty Name="Region" ColumnName="Region" />
      <ScalarProperty Name="City" ColumnName="City" />
      <ScalarProperty Name="Address" ColumnName="Address" />
      <ScalarProperty Name="CustomerID" ColumnName="CustomerID" />
    </MappingFragment>
  </EntityTypeMapping>
</EntitySetMapping>
```

With these conceptual and mapping model definitions, you can easily query all users (this returns both User and Customer entity objects):

```
var query = from u in context.Users
            select u;
```

On the other hand, if we are interested only in Customers, we can use the OfType extension method, which returns only the entities of a given type:

```
var query = from c in context.Users.OfType<Customer>()
            select c;
```

Inheritance Mapping

Three different approaches to mapping inheritance hierarchies to database tables exist—table-per-type, table-per-concrete-type, and table-per-hierarchy.

With the *table-per-type* approach, used in the previous example, each entity type in the conceptual model is mapped to a separate database table. To retrieve a derived entity such as Customer, the Entity Framework performs a SQL join of all tables storing properties of parent entity types.

With the *table-per-concrete-type* approach, each nonabstract type in the inheritance hierarchy gets its own table with a full set of columns necessary to store properties of the entity type itself and all of its parent types. This allows the Entity Framework to query only one table to retrieve entity of any given type. However, if you query instances of a base type, such as User in the previous example, the Entity Framework has to perform a SQL union of all tables to which the derived entity types are mapped.

With the *table-per-hierarchy* approach, all entity types derived from a common base are stored in a single table, with one or more columns serving as discriminators that identify the entity type stored in each particular row. This approach results in having columns required to store all properties of all types in a hierarchy in a single table, which could easily become quite wide as the number of entity types increases.

Each of these approaches has unique trade-offs that can have a significant effect on performance and data storage requirements of your application. Assess them carefully before making a decision. See Chapter 9, "Implementing Business Logic," for a closer look at this advanced topic.

Stored Procedures

Although LINQ to Entities is a very powerful mechanism for creating database queries, you might find yourself in a situation where it is not enough and use of database stored procedures is desirable. The most common reasons for using stored procedures in database applications are performance optimization and security. Both of these reasons are still applicable but not as relevant as in classic ADO.NET applications because Entity Framework generates well-performing and secure SQL code out of the box. When optimizing performance, your first choice should be to simplify and speed-up the LINQ queries. Making sure that LINQ queries take advantage of indexes, return a minimal number of rows, and use projections to limit the size of result sets goes a long way to improve application performance. Although stored procedures are fully supported by the Entity Framework, they require additional effort to implement and maintain, so you should resort to using them for improved performance only after exhausting the LINQ optimization options.

Consider the following LINQ query that returns products that need to be re-ordered:

```
var query = from p in context.Products
            where p.UnitsInStock < p.ReorderLevel
            select p;
```

Similar logic can be implemented using T-SQL in the following stored procedure:

```
CREATE PROCEDURE dbo.GetProductsToReorder
AS
  SELECT * FROM dbo.Products
  WHERE UnitsInStock < ReorderLevel;
```

Code in this example would not benefit from using a stored procedure. Any performance improvement from rewriting it in a stored procedure using raw T-SQL would not be noticeable. It is used here only for simplicity.

Having this procedure defined in the Northwind database, you can import its definition as a *function* to the model. To do that, open the Update Wizard that was discussed earlier by right-clicking the design surface in Entity Designer and selecting the Update Model from Database item from the context menu. On the Add tab of the Update Wizard, shown in Figure 2.14, expand Stored Procedures, select the GetProductsToReorder stored procedure, and click the Finish button.

FIGURE 2.14 Adding stored procedures to the entity model.

When the Update Model wizard closes, the stored procedure is added to the storage section of the entity model shown in Figure 2.15. However, before it can be used in the application code, you must add it as a *function import* to the conceptual section of the entity model. Right-click the stored procedure in the storage section of the Model Browser and select Add Function Import from the context menu—this opens a dialog similar to that shown in Figure 2.16.

FIGURE 2.15 Stored procedure in storage section of the entity model.

In the Add Function Import dialog (see Figure 2.16), you can specify the name of the function that will be added to the conceptual model. By default, it will match the name of the stored procedure, but you have the option of changing it. It is common for organizations to use the Hungarian naming convention for stored procedure names, with prefixes such as usp_ to distinguish custom stored procedures from system stored procedures, which have prefix sp_. However, the Hungarian notation is discouraged in .NET applications to improve readability of the code. Function import mapping option in Entity Framework allows you to follow .NET naming conventions in the application code without having to rename the stored procedure.

In addition to the function name, another design decision you need to make when importing a stored procedure is to specify the type of objects returned by the stored procedure. The Get Column Information button allows you to quickly see the definition of its result set. In this case, the GetProductsToReorder procedure returns a set of Products, and you can have the function return a collection of Product entities. If the set of columns returned by a stored procedure does not match any of the entity types defined in the model, you can choose the option to return a collection of *complex* (non-entity) objects and have the tool automatically create a new complex type definition. Function imports returning collections of complex objects are similar to LINQ queries that use projection to return sets of anonymous or named objects. Similar to projection, having a stored procedure return a specific set of columns helps to reduce the size of the result set but does not take advantage of the identity tracking, which is only supported for entities.

FIGURE 2.16 Add function import.

When you click the OK button in the Add Function Import dialog, the function import is added to the conceptual section of the model. You can find it under Entity Container/Function Imports in the model browser; Figure 2.17 shows an example.

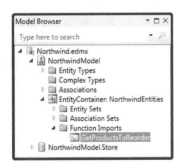

FIGURE 2.17 Function import in the conceptual section of model browser.

For each function import, the Entity Designer generates a strongly-typed method in the ObjectContext class. Following is an example of using the newly added GetProductsToReorder method to list all products returned by the stored procedure:

```
using (NorthwindEntities context = new NorthwindEntities())
{
  IEnumerable<Product> products = context.GetProductsToReorder();
  foreach (Product p in products)
    Console.WriteLine(p.ProductName);
}
```

The generated method returns an IEnumerable and not an IQueryable. Although you can use the familiar LINQ operators to manipulate it further, keep in mind that these operations are performed in the application memory and not by the database server. Instead, it is often best to modify the definition of the stored procedure itself and have it return a more focused result set.

Insert, Update, and Delete Stored Procedures

The Entity Framework also allows you to use stored procedures to perform insert, update, and delete operations instead of generating SQL statements dynamically. When combined with restriction of the application permissions to only read data, this technique can help reduce accidental data corruption and locking due to casual browsing, when developers or administrators use a tool, such as SQL Server Management Studio to interactively explore live data in a production system.

Here's an example of the stored procedure that inserts a new Product entity into the Products table:

```
CREATE PROCEDURE [dbo].[Products_Insert]
  @ProductName nvarchar(40), @SupplierID int, @CategoryID int,
  @QuantityPerUnit nvarchar(20), @UnitPrice money, @UnitsInStock smallint,
  @UnitsOnOrder smallint, @ReorderLevel smallint, @Discontinued bit
AS
BEGIN
  INSERT INTO Products
    (ProductName, SupplierID, CategoryID,
    QuantityPerUnit, UnitPrice, UnitsInStock,
    UnitsOnOrder, ReorderLevel, Discontinued)
  VALUES
    (@ProductName, @SupplierID, @CategoryID,
    @QuantityPerUnit, @UnitPrice, @UnitsInStock,
    @UnitsOnOrder, @ReorderLevel, @Discontinued);

  SELECT SCOPE_IDENTITY() as ProductID;
END
```

Notice that this stored procedure takes a set of parameters, each representing a particular table column, such as ProductName and SupplierID. The stored procedure performs the INSERT statement and a SELECT statement to return the ProductID value of the newly inserted row.

For the Entity Framework to take advantage of this stored procedure, it needs to be added to the storage section of the entity model, similar to the `GetProductsToReorder` stored procedure discussed earlier. However, instead of adding it as a function import to the conceptual model, right-click the Product entity in the Entity Designer and select Stored Procedure Mapping from the context menu. You will see the Mapping Details window similar to that shown in Figure 2.18.

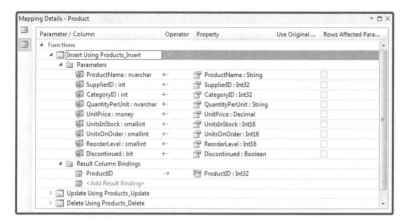

FIGURE 2.18 Insert function mapping.

The Functions tab of the Mapping window allows you to map the stored procedure parameters (shown on the left) to the entity properties (shown on the right). In this example, the generated `ProductID` value is mapped in the Result Column Bindings section.

The *Update* stored procedures are somewhat more complex because they need to implement the optimistic locking normally performed by the Entity Framework. In addition to the primary key value required to uniquely identify the target row and the current values of all fields, the update procedure needs to provide a separate parameter for each entity property that has Concurrency Mode set to Fixed in the entity model. In the following example, the `Products_Update` procedure provides a separate set of parameters for all properties, one set for the *new* values, used to update the row, and the other set of *old* values, used to make sure that the entity has not been modified since it was last retrieved from the database.

The update stored procedure also needs to be added to the model and used to map the Product entity as shown in Figure 2.19. Each property of the Product entity is mapped twice—first to the parameter that receives the "old" value of the entity property as it was originally retrieved from the database and then to the parameter that receives the "new" value that needs to be persisted. Notice that the `@RowsAffected` output parameter of the stored procedure, which returns the number of rows actually modified by the stored procedure, has a checkbox in the Rows Affected Parameter column. This parameter is used by the Entity Framework to determine if the optimistic locking was performed successfully and throw the `OptimisticConcurrencyException` if it returns zero.

```
CREATE PROCEDURE [dbo].[Products_Update]
  @ProductID int, @RowsAffected int out,

  @OldProductName nvarchar(40), @OldSupplierID int, @OldCategoryID int,
  @OldQuantityPerUnit nvarchar(20), @OldUnitPrice money,
  @OldUnitsInStock smallint, @OldUnitsOnOrder smallint,
  @OldReorderLevel smallint, @OldDiscontinued bit,

  @NewProductName nvarchar(40), @NewSupplierID int, @NewCategoryID int,
  @NewQuantityPerUnit nvarchar(20), @NewUnitPrice money,
  @NewUnitsInStock smallint, @NewUnitsOnOrder smallint,
  @NewReorderLevel smallint, @NewDiscontinued bit
AS
BEGIN
  UPDATE Products SET
    ProductName = @NewProductName,
    SupplierID = @NewSupplierID,
    CategoryID = @NewCategoryID,
    QuantityPerUnit = @NewQuantityPerUnit,
    UnitPrice = @NewUnitPrice,
    UnitsInStock = @NewUnitsInStock,
    UnitsOnOrder = @NewUnitsOnOrder,
    ReorderLevel = @NewReorderLevel,
    Discontinued = @NewDiscontinued
  WHERE
    ProductID = @ProductID AND
    SupplierID = @OldSupplierID AND
    CategoryID = @OldCategoryID AND
    QuantityPerUnit = @OldQuantityPerUnit AND
    UnitPrice = @OldUnitPrice AND
    UnitsInStock = @OldUnitsInStock AND
    UnitsOnOrder = @OldUnitsOnOrder AND
    ReorderLevel = @OldReorderLevel AND
    Discontinued = @OldDiscontinued;

  SET @RowsAffected = @@ROWCOUNT;
END
```

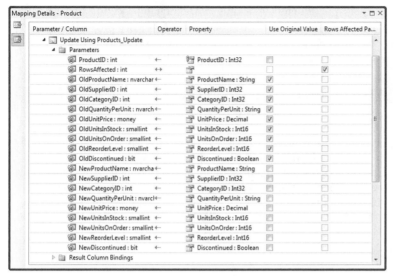

FIGURE 2.19 Update function mapping.

The *Delete* stored procedures are similar to the update stored procedures in that they also need to implement optimistic locking and make sure that the deleted entity has not been modified since it was last retrieved from the database. However, because there are no *new* values to persist, their parameter lists are usually much shorter. Here is an example of the delete procedure for the Product entity:

```
CREATE PROCEDURE [dbo].[Products_Delete]
    @ProductID int, @ProductName nvarchar(40), @SupplierID int, @CategoryID
int,
    @QuantityPerUnit nvarchar(20), @UnitPrice money, @UnitsInStock smallint,
    @UnitsOnOrder smallint, @ReorderLevel smallint, @Discontinued bit,
    @RowsAffected int out
AS
BEGIN
  DELETE FROM Products
  WHERE
    ProductID = @ProductID AND
    SupplierID = @SupplierID AND
    CategoryID = @CategoryID AND
    QuantityPerUnit = @QuantityPerUnit AND
    UnitPrice = @UnitPrice AND
    UnitsInStock = @UnitsInStock AND
    UnitsOnOrder = @UnitsOnOrder AND
    ReorderLevel = @ReorderLevel AND
    Discontinued = @Discontinued;

  SET @RowsAffected = @@ROWCOUNT
END
```

Because there is only one set of parameters, mapping of the delete procedures is also straightforward. If the parameter names match the names of the entity properties, the Entity Designer maps them automatically. You only need to make sure that the `RowsAffected` parameter has a check mark in the Rows Affected Parameter column.

> **NOTE**
>
> Although it would be possible to revoke direct data access permissions from an application using Entity Framework and force it to rely strictly on the Select, Insert, Update, and Delete stored procedures, doing so would require an additional effort to implement and take away most of the strengths and productivity improvements offered by the Entity Framework. Stored procedures are a great performance and security optimization option, but when followed to the extreme, this approach defeats most of the reasons to use a LINQ-based framework in the first place.

Summary

The ADO.NET Entity Framework is an ORM framework developed by Microsoft as part of the .NET Framework. It is built on top of the Entity Data Model, which includes a storage model, describing database tables, views, and stored procedures; a conceptual model, describing application entity types and functions; and a mapping model that connects conceptual definitions to their physical implementation in the storage model.

The Entity Framework has first-class design tools in Visual Studio for working with entity data models, including the Entity Designer, Model Browser, and Mapping tool windows as well as the Update Wizard. Together, these tools allow developers to use the database-first approach, where the entity model is reverse-engineered from an existing database, as well as the model-first approach, where the database is generated from an entity data model created from scratch.

Based on the conceptual model, the Entity Framework generates strongly-typed application classes, including entity classes, which encapsulate individual rows of data, and an `ObjectContext`, which encapsulates a collection of entity sets (tables) and functions (stored procedures). Entity Framework allows using LINQ queries to retrieve entity instances from the database. The LINQ queries are compiled in a form of LINQ expressions. At run time, the LINQ expressions are translated into dynamic, parameterized SQL statements and sent to the underlying database engine for execution. Upon return, the `ObjectContext` materializes the records returned by the SQL queries are in the form of entity instances, allowing using strongly-typed .NET code to query and manipulate database information.

Entity Framework provides an abstraction layer that allows you to build a holistic view of the information in a conceptual model independent from the underlying storage schema. In particular, a single entity type can be mapped to multiple tables. Entity Framework also supports entity inheritance and allows mapping class hierarchies using table-per-type, table-per-concrete type, and table-per-hierarchy strategies.

The Entity Framework is optimized for rich-client applications that retrieve and manipulate a relatively small number of records at a time. However, by turning off the object tracking options, its performance can be improved for multi-threaded web applications as well as applications working with a large number of records in batch mode. Although the Entity Framework generates high-quality, parameterized SQL code appropriate for most common data access scenarios, it also allows the use of stored procedures to create, read, update, and delete entities/database records.

Entity Framework supports the `TransactionScope` class from the `System.Transactions` namespace and optimistic concurrency for conflict detection in multi-user scenarios. It does not support pessimistic locking out of the box; however, implementing it is possible with the help of custom stored procedures.

The Entity Framework represents a long-term strategic investment for Microsoft. As of .NET version 4, it is a powerful framework appropriate for use on most enterprise application projects. It offers significant productivity improvements compared to the classic ADO.NET and has become a recommended choice with some of the new technologies developed by Microsoft, including ASP.NET Dynamic Data. The Entity Framework is under active development. Version 4.1, added support for Code-First approach, making it possible to define entity model directly in application code, as classes. The upcoming version 4.5 will bring significant enhancements to the Entity Designer, including support for enumerated types and multiple diagrams, making developers using the database-first approach, discussed in this chapter, as well as the model-first approach, much more productive.

CHAPTER 3

Field Templates

Enterprise applications deal with employees, managers, emergency contacts, prospects, customers, suppliers, and vendors—in other words, people and organizations, who all have names, addresses, and phone numbers. Implementing data entry logic for these attributes is repetitive, and for years, the ASP.NET developers have been developing user controls to reduce the code duplication. It is common to see user controls with text boxes and validators for entering street, city, state, and postal code in many web applications today.

Although they are a great mechanism for reusing presentation and validation logic, user controls require a certain amount of plumbing before they can be used on a web page. At the very minimum, user controls must be registered, and because even the simplest controls need to provide slightly varying functionality in different contexts, they also usually have one or more properties that need to be configured. As the user controls get more and more granular, the amount of plumbing work required to apply them increases. It quickly reaches the point of diminishing returns, and developers usually stop short of implementing user controls for the individual data entry fields.

Field template is a special type of ASP.NET user control that encapsulates presentation and validation logic for a single field. Unlike the traditional user controls, field templates do not require registration. Instead, a simple `DynamicControl` or a `DynamicField` placed on a web page automatically loads and configures an appropriate field template based the column name and metadata.

Metadata information, readily available in Dynamic Data web applications, dramatically lowers the amount of plumbing code developers have to write when working with user controls, enables effective use of smaller user controls, and takes code reuse to an unprecedented new level.

Read-Only Templates

By convention, field templates are located in the `DynamicData\FieldTemplates` folder of the Dynamic Data web application projects and websites. A single instance of a field template provides user interface for one particular field value. Consider Listing 3.1, which shows markup file of the `DateTime` field template.

LISTING 3.1 DateTime Field Template (Markup)

```
<%@ Control Language="C#" CodeBehind="DateTime.ascx.cs"
  Inherits="WebApplication.DynamicData.FieldTemplates.DateTimeField" %>

<asp:Literal runat="server" ID="literal" Text="<%# FieldValueString %>" />
```

This is a *read-only* field template, the simplest type of field template. It relies on ASP.NET data binding syntax `<%# %>` to display the field value in a single `Literal` control. Listing 3.2 shows the code-behind of the `DateTime` field template. You can see that it inherits from the `FieldTemplateUserControl`, a special base class provided for field templates by Dynamic Data. This class defines the `FieldValueString` property to which the `Literal` control is bound.

LISTING 3.2 DateTime Field Template (Code-behind)

```
using System.Web.DynamicData;
using System.Web.UI;

namespace WebApplication.DynamicData.FieldTemplates
{
  public partial class DateTimeField : FieldTemplateUserControl
  {
    public override Control DataControl
    {
      get { return this.literal; }
    }
  }
}
```

Code-behind files perform most of the work required to make the generated web pages dynamic. In this simplest example, the template overrides the `DataControl` property defined by the base class. Entity templates (see Chapter 4, "Entity Templates") use this property when dynamically generating entity forms, to associate each field template with a matching `Label` control.

Field Value Display Format

In addition to the `FieldValueString` property, the `FieldTemplateUserControl` class also provides another property called `FieldValue`, which returns the raw value object. At a cursory glance, the `FieldValue` property could be used to bind the `Literal` control as well. However, it is important to use the `FieldValueString` property as it automatically takes into account additional display format properties when converting the raw field value to a string:

▶ `DataFormatString` specifies a .NET format string that will be passed to the `String.Format` method to convert the field value to a display string.

▶ `NullDisplayText` specifies a replacement string that will be used when the raw field value is null.

▶ `ConvertEmptyStringToNull` is a Boolean value that determines whether an empty string value should treated as null and if the `NullDisplayText` will be used as a replacement for empty strings as well as null values. This property is `true` by default.

▶ `HtmlEncode` is a Boolean value that determines whether any special HTML symbols in the raw field value, such as `'<'` or `'>'`, will be encoded using escape sequences, such as `&lt;` and `&gt;`. This property is `true` by default.

Display format properties can be specified in the data model by applying the `DataTypeAttribute` or the `DisplayFormatAttribute` to a particular column, as shown in Listing 3.3. The `DisplayFormatAttribute`, applied to the OrderDate column, specifies a long date `{0:D}` format string. The `DataTypeAttribute`, applied to the RequiredDate column, does not have its own `DataFormatString` property. Instead, it offers the `DisplayFormat` property, which gets a default `DisplayFormatAttribute` generated, based on the specified data type. For `DataType.Date`, the default data format string will be a short date `{0:d}`.

LISTING 3.3 Specifying Display Format Using Data Annotations

```
using System.ComponentModel.DataAnnotations;

namespace DataModel
{
  [MetadataType (typeof(Order.Metadata))]
  partial class Order
  {
```

LISTING 3.3 Continued

```
    public class Metadata
    {
      [DisplayFormat(DataFormatString = "{0:D}")]
      public object OrderDate;

      [DataType(DataType.Date)]
      public object RequiredDate;
    }
  }
}
```

Display format properties can be also specified in page markup by setting the correspond-ing properties of the DynamicControl or DynamicField classes, similar to the properties of the "non-dynamic" BoundField. Listing 3.4 shows an example where a DynamicField is used in a GridView control and specifies a custom date format string {0:MM/dd/yy} for the ShippedDate column.

LISTING 3.4 Specifying Data Format Using DynamicField

```
<%@ Page Language="C#"
  MasterPageFile="~/Site.master" CodeBehind="SamplePage.aspx.cs"
  Inherits="WebApplication.Samples.Ch01.DataFormatString.SamplePage" %>

<asp:Content ContentPlaceHolderID="ContentPlaceHolder1" runat="server">
  <asp:GridView ID="gridView" runat="server" DataSourceID="dataSource"
    AutoGenerateColumns="false" AllowPaging="true">
    <columns>
      <asp:DynamicField DataField="OrderDate" />
      <asp:DynamicField DataField="RequiredDate" />
      <asp:DynamicField DataField="ShippedDate" DataFormatString="{0:MM/dd/yy}" />
    </columns>
  </asp:GridView>
  <asp:EntityDataSource ID="dataSource" runat="server"
    ConnectionString="name=NorthwindEntities"
    DefaultContainerName="NorthwindEntities" EntitySetName="Orders" />
</asp:Content>
```

Figure 3.1 shows the web page generated by this code. As you can see, the OrderDate values use the long format specified in the DisplayFormatAttribute in the model; the RequiredDate values use the short format provided by the DataTypeAttribute; and the ShippedDate values use the custom format specified in the page markup.

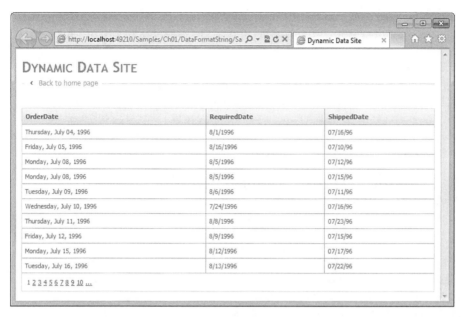

FIGURE 3.1 GridView with `DataType` and `DisplayFormat` attributes applied.

Inside of the field templates, the display format properties are available via the `FormattingOptions` property inherited from the `FieldTemplateUserControl`. The base class automatically initializes them based on the formatting options of the host—`DynamicControl` or `DynamicField`.

As you might expect, a fair amount of logic is involved in converting the raw field value to the final display string. By using the `FieldValueString` property of the `FieldTemplateUserControl` class, field templates ensure consistent behavior that offers application developers great flexibility in defining the presentation aspects of their data. The `DataTypeAttribute` allows specifying default display properties for a column in the data model based on its data type. The `DisplayFormatAttribute` allows fine-tuning it with the standard or custom format strings. Finally, the `DynamicControl` and `DynamicField` controls allow tailoring the display of column values for a specific page in a web application.

Edit and Insert Mode Templates

In addition to the read-only field templates, Dynamic Data has *Edit* and *Insert* field templates. Unlike the Read-Only templates, where the field value is simply displayed on the page, the Edit templates allow the user to modify it using a data entry control, such as a `TextBox`. By convention, Dynamic Data distinguishes Edit and Insert templates by the `_Edit` and `_Insert` they have at the end of their file names, respectively. The Insert templates are a special case of Edit templates, used for editing field values of rows that have not been saved to the database. However, most Edit mode field templates can be used in Insert mode as well.

The Edit field templates are significantly more complex than their read-only counterparts. Consider Listing 3.5, which shows the Edit version of the DateTime field template.

LISTING 3.5 DateTime_Edit Field Template (Markup)

```
<%@ Control Language="C#" CodeBehind="DateTime_Edit.ascx.cs"
  Inherits="WebApplication.DynamicData.FieldTemplates.DateTime_EditField" %>

<asp:TextBox ID="textBox" runat="server" Text='<%# FieldValueEditString %>'
  Columns="20" />

<asp:RequiredFieldValidator runat="server" ID="requiredFieldValidator"
  ControlToValidate="textBox" Enabled="false" />
<asp:RegularExpressionValidator runat="server" ID="regularExpressionValidator"
  ControlToValidate="textBox" Enabled="false" />
<asp:DynamicValidator runat="server" ID="dynamicValidator"
  ControlToValidate="textBox" />
<asp:CustomValidator runat="server" ID="dateValidator" ControlToValidate="textBox"
  EnableClientScript="false" Enabled="false"
  OnServerValidate="DateValidator_ServerValidate" />
```

In addition to the data entry control, the edit field templates typically have one or more validation controls. The DateTime_Edit template includes a RequiredFieldValidator, a RegularExpressionValidator, a DynamicValidator, and a CustomValidator control. Notice that with the exception of the DynamicValidator, these controls are not enabled by default. They are configured dynamically by the Page_Load event handler defined in the code-behind file shown in Listing 3.6.

Each validator control is configured by a call to the SetUpValidator method of the FieldTemplateUserControl base class. This method enables and configures the validator if the column metadata contains an appropriate data annotation attribute. In particular, the RequiredFieldValidator will be enabled when the column is marked with a RequiredAttribute that does not allow empty strings, and the RegularExpressionValidator will be enabled when the column is marked with a RegularExpressionAttribute. In addition to enabling the validator, the SetUpValidator method also assigns its ErrorMessage and ToolTip properties with an error message either explicitly specified in the data annotation attribute or generated based on the column's display name.

DynamicValidator is a special validation control provided by Dynamic Data. It ensures all validation attributes applied to the column are invoked to verify its value is correct. This andincludes not only the well-known RequiredAttribute, RangeAttribute, and CustomValidationAttribute, but also all other descendants of the ValidationAttribute that may be applied to the column and are not covered by a specific ASP.NET validator control in this field template.

The `CustomValidator` control in this field template performs the job you would normally expect the `DataTypeAttribute` to do. Even though `DataTypeAttribute` inherits from the `ValidationAttribute` class, it does not actually perform any validation. Its `IsValid` method always returns `true`, which is why the `DateTime_Edit` template uses the `CustomValidator` control to ensure that the value entered by the user matches the type specified by the `DataTypeAttribute`. The `SetUpCustomValidator` method enables the validator if the column was marked with a `DataTypeAttribute` and the `DateValidator_ServerValidate` method performs the actual validation.

LISTING 3.6 DateTime_Edit Field Template (Code-Behind)

```
using System;
using System.Collections.Specialized;
using System.ComponentModel.DataAnnotations;
using System.Web;
using System.Web.DynamicData;
using System.Web.UI;
using System.Web.UI.WebControls;

namespace WebApplication.DynamicData.FieldTemplates
{
  public partial class DateTime_EditField : FieldTemplateUserControl
  {
    private static DataTypeAttribute DefaultDateAttribute =
      new DataTypeAttribute(DataType.DateTime);

    public override Control DataControl
    {
      get { return this.textBox; }
    }

    protected void Page_Load(object sender, EventArgs e)
    {
      this.textBox.ToolTip = this.Column.Description;

      this.SetUpValidator(this.requiredFieldValidator);
      this.SetUpValidator(this.regularExpressionValidator);
      this.SetUpValidator(this.dynamicValidator);
      this.SetUpCustomValidator(this.dateValidator);
    }

    protected override void ExtractValues(IOrderedDictionary dictionary)
    {
      dictionary[Column.Name] = this.ConvertEditedValue(this.textBox.Text);
    }
```

LISTING 3.6 Continued

```
protected void DateValidator_ServerValidate(object source,
  ServerValidateEventArgs args)
{
  DateTime dummyResult;
  args.IsValid = DateTime.TryParse(args.Value, out dummyResult);
}

private void SetUpCustomValidator(CustomValidator validator)
{
  if (this.Column.DataTypeAttribute != null)
  {
    switch (this.Column.DataTypeAttribute.DataType)
    {
      case DataType.Date:
      case DataType.DateTime:
      case DataType.Time:
        this.EnableCustomValidator(validator, this.Column.DataTypeAttribute);
        break;
    }
  }
  else if (this.Column.ColumnType.Equals(typeof(DateTime)))
  {
    this.EnableCustomValidator(validator, DefaultDateAttribute);
  }
}

private void EnableCustomValidator(CustomValidator validator,
  DataTypeAttribute attribute)
{
  validator.Enabled = true;
  validator.ErrorMessage = HttpUtility.HtmlEncode(
    attribute.FormatErrorMessage(this.Column.DisplayName));
}
  }
}
```

Field Value Edit Format

You might have noticed that the `DateTime_Edit` template uses the `FieldValueEditString` property of the `FieldTemplateUserControl` base class. This property is similar to the `FieldValueString` property discussed earlier in that it respects the `FormattingOptions` when converting the raw column value to a display string. However, it was specifically designed for use in the Edit mode templates, and an additional property is used to control its behavior.

▸ `ApplyFormatInEditMode` is a Boolean value that determines whether the `DataFormatString`, `NullDisplayText`, `ConvertEmptyStringToNull`, and `HtmlEncode` display format properties will be used in Edit mode. This property is `false` by default.

Similar to using the `FieldValueString` property when implementing Read-only field templates, it is also important to rely on the `FieldValueEditString` property as much as possible when implementing the Edit and Insert mode templates. This helps the field templates to behave consistently and allow the application developers to change presentation aspects of column values using metadata attributes as well as explicit configuration in page markup.

Changing Existing Field Template

Dynamic Data uses the same field template for all matching columns in the model. The `DateTime_Edit` field template is automatically used for all columns of type `DateTime` in the Northwind data model, including OrderDate, RequiredDate, and ShippedDate columns of the Order table as well as BirthDate and HireDate columns of the Employee table. By changing definition of the field template, you affect all web pages where it is used. Figure 3.2 shows how the experience of entering date values can be improved by allowing the users to select a date from a calendar drop-down.

FIGURE 3.2 Modified DateTime field template with calendar drop-down.

The modified field template, `DateTime_Edit.ascx`, is shown in Listing 3.7. This example uses the `CalendarExtender` control from the AJAX Control Toolkit, but you can use any other ASP.NET control from your favorite component vendor. The `CalendarExtender` is associated with the `TextBox` by specifying its `TagetControlID` property. Using the `PopupButtonID` property, it is also associated with an `ImageButton` that users can click to display the calendar drop-down.

> **NOTE**
>
> The AJAX (Asynchronous JavaScript and XML) Control Toolkit is an extension of the ASP.NET framework developed by Microsoft to enhance client-side behavior of the standard WebForms controls. It is an open source project hosted on CodePlex and available for download at `http://AjaxControlToolkit.CodePlex.com`.
>
> The AJAX Control Toolkit comes in a ZIP archive that you need to extract to a directory on your hard drive. Before you can begin using AJAX controls, you need to add the downloaded AjaxControlToolkit.dll as a reference to your web application project in Visual Studio.

LISTING 3.7 Extended DateTime_Edit Field Template (Markup)

```
<%@ Control Language="C#" CodeBehind="DateTime_Edit.ascx.cs"
  Inherits="WebApplication.DynamicData.FieldTemplates.DateTime_EditField" %>


<asp:TextBox ID="textBox" runat="server" Text='<%# FieldValueEditString %>'
  Columns="20" />
<asp:ImageButton ID="calendarButton" runat="server"
  ImageUrl="../Content/Images/Calendar.png" />
<ajax:CalendarExtender runat="server" TargetControlID="textBox"
  PopupButtonID="calendarButton" />


<asp:RequiredFieldValidator runat="server" ID="requiredFieldValidator"
  ControlToValidate="textBox" Enabled="false" />
<asp:RegularExpressionValidator runat="server" ID="regularExpressionValidator"
  ControlToValidate="textBox" Enabled="false" />
<asp:DynamicValidator runat="server" ID="dynamicValidator"
  ControlToValidate="textBox" />
<asp:CustomValidator runat="server" ID="dateValidator" ControlToValidate="textBox"
  EnableClientScript="false" Enabled="false"
  OnServerValidate="DateValidator_ServerValidate" />
```

Notice that this example uses a custom ajax: tag prefix with the CalendarExtender
without actually registering it. We could have used the ASP.NET <%@ Register %> directive
to register this tag prefix directly in the DateTime_Edit.ascx. However, because the AJAX
Control Toolkit is used in other field templates of this sample project, it is better to register it in the Web.config as shown in Listing 3.8. This makes the AJAX controls available in
all pages and controls of the web application and helps you avoid having to register the
same tag prefix in multiple pages and user controls.

LISTING 3.8 Registering AJAX Controls in the Web Configuration File

```
<?xml version="1.0"?>
<configuration>
  <system.web>
    <compilation debug="true" targetFramework="4.0"/>
    <pages styleSheetTheme="Default">
      <controls>
        <add tagPrefix="ajax" assembly="AjaxControlToolkit"
          namespace="AjaxControlToolkit"/>
      </controls>
    </pages>
  </system.web>
  <system.webServer>
    <modules runAllManagedModulesForAllRequests="true"/>
  </system.webServer>
  <connectionStrings>
```

LISTING 3.8 Continued

```
    <add name="NorthwindEntities"
      providerName="System.Data.EntityClient"
      connectionString="
        metadata=res://*/Northwind.csdl¦
                 res://*/Northwind.ssdl¦
                 res://*/Northwind.msl;
        provider=System.Data.SqlClient;
        provider connection string=&quot;
          data source=.\sqlexpress;
          initial catalog=Northwind;
          integrated security=True;
          multipleactiveresultsets=True&quot;"/>
  </connectionStrings>
</configuration>
```

Data Binding

Several of the built-in Dynamic Data field templates, including the DateTime and DateTime_Edit templates, rely on data binding to display column value on the page.

```
<asp:TextBox ID="textBox" runat="server" Text='<%# FieldValueEditString %>' />
```

In addition, the field template controls themselves are data bound, and several properties of the FieldTemplateUserControl base class rely on the data binding mechanics. These properties can be used safely *only* from the DataBind method and will throw an InvalidOperationException when used outside of the data binding context, such as during a post-back:

▶ Row provides access to the entity instance the field template is bound to, such as an Order object. In Read-only and Edit modes, it is an equivalent of calling the Page.GetDataItem method. In Insert mode, this property returns a CustomTypeDescriptor object that provides access to default field values extracted by the page template from the page request URL (more on this in Chapter 6, "Page Templates").

▶ FieldValue returns value of the column property, such as Order.OrderDate. It is an equivalent of calling DataBinder.Eval(Row, Column.Name).

▶ FieldValueString converts the field value to a display string in Read-only mode, using the formatting options specified in the data model or page markup. It is an equivalent of calling FormattingOptions.FormatValue(FieldValue).

▶ `FieldValueEditString` converts the field value to a string in Edit or Insert mode, using the formatting options specified in the data model or page markup. It is an equivalent of calling `FormattingOptions.FormatEditField(FieldValue)`.

During a post-back, a field template itself does not actually save the new column value back in its `Row` object. Instead, the `FieldTemplateUserControl` class implements the `IBindableControl` interface and relies on the parent `FormView`, `DetailsView`, and `GridView` controls to perform this task. When the parent control is handling an Insert or an Update command, it iterates through the list of its child controls and calls the `ExtractValues` of each child that implements `IBindableControl` interface.

```csharp
protected override void ExtractValues(IOrderedDictionary dictionary)
{
  dictionary[this.Column.Name] =
    this.ConvertEditedValue(this.textBox.Text);
}
```

The `ExtractValues` method receives a dictionary object used to store column name and value pairs. The extract from the `DateTime_Edit` field template just shown is a typical implementation of this method. The `ConvertEditedValue` method is provided by the `FieldTemplateUserControl` base class. It can automatically convert the field value to null based on the `ConvertEmptyStringToNull` and `NullDisplayText` formatting options.

Notice that by providing the dictionary argument, `ExtractValue` method allows a field template to return values of other columns or even multiple column values. This capability is important for the foreign key templates used for navigation properties, such as the Customer property of the `Order` class in the Northwind data model, that need to return values of the corresponding primitive properties, such as CustomerID. Consider Listing 3.9, which shows the markup of the `ForeignKey_Edit` template.

LISTING 3.9 ForeignKey_Edit Field Template (Markup)

```
<%@ Control Language="C#" CodeBehind="ForeignKey_Edit.ascx.cs"
  Inherits="WebApplication.DynamicData.FieldTemplates.ForeignKey_EditField" %>

<asp:DropDownList ID="dropDownList" runat="server"/>

<asp:RequiredFieldValidator runat="server" ID="requiredFieldValidator"
  ControlToValidate="dropDownList" Enabled="false" />
<asp:DynamicValidator runat="server" ID="dynamicValidator"
  ControlToValidate="dropDownList" />
```

Notice that the `ForeignKey_Edit` template uses a `DropDownList` control, which allows users to select from a list of items created programmatically, in the `Page_Load` method shown in Listing 3.10. Each `ListItem` object in the `DropDownList` represents a single foreign key, with `Text` property storing value of the display column from the referenced table and `Value` property storing a comma-separated list of its primary key columns. This code relies on the convenience method, called `PopulateListControl`, provided by the `FieldTemplateUserControl` base class, which does all the heavy lifting required to query the referenced table, create the `ListItem` objects, and add them to the `DropDownList`.

LISTING 3.10 ForeignKey_Edit Field Template (Code-Behind)

```
using System;
using System.Collections.Specialized;
using System.Web.DynamicData;
using System.Web.UI;
using System.Web.UI.WebControls;

namespace WebApplication.DynamicData.FieldTemplates
{
  public partial class ForeignKey_EditField : FieldTemplateUserControl
  {
    public override Control DataControl
    {
      get { return this.dropDownList; }
    }

    protected void Page_Load(object sender, EventArgs e)
    {
      if (this.dropDownList.Items.Count == 0)
      {
        if (this.Mode == DataBoundControlMode.Insert || !this.Column.IsRequired)
          this.dropDownList.Items.Add(new ListItem("[Not Set]", string.Empty));
        this.PopulateListControl(this.dropDownList);
      }

      this.SetUpValidator(this.requiredFieldValidator);
      this.SetUpValidator(this.dynamicValidator);
    }

    protected override void OnDataBinding(EventArgs e)
    {
      base.OnDataBinding(e);
      string selectedValueString = this.GetSelectedValueString();
      if (this.dropDownList.Items.FindByValue(selectedValueString) != null)
        this.dropDownList.SelectedValue = selectedValueString;
```

```
    }

    protected override void ExtractValues(IOrderedDictionary dictionary)
    {
        this.ExtractForeignKey(dictionary, this.dropDownList.SelectedValue);
    }
  }
}
```

To display the current field value, the ForeignKey_Edit template cannot rely on the FieldValueEditString property because the FieldValue in this case consists of one or more values of the underlying primitive columns. For the Customer column of the Order table, this would mean displaying CustomerID, "ALFKI", instead of the Customer's CompanyName, "Alfreds Futterkiste", which is not very user friendly. Instead, the ForeignKey_Edit template overrides the OnDataBinding method to select the matching item in the DropDownList. It calls the GetSelectedValueString, a convenience method provided by the FieldTemplateUserControl base class. For foreign key columns, this method is equivalent to calling ForeignKeyColumn.GetForeignKeyString(Row) and returns a comma-separated list of values of the primitive columns in the foreign key.

The ForeignKey_Edit template also overrides the ExtractValues method and calls the ExtractForeignKey provided by the FieldTemplateUserControl base class. Given a comma-separated list of column values, this method stores them in the dictionary under the names of the foreign key columns. Under the hood, this method simply calls ForeignKeyColumn.ExtractForeignKey(dictionary, selectedValue).

Creating a New Field Template

The set of field templates provided by Dynamic Data can be extended whenever a special data entry control is needed to handle values of a certain type. For example, the Northwind database uses regular string columns to store phone numbers for customers, employees, suppliers, and shippers. The phone numbers already stored in the database are in a consistent (###)###-#### format; however, Dynamic Data uses the regular Text_Edit field template for these columns, which does not enforce the phone number format. It would be nice to create a field template that would help users enter the phone numbers correctly.

You create a new field template by adding a new user control to the DynamicData\FieldTemplates folder of your project. You can also copy an existing field template that most closely matches the desired functionality. If you do copy an existing field template, remember to change the class name in both markup and code-behind files. In this example, however, we will start from scratch and create a new user control called PhoneNumber_Edit, shown in Listing 3.11.

LISTING 3.11 PhoneNumber_Edit Field Template (Markup)

```
<%@ Control Language="C#" CodeBehind="PhoneNumber_Edit.ascx.cs"
    Inherits="WebApplication.DynamicData.FieldTemplates.PhoneNumberEditField" %>

<asp:TextBox ID="textBox" runat="server" Text='<%# FieldValueEditString %>'/>
<ajax:FilteredTextBoxExtender TargetControlID="textBox" runat="server"
    FilterType="Custom" ValidChars="+()-1234567890" />

<asp:RequiredFieldValidator runat="server" ID="requiredFieldValidator"
    ControlToValidate="textBox" Enabled="false" />
<asp:RegularExpressionValidator runat="server" ID="regularExpressionValidator"
    ControlToValidate="textBox" />
<asp:DynamicValidator runat="server" ID="dynamicValidator"
    ControlToValidate="textBox" />
```

As you can see, the PhoneNumber_Edit field template is similar to the DateTime template discussed earlier. It has a TextBox control used to enter the phone number, a FilteredTextBoxExtender, another AJAX control used to prevent users from entering symbols that would not be valid in a phone number, as well as several validator controls.

Although having a single DynamicValidator control is sufficient to enforce all validation attributes applied to the column in the data model, this control performs validation only on the server side, which requires a post-back before the error can be reported. Other ASP.NET validation controls, such as the RequiredFieldValidator, are optional, but because they also offer client-side validation logic, it's best to include them in field templates to provide immediate feedback to the user, and improve the data entry experience.

Listing 3.12 shows the code-behind of the PhoneNumber_Edit field template.

LISTING 3.12 PhoneNumber_Edit Field Template (Code-Behind)

```
using System;
using System.Collections.Specialized;
using System.ComponentModel.DataAnnotations;
using System.Linq;
using System.Web;
using System.Web.DynamicData;
using System.Web.UI;
using System.Web.UI.WebControls;

namespace WebApplication.DynamicData.FieldTemplates
{
    public partial class PhoneNumberEditField : FieldTemplateUserControl
    {
        public override Control DataControl
        {
```

```
    get { return this.textBox; }
  }

  protected void Page_Load(object sender, EventArgs e)
  {
    this.textBox.ToolTip = this.Column.Description;

    this.SetUpValidator(this.requiredFieldValidator);
    this.SetUpValidator(this.dynamicValidator);
    this.SetUpRegexValidator(this.regularExpressionValidator);
  }

  protected override void ExtractValues(IOrderedDictionary dictionary)
  {
    dictionary[this.Column.Name] = this.ConvertEditedValue(this.textBox.Text);
  }

  private void SetUpRegexValidator(RegularExpressionValidator validator)
  {
    RegularExpressionAttribute attribute = this.Column.Attributes
      .OfType<RegularExpressionAttribute>().FirstOrDefault();
    if (attribute == null)
    {
      attribute = new RegularExpressionAttribute(@"\(\d{3}\)\d{3}-\d{4}");
      attribute.ErrorMessage = "The field {0} must be a valid phone number.";
    }

    validator.Enabled = true;
    validator.Text = "*";
    validator.ValidationExpression = attribute.Pattern;
    validator.ErrorMessage = HttpUtility.HtmlEncode(
      attribute.FormatErrorMessage(this.Column.DisplayName));
    validator.ToolTip = validator.ErrorMessage;

    this.IgnoreModelValidationAttribute(attribute.GetType());
  }
}
}
```

Most of the phone number validation in the new field template is performed by the standard ASP.NET control, RegularExpressionValidator, which ensures that the value entered by the user matches the regular expression pattern that defines a valid phone number. In addition to the server-side validation based on the .NET implementation of regular expressions in the System.Text.RegularExpressions namespace, it also works on the client side taking advantage of the regular expression functionality in JavaScript.

The `RegularExpressionValidator` is configured by the `SetUpRegexValidator` method defined in the code-behind. This method first searches the list of attributes applied to the column in the data model, `Column.Attributes`, for a `RegularExpressionAttribute` that might have been supplied by the application developer to indicate the expected phone number pattern. If no such attribute exists, this method creates a default `Regular ExpressionAttribute` with the pattern, `\(\d{3}\)\d{3}-\d{4}`, that matches U.S. phone numbers, such as (877)514-9180, with a three-digit area code in parentheses, followed by a seven-digit local number. The default attribute also has a generic error message that says that a column must be a valid phone number.

Having obtained the `RegularExpressionAttribute` instance, the `SetUpRegexValidator` method configures the `RegularExpressionValidator` control consistently with how the `SetUpValidator` method of the `FieldTemplateUserControl` base class does it—the `Text` displayed by the validator itself is always a star symbol; its `ErrorMessage` is reported through a `ValidationSummary` control on the page and the `ToolTip` contains the complete error message.

The last step in setting up the `RegularExpressionValidator` is to call the `IgnoreModel ValidationAttribute` method of the `FieldTemplateUserControl` base class. This allows the `DynamicValidator` to ignore the `RegularExpressionAttribute` during its validation because this attribute is already covered by the `RegularExpressionValidator`. Aside from helping to avoid doing the same validation check twice, this also prevents the regular expression validation error from being reported twice—first by the `RegularExpression Validator` and then by the `DynamicValidator` control.

Listing 3.13 shows an example of how the new `PhoneNumber_Edit` field template can be associated with a column using data annotation attributes.

LISTING 3.13 Associating PhoneNumber Template with a Column

```
using System.ComponentModel.DataAnnotations;

namespace DataModel
{
  [MetadataType(typeof(Employee.Metadata))]
  partial class Employee
  {
    public class Metadata
    {
      [DataType(DataType.Date)]
      public object BirthDate;

      [DataType(DataType.Date)]
      public object HireDate;

      [DataType(DataType.PhoneNumber)]
      [RegularExpression(@"\(\d{2,3}\)\d{3}-\d{4}",
        ErrorMessage = "The Home Phone must be a valid phone number.")]
```

```
        public object HomePhone;
    }
  }
}
```

DataTypeAttribute, applied to the HomePhone column, specifies this string column's actual data type is `PhoneNumber`. Dynamic Data uses this information as a hint when looking for a matching field template for this column and chooses the new `PhoneNumber_Edit` template instead of the default `Text_Edit`. In this example, `RegularExpressionAttribute` is also applied to the HomePhone column to provide a pattern that matches not only U.S. phone numbers, which have three-digit area codes, but also UK numbers, which might have two-digit area codes.

Figure 3.3 shows the Employee Edit page after the implementation of the `PhoneNumber_Edit` field template has been completed. Although you cannot tell from this screenshot, thanks to the `FilteredTextBoxExtender`, you cannot type any alphabetical symbols in the phone number text box. The pattern validation is performed on the client side as soon as you tab out of the text box, such as in this case, where one digit was removed from an otherwise valid UK phone number.

FIGURE 3.3 Employee Edit page with the New PhoneNumber_Edit field template.

Field Template Lookup Rules

Dynamic Data tries to find the most specific template that matches the field based on the column type and control mode. If such a field template does not exist, Dynamic Data will gradually relax the matching rules until it finds the best possible match among the field templates in the project.

Data Annotations

Consider the RequiredDate column of the Order table used in Listing 3.3 earlier in this chapter. If the developer specifies the exact template name by applying the UIHintAttribute as shown in Listing 3.14, Dynamic Data first checks to see if a template with the specified name, MyDate.ascx, exists. If this template does not exist, Dynamic Data then checks if a DataTypeAttribute is applied to the column and tries using the specified DataType value as the template name. In this example, it checks to see if a field template called Date.ascx exists.

LISTING 3.14   Data Annotations That Affect Field Template Lookup

```
using System.ComponentModel.DataAnnotations;

namespace DataModel
{
  [MetadataType(typeof(Order.Metadata))]
  partial class Order
  {
    public class Metadata
    {
      [UIHint("MyDate")]
      [DataType(DataType.Date)]
      public object RequiredDate;
    }
  }
}
```

Type Names

If the column has no data annotation attributes, Dynamic Data then tries to find a matching template based on the name of its type. First, it looks for a template whose name matches the full name of the type, including the namespace where the type is defined. In the example of RequiredDate, when looking for a template for a column of DateTime type, it checks to see if a template called System.DateTime.ascx exists. If not, Dynamic Data then tries the short type name, without the namespace, and finally chooses the template called DateTime.ascx provided by Dynamic Data out of the box.

Type Aliases

Dynamic Data allows template names to use special aliases instead of actual type names for two built-in .NET types, Int32 and String. When looking for a field template for a column of type String, Dynamic Data considers the template called Text.ascx to be a match. In the Northwind data model, this means that the Text.ascx template will be used for the ProductName column of the Product table. Likewise, when looking for a template for an Int32 column, Dynamic Data considers Integer.ascx to be a match as well. Table 3.1 shows the built-in type aliases at a glance.

TABLE 3.1 Type Name Aliases

Type Name	Alias
Int32	Integer
String	Text

Type aliases are considered less specific than the type names, and type *names* take precedence over *aliases* during template lookup. For example, if the Dynamic Data project contains templates called Int32.ascx and Integer.ascx, only the one called Int32.ascx will be used for an integer column.

Type Fallback

If there is no matching field template for a particular data type, Dynamic Data uses *fallback logic* to find a template for a more generic type that could be used instead. Consider the UnitsInStock column of the Product entity, which is of type Int16. When looking for a field template for this column, Dynamic Data first checks to see if a template called Int16.ascx exists. Because there is no template with this name, it uses the fallback rules shown in Table 3.2 to determine the fallback type, Int32, and tries to find a matching template for that type.

TABLE 3.2 Type Fallback Rules

Data Type	Fallback Type
Double, Float	Decimal
Byte, Int16, Int64	Int32
Char, Decimal, DateTime, DateTimeOffset, Guid Int32, TimeSpan	String

Both type names and aliases are used during template lookup for the fallback type, just as they were used for the original type. For the UnitsInStock column, this means that Dynamic Data will then try System.Int32.ascx, Int32.ascx, and Integer.ascx. Because none of these field templates exist in the default Dynamic Data project, it falls back to the next type—String and tries System.String.ascx, String.ascx, and finally choosing Text.ascx.

Control Mode

Control mode defines the context where the field template will be used. It can be one of the members of the ASP.NET `DataBoundControlMode` enumeration:

▶ `ReadOnly` templates are used by the `Details.aspx` page template or custom pages to display field values in Read-only mode.

▶ `Edit` templates are used by the `Edit.aspx` page template or custom pages to change field values of an existing row.

▶ `Insert` are used by the `Insert.aspx` page template or custom pages to collect field values for a new row.

When looking for a `ReadOnly` field template for the ShippedDate column of the Order table, which has `DateTime` data type and no additional metadata attributes in the sample data model, Dynamic Data finds the `DateTime.ascx` template. `Edit` mode is considered more specific because it requires the field template to not only display the current field value, but also allow changing it. Therefore, when looking for an Edit field template for the ShippedDate column, Dynamic Data chooses the template called `DateTime_Edit.ascx` if it exists. Note that Dynamic Data uses the `"_Edit"` suffix for Edit templates and no suffix for the `ReadOnly` templates. The Insert mode is even more specific because it might require special logic to deal with rows that have not been submitted to the database, and Dynamic Data chooses the template called `DateTime_Insert.ascx` if it exists.

Mode Fallback

If there is no matching field template for a particular control mode, Dynamic Data uses fallback logic to find another template for a more generic mode. In this ongoing example, when looking for an Insert template for the ShippedDate column, Dynamic Data will first try to find the template called `DateTime_Insert.ascx`. Because there is no field template with this name, it falls back from the Insert to the Edit mode and ends up using the template called `DateTime_Edit.ascx`, assuming it can handle both Edit and Insert modes. Similarly, if an Edit mode template cannot be found, Dynamic Data falls back to Read-only mode.

However, before Dynamic Data falls back to the next *mode*, it performs the *type* fallback. Consider UnitsInStock, an Int16 column from the Products table. When looking for an Edit template for this field, it tries using `System.Int16_Edit.ascx` and `Int16_Edit.ascx` templates first, but because they do not exist, it falls back to type `Int32` and checks for `System.Int32_Edit.ascx` and `Int32_Edit.ascx` and eventually finds `Integer_Edit.ascx`. If Dynamic Data performed the mode fallback first, it would skip this template and try to look for a ReadOnly template called `System.Int16.ascx` instead.

Navigation Columns

So far, our discussion has been about the lookup rules Dynamic Data uses for columns of *primitive* types that can be stored using built-in system types like Int32 and String. The Dynamic Data metadata API represents them using the MetaColumn class.

Navigation columns, on the other hand, are columns that provide access to one or more entities that are defined as custom classes in the data model itself. There are three types of navigation columns from the Dynamic Data prospective:

▶ MetaForeignKeyColumn represents a navigation property that returns a single entity referenced by the underlying foreign key field. In the Northwind example, Product is a foreign key column of the Order_Detail entity that represents the Product entity referenced by the ProductID foreign key field.

▶ MetaChildrenColumn is an opposite of a foreign key. In the Northwind example, Order_Details column of the Product entity returns all Order_Detail items that reference a particular product instance.

▶ Many-to-Many column is a special case of a MetaChildrenColumn where the IsManyToMany property is set to true. In the Northwind example, the Territories column of the Employees entity returns all territories assigned to a particular employee. Likewise, the Employees column of the Territory entity returns all employees assigned to work in a particular Territory. Dynamic Data considers both of these columns as Many-to-Many.

Navigation columns get special treatment during field template lookup. Unless the developer already placed a UIHintAttribute on a navigation property, Dynamic Data uses the rules shown in Table 3.3 to come up with a default UI Hint.

TABLE 3.3 Navigation Column Rules

Column Type	UI Hint
MetaForeignKeyColumn	ForeignKey
MetaChildrenColumn	Children
MetaChildrenColumn, IsManyToMany = true	ManyToMany

In this example, it means that for the Product column of the Order_Details table, Dynamic Data uses a template called ForeignKey.ascx; for the Order_Details column of the Product table, it uses a template called Children.ascx; and for both Employee.Territories and Territory.Employees columns, it uses the template called ManyToMany.ascx.

Effectively, there is no type fallback during template lookup for navigation columns. However, Dynamic Data does perform mode fallback, so if your page needs a foreign key template in Insert mode, it first tries ForeignKey_Insert.ascx, then ForeignKey_Edit.ascx, and then ForeignKey.ascx if necessary. The default Dynamic Data project template actually takes advantage of this to disable user interface for the children columns in Insert mode. If you open the `Children_Insert.ascx` field template, you see that it is empty. If this empty field template did not exist, `Children.ascx` would be used in its place, causing runtime errors because this template is not prepared to handle the scenario when the parent row does not exist.

Field Template Lookup Algorithm

Although the lookup rules for field templates might seem complex at a first, they are based on common-sense logic, and when you understand the idea behind them, the results will feel intuitive. Just remember that Dynamic Data tries to choose the most specific field template based on the column definition and control mode, and if such a field template does not exist, it gradually relaxes the matching rules until it finds a match or reports an error. The resulting behavior allows you to easily add new field templates where unique behavior is required to support a particular column type while allowing you to reuse existing templates with common behavior such as displaying read-only field values. Figure 3.4 shows the actual algorithm used by Dynamic Data. `FieldTemplateFactory`, a special class defined in the `System.Web.DynamicData` namespace, performs this task.

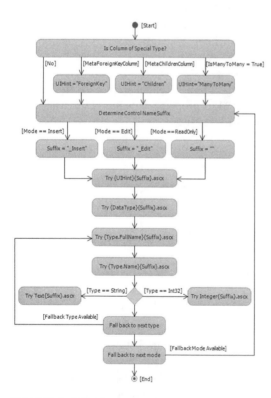

FIGURE 3.4 Field template lookup algorithm.

As an example, consider Table 3.4, which shows the sequence of template file names Dynamic Data will try when looking for a matching field template for the HomePhone property of the Employee entity.

TABLE 3.4 Example of Field Template Lookup for String Column

Mode="Insert"	Mode="Edit"	Mode="ReadOnly"
PhoneNumber_Insert.ascx	**PhoneNumber_Edit.ascx**	PhoneNumber.ascx
System.String_Insert.ascx	System.String_Edit.ascx	System.String.ascx
String_Insert.ascx	String_Edit.ascx	String.ascx
Text_Insert.ascx	Text_Edit.ascx	**Text.ascx**
PhoneNumber_Edit.ascx	PhoneNumber.ascx	
System.String_Edit.ascx	System.String.ascx	
String_Edit.ascx	String.ascx	
Text_Edit.ascx	Text.ascx	
PhoneNumber.ascx		
System.String.ascx		
String.ascx		
Text.ascx		

Because the HomePhone property has no UIHintAttribute and UIHint property is not specified for DynamicControl or DynamicField in page markup, the search sequence does not include the file names based on the UIHint. However, the HomePhone property does have the DataType specified in the data model using the [DataType(DataType.PhoneNumber)] attribute.

In Insert mode, the FieldTemplateFactory checks to see if PhoneNumber_Insert.ascx, System.String_Insert.ascx, String_Insert.ascx, and Text_Insert.ascx field templates exist before finding the PhoneNumber_Edit.ascx template created earlier in this chapter. If this template didn't exist, the FieldTemplateFactory would continue checking for System.String_Edit.ascx, String_Edit.ascx, and eventually find the Text_Edit.ascx field template provided by Dynamic Data projects out of the box.

In Edit mode, the FieldTemplateFactory starts with PhoneNumber_Edit.ascx and because it exists, uses it immediately. Likewise, had this field template not been defined, it would continue the search and eventually find the Text_Edit.ascx template provided by Dynamic Data.

In ReadOnly mode, the FieldTemplateFactory starts with PhoneNumber.ascx. Because the read-only version of the phone number field template does not exist, it continues by trying System.String.ascx and String.ascx and finally finds the Text.ascx field template provided by Dynamic Data out of the box.

Table 3.5 shows another example of field template lookup sequence, this time for the UnitsInStock property of the Product entity. This column is of type Int32 and, unlike the HomePhone in the previous example, doesn't have a DataTypeAttribute applied to it.

Instead, this field template takes advantage of the fallback logic Dynamic Data uses for types and modes.

TABLE 3.5 Example of Field Template Lookup for Integer Column

Mode="Insert"	Mode="Edit"	Mode="ReadOnly
System.Int32_Insert.ascx	System.Int32_Edit.ascx	System.Int32.ascx
Int32_Insert.ascx	Int32_Edit.ascx	Int32.ascx
Integer_Insert.ascx	**Integer_Edit.ascx**	Integer.ascx
System.String_Insert.ascx	System.String_Edit.ascx	System.String.ascx
String_Insert.ascx	String_Edit.ascx	String.ascx
Text_Insert.ascx	Text_Edit.ascx	**Text.ascx**
System.Int32_Edit.ascx	System.Int32.ascx	
Int32_Edit.ascx	Int32.ascx	
Integer_Edit.ascx	Integer.ascx	
System.String_Edit.ascx	System.String.ascx	
String_Edit.ascx	String.ascx	
Text_Edit.ascx	Text.ascx	
System.Int32.ascx		
Int32.ascx		
Integer.ascx		
System.String.ascx		
String.ascx		
Text.ascx		

In Insert mode, the `FieldTemplateFactory` starts with the most specific template name (System.Int32) and mode (Insert). It tries `System.Int32_Insert`, `Int32_Insert`, and `Integer_Insert` before falling back to the next type—`String`. It continues trying `System.String_Insert`, `String_Insert`, and `Text_Insert` before falling back to the next mode, Edit, and repeating the steps starting with the most specific template name, `System.Int32`. Eventually, it finds `Integer_Edit.ascx`, the built-in field template provided by Dynamic Data for integer columns.

> **NOTE**
>
> For the UnitsInStock column, Dynamic Data uses both type aliases during the lookup sequence—Integer, which represents Int32, and Text, which represents String.

The Edit mode lookup sequence for the UnitsInStock column is very similar to that of Insert mode's. It starts with `System.Int32_Edit` and finds the built-in `Integer_Edit` template. The Read-only mode is different, however. Because Dynamic Data doesn't provide a built-in read-only template for integer columns, the `FieldTemplateFactory` falls back from `Integer` to `String` data type and eventually finds `Text.ascx`, a read-only template that can display field values of all types.

Built-in Field Templates

Dynamic Data web project templates in Visual Studio 2010 include a large number of ready-to-use field templates.

Boolean

The `Boolean.ascx` field template is used for Boolean columns in Read-only mode. It contains a disabled `CheckBox` control, checked when the field value is `true`.

Boolean_Edit

The `Boolean_Edit.ascx` field template is used for Boolean columns in Edit and Insert modes. It contains a `CheckBox` control users can use to set field value to `true` or `false`. This field template does not support null values and, unlike other well-behaved field templates, does not perform validation.

Children

The `Children.ascx` field template is used in Read-only and Edit modes for navigation properties that represent the many side of one-to-many relationships between entities. For example, the Customer entity in the Northwind sample data model has a children navigation property called `Orders`, which returns a collection of all orders placed by a given customer. In Read-only and Edit modes, the `Children.ascx` entity template displays a hyperlink to the dynamic `List.aspx` page that displays all child rows of the parent entity.

Children_Insert

The `Children_Insert.ascx` field template is empty. Because the dynamic `List.aspx` page cannot display child rows of a parent entity that has not been submitted to the database, this template prevents the `Children.ascx` field template from being used in Insert mode.

DateTime

Shipped Date	7/5/1996 12:00:00 AM

The DateTime.ascx field template is used in Read-only mode to display DateTime field values. This field template contains a Literal control that injects the field value directly into the web page without any adorning HTML elements. This template is nearly identical to the Text.ascx template described in the following sections and could be removed, making Text.ascx responsible for displaying DateTime field values in Read-only mode as well.

DateTime_Edit

Shipped Date	7/23/1996 12:00:00 AM

The DateTime_Edit.ascx field template is used for DateTime columns in Edit and Insert mode. It contains a TextBox control, accompanied by a CustomValidator, used to make sure that the value entered in the TextBox is a valid DateTime. It also contains a RequiredFieldValidator, used to enforce values for columns marked with the RequiredAttribute, a RegularExpressionValidator, used to enforce regular expression patterns for columns marked with the RegularExpressionAttribute and a DynamicValidator, used to enforce all other validation attributes applied to this column.

Decimal_Edit

Freight	32.3800

The Decimal_Edit.ascx field template is used for Decimal, Float, and Double columns in Edit and Insert mode. It contains a TextBox control, accompanied by a CompareValidator, used to ensure that values entered in the TextBox are valid numbers. It also contains a RequiredFieldValidator, used to enforce values for columns marked with the RequiredAttribute; a RangeValidator, used to enforce range of values for columns marked with the RangeAttribute; a RegularExpressionValidator, used to enforce regular expression patterns for columns marked with the RegularExpressionAttribute; and a DynamicValidator, used to enforce all other validation attributes applied to this column.

EmailAddress

Email Address	nancy.davolio@northwind.com

The EmailAddress.ascx field template is a read-only template used for String columns marked with the DataType(DataType.EmailAddress) attribute. It includes a HyperLink control that displays the field value as a link with the URL scheme "mailto:". When the user clicks this link, most web browsers launch the default e-mail client installed on the computer and create a new message with the field value automatically added in the "To" list.

Enumeration

Order Status	Submitted

The Enumeration.ascx field template is used for enumeration columns in Read-only mode. It contains a Literal control that displays the underlying integral field value converted to its equivalent enumerated value and then converted to a String.

> **NOTE**
>
> Enumeration columns represent properties with an actual enumerated .NET data type (supported only by LINQ to SQL today) or integer properties that have been marked with the EnumDataTypeAttribute (supported by both LINQ to SQL and Entity Framework). As an example, consider the following enumerated type that could be used to track status of Orders in the Northwind database:
>
> ```
> public enum OrderStatus: byte
> {
>   Draft = 0,
>   Submitted = 1,
>   PaymentProcessed = 2,
>   Fulfilled = 3
> }
> ```
>
> In the sample data model, it could be expressed as an integer property called OrderStatus in the Order entity:
>
> ```
> [EnumDataType(typeof(OrderStatus))]
> public byte OrderStatus { get; set; }
> ```
>
> By marking the OrderStatus property with the EnumDataTypeAttribute, you can make Dynamic Data treat it as enumeration instead of an integer and use the Enumeration.ascx field template, which displays OrderStatus field values as "Draft" and "Submitted," instead of "1" and "2."

Enumeration Edit

The Enumeration_Edit.ascx field template is used for enumeration columns in Edit and Insert modes. It contains a DropDownList control, populated with enumerated items converted to string, plus "[Not Set]" if the column allows null values. This field template also includes a RequiredFieldValidator to enforce values for columns marked with the RequiredAttribute and a DynamicValidator to enforce all other validation attributes applied to this column.

> **NOTE**
>
> When converting enumeration values to string, the Enumeration field templates do not automatically separate words concatenated to form a valid programmatic identifier. For example, an enumerated value ReadOnly would be normally displayed as "read-only" in a hand-coded web page. To make display names of the enumeration values more user-friendly, you can modify the Enumeration field templates to implement appropriate logic based either on the naming convention used to define the enumerated values, commonly PascalCase in .NET programs. Alternatively, you can use metadata attributes, such as DisplayAttribute, that can be applied to the enumerated values to specify the exact display string. Chapter 11, "Building Dynamic Forms," shows how to implement this.

ForeignKey

The `ForeignKey.ascx` is used for foreign key columns in Read-only mode. It contains a `HyperLink` control that displays the field value of the "display" column of the parent table. You can specify the display column explicitly by applying the `DisplayColumnAttribute` to the parent entity class, or it can be selected automatically based on the Dynamic Data heuristics. Users can click the link generated by the control to navigate to the `List.aspx` page of the parent table.

ForeignKey_Edit

The `ForeignKey_Edit.ascx` field template is used for foreign key columns in Edit and Insert modes. It contains a `DropDownList` control that displays all rows from the parent table. The display column of the parent table determines the `Text` of each `ListItem`, and its primary key columns determine its `Value`.

Integer_Edit

The `Integer_Edit.ascx` field template is used for `Byte`, `Int16`, `Int32`, and `Int64` columns in Edit and Insert modes. It contains a `TextBox` control, accompanied by a `CompareValidator`, which is used to ensure that values entered in the `TextBox` are valid numbers. It also contains a `RequiredFieldValidator`, used to enforce values for columns marked with the `RequiredAttribute`; a `RangeValidator`, used to enforce range of values for columns marked with the `RangeAttribute`; a `RegularExpressionValidator`, used to enforce regular expression patterns for columns marked with the `RegularExpressionAttribute`; and a `DynamicValidator`, used to enforce all other validation attributes applied to the column.

ManyToMany

The `ManyToMany.ascx` field template is used for children columns in a many-to-many relationship, such as the Employees column of the Territory entity in the Northwind sample database. This template contains a `Repeater` control that generates a `DynamicHyperLink` for every child entity. On the actual page, this looks like a list of hyperlinks that the user can click to navigate to the `Details.aspx` page of a particular child entity.

> **NOTE**
>
> Many-to-many relationships are natively supported in Entity Framework but not in LINQ to SQL. Therefore, only the Entity Framework flavors of the Dynamic Data project templates in Visual Studio include the `ManyToMany` field template. Unlike other field templates, which work equally well with both data access frameworks, the `ManyToMany` field template uses Entity Framework APIs directly.

LINQ to SQL natively supports only one-to-many relationships and requires you to have an explicit many-to-many entity in the model. However, it is possible to mimic many-to-many relationships by implementing a simple coding pattern as Eric Smith and Shannon Davidson describe in the article published on the Code Project, which can be found at the following location online:

`http://www.codeproject.com/KB/linq/linq-to-sql-many-to-many.aspx`

It is possible to create Dynamic Data many-to-many field templates for LINQ to SQL based on this approach. However, this exercise is outside the scope of this chapter.

ManyToMany_Edit

The `ManyToMany_Edit.ascx` field template is used for many-to-many children columns in Edit and Insert modes. This template contains a `CheckBoxList` control that generates a check box for every entity the user can check to add it to the list of children.

MultilineText_Edit

The `MultilineText_Edit.ascx` field template is used for long string columns in Edit and Insert modes. It contains a `TextBox` control with `TextMode` property set to `MultiLine`. It also contains a `RequiredFieldValidator`, used to enforce values for columns marked with the `RequiredAttribute`, a `RegularExpressionValidator`, used to enforce regular expression patterns for columns marked with the `RegularExpressionAttribute` and a `DynamicValidator`, used to enforce all other validation attributes applied to the column.

String columns are considered *long* when they do not have maximum length specified in the data model, such as the Notes column of the Employee entity in the Northwind sample, which has type `NTEXT`. You can also force Dynamic Data to use the `MultilineText_Edit` field template for columns that do have maximum length by applying the `DataType(DataType.MultilineText)` attribute to their properties in the data model.

Text

Due to the data type fallback used during template lookup, the `Text.ascx` field template can be used in Read-only mode for columns of all primitive types with the exception of Boolean and DateTime columns, for which Dynamic Data provides specific templates. This field template includes a `Literal` control that displays the field value converted to a string.

Text_Edit

Product Name   Chai

The `Text_Edit.ascx` field template is used for string columns in Edit and Insert modes. It includes a `TextBox` control, accompanied by a `RequiredFieldValidator`, used to enforce values for columns marked with the `RequiredAttribute`; a `RegularExpressionValidator`, used to enforce regular expression patterns for columns marked with the `RegularExpressionAttribute`; and a `DynamicValidator`, used to enforce all other validation attributes applied to the column.

PhotoPath   http://accweb/emmployees/davolio.bmp

Url

The `Url.ascx` field template is used for columns marked with the `DataType(DataType.Url)` attribute. It contains a `HyperLink` control that displays the field value as a link in the generated HTML. The `"http://"` scheme is automatically added to the URL unless the field value already contains it. Only HTTP and HTTPS schemes are recognized automatically. Although this field template does not require the column type to be only `String`, the field value converted to string must be a valid URL for the generated hyperlink to work correctly.

Summary

A field template is a special type of ASP.NET user control that inherits from the `FieldTemplateUserControl` base class provided by Dynamic Data. Multiple columns can reuse the same field template based on its compatibility with the column type and control mode. Changing a single field template automatically affects the user interface generated for all matching columns in the data model. Dynamic Data project template comes with a reasonable number of field templates that allow developers to create working web applications for many data types out of the box. Developers can easily modify the default field templates as well as add new ones to meet specific requirements of their projects.

Dynamic Data supports separate templates for Read-only, Edit, and Insert modes. Although a single template can support all three modes and programmatically display different versions of child controls, separating this logic into different templates helps to keep them simple and lightweight. Dynamic Data uses common-sense logic to find the best matching field template based on the column type and required control mode. If the most specific template does not exist, Dynamic Data gradually relaxes the matching rules and tries to find templates for a more generic column type and control mode.

CHAPTER 4

Entity Templates

Most web applications that work with data have pages that display information pertaining to a single item, as well as allow users to create new or modify existing items one at a time. Figure 4.1 shows an example of such page, which displays a single customer record from the Northwind sample database. Aside from the obvious lack of visual polish, driven by the need to keep the code examples simple, this type of page is common in internal, commercial, and packaged web applications today. You can easily find similar pages that display customer profiles on online retailers' websites or customer information in commercial CRM (customer relationship management) systems.

Implementing pages like this with ASP.NET is straightforward. Typical pages, like the one shown in Figure 4.1, can use a data source control, the `EntityDataSource` in this example, to retrieve the record from the database. The data source control is associated with a presentation control, such as the `FormView`, which uses one or more databound controls to display the field values.

In Chapter 3, "Field Templates," you saw how Dynamic Data makes the task of creating data-driven pages easier by providing Field Templates, a special type of user control that encapsulate presentation and business logic for individual field values of different column types. You can use field templates by adding `DynamicControl` instances to the page and specifying their `DataField` properties to indicate the column for which a field template is needed. `DynamicControl` chooses an appropriate field template based on the metadata information that describes the column, and the field template uses appropriate controls to format and display the field value.

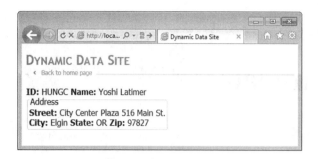

FIGURE 4.1 Customer Information page.

The markup in Listing 4.1 takes advantage of the field templating functionality, making it clearer and more concise than its equivalent based on regular ASP.NET controls. However, in this example, only the read-only template is defined. If you were to reuse this page and allow users to edit information of existing customers or create new customer records as well, you would also need to define the `EditItemTemplate` and `InsertItemTemplate` in the `FormView` control, in addition to the read-only `ItemTemplate` that exists now. Defining multiple item templates in a single `FormView` control significantly increases the amount of code and complexity of the page. However, even if you split this page into separate Customer Details, Customer Edit, and Customer Insert pages, the problem still stands—the amount of code will grow even more, except that it will be split among multiple files. It would be great to have this *entity-level* presentation logic (that is, how a Customer Information form is laid out) defined separately so you could reuse the rest of the presentation and data access logic on this page without duplicating it.

LISTING 4.1   Customer Information Page (Markup)

```
<%@ Page Language="C#"
  MasterPageFile="~/Site.master" CodeBehind="SamplePage.aspx.cs"
  Inherits="WebApplication.Samples.Ch04.FormView.SamplePage" %>

<asp:Content runat="server" ContentPlaceHolderID="main">
  <asp:ValidationSummary runat="server" />
  <asp:FormView ID="form" runat="server" DataSourceID="dataSource">
    <ItemTemplate>
      <label>ID:</label>
      <asp:DynamicControl runat="server" DataField="CustomerID" />
      <label>Name:</label>
      <asp:DynamicControl runat="server" DataField="ContactName" />

      <fieldset><legend>Address</legend>
        <label>Street:</label>
        <asp:DynamicControl runat="server" DataField="Address" /><br />
```

```
      <label>City:</label>
      <asp:DynamicControl runat="server" DataField="City" />
      <label>State:</label>
      <asp:DynamicControl runat="server" DataField="Region" />
      <label>Zip:</label>
      <asp:DynamicControl runat="server" DataField="PostalCode" />
    </fieldset>
  </ItemTemplate>
</asp:FormView>
<asp:EntityDataSource ID="dataSource" runat="server"
  ConnectionString="name=NorthwindEntities" AutoGenerateWhereClause="true"
  DefaultContainerName="NorthwindEntities" EntitySetName="Customers">
  <WhereParameters>
    <asp:QueryStringParameter QueryStringField="ID" Name="CustomerID" />
  </WhereParameters>
</asp:EntityDataSource>
</asp:Content>
```

As discussed in Chapter 1, "Getting Started," the code-behind of pages that use dynamic controls need to associate the databound control, such as the FormView in this example, with the MetaTable instance describing the entity class. The MetaTable is typically retrieved using the MetaModel instance created in the Global.asax and exposed by the DefaultModel static property, as shown in Listing 4.2.

LISTING 4.2   Customer Information Page (Code-Behind)

```
using System;
using System.Web.DynamicData;

namespace WebApplication.Samples.Ch04.ReadOnlyTemplate
{
  public partial class SamplePage : System.Web.UI.Page
  {
    protected void Page_Init(object sender, EventArgs e)
    {
      MetaTable table = Global.DefaultModel.GetTable("Customers");
      this.form.SetMetaTable(table);
    }
  }
}
```

Creating an Entity Template

Entity Template is a special type of user control used by Dynamic Data to encapsulate presentation logic for a single entity or a class that represents a single row from a database table. You can create a custom entity template for the Customers table by simply extracting the highlighted code from Listing 4.1 and placing it into a new user control, `Customers.ascx`, in the `DynamicData\EntityTemplates` folder of the web project, which is where Dynamic Data looks for entity templates by default. Listing 4.3 shows markup of the new entity template.

LISTING 4.3   Customer Entity Template (Markup)

```
<%@ Control Language="C#" CodeBehind="Customers.ascx.cs"
  Inherits="WebApplication.DynamicData.EntityTemplates.CustomerEntityTemplate" %>
<label>ID:</label>
<asp:DynamicControl runat="server" DataField="CustomerID" />
<label>Name:</label>
<asp:DynamicControl runat="server" DataField="ContactName" />
<fieldset><legend>Address</legend>
  <label>Street:</label>
  <asp:DynamicControl runat="server" DataField="Address" /><br />
  <label>City:</label>
  <asp:DynamicControl runat="server" DataField="City" />
  <label>State:</label>
  <asp:DynamicControl runat="server" DataField="Region" />
  <label>Zip:</label>
  <asp:DynamicControl runat="server" DataField="PostalCode" />
</fieldset>
```

Aside from the `<%@ Control %>` directive, markup of the new Customers entity template is a true copy and paste of the code from Listing 4.1.

> **NOTE**
>
> Note that the name of the control file, Customers.ascx, is significant. The file name, without extension, needs to match the name of the MetaTable that describes the Customer entity in the metadata, which is *Customers* (plural).

The user control must inherit from a special class provided by the Dynamic Data, called `EntityTemplateUserControl`, as shown in Listing 4.4. This simple base class provides several properties, including `Table`, which returns a `MetaTable` instance describing the entity and `Mode`, which could be Read Only, Insert, or Edit.

LISTING 4.4   Customer Entity Template (Code-Behind)

```
using System.Web.DynamicData;

namespace WebApplication.DynamicData.EntityTemplates
{
    public partial class CustomerEntityTemplate : EntityTemplateUserControl
    {
    }
}
```

Having defined the entity template, you can modify the Customer Information page to take advantage of it by replacing the entire contents of the FormView with a DynamicEntity control, as shown in Listing 4.5.

LISTING 4.5   Customer Information Page with Entity Template (Markup)

```
<%@ Page Language="C#"
  MasterPageFile="~/Site.master" CodeBehind="SamplePage.aspx.cs"
  Inherits="WebApplication.Samples.Ch04.ReadOnlyTemplate.SamplePage" %>

<asp:Content runat="server" ContentPlaceHolderID="main">
  <asp:ValidationSummary runat="server" />
  <asp:FormView ID="form" runat="server" DataSourceID="dataSource">
    <ItemTemplate>
      <asp:DynamicEntity runat="server" />
    </ItemTemplate>
  </asp:FormView>
  <asp:EntityDataSource ID="dataSource" runat="server"
    ConnectionString="name=NorthwindEntities" AutoGenerateWhereClause="true"
    DefaultContainerName="NorthwindEntities" EntitySetName="Customers">
    <WhereParameters>
      <asp:QueryStringParameter QueryStringField="ID" Name="CustomerID" />
    </WhereParameters>
  </asp:EntityDataSource>
</asp:Content>
```

DynamicEntity is a new control defined in the System.Web.DynamicData namespace. At run time, it automatically determines the MetaTable associated with its parent FormView control and locates a template with a matching name in the DynamicData\EntityTemplates folder of the web application. If the matching entity template exists, DynamicEntity loads and includes it the web page, which in this example makes it look identical to the one shown in Figure 4.1.

Composite Entity Templates

There is no requirement to have a single entity template per entity. You can create multiple entity templates for a single entity, where each template contains presentation of the entire entity or just a part of it. This is particularly useful for large entities, where it makes sense to present the information on multiple pages or on multiple tabs of a single page. You can further decompose the Customer entity template by separating contact and address information into separate entity templates shown in Listing 4.6 and Listing 4.7, respectively.

LISTING 4.6   Contact Entity Template (Markup)

```
<%@ Control Language="C#" CodeBehind="Contact.ascx.cs"
  Inherits="WebApplication.DynamicData.EntityTemplates.ContactTemplate" %>


<label>Name:</label>
<asp:DynamicControl runat="server" DataField="ContactName" />
<br />

<label>Company:</label>
<asp:DynamicControl runat="server" DataField="CompanyName" />
<br />

<label>Title:</label>
<asp:DynamicControl runat="server" DataField="ContactTitle" />
<br />
```

As you can see, the Contact entity template contains only name, company, and title fields, and the Address entity template contains only the address fields.

LISTING 4.7   Address Entity Template (Markup)

```
<%@ Control Language="C#" CodeBehind="Address.ascx.cs"
  Inherits="WebApplication.DynamicData.EntityTemplates.AddressTemplate" %>

<fieldset><legend>Address</legend>
  <label>Street:</label>
  <asp:DynamicControl runat="server" DataField="Address" />
  <br />

  <label>City:</label>
  <asp:DynamicControl runat="server" DataField="City" />
  <label>State:</label>
  <asp:DynamicControl runat="server" DataField="Region" />
  <label>Zip:</label>
  <asp:DynamicControl runat="server" DataField="PostalCode" />
</fieldset>
```

Having the contact and address fields encapsulated in two separate entity templates, it's time to update the main Customers entity template to instantiate them with the help of the DynamicEntity control, as shown in Listing 4.8.

LISTING 4.8   Composite Customer Entity Template (Markup)

```
<%@ Control Language="C#" CodeBehind="Customers.ascx.cs"
  Inherits="WebApplication.DynamicData.EntityTemplates.CustomerEntityTemplate" %>

<label>ID:</label>
<asp:DynamicControl runat="server" DataField="CustomerID" />

<asp:DynamicEntity runat="server" UIHint="Contact" />
<asp:DynamicEntity runat="server" UIHint="Address" />
```

Notice that because the names of the Contact and Address entity templates do not match the name of the Customers table, you reference them explicitly by specifying the UIHint attribute of the DynamicEntity control.

Generic Entity Templates

If you notice, nothing is tying these new Contact and Address templates to the Customer entity aside from the names of the fields they display. Different pages can take advantage of the fact that DynamicControl performs all initialization tasks at run time by reusing these templates for any other entity that has fields with the same names. In the Northwind sample database, the Suppliers table is similar to the Customers table; you can reuse both Contact and Address entity templates to implement the UI, as shown in Listing 4.9.

LISTING 4.9   Supplier Information Page (Markup)

```
<%@ Page Language="C#"
  MasterPageFile="~/Site.master" CodeBehind="SamplePage.aspx.cs"
  Inherits="WebApplication.Samples.Ch04.GenericTemplates.SamplePage" %>

<asp:Content runat="server" ContentPlaceHolderID="main">
  <asp:FormView ID="form" runat="server" DataSourceID="dataSource">
    <ItemTemplate>
      <asp:DynamicEntity runat="server" UIHint="Contact" />
      <asp:DynamicEntity runat="server" UIHint="Address" />
    </ItemTemplate>
  </asp:FormView>
  <asp:EntityDataSource ID="dataSource" runat="server"
    ConnectionString="name=NorthwindEntities" AutoGenerateWhereClause="true"
    DefaultContainerName="NorthwindEntities" EntitySetName="Suppliers">
```

LISTING 4.9   Continued

```
  <WhereParameters>
    <asp:QueryStringParameter QueryStringField="ID"
      Name="SupplierID" DbType="Int32" />
  </WhereParameters>
  </asp:EntityDataSource>
</asp:Content>
```

You can see the actual page produced by the markup from Listing 4.9 in Figure 4.2.

FIGURE 4.2   Supplier Information page.

Note that you could have achieved the same result by creating a composite Supplier entity template, `Suppliers.ascx`, similar to the Customer entity template shown in Listing 4.8. The advantage of creating a supplier entity template is that it will work with the built-in page templates, discussed in Chapter 6, "Page Templates," which implement data access logic and eliminate the need to create custom pages altogether.

Dynamic Entity Templates

If you need to display all fields for a particular entity and the exact layout of the fields on the form is not very important, you can take advantage of the dynamic entity templates instead of creating custom templates discussed earlier in this chapter.

Dynamic entity templates are included in each Dynamic Data project out of the box. Figure 4.3 shows the Supplier page produced by the dynamic template, called `Default.ascx`, located in the `DynamicData\EntityTemplates` folder of the Web Application.

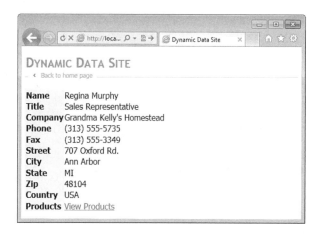

FIGURE 4.3   Supplier Information page produced by dynamic entity template.

Listing 4.10 shows the markup of the dynamic entity template.

LISTING 4.10   Default Entity Template (Markup)

```
<%@ Control Language="C#" CodeBehind="Default.ascx.cs"
  Inherits="WebApplication.DynamicData.EntityTemplates.DefaultEntityTemplate" %>

<asp:EntityTemplate runat="server" ID="entityTemplate">
  <ItemTemplate>
    <tr>
      <td><asp:Label runat="server" OnInit="Label_Init" /></td>
      <td><asp:DynamicControl runat="server" OnInit="DynamicControl_Init" /></td>
    </tr>
  </ItemTemplate>
</asp:EntityTemplate>
```

Dynamic entity templates take advantage of the metadata information provided by
Dynamic Data, which includes the list of all columns for each table in the registered data
model. The EntityTemplate control used in this markup is a lightweight template control,
similar to the ASP.NET Repeater. The OnLoad method shown in Listing 4.11 uses it to
create a Label and a DynamicControl for each entity column programmatically. Because
the same template is used for all columns, the DataField property of the DynamicControl
as well as the Text property of the Label is initialized programmatically in their respective
OnInit event handlers.

LISTING 4.11   Default Entity Template (Code-Behind)

```csharp
using System;
using System.Collections.Generic;
using System.Web.DynamicData;
using System.Web.UI;
using System.Web.UI.WebControls;

namespace WebApplication.DynamicData.EntityTemplates
{
  public partial class DefaultEntityTemplate : EntityTemplateUserControl
  {
    private MetaColumn currentColumn;

    protected override void OnLoad(EventArgs e)
    {
      IEnumerable<MetaColumn> scaffoldColumns = this.Table.GetScaffoldColumns(
        this.Mode, this.ContainerType);
      foreach (MetaColumn column in scaffoldColumns)
      {
        this.currentColumn = column;
        NamingContainer container = new NamingContainer();
        this.entityTemplate.ItemTemplate.InstantiateIn(container);
        this.entityTemplate.Controls.Add(container);
      }
    }

    protected void Label_Init(object sender, EventArgs e)
    {
      ((Label)sender).Text = this.currentColumn.DisplayName;
    }

    protected void DynamicControl_Init(object sender, EventArgs e)
    {
      ((DynamicControl)sender).DataField = this.currentColumn.Name;
    }
  }
}
```

NOTE

Note that NamingContainer is a custom control that inherits directly from the built-in Control and implements the INamingContainer marker interface. The ASP.NET runtime relies on this interface to determine naming boundaries and generate control IDs unique across the entire page.

The `OnLoad` method uses the `Table` property, provided by the `EntityTemplateUserControl` base class, to access the `MetaTable` object describing the entity. Its `GetScaffoldColumns` method returns a list of `MetaColumn` objects representing all "scaffolded" properties of the entity class. Scaffolded properties are the properties that need their field controls generated automatically. This list includes

- ▶ Primitive properties of type `String`, `Char`, `Byte`, `Int16`, `Int32`, `Int64`, `Float`, `Double`, `Decimal`, `DateTime`, `TimeSpan`, `DateTimeOffset`, `Boolean`, as well as enumerated types.

- ▶ Navigation properties that represent foreign keys and collections of child rows.

- ▶ Properties that have `DisplayAttribute` where `AutoGenerateField` property is set to true.

- ▶ Properties that have `ScaffoldColumnAttribute` where `Scaffold` property is set to true.

- ▶ Properties that have `UIHintAttribute` where `UIHint` property is not blank.

By default, the list of scaffolded columns *excludes*

- ▶ Automatically generated properties, such as identity columns used as primary keys.

- ▶ Primitive properties that support navigation properties, such as the `CustomerID`, which supports the Customer navigation property of the Order entity. Since the navigation property will be scaffolded by default, there is no need to scaffold its underlying primitive properties.

- ▶ Children navigation properties in insert mode. Child rows cannot be inserted before their parent rows.

- ▶ Foreign key navigation properties if the current user has no read access to the parent table (more on this in Chapter 14, "Implementing Security").

The order of columns returned by the `GetScaffoldColumns` method matches the order in which the properties appear in the entity class. You can change the order by applying the `DisplayAttribute` to the entity properties and specifying its `Order` property. Listing 4.12 shows an example of doing that for the Supplier entity. Columns that do not have the `Order` value specified explicitly appear *after* the columns that do, in the same order they are declared in the entity class. The example in Listing 4.12 takes advantage of this fact by specifying the `Order` values for the Phone and Fax columns so they appear immediately after ContactName, ContactTitle, and CompanyName and before the address columns.

Another metadata property you commonly need to specify when relying on dynamic entity templates is the *display name* of the column. This is necessary when the underlying property name of a particular column does not match what you want your users to see on the web pages of the application. For example, column names often contain multiple words concatenated using underscores or Pascal naming convention, such as the `ContactName` property of the Supplier entity. By setting the `Name` property of the `DisplayAttribute`, you can specify the human-readable column name that will be displayed by the Label control dynamically generated by the entity template as well as in the ValidationSummary control when the validation errors are reported. The Supplier example in Listing 4.12 specifies display names for ContactName, ContactTitle, CompanyName, and several other columns.

You can prevent displaying a particular column altogether by setting the AutoGenerateField property of the DisplayAttribute to false. Alternatively but to achieve the same result, you can apply the ScaffoldColumnAttribute to the entity property and specify false as its Scaffold property value. Listing 4.12 (Supplier example) shows how to use this method to hide the HomePage column.

> **NOTE**
>
> The ScaffoldColumnAttribute was introduced in the first version of the ASP.NET Dynamic Data, released as part of the Service Pack 1 for .NET Framework 3.5. The DisplayAttribute was introduced in the second version (released with the .NET Framework 4), leaving the ScaffoldColumnAttribute available for backward compatibility.

LISTING 4.12   Supplier Metadata Attributes

```csharp
using System.ComponentModel.DataAnnotations;

namespace DataModel
{
  [MetadataType(typeof(Supplier.Metadata))]
  partial class Supplier
  {
    public class Metadata
    {
      [Display(Name = "Name", Order = 1)]
      public object ContactName { get; set; }

      [Display(Name = "Title", Order = 2)]
      public object ContactTitle { get; set; }

      [Display(Name = "Company", Order = 3)]
      public object CompanyName { get; set; }

      [Display(Order = 4)]
      public object Phone { get; set; }

      [Display(Order = 5)]
      public object Fax { get; set; }
```

```
        [Display(Name = "Street")]
        public object Address { get; set; }

        [Display(Name = "State")]
        public object Region { get; set; }

        [Display(Name = "Zip")]
        public object PostalCode { get; set; }

        [ScaffoldColumn(false)]
        public object HomePage { get; set; }
    }
  }
}
```

Edit and Insert Entity Templates

In addition to the Read-only entity templates that have been discussed so far, Dynamic Data also supports entity templates in Edit and Insert modes. Consider the FormView control in Listing 4.13, which in addition to the Read-only ItemTemplate used earlier also defines the EditItemTemplate and InsertItemTemplate sections. All three of these sections use the DynamicEntity control to load an appropriate entity template dynamically, based on the MetaTable associated with the FormView and the Mode property, which can be Insert, Edit, or ReadOnly (default).

LISTING 4.13   Customer Information Page with Support for Edit and Insert Modes

```
<%@ Page Language="C#"
  MasterPageFile="~/Site.master" CodeBehind="SamplePage.aspx.cs"
  Inherits="WebApplication.Samples.Ch04.EditTemplates.SamplePage" %>

<asp:Content runat="server" ContentPlaceHolderID="main">
  <asp:ValidationSummary runat="server" />
  <asp:FormView ID="form" runat="server" DataSourceID="dataSource"
    DataKeyNames="CustomerID">
    <ItemTemplate>
      <asp:DynamicEntity runat="server" />
      <tr><td>
        <asp:LinkButton runat="server" CommandName="Edit" Text="Edit" />
        <asp:LinkButton runat="server" CommandName="New" Text="New" />
      </td></tr>
    </ItemTemplate>
    <InsertItemTemplate>
      <asp:DynamicEntity runat="server" Mode="Insert"/>
```

LISTING 4.13 Continued

```
      <tr><td>
        <asp:LinkButton runat="server" CommandName="Insert" Text="Insert" />
      </td></tr>
    </InsertItemTemplate>
    <EditItemTemplate>
      <asp:DynamicEntity runat="server" Mode="Edit" />
      <tr><td>
        <asp:LinkButton runat="server" CommandName="Update" Text="Update" />
      </td></tr>
    </EditItemTemplate>
  </asp:FormView>
  <asp:EntityDataSource ID="dataSource" runat="server"
    EnableInsert="true" EnableUpdate="true"
    ConnectionString="name=NorthwindEntities" AutoGenerateWhereClause="true"
    DefaultContainerName="NorthwindEntities" EntitySetName="Customers">
    <WhereParameters>
      <asp:QueryStringParameter QueryStringField="ID" Name="CustomerID" />
    </WhereParameters>
  </asp:EntityDataSource>
</asp:Content>
```

Similar to field templates, Dynamic Data uses the last part of the template file name to determine its mode. For the Customer page, you might need to have the following three templates in the DynamicData\EntityTemplates folder of the web application:

▶ Customers.ascx, the read-only template

▶ Customers_Edit.ascx, the edit template

▶ Customers_Insert.ascx, the insert template

Creating the Customers_Edit and Customers_Insert entity templates is straightforward; they are nearly identical to the Read-only Customers template (see Listing 4.3) except that the Mode property of the DynamicControl instances is set to Edit and Insert respectively. Listing 4.14 shows the Edit mode template for the Customer entity.

LISTING 4.14   Customers_Edit Entity Template (Markup)

```
<%@ Control Language="C#" CodeBehind="Customers_Edit.ascx.cs"
  Inherits="WebApplication.DynamicData.EntityTemplates.CustomerEditEntityTemplate"%>

<label>ID:</label>
<asp:DynamicControl runat="server" DataField="CustomerID" Mode="Edit"/>
<label>Name:</label>
<asp:DynamicControl runat="server" DataField="ContactName" Mode="Edit"/>
<fieldset><legend>Address</legend>
```

```
<label>Street:</label>
<asp:DynamicControl runat="server" DataField="Address" Mode="Edit"/><br />
<label>City:</label>
<asp:DynamicControl runat="server" DataField="City" Mode="Edit"/>
<label>State:</label>
<asp:DynamicControl runat="server" DataField="Region" Mode="Edit"/>
<label>Zip:</label>
<asp:DynamicControl runat="server" DataField="PostalCode" Mode="Edit"/>
</fieldset>
```

Although you could easily create the Insert mode template as well, the only difference between them would be the Insert mode specified for DynamicControl instances. As discussed in Chapter 3, Dynamic Data automatically falls back to use an Edit field template when an Insert template for a particular field is not available. In case of the Customer entity template, it means that the Text_Edit field template instances will be used in both Insert and Edit modes. Therefore, defining a separate entity template for Insert mode would be redundant in this case. Luckily, you can take advantage of the fact that Dynamic Data uses a similar fallback algorithm for entity templates as well, which allows you to reuse Edit templates, such as Customers_Edit in Insert mode. You need only define Insert entity templates when they need to look and work differently from their Edit mode counterparts.

Entity Template Lookup Rules

When looking for an entity template, Dynamic Data looks in the DynamicData\EntityTemplates folder of the web application and tries to find the best match based on the template name and mode. Template file names consist of the template name, followed by the optional mode suffix:

```
DynamicData\EntityTemplates\{TemplateName}{_Mode}.ascx
```

Template Name

By default, the template name is determined by the name of the MetaTable describing the entity class. This name usually matches the name of the property provided by the context class that you would use to query it. In the Northwind sample, the context class, NorthwindEntities, has a property called Customers that you would normally use to query Customer entities, as illustrated here. Therefore, for the Customer entity, the table name and the default template name is *Customers*, plural:

```
using (NorthwindEntities context = new NorthwindEntities())
{
    var customers = from c in context.Customers
                    select c;
}
```

In data models that use inheritance, derived entity classes are represented slightly differently. Imagine a CRM (Customer Relationship Management) system that has a base class Contact and derived classes Prospect and Customer. Even though both Prospect and Customer entities might be stored in the same database table called Contacts, Dynamic Data provides a separate MetaTable object for each entity class. The name of each MetaTable matches the name of the derived class, so for the Prospect entity, the MetaTable name and the default template name is *Prospect*, singular:

```
using (CrmEntities context = new CrmEntities())
{
   var prospects = from p in context.Contacts.OfType<Prospect>()
                   select p;
}
```

Template name can also be specified explicitly by setting the UIHint attribute of the DynamicEntity control, in which case it does not have to match the table name of the entity class at all:

```
<asp:DynamicEntity runat="server" UIHint="Contact"/>
```

An explicitly specified template name is a more specific match than the *table* name. Therefore, if the previous code snipped is used for the Customer entity, the Contact.ascx entity template is used even though the Customers.ascx entity template is also available.

If a matching template cannot be found based explicitly on the specified template name or the table name, *Default* is used. Because Dynamic Data projects come with a set of default entity templates out of the box, this guarantees that a matching template exists for any entity.

Template Mode

Similar to the control mode for field templates, template mode defines the context where the entity template will be used. It is defined by the members of the ASP.NET DataBoundControlMode enumeration and used by Dynamic Data to determine the suffix of the template file name:

▶ ReadOnly templates are used to implement the ItemTemplate of the FormView and ListView controls. Read-only entity templates have no mode-based suffix in their file names.

▶ Edit templates are used to implement the EditItemTemplate of the FormView and ListView controls. Edit templates have _Edit at the end of their file names, such as Default_Edit.ascx.

▶ Insert templates are used to implement InsertItemTemplate of the FormView and ListView controls and have _Insert at the end of their file names, such as Default_Insert.ascx.

Insert templates are considered the most specific, whereas in many cases the Edit templates can be safely used in both Edit and Insert modes. Read-only templates are considered the most generic and can be used as a fallback if neither the Edit nor Insert template is available.

Entity Template Lookup Algorithm

Figure 4.4 shows the actual algorithm used by Dynamic Data to look up entity templates. This algorithm is implemented by the EntityTemplateFactory class in the System.Web.DynamicData namespace.

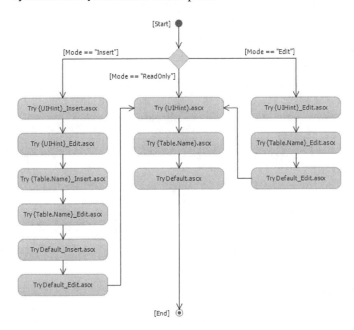

FIGURE 4.4   Entity template lookup algorithm.

Dynamic Data starts searching for an entity template with the most specific template name and the most specific mode. If there is no match, it tries more generic template names and modes. Here is a specific example:

```
<asp:DynamicEntity runat="server" UIHint="Contact" />
```

Imagine that the markup just shown is used on a FormView that displays the Customer entity rows. Because Mode property of the DynamicEntity control has value ReadOnly by default, Dynamic Data will try Contact.ascx, Customers.ascx, and Default.ascx file names to find the matching entity template.

If the Mode property of the DynamicEntity control were set to Edit, Dynamic Data would first try Contact_Edit.ascx, Customers_Edit.ascx, and Default_Edit.ascx before falling back to the read-only templates.

If the `Mode` property is set to `Insert`, Dynamic Data will also try Insert mode templates in the order shown in Table 4.1.

Notice that in Insert mode, the lookup algorithm breaks the pattern used in Read-only and Edit modes. Instead of trying different template names for Insert mode first, such as `Contact_Insert.ascx`, `Customers_Insert.ascx`, and `Default_Insert.ascx` and then repeating the process with Edit mode, it tries Insert and Edit modes for each template name. This is unfortunate because it makes the lookup algorithm much more confusing and difficult to understand. On the other hand, this twist allows you to reuse Edit mode templates in Insert mode. If it were not in place, the `Default_Insert.ascx` field template would always be used in Insert mode unless you defined `Contact_Insert.ascx` or `Customers_Insert.ascx`.

TABLE 4.1   Example of Entity Template Lookup

Mode="Insert"	Mode="Edit"	Mode="ReadOnly"
`Contact_Insert.ascx`	`Contact_Edit.ascx`	`Contact.ascx`
`Contact_Edit.ascx`	`Customers_Edit.ascx`	`Customers.ascx`
`Customers_Insert.ascx`	`Default_Edit.ascx`	`Default.ascx`
`Customers_Edit.ascx`	`Contact.ascx`	
`Default_Insert.ascx`	`Customers.ascx`	
`Default_Edit.ascx`	`Default.ascx`	
`Contact.ascx`		
`Customers.ascx`		
`Default.ascx`		

Built-in Entity Templates

Out of the box, Dynamic Data projects offer three dynamic entity templates, one for each mode:

▶ `Default.ascx`

▶ `Default_Edit.ascx`

▶ `Default_Insert.ascx`

All three dynamic entity templates generate a table with two columns, where the left column contains `Label` controls and the right column contains `DynamicControl` instances. One table row is generated for each scaffolded column in the entity `MetaTable`. Aside from the `Mode` property of the `DynamicControl`, which they set to `ReadOnly`, `Edit`, and `Insert`, respectively, these three entity templates are nearly identical and designed to present a consistent view of the entity in all three different modes.

Summary

Entity templates are a special type of ASP.NET user control, used by Dynamic Data to encapsulate presentation logic of displaying a single entity instance or, using database terminology, a single row from database table. Entity templates are used with web pages that display a single item at a time, typically in a form-based format.

By default, Dynamic Data expects to find entity templates in the `DynamicData\EntityTemplates` folder of the web application. A set of default entity templates is provided out of the box in this folder by the Dynamic Data web project templates in Visual Studio 2010. The default templates dynamically generate labels and controls for any given entity based on the metadata information extracted from a LINQ-based data model, such as Entity Framework or LINQ to SQL.

Metadata information defines the list of columns that should be displayed based on the `DisplayAttribute` in the `System.ComponentModel.DataAnnotations` namespace. Data annotation attributes can be used to change display names and order of the columns on a page produced by the default entity templates. When fine-grained control of the form layout is required, custom entity templates can be created.

4

Filter Templates

Search functionality is essential for most database applications. Whether it is a customer browsing the product catalog or a service representative looking up a customer record, users need a fast and convenient mechanism for finding the information they need. For more than a decade now, ASP.NET developers have been using stored procedures to implement data access code in general and search functionality in particular. For each search screen, such as the Customer search page shown in Figure 5.1, one or more stored procedures would be created, each accepting a number of parameters representing the search criteria and executing an appropriate SELECT statement.

Although implementing a simple page using stored procedures is easy, complexity grows exponentially with the number of additional parameters in the search criteria. Consider the Customer search page shown in Figure 5.1. With only 2 search parameters, City and Title, this search page needs to support 3 different combinations of their values—only City, only Title, and both City and Title. This requires placing conditional logic either in the form of IF statements in the stored procedure body or in the form of logical conditions in the WHERE clause of the SELECT statement to handle each of the 3 combinations. With 3 search parameters, the number of combinations jumps to 7; with 4 parameters, it is already 15; and with only 5 parameters, (a very modest number for an advanced search page in a typical application), the number of possible combination is a formidable 31.

The number of possible combinations of parameter values is important for two reasons. On one hand, it directly affects the complexity of the database code developers have to write. But more importantly, conditional logic in queries and stored procedures defeats the query optimization logic the database engines use to improve performance. When a query designed to handle all 31 combinations of 5 parameters is executed for the first time, the probability of having the same combination of parameter values next can be as low as 3%, so the execution plan cached for the first query is likely to be invalid next time.

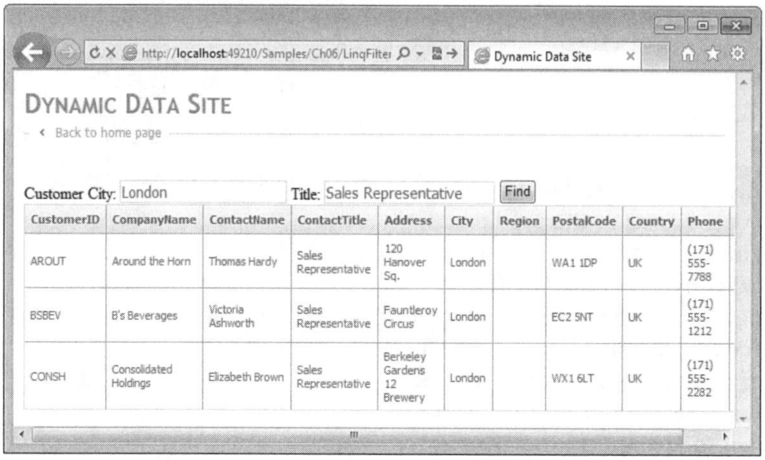

FIGURE 5.1   Customer Search page.

A better alternative to placing conditional logic in a static query code is to create the query dynamically, based on the specific combination of the parameter values. This approach leads to smaller, more focused queries that can be processed by the query optimizer effectively. Although dynamic queries can be created in the database and application code, this approach could open the application to SQL injection attacks if the developers are not careful to use parameters and not string concatenation to build the queries. This and the long entrenched assumption that dynamic SQL queries are slower than stored procedures are the reasons why database administrators often resist use of dynamic queries in internal applications.

Filtering with LINQ

Implementing search functionality became a lot easier with the advent of LINQ (Language Integrated Query) and LINQ-based data access frameworks, such as Entity Framework and LINQ to SQL. LINQ enables using SQL-like queries directly in C# and Visual Basic code:

```
using (NorthwindEntities context = new NorthwindEntities())
{
   IQueryable<Customer> query = from c in context.Customers
                                where c.City == "London"
                                select c;
```

```
    gridView.DataSource = customers.ToArray();
    gridView.DataBind();
}
```

With the help of strongly typed classes, LINQ takes advantage of the compiler and eliminates the simple, but all too common, errors caused by misspelled table and column
names in SQL queries. However, its biggest advantage is not the convenience of having
the compiler check your code for typos. LINQ queries are first compiled into expression
trees before they are translated into dynamic, parameterized SQL statements and sent to
the database server for execution.

Although having the query compiled into an expression might seem like overhead at first,
it offers two important advantages. On one hand, it protects the application against SQL
injection attacks. Any malicious search string provided by the user, such as "'; drop
table Customers;'" are passed to the database server as a *parameter value* and not as part
of the query itself. On the other hand, LINQ expressions can be manipulated to customize
the query. The following code snippet shows how you could implement filtering logic for
this sample Customer search page using LINQ:

```
using (NorthwindEntities context = new NorthwindEntities())
{
    IQueryable<Customer> customers = context.Customers;

    if (this.cityFilter.Text.Length > 0)
        customers = customers.Where(c => c.City == this.cityFilter.Text);

    if (this.titleFilter.Text.Length > 0)
        customers = customers.Where(c=>c.ContactTitle==this.titleFilter.Text);

    gridView.DataSource = customers.ToArray();
    gridView.DataBind();
}
```

This code uses the Where extension method instead of the where keyword. The first parameter of this generic method is an IQueryable<T> object, such as the
IQueryable<Customer> in this example. An IQueryable<T> can be obtained from a regular
LINQ query or directly from the Customers property of the context object. The second
parameter of the Where method is a *lambda expression*, a mini-method that takes a
Customer as a parameter and returns a Boolean value that indicates whether or not it
matches the search condition.

LINQ allows you to compose queries from multiple parts. In this ongoing example, the
Where method is first called if the user entered a search string for City, producing a SQL
query that looks like this:

```
select * from Customers where City = @City
```

If the user enters a search string for `Title`, the second `Where` method is called, and the SQL query looks like the following:

```
select * from Customers where ContactTitle = @Title
```

Only if the user entered both `City` and `Title` search strings, both `Where` methods are called, and the SQL query includes conditions for both columns:

```
select * from Customers where City = @City and ContactTitle = @Title
```

In other words, with the help of LINQ, you can build focused queries that include only those conditions required for the search values supplied by the user. This helps the database server choose a more efficient execution plan than a typical hand-coded SQL (shown next) that tries to handle both search conditions and usually requires the database server to perform a full table scan:

```
select * from Customers
where City = ISNULL(@City, City)
   and ContactTitle = ISNULL(@Title, ContactTitle)
```

Creating a Filter Template

A filter template is a user control that encapsulates both presentation and data access logic necessary to implement query filtering for a single column. In traditional search pages, this logic is usually spread over the markup and code-behind files. Consider the filtering logic required for the City column in our Customer search page (see the markup in Listing 5.1).

LISTING 5.1   Simple Search Page (Markup)

```
<%@ Page Title="" Language="C#"
  MasterPageFile="~/Site.master" CodeBehind="SamplePage.aspx.cs"
  Inherits="WebApplication.Samples.Ch05.LinqFilter.SamplePage" %>

<asp:Content ContentPlaceHolderID="main" runat="server">
  Customer City: <asp:TextBox runat="server" ID="cityFilter" />
  Title: <asp:TextBox runat="server" ID="titleFilter" />
  <asp:Button runat="server" Text="Find" OnClick="Find_Click" />
  <asp:GridView ID="gridView" runat="server" />
</asp:Content>
```

The traditional page includes a `TextBox` control where the user can enter a value to search for in the City column. The data access logic for filtering rows based on this value is a part of the `Find_Click` event handler shown in Listing 5.2.

LISTING 5.2 Simple Search Page (Code-Behind)

```
using System;
using System.Linq;
using DataModel;

namespace WebApplication.Samples.Ch05.LinqFilter
{
  public partial class SamplePage : System.Web.UI.Page
  {
    protected void Find_Click(object sender, EventArgs e)
    {
      using (NorthwindEntities context = new NorthwindEntities())
      {
        IQueryable<Customer> customers = context.Customers;

        if (this.cityFilter.Text.Length > 0)
        {
          customers = customers.Where(c => c.City == this.cityFilter.Text);
        }

        if (this.titleFilter.Text.Length > 0)
        {
          customers = customers.Where(c=>c.ContactTitle==this.titleFilter.Text);
        }

        this.gridView.DataSource = customers.ToArray();
        this.gridView.DataBind();
      }
    }
  }
}
```

To create a filter template for the City column, you need to extract both the markup and the code into a new user control and save it in the DynamicData\Filters folder of the web project. Note that the markup and code-behind for the ContactTitle column is nearly identical to that of the City column. The filter template created here works for both of these columns. Listings 5.3 and 5.4 show its markup and code-behind respectively.

LISTING 5.3 Text Filter Template (Markup)

```
<%@ Control Language="C#" CodeBehind="Text.ascx.cs"
  Inherits="WebApplication.DynamicData.Filters.TextFilter" %>

<asp:TextBox runat="server" ID="textBox" OnTextChanged="TextBox_TextChanged" />
```

You can use any of the built-in or third-party ASP.NET controls to implement user interface appropriate for entering search values for a data type the template is designed to handle. This template is designed for String columns. It uses a TextBox control similar to the one used in the sample search page earlier. The OnTextChanged event handler is used to refresh the query results when the user changes the search value.

LISTING 5.4   Text Filter Template (Code-Behind)

```csharp
using System;
using System.Linq;
using System.Linq.Dynamic;
using System.Web.DynamicData;
using System.Web.UI;

namespace WebApplication.DynamicData.Filters
{
  public partial class TextFilter : QueryableFilterUserControl
  {
    public override IQueryable GetQueryable(IQueryable query)
    {
      if (!string.IsNullOrEmpty(this.textBox.Text))
      {
        string filter = this.Column.Name + " == @0";
        query = query.Where (filter, this.textBox.Text);
      }

      return query;
    }

    protected override void OnInit(EventArgs e)
    {
      base.OnInit(e);
      this.textBox.MaxLength = this.Column.MaxLength;
      this.textBox.Text = this.DefaultValue;
    }

    protected void TextBox_TextChanged(object sender, EventArgs e)
    {
      this.OnFilterChanged();
    }
  }
}
```

Filter templates inherit from a special base class provided by Dynamic Data called QueryableFilterUserControl. This class defines several virtual methods and properties that child classes need to override and offers several helper methods designed to help with implementation of concrete filter templates.

GetQueryable Method

The GetQueryable method is the heart of a filter template. It is defined as abstract in the QueryableFilterUserControl base class and must be overridden by all filter templates to implement the data access logic. This method receives a query object, an instance of IQueryable, which it needs to modify based on the search value entered by the user. If the user did not enter any search criteria for this particular column, the GetQueryable method should return the original query. Notice how the code in Listing 5.4 checks the contents of the TextBox control and modifies the query only if it is not empty.

OnFilterChanged Method

The OnFilterChanged method of the QueryableFilterUserControl base class notifies the data source control responsible for executing the query and fetching rows from the database that the query might have changed. The base class calls the GetQueryable method in response to the OnFilterChanged.

In this example, the OnFilterChanged method is called from the TextBox_TextChanged method, which handles the OnTextChanged event of the TextBox control. This ensures that any change to the search value entered in the text box is detected during the post-back, and the GetQueryable method is invoked to apply the filter.

DefaultValue Property

The DefaultValue property provides the initial filter value. When instantiated as part of the List page template, which is discussed in Chapter 6, "Page Templates," filters can be initialized by passing column names and values through the page request URL. Although not required for new filter templates, supporting this functionality is important to make them behave consistently with the built-in templates provided by Dynamic Data project templates.

Dynamic LINQ Queries

Most filter templates, such as the Text.ascx in this example, can be reused for any column of a matching type. Dynamic filter templates, such as this, cannot hardcode the column name in the query. Instead, use the column metadata, available through the Column property of the QueryableFilterUserControl base class, to get the column name and build the query dynamically:

```
public override IQueryable GetQueryable(IQueryable query)
{
  if (!string.IsNullOrEmpty(this.textBox.Text))
  {
    string filter = this.Column.Name + " == @0";
    query = query.Where(filter, this.textBox.Text);
  }

  return query;
}
```

In this example, a *dynamic* version of the `Where` extension method is used. This method takes a `string` that represents a logical condition and converts it into a lambda expression LINQ needs to execute this query. Notice the use of the `MetaColumn.Name` property; it specifies the actual column name dynamically. With the City column, the filter string will be `"City==@0"`, and with ContactTitle, it will be `"ContactTitle==@0"`. `@0` is a placeholder for the first parameter of the lambda expression, similar to parameters in dynamic SQL statements. The actual parameter value, `TextBox.Text`, is passed as the second argument in the call to the `Where` method.

NOTE

The `System.Linq.Dynamic` namespace, which provided the dynamic version of the `Where` extension method in this filter template, is *not* a part of the .NET Framework. It is a C# sample project called `DynamicQuery` and can be found in the following folder of the Visual Studio installation:

```
Microsoft Visual Studio 10.0
    \Samples
        \1033
            \CSharpSamples.zip
                \LinqSamples
                    \DynamicQuery
```

Before you can start using dynamic LINQ extensions in your project, you need to extract the sample project from the following folder on your computer and add it to your solution. When compiled, the assembly can be used in both C# and Visual Basic projects.

The dynamic LINQ extensions make the task of creating queries dynamically almost as easy as writing regular LINQ code. Compare the statically typed code shown here:

```
IQueryable<Customer> query = // …
query = query.Where(customer => customer.City == "London");
```

with its dynamic equivalent.

```
IQueryable query = // …
query = query.Where("City == @0", "London");
```

The dynamic Where method parses the string and creates a strongly-typed LINQ expression tree that can be used by a LINQ-enabled data access framework, such as the ADO.NET Entity Framework in this example. Following is the equivalent code that uses LINQ expression classes to accomplish the same result:

```
IQueryable query = // …


ParameterExpression parameter = Expression.Parameter(
    query.ElementType, string.Empty);
Expression property = Expression.PropertyOrField(parameter, "City");
Expression comparison = Expression.Equal(
    property, Expression.Constant("London"));
LambdaExpression lambda = Expression.Lambda(
    comparison, new ParameterExpression[] { parameter });

MethodCallExpression where = Expression.Call(
    typeof(Queryable), "Where",
    new Type[] { query.ElementType },
    new Expression[] { query.Expression, Expression.Quote(lambda) });

query = query.Provider.CreateQuery(where);
```

Compared to raw expressions, dynamic LINQ extensions make implementing filter templates much, much easier. However, parsing strings requires additional CPU resources on the web server, and you might want to consider implementing filter templates with LINQ expressions as an optimization. You might also need to use LINQ expressions if the dynamic extensions do not support the LINQ functionality you need in your filter template, such as joins. However, this topic is too vast and complex to cover here; it is revisited in Chapter 12, "Building Custom Search Pages."

Building Search Pages with Filter Templates

Now that you have implemented the filter template, Text.ascx, and saved it in the DynamicData\Filters folder of this web project, you can rewrite the sample search page to take advantage of its functionality. Compare Listing 5.5, which shows markup of the new version of this page, with Listing 5.1, which shows the original version.

LISTING 5.5 Simple Search Page with DynamicFilter Controls (Markup)

```
<%@ Page Title="" Language="C#"
  MasterPageFile="~/Site.master" CodeBehind="SamplePage.aspx.cs"
  Inherits="WebApplication.Samples.Ch05.DynamicFilter.SamplePage" %>

<asp:Content ContentPlaceHolderID="main" runat="server">
  Customer City:
  <asp:DynamicFilter runat="server" ID="cityFilter"
    DataField="City" FilterUIHint="Text" />
  Title:
  <asp:DynamicFilter runat="server" ID="titleFilter"
    DataField="ContactTitle" FilterUIHint="Text" />
  <asp:Button runat="server" Text="Find" />
  <asp:GridView ID="gridView" runat="server" DataSourceID="dataSource" />
  <asp:EntityDataSource runat="server" ID="dataSource"
    ConnectionString="name=NorthwindEntities"
    DefaultContainerName="NorthwindEntities" EntitySetName="Customers" />
  <asp:QueryExtender runat="server" TargetControlID="dataSource">
    <asp:DynamicFilterExpression ControlID="cityFilter" />
    <asp:DynamicFilterExpression ControlID="titleFilter" />
  </asp:QueryExtender>
</asp:Content>
```

At run time, the new version of the page looks identical to the original shown in Figure 5.1. However, notice that the DynamicFilter controls are used instead of text boxes. DynamicFilter is a new ASP.NET control provided by Dynamic Data. At run time, it dynamically loads an appropriate filter template for the column specified in its DataField property. On this page, you have two instances of the DynamicFilter control, one for the City column and one for the ContactTitle.

Each DynamicFilter control must be ultimately connected to a LINQ-based data source control that queries the database. In this example, Entity Framework is used, and there is an EntityDataSource control on this page, configured to retrieve rows from the Customers table. EntityDataSource class inherits the QueryCreated event from its base class, QueryableDataSource. The control fires this event *after* it has created the initial LINQ query, an IQueryable instance, but *before* the query is converted to SQL and sent to the database server for execution. During this event, the query can be modified by the DynamicFilter controls.

In addition to the data source control, there's also a QueryExtender control on the page. This control is associated with a QueryableDataSource by specifying its ID in the TargetControlID property of the query extender. At run time, the query extender handles the QueryCreated of the data source control and passes the IQueryable instance to every one of its data source expressions. This page uses two DynamicFilterExpression instances to associate both of the DynamicFilter controls with the QueryExtender. Each

DynamicFilterExpression passes the query to its DynamicFilter, which in turn passes it to its filter template, Text.ascx, in this example.

Figure 5.2 illustrates how the whole process works, starting with the EntityDataSource on the left and ending with the filter template, a QueryableFilterUserControl, on the right.

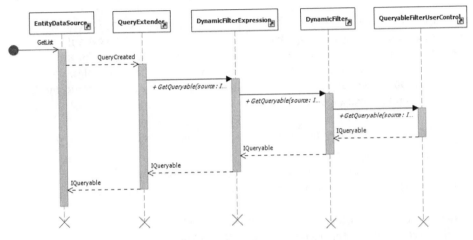

FIGURE 5.2   Query modification sequence diagram.

It might seem this markup is more complex than the original version shown in Listing 5.1. However, keep in mind, unlike in the original page where there was a significant amount of data access logic hard-coded in the code-behind file, the new page has most of this logic in the markup, leaving the code-behind (see Listing 5.6) almost empty. Implementing filtering for additional columns is also easier. Should you need to support filtering for additional columns on this page, you can simply add more DynamicFilter controls to the markup without having to modify the code-behind.

LISTING 5.6   Sample Search Page with DynamicFilter Controls (Code-Behind)

```
using System;
using System.Web.DynamicData;

namespace WebApplication.Samples.Ch05.DynamicFilter
{
    public partial class SamplePage : System.Web.UI.Page
    {
        protected void Page_Init(object sender, EventArgs e)
        {
            MetaTable table = Global.DefaultModel.GetTable("Customers");
            this.gridView.SetMetaTable(table);
        }
    }
}
```

The code-behind only needs to associate the required `MetaTable` object with the `GridView` control. This allows the `DynamicFilter` controls to locate the `MetaColumn` objects based on the column names specified in their `DataField` properties.

QueryableFilterRepeater Control

The `DynamicFilter` control is the right choice for implementing filtering functionality if you need to build a custom search page with specific search criteria. However, if you need to build an advanced search page where users can search for data using *any* of the supported columns or a dynamic search page that can work for different tables, you can also use the `QueryableFilterRepeater` control. Listing 5.7 shows how you could modify the search page to take advantage of it.

LISTING 5.7   Search Page with QueryableFilterRepeater Control (Markup)

```
<%@ Page Title="" Language="C#"
  MasterPageFile="~/Site.master" CodeBehind="SamplePage.aspx.cs"
  Inherits="WebApplication.Samples.Ch05.QueryableFilterRepeater.SamplePage" %>

<asp:Content ContentPlaceHolderID="main" runat="server">
  <asp:QueryableFilterRepeater runat="server" ID="filterRepeater">
    <ItemTemplate>
      <%# Eval("DisplayName") %>:
      <asp:DynamicFilter ID="DynamicFilter" runat="server" />
    </ItemTemplate>
  </asp:QueryableFilterRepeater>
  <asp:Button runat="server" Text="Find" />
  <asp:GridView ID="gridView" runat="server" DataSourceID="dataSource" />
  <asp:EntityDataSource runat="server" ID="dataSource"
    ConnectionString="name=NorthwindEntities"
    DefaultContainerName="NorthwindEntities" EntitySetName="Customers" />
  <asp:QueryExtender runat="server" TargetControlID="dataSource">
    <asp:DynamicFilterExpression ControlID="filterRepeater" />
  </asp:QueryExtender>
</asp:Content>
```

Similar to the regular `Repeater` control, `QueryableFilterRepeater` enables you to define a markup template that it will use to generate filtering controls for each supported column in the table. Each instance of the `ItemTemplate` it defines is bound to a `MetaColumn` object describing a column that can be filtered by Dynamic Data. This allows you to use ASP.NET data-binding syntax `<%# Eval("DisplayName")%>` to generate a text label for each column. Inside of the `ItemTemplate`, you also need to have a single instance of the `DynamicFilter` control that has ID property set to "DynamicFilter". This allows the `QueryableFilterRepeater` to find the `DynamicFilter` control inside of each `ItemTemplate` instance and configure it based on the current `MetaColumn`; the `QueryableFilterRepeater` will initialize the filter control at run time.

The `QueryableFilterRepeater` control also needs to be connected to the `QueryExtender` with the help of the `DynamicFilterExpression`. Notice that in this example, there are no `DynamicFilterExpression` instances for the individual `DynamicFilter` controls, only one for the `QueryableFilterRepeater`. The `DynamicFilterExpression` calls the `GetQueryable` method of the `QueryableFilterRepeater` control, which in turn invokes the `GetQueryable` method of each `DynamicFilter` it created to modify the query.

The overall process of applying filters to a LINQ query, shown in Figure 5.3, is similar to the process involving only `DynamicFilter` controls reviewed earlier, except that here, a `QueryableFilterRepeater` is between a single `DynamicFilterExpresssion` and multiple `DynamicFilter` controls.

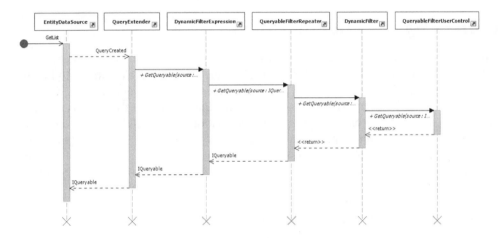

FIGURE 5.3   QueryableFilterRepeater query modification sequence diagram.

Notice that in addition to the `DataField` property of the `DynamicFilter` control, which the `QueryableFilterRepeater` initializes programmatically, the code in Listing 5.7 also does not specify the `FilterUIHint` property. For the Text filter template to work, this information needs to be specified in column metadata by applying the `FilterUIHintAttribute` to the property of the column. Listing 5.8 shows an example of doing that for the City and ContactTitle columns of the Customer entity.

LISTING 5.8   Specifying FilterUIHintAttribute

```
using System.ComponentModel.DataAnnotations;

namespace DataModel
{
  [MetadataType(typeof(Customer.Metadata))]
  partial class Customer
  {
    public abstract class Metadata
    {
```

LISTING 5.8   Continued

```
    [FilterUIHint("Text")]
    public object City { get; set; }

    [FilterUIHint("Text")]
    public object ContactTitle { get; set; }
    }
  }
}
```

Filter Template Lookup Rules

Compared to the lookup rules for field templates, lookup rules for filter templates are simple. Dynamic Data uses only the FilterUIHint associated with the column and has an intrinsic knowledge of several column types. If the FilterUIHint is not specified in the data model, and the column is Foreign Key (a column that represents the parent navigation property of a many-to-one or a one-to-one association in the child entity), a Boolean, or an enumeration, Dynamic Data chooses a predefined FilterUIHint value, ForeignKey, Boolean, or Enumeration, respectively. Having the FilterUIHint value, Dynamic Data tries to locate a user control with the matching name in the DynamicData\Filters directory of the web application project. If the user control does not exist, the lookup process ends, and filtering is considered to be unsupported for this column. Figure 5.4 illustrates the algorithm used by Dynamic Data for filter template lookup.

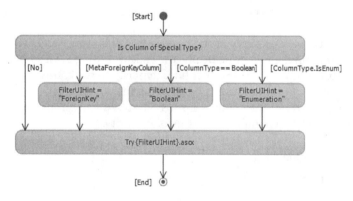

FIGURE 5.4 Filter template lookup algorithm.

Built-in Filter Templates

Perhaps the reason why the lookup algorithm for filter templates is so simplistic compared to field templates is that only three filter templates come with a Dynamic Data web project by default.

Boolean

The `Boolean` filter template is used for columns of Boolean type. It contains a DropDownList control that allows the user to choose filter value from `All`, `True`, `False`, and `[Not Set]` if the column allows `null` values.

Enumeration

The `Enumeration` filter template is used for columns of enum types or integer columns marked with the `EnumDataTypeAttribute` that specifies an enum type. It contains a DropDownList control that allows users to choose filter value from All, `[Not Set]` (if the column allows `null` values), as well as the string names of all items in the enumerated type.

ForeignKey

The `ForeignKey` filter template is used for foreign key columns. It displays all records from the parent table referenced by the foreign key column in a `DropDownList` control, plus `All` and `[Not Set]` (if the column allows `null` values). Each `ListItem` represents a single row from the parent table. Its `Value` property contains a comma-separated list of primary key column values. The `Text` property value is determined by calling the `GetDisplayString` method of the `MetaTable` instance describing the parent table. If the parent entity class overrides the `ToString` method, the value returned by this method is used; otherwise, the value of the display column of the parent entity class is used. Display column can be specified explicitly, by applying the `DisplayColumnAttribute` to the entity class, or determined heuristically, in which case the value of the first string property is used.

Summary

A filter template is a special type of user control that encapsulates both user interface and data access logic required to filter rows of a particular table based on the values of a single column. Filter template modifies the LINQ query created by a data source control to apply the filter criteria dynamically, based on the search parameter entered by the user. Multiple instances of the same filter template can be used in an application for different columns of the same type. Dynamic Data includes a small number of ready-to-use filter templates, including templates for Boolean, enumeration, and foreign key columns. New filter templates can be implemented using built-in or third-party ASP.NET controls and LINQ expressions or dynamic LINQ extensions.

CHAPTER 6

Page Templates

Implementation of CRUD (Create, Read, Update and Delete) operations has been an ongoing challenge in web applications. The problem is not so much their complexity, but rather a sheer number of the pages that have to be implemented in a typical enterprise application. It is common in web applications to have a separate web page for implementing each type of operation, with one page for editing a particular entity type and another for displaying it in Read-only mode. The resulting number of pages can quickly become unmanageable in enterprise applications that have dozens and sometimes hundreds of entity types.

In traditional ASP.NET WebForms applications, developers sometimes try to address this problem by creating multi-purpose pages, such as a single page that allows users to both *create* and *modify* instances of a particular entity type. Visual Studio even offers limited support for creating multi-purpose pages by generating the Item, Edit, and Insert templates for FormView controls. Although this approach reduces the overall number of pages in the application, it does so at the cost of significantly increasing complexity of the individual pages.

The ASP.NET MVC framework attempts to solve this problem by offering scaffolding functionality in Visual Studio, which generates separate CRUD pages for a given entity at design time. Although design-time scaffolding helps create the initial version of the CRUD pages, the task of maintaining the generated code falls back onto developers' shoulders. In a way, the design-time scaffolding solves the problem of supporting CRUD operations by creating a bigger problem of rapidly increasing the number of pages and amount of code developers have to maintain.

ASP.NET Dynamic Data offers an alternative solution to the CRUD problem. Instead of generating pages at design time, like the WebForms and MVC tools do, it generates pages at runtime with the help of *page templates*.

Built-in Page Templates

When users of a web application need to perform a particular action, such as creating, reading, or modifying an instance of a particular entity type, Dynamic Data can use a single dynamic page template to handle this action across all entity types:

```
namespace System.Web.DynamicData
{
  public static class PageAction
  {
    public static string Details { get { return "Details"; } }
    public static string Edit    { get { return "Edit";    } }
    public static string Insert  { get { return "Insert";  } }
    public static string List    { get { return "List";    } }
  }
}
```

Out of the box, Dynamic Data understands actions defined in the `PageAction` class and provides page templates (see Figure 6.1) for inserting, displaying details, editing, and listing entities as part of the new website and web application projects in Visual Studio.

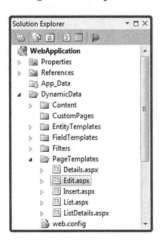

FIGURE 6.1 Page templates in a Dynamic Data web application project.

Page templates are special ASPX forms located in the `DynamicData/PageTemplates` folder of the web application. They rely on URL routing functionality of ASP.NET to handle page requests for different entity types. Dynamic Data applications register at least one

`DynamicDataRoute` during the application startup. Here is an example of the route registration code you normally find in the `Global.asax`:

```
RouteTable.Routes.Add(new DynamicDataRoute("{table}/{action}.aspx"));
```

The static `Routes` property of the `RouteTable` class provides access to the global collection of `Route` objects. This code uses it to register a new `DynamicDataRoute` that defines a URL as a combination of a table name and a page action. The `{table}` marker defines the place where you expect to find a table name in the URL, and the `{action}` marks the place where you expect to find the page action. If an incoming request has a URL in this format, the default `MetaModel` of the web application contains a table with the matching name, and a page template exists matching the action, Dynamic Data uses this page template to handle the request. In the following URL, *Products* matches the table parameter, and *List* matches the action:

```
http://localhost/Products/List.aspx
```

Details Page Template

The Details page template generates web pages that display a single entity instance in a form view. Figure 6.2 shows an example of such page generated for the Product entity. Notice the URL in the address bar of the web browser; it includes the name of the table (Products) and a query string that specifies value of the entity's primary key (ProductID). The Details page template uses this information to retrieve the appropriate entity instance from the database.

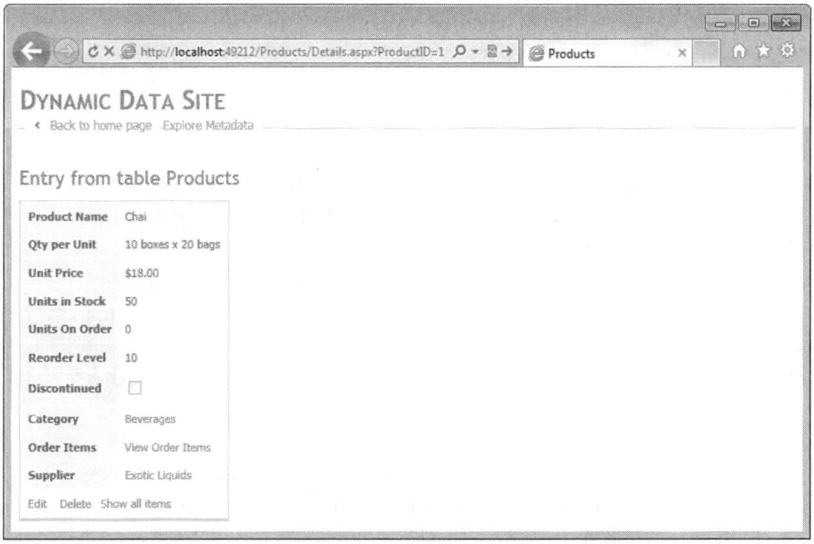

FIGURE 6.2 Web page generated by the Details page template.

Listing 6.1 shows the source code of the Details page template, `Details.aspx`, located in the `DynamicData\PageTemplates` folder of the web application. Most of its contents should be already familiar to you from Chapter 2, "Entity Framework," and Chapter 4, "Entity Templates."

LISTING 6.1 Details Page Template (Markup)

```
<%@ Page Language="C#"
  MasterPageFile="~/Site.master" CodeBehind="Details.aspx.cs"
  Inherits="WebApplication.DynamicData.PageTemplates.Details" %>

<asp:Content ContentPlaceHolderID="main" runat="Server">
  <asp:DynamicDataManager runat="server">
    <DataControls>
      <asp:DataControlReference ControlID="formView" />
    </DataControls>
  </asp:DynamicDataManager>

  <h2>Entry from table <%= table.DisplayName %></h2>

  <asp:UpdatePanel runat="server">
    <ContentTemplate>
      <asp:ValidationSummary runat="server" HeaderText="List of validation errors"/>
      <asp:DynamicValidator runat="server" ControlToValidate="formView"
        Display="None" />

      <asp:FormView runat="server" ID="formView" DataSourceID="dataSource"
        OnItemDeleted="FormView_ItemDeleted">
        <ItemTemplate>
          <asp:DynamicEntity runat="server" />
          <div class="DDFormActions">
            <asp:DynamicHyperLink runat="server" Action="Edit" Text="Edit" />
            <asp:LinkButton runat="server" CommandName="Delete" Text="Delete"
              OnClientClick='return
                confirm("Are you sure you want to delete this item?");'/>
            <asp:DynamicHyperLink runat="server" Action="List" Text="Back to List"/>
          </div>
        </ItemTemplate>
      </asp:FormView>

      <asp:EntityDataSource ID="dataSource" runat="server" EnableDelete="true" />
      <asp:QueryExtender TargetControlID="dataSource" runat="server">
        <asp:DynamicRouteExpression />
      </asp:QueryExtender>
```

```
    </ContentTemplate>
  </asp:UpdatePanel>
</asp:Content>
```

The `EntityDataSource` control is used to retrieve the required entity instance from the database. However, as you probably noticed, it does not specify the `DefaultContainerName` and the `EntitySetName` properties normally required for the control to know which `ObjectContext` to instantiate and which object set to query. This information is supplied to the `EntityDataSource` by the `DynamicDataManager`, one of the new controls provided by Dynamic Data.

The `DynamicDataManager` control has a `DataControls` collection that stores one or more `DataControlReference` objects. In the Details page template, it stores a single reference to the `FormView` control. During the initialization phase of the page lifecycle, the `DynamicDataManager` uses this reference to find the `EntityDataSource` control associated with the `FormView` and configures it. In particular, it extracts the table name from the current URL route and obtains the `MetaTable` object describing the table. The `MetaTable` object provides the information necessary to initialize the `EntityDataSource`, including the type of the `ObjectContext` as well as the name of the entity set to query.

Knowing the context type and the entity set is not enough to retrieve a specific entity from the database. The query sent to the database server must also include a `WHERE` clause that identifies the table row where it is stored. This task is performed by the `QueryExtender` control, which is associated with the `EntityDataSource`. In the Details page template, the `QueryExtender` uses a special type of data source expression, called `DynamicRouteExpression`. At runtime, this object extracts the values of the primary key columns from the URL and modifies the query generated by the `EntityDataSource` to include appropriate filter criteria.

The `FormView` control defines an **ItemTemplate** to display the entity with the help of the `DynamicEntity` control. As you remember, this control uses Dynamic Data entity templates to generate either a generic, single column view of the entity or a custom view if a custom template was defined for the entity. In the Details page template, the `DynamicEntity` control does not specify the `Mode` property, so a *read-only* entity template is used.

In addition to the `DynamicEntity`, the `ItemTemplate` of the `FormView` control also includes a set of links for users to edit or delete the entity or to go back to the List page. The Edit and List actions are implemented by the `DynamicHyperLink` controls. When databound to an entity instance, a `DynamicHyperLink` control generates a URL that points to another dynamic page based on the value of the control's `Action` property. In this example, the URL generated by the first `DynamicHyperLink` control looks like this:

```
http://localhost:49212/Products/Edit.aspx?ProductID=1
```

In this URL, `Products` is the name of the `MetaTable` describing the current entity instance, `Edit` is the name of the action specified in the `Action` property of the `DynamicHyperLink` control, and `ProductID=1` is the name and value of the primary key column of the current entity instance. Because the second DynamicHyperLink's Action property set to List, the URL it generates looks like this instead:

```
http://localhost:49212/Products/List.aspx?ProductID=1
```

The *Delete* action, on the other hand, is implemented by a traditional LinkButton. This control specifies the CommandName property and takes advantage of the deletion support built into the FormView. When the user clicks the link generated by this control, a Delete command is submitted back to the FormView, which in turn passes the deletion request to the data source control associated with it. To allow deletion, the EntityDataSource control has its EnableDelete property set to true.

Not all of the functionality is implemented directly in the markup of the Details page template. You might have noticed that the caption line relies on the table field defined in the code-behind.

```
<h2>Entry from table <%= table.DisplayName %></h2>
```

Additional code is required to initialize controls and handle entity deletion. Listing 6.2 shows the code-behind of the Details page template.

LISTING 6.2 Details Page Template (Code-Behind)

```csharp
using System;
using System.Web.DynamicData;
using System.Web.UI.WebControls;

namespace WebApplication.DynamicData.PageTemplates
{
  public partial class Details : System.Web.UI.Page
  {
    protected MetaTable table;

    protected void Page_Init(object sender, EventArgs e)
    {
      this.table = DynamicDataRouteHandler.GetRequestMetaTable(this.Context);
      this.Title = this.table.DisplayName;
      this.dataSource.EntityTypeFilter = this.table.EntityType.Name;
      this.dataSource.Include = this.table.ForeignKeyColumnsNames;
    }

    protected void FormView_ItemDeleted(object sender, FormViewDeletedEventArgs e)
    {
      if (e.Exception == null ¦¦ e.ExceptionHandled)
        this.Response.Redirect(this.table.ListActionPath);
    }
  }
}
```

The `Page_Init` event handler initializes the `table` field by extracting the table name from the URL route and looking up the matching `MetaTable` object in the default `MetaModel`. `DisplayName` of the table is used to initialize the `Title` of the page, but more importantly, this code performs the missing initialization steps required for the `EntityDataSource`.

The `EntityTypeFilter` property of the `EntityDataSource` specifies the name of the entity *type*, which might be different from the entity *set* if your data model uses entity inheritance. The Northwind sample data model doesn't take advantage of this feature, but imagine that a Contact table was used to store both Customer and Employee information with a ContactType column serving as the discriminator. The same entity set, Contacts, could be used to retrieve both Customer and Employee entity type, and you would need to specify the `EntityTypeFilter` to make sure a Customer entity is not displayed as if it were an Employee. The `Page_Init` handler sets the `EntityTypeFilter` property using the entity type name retrieved from the `MetaTable` object.

The `Include` property of the `EntityDataSource` determines whether related entities will be retrieved along with the main one. In the case of the Product entity, Category and Supplier entities also need to be retrieved from the database to display the category and supplier names in human-readable form, as opposed to the raw numeric values of the CategoryID and SupplierID columns. The `Page_Init` handler sets the Include property using the names of the foreign key navigation properties of the entity type, retrieved from the `MetaTable` object.

The `FormView_ItemDeleted` event handler is invoked when the user clicks the *Delete* `LinkButton` and the current entity instance has been successfully deleted. Instead of displaying an empty page, this method redirects the user back to the List page that displays all remaining entities of that type.

Edit Page Template

The Edit page template generates a web page for editing a single entity instance. Figure 6.3 shows such a page generated for a Product entity.

This page is quite similar to the Details page discussed earlier. The URL also includes table and action names as well as the names and values of the primary key columns of the current entity instance.

```
http://localhost:49212/Products/Edit.aspx?ProductID=1
```

Users can navigate to this page by clicking the Edit link on the pages generated by the Details page template, as well as on the pages produced by the List page template, which is discussed shortly.

As you would expect, implementation of the Edit page template is similar to the Details page template. Listing 6.3 shows the markup file of this template, with significant differences between the templates indicated by bold font.

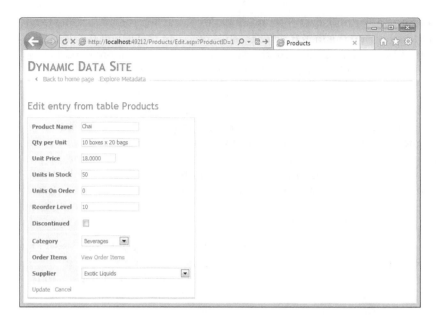

FIGURE 6.3 Web page generated by the Edit page template.

LISTING 6.3 Edit Page Template (Markup)

```
<%@ Page Language="C#" MasterPageFile="~/Site.master" CodeBehind="Edit.aspx.cs"
  Inherits="WebApplication.DynamicData.PageTemplates.Edit" %>

<asp:Content ContentPlaceHolderID="main" runat="Server">
  <asp:DynamicDataManager runat="server">
    <DataControls>
      <asp:DataControlReference ControlID="formView" />
    </DataControls>
  </asp:DynamicDataManager>

  <h2>Edit entry from table <%= table.DisplayName %></h2>

  <asp:UpdatePanel runat="server">
    <ContentTemplate>
      <asp:ValidationSummary runat="server" HeaderText="List of validation errors"/>
      <asp:DynamicValidator runat="server" ControlToValidate="formView"
        Display="None"/>

      <asp:FormView runat="server" ID="formView" DataSourceID="dataSource"
        DefaultMode="Edit" OnItemCommand="FormView_ItemCommand"
        OnItemUpdated="FormView_ItemUpdated">
        <EditItemTemplate>
```

```
        <asp:DynamicEntity runat="server" Mode="Edit" />
        <div class="DDFormActions">
          <asp:LinkButton runat="server" CommandName="Update" Text="Update" />
          <asp:LinkButton runat="server" CommandName="Cancel" Text="Cancel"
            CausesValidation="false" />
        </div>
      </EditItemTemplate>
    </asp:FormView>

    <asp:EntityDataSource ID="dataSource" runat="server" EnableUpdate="true" />
    <asp:QueryExtender TargetControlID="dataSource" runat="server">
      <asp:DynamicRouteExpression />
    </asp:QueryExtender>
  </ContentTemplate>
  </asp:UpdatePanel>
</asp:Content>
```

The Edit page also includes an EntityDataSource and QueryExtender controls to implement data access logic as well as a FormView and DynamicEntity controls to render the user interface. However, unlike the read-only Details page template, which allows deleting the current entity, the Edit page template enables you to edit the current entity, but not delete it. Consequently, it sets the Mode property of the FormView and DynamicEntity controls to Edit and sets EnableUpdate property of the EntityDataSource control to true.

As you recall from the discussion of entity templates in Chapter 5, "Filter Templates," setting the Mode of the DynamicEntity control to Edit instructs this control to choose an appropriate edit-mode entity template, which includes editable controls, like TextBox and DropDownList instead of the read-only Literal and DynamicHyperLink controls generated by the read-only entity templates.

Setting DefaultMode of the FormView control to Edit makes it instantiate the EditItemTemplate, which contains the DynamicEntity control along with two LinkButton controls. The FormView control has built-in support for the Update command, so when the user clicks the Update link, the current property values of the entity displayed by the FormView are automatically validated and submitted to the EntityDataSource control to be saved in the database. The Cancel link is used to abandon editing the current entity and go back to the List page.

The Edit page template includes the ValidationSummary and DynamicValidator controls. Although these controls are also included in the Details page template, they haven't been discussed because validation plays a much more prominent role in the process of editing entities compared to deletion. As you recall from the discussion of field templates in Chapters 4, the individual field values are validated by the field templates with the help of the ASP.NET validation controls, including the new DynamicValidator control, which enforces validation rules based on the Data Annotation attributes. If any validation errors are encountered, the validators embedded in the field templates indicate invalid fields by displaying an asterisk next to the corresponding data entry controls. However, the complete error messages are displayed by the ValidationSummary control on the Edit page template.

In field templates, the DynamicValidator controls are associated with MetaColumn objects describing specific entity properties. However, the DynamicValidator control used by the Edit page template is not associated with any particular column and specifies the FormView as its ControlToValidate. When configured this way, the DynamicValidator control catches unhandled validation exceptions thrown by the EntityDataSource associated with the FormView. Chapter 8, "Implementing Entity Validation," provides detailed discussion of this topic.

Listing 6.4 shows the code-behind file of the Edit page template.

LISTING 6.4 Edit Page Template (Code-Behind)

```
using System;
using System.Web.DynamicData;
using System.Web.UI.WebControls;

namespace WebApplication.DynamicData.PageTemplates
{
  public partial class Edit : System.Web.UI.Page
  {
    protected MetaTable table;

    protected void Page_Init(object sender, EventArgs e)
    {
      this.table = DynamicDataRouteHandler.GetRequestMetaTable(Context);
      this.Title = table.DisplayName;
      this.dataSource.EntityTypeFilter = this.table.EntityType.Name;
      this.dataSource.Include = this.table.ForeignKeyColumnsNames;
    }

    protected void FormView_ItemCommand(object sender, FormViewCommandEventArgs e)
    {
      if (e.CommandName == DataControlCommands.CancelCommandName)
        this.Response.Redirect(this.table.ListActionPath);
    }

    protected void FormView_ItemUpdated(object sender, FormViewUpdatedEventArgs e)
    {
      if (e.Exception == null || e.ExceptionHandled)
        this.Response.Redirect(this.table.ListActionPath);
    }
  }
}
```

Initialization code in the Page_Init event handler is identical to that in the Details page template. The FormView_ItemUpdated event handler redirects the user to the List page after he clicks the Update link on the Edit page and the modified entity has been successfully saved in the database. The `FormView_ItemCommand` event handler also redirects the user to the List page, but in response to him clicking the page's Cancel link.

List Page Template

The List page template generates web pages that display a list of entities and allow searching and sorting the list by individual columns. Figure 6.4 shows an example of such a page generated for the Products table. At the top of the page, a dynamically generated set of filter controls is displayed for all properties of the entity type for which Dynamic Data has appropriate filter templates. The list of entities occupies the main part of the page. Changing any of the filter controls automatically refreshes the list of entries. The grid columns can be sorted in ascending or descending order by clicking their headers; a set of action links for editing, deleting, or displaying details of individual entity instances is displayed in the left-most column for each row. At the bottom of the grid, there are controls for navigating between pages and changing the number of rows displayed per page.

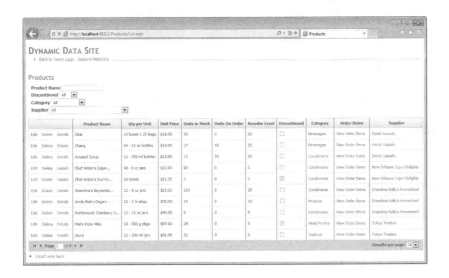

FIGURE 6.4 Web page generated by the List page template.

The Edit and Details links point to the dynamic Edit and Details pages discussed earlier. Examples of these pages can be found in Figures 6.3 and 6.2, respectively. The foreign key navigation properties, such as the Category and Supplier, are also displayed in the form of hyperlinks that, when clicked, take users to the corresponding Details pages. One-to-many navigation properties, such as the Order Items, take users to the List page of the target entity where the search criteria has been prepopulated to display only the child entities of the parent entity clicked. For example, when a user clicks View Order Items of the product with the name Chai, an Order Items list page is displayed with the Product filter control preset to Chai, as shown in Figure 6.5.

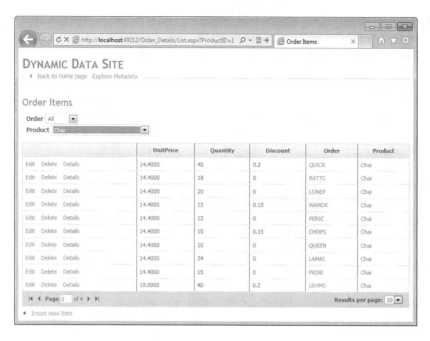

FIGURE 6.5 Prefiltered List page.

The List page template is implemented in List.aspx, located in the DynamicData\PageTemplates folder of the web application. Listing 6.5 shows the markup of the built-in template after some cleanup to improve readability and highlight important sections in bold.

The structure of the List page template is actually quite similar to the structure of the Details page template. It also includes DynamicDataManager, EntityDataSource, and QueryExtender controls. The only significant differences are the GridView control, which this template uses to display entities, and the QueryableFilterRepeater used to generate the filter controls.

LISTING 6.5 List Page Template (Markup)

```
<%@ Page Language="C#" MasterPageFile="~/Site.master" CodeBehind="List.aspx.cs"
  Inherits="WebApplication.DynamicData.PageTemplates.List" %>
<%@ Register Src="~/DynamicData/Content/GridViewPager.ascx"
  TagName="GridViewPager" TagPrefix="dd" %>
<asp:Content ContentPlaceHolderID="main" runat="Server">
  <asp:DynamicDataManager runat="server">
    <DataControls>
      <asp:DataControlReference ControlID="gridView" />
    </DataControls>
  </asp:DynamicDataManager>
```

```
<h2><%= table.DisplayName %></h2>

<asp:UpdatePanel runat="server">
  <ContentTemplate>
    <div class="DD">
      <asp:ValidationSummary runat="server" HeaderText="Validation errors" />
      <asp:DynamicValidator runat="server" ControlToValidate="gridView"
        Display="None"/>

      <asp:QueryableFilterRepeater runat="server" ID="FilterRepeater">
        <ItemTemplate>
          <asp:Label runat="server" Text='<%# Eval("DisplayName") %>'
            OnPreRender="Label_PreRender" />
          <asp:DynamicFilter runat="server" ID="DynamicFilter"
            OnFilterChanged="DynamicFilter_FilterChanged" />
          <br />
        </ItemTemplate>
      </asp:QueryableFilterRepeater>
      <br />
    </div>

    <asp:GridView ID="gridView" runat="server" DataSourceID="dataSource"
      EnablePersistedSelection="true" AllowPaging="True" AllowSorting="True">
      <Columns>
        <asp:TemplateField>
          <ItemTemplate>
            <asp:DynamicHyperLink runat="server" Action="Edit" Text="Edit" />
            <asp:LinkButton runat="server" CommandName="Delete" Text="Delete"
              OnClientClick='return
                confirm("Are you sure you want to delete this item?");'/>
            <asp:DynamicHyperLink runat="server" Text="Details" />
          </ItemTemplate>
        </asp:TemplateField>
      </Columns>
      <PagerTemplate>
        <dd:GridViewPager runat="server" />
      </PagerTemplate>
    </asp:GridView>

    <asp:EntityDataSource ID="dataSource" runat="server" EnableDelete="true" />
    <asp:QueryExtender TargetControlID="dataSource" runat="server">
      <asp:DynamicFilterExpression ControlID="FilterRepeater" />
    </asp:QueryExtender>

    <div class="DDBottomHyperLink">
      <asp:DynamicHyperLink ID="insertLink" runat="server" Action="Insert">
```

LISTING 6.5 Continued

```
          <img runat="server" src="~/DynamicData/Content/Images/plus.gif"/>
          Insert new item
        </asp:DynamicHyperLink>
      </div>
    </ContentTemplate>
  </asp:UpdatePanel>
</asp:Content>
```

The GridView control is configured to allow paging and sorting. It includes a single TemplateField to define a column that displays action links—Edit, Delete, and Details. The actual data columns are generated dynamically by a DefaultAutoFieldGenerator. During page initialization, the DynamicDataManager control sets the ColumnsGenerator property of the GridView with a new instance of the DefaultAutoFieldGenerator class. So, instead of being specified explicitly in page markup, as shown in the example below, the DynamicField instances are created dynamically, based on the metadata information describing properties of the current entity type.

```
<Columns>
  <asp:DynamicField DataField="ProductName"/>
  <asp:DynamicField DataField="UnitsInStock"/>
</Columns>
```

Paging functionality is implemented by the GridViewPager control. This is not a built-in ASP.NET control; it is a user control included in the Dynamic Data project templates of Visual Studio and created in the DynamicData\Content folder of your web application when you first create the project.

The QueryableFilterRepeater control, which was discussed in Chapter 5, is used to generate a set of DynamicFilter controls, one for each property that can be filtered using filter templates available in the DynamicData\Filters folder of the web application. Notice that this markup does not specify the DataField property of the DynamicFilter control. This is done automatically when the QueryableFilterRepeater instantiates its ItemTemplate for each filterable property in the entity type. The ID property of the DynamicFilter control has to be "DynamicFilter," which is what the QueryableFilterRepeater looks for by default.

The QueryableFilterRepeater control is associated with the QueryExtender by the DynamicFilterExpression in the page markup. In its turn, the QueryExtender control is associated with the EntityDataSource, which allows the individual filter templates to modify the LINQ query it generates at run time based on the values selected by the user.

Listing 6.6 shows the code-behind file of the List page template, again, cleaned-up to improve readability and highlight important points.

LISTING 6.6 List Page Template (Code-Behind)

```csharp
using System;
using System.Collections.Generic;
using System.Web.DynamicData;
using System.Web.Routing;
using System.Web.UI.WebControls;

namespace WebApplication.DynamicData.PageTemplates
{
  public partial class List : System.Web.UI.Page
  {
    protected MetaTable table;

    protected void Page_Init(object sender, EventArgs e)
    {
      this.table = DynamicDataRouteHandler.GetRequestMetaTable(this.Context);
      this.Title = this.table.DisplayName;
      this.dataSource.EntityTypeFilter = this.table.EntityType.Name;
      this.dataSource.Include = table.ForeignKeyColumnsNames;

      IDictionary<string, object> columnValues =
        this.table.GetColumnValuesFromRoute(this.Context);
      this.gridView.SetMetaTable(this.table, columnValues);

      this.insertLink.NavigateUrl = this.table.GetActionPath(
        PageAction.Insert, new RouteValueDictionary(columnValues));
    }

    protected void Label_PreRender(object sender, EventArgs e)
    {
      var label = (Label)sender;
      var dynamicFilter = (DynamicFilter)label.FindControl("DynamicFilter");
      var template = dynamicFilter.FilterTemplate as QueryableFilterUserControl;
      if (template != null && template.FilterControl != null)
      {
        label.AssociatedControlID =
          template.FilterControl.GetUniqueIDRelativeTo(label);
      }
    }

    protected void DynamicFilter_FilterChanged(object sender, EventArgs e)
    {
      this.gridView.PageIndex = 0;
    }
  }
}
```

The Page_Init event handler performs the familiar tasks of finding the MetaTable describing the current entity type using information in the URL route, updating the page title with the display name of the entity, and configuring the EntityDataSource. However, this code also performs an important additional step, which was not necessary in the Details and Edit page templates discussed so far.

The code in the Page_Init event handler calls the GetColumnValuesFromRoute method of the MetaTable class to obtain a dictionary of property names and values from the request URL. This is important when the user navigates to a list page by clicking a "View Children" link on any of the other dynamically generated pages, such as the View Order Items link on the Product list page in Figure 6.4. In this scenario, the primary key of the parent entity is passed to the page template in a request URL similar to the one shown here:

```
http://localhost:49212/Order_Details/List.aspx?ProductID=1
```

When the dictionary of property names and values has been obtained, the Page_Init code calls the SetMetaTable extension method defined in the DynamicDataExtensions class to associate both the MetaTable object and the dictionary of what it calls *default values* with the GridView control. The filter templates rely on this information to provide initial values in filter controls (see the DefaultValue property of the QueryableFilterUserControl class).

> **NOTE**
>
> Normally it is not necessary to call the SetMetaTable extension method if you have a DynamicDataManager control associated with a databound control, such as the GridView in this example. The DynamicDataManager calls this method automatically, but in this case, the template calls it explicitly to pass the default values to filter templates.

The rest of the code in the Page_Init event handler deals with initializing the Insert new item hyperlink at the bottom of the page. Using the same dictionary of property names and values, this code generates a link to the dynamic Insert page, with the default values in the URL. As you see shortly, the Insert page template also supports column values passed through the request URL and relies on them to prepopulate some of the field values.

The Label_PreRender method handles the PreRender event of the Label controls generated by the QueryableFilterRepeater. It associates each label with the filter control generated by its matching DynamicFilter. This makes the generated label behave like a true control label as opposed to regular selectable text content on the page. Clicking a label in the web browser automatically selects the corresponding control.

The DynamicFilter_FilterChanged method handles the FilterChanged event of the DynamicFilter controls, which fires any time the user changes the filter criteria. Although the QueryableFilterRepeater automatically notifies the EntityDataSource control and causes the query to be reloaded, this method flips the GridView to the first page to avoid confusion and errors when the new filter criteria makes the number of pages in the result set less than the current page number.

Insert Page Template

The Insert page template is the last of the built-in page templates Dynamic Data projects provide out of the box. This page template generates web pages that allow users to create new entity instances, such as the Add Product page shown in Figure 6.6. From a user interface and behavior standpoint, the Insert pages are similar to the Edit pages discussed earlier in this chapter. However, they are integrated with the List pages, and it will be easier to discuss the Insert page template now that you have reviewed implementation of its List cousin.

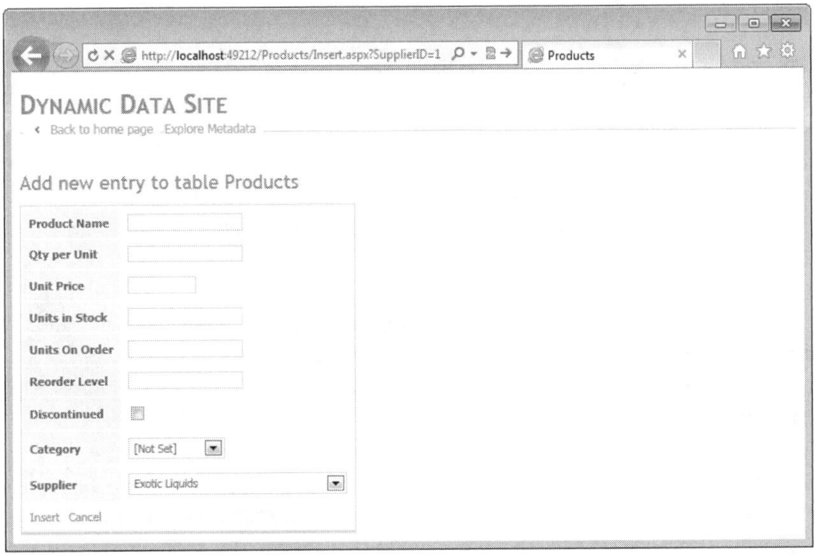

FIGURE 6.6 Web page generated by the Insert page template.

One subtle but important difference between Insert and Edit pages is the meaning of the query parameters in their URLs. For the Edit pages, the URL contains the names and values of the primary key properties of an existing entity. For the Insert pages, however, either there are no parameters, or the URL contains the default values for the foreign key properties of the new entity to be created. Notice how in Figure 6.6, the URL for the Add Product page contains a SupplierID value of 1. This is because the page in this screenshot was displayed by clicking the Insert new item link on the Products List page that displayed all products offered by a specific supplier, *Exotic Liquids*. The List page passed the SupplierID to the Insert page via the generated Insert new item link. This requires the Insert page template to have logic similar to that of the List page template for extracting parameter values from the request URL and sharing it with the field templates.

The Insert page template is implemented in the Insert.aspx located in the DynamicData\ PageTemplates folder of the web application. Listing 6.7 shows the markup of this template. Most of it is very similar to the markup of the Edit.aspx shown in Listing 6.3, except that the FormView, DynamicEntity, and EntityDataSource are used in *Insert* mode. Because the Insert page does not need to retrieve an existing entity instance from the database, it does not need a QueryExtender, only the data source control.

LISTING 6.7 Insert Page Template (Markup)

```
<%@ Page Language="C#" MasterPageFile="~/Site.master" CodeBehind="Insert.aspx.cs"
  Inherits="WebApplication.DynamicData.PageTemplates.Insert" %>

<asp:Content ContentPlaceHolderID="main" runat="Server">
  <asp:DynamicDataManager runat="server">
    <DataControls>
      <asp:DataControlReference ControlID="formView" />
    </DataControls>
  </asp:DynamicDataManager>
  <h2>Add new entry to table <%= table.DisplayName %></h2>

  <asp:UpdatePanel runat="server">
    <ContentTemplate>
      <asp:ValidationSummary runat="server" HeaderText="List of validation errors"/>
      <asp:DynamicValidator runat="server" ControlToValidate="formView"
        Display="None" />

      <asp:FormView runat="server" ID="formView" DataSourceID="dataSource"
        DefaultMode="Insert" OnItemCommand="FormView_ItemCommand"
        OnItemInserted="FormView_ItemInserted">
        <InsertItemTemplate>
          <asp:DynamicEntity runat="server" Mode="Insert" />
          <div class="DDFormActions">
            <asp:LinkButton runat="server" CommandName="Insert" Text="Insert" />
            <asp:LinkButton runat="server" CommandName="Cancel" Text="Cancel"
              CausesValidation="false" />
          </div>
        </InsertItemTemplate>
      </asp:FormView>

      <asp:EntityDataSource ID="dataSource" runat="server" EnableInsert="true" />
    </ContentTemplate>
  </asp:UpdatePanel>
</asp:Content>
```

The most important difference between the code-behinds of the Insert (see Listing 6.8) and Edit (see Listing 6.4) page templates is the additional initialization step the Insert page templates performs for the FormView control. Just like the List page template, it extracts the names and values of the entity properties from the request URL and associates them with the FormView control by calling the SetMetaTable extension method. The field templates generated by the DynamicEntity control use this information to provide default field values in their data entry controls. The FieldValue and FieldValueEditString properties of the FieldTemplateUserControl class respect the default values associated with their parent databound control, such as the FormView in this example. This is why the Supplier drop-down list generated by the ForeignKey_Edit field template in Figure 6.6 has been prepopulated with *Exotic Liquids*.

LISTING 6.8 Insert Page Template (Code-Behind)

```
using System;
using System.Web.DynamicData;
using System.Web.UI.WebControls;

namespace WebApplication.DynamicData.PageTemplates
{
  public partial class Insert : System.Web.UI.Page
  {
    protected MetaTable table;

    protected void Page_Init(object sender, EventArgs e)
    {
      this.table = DynamicDataRouteHandler.GetRequestMetaTable(Context);
      this.Title = this.table.DisplayName;
      this.dataSource.EntityTypeFilter = table.EntityType.Name;
      this.formView.SetMetaTable(this.table,
        this.table.GetColumnValuesFromRoute(Context));
    }

    protected void FormView_ItemCommand(object sender, FormViewCommandEventArgs e)
    {
      if (e.CommandName == DataControlCommands.CancelCommandName)
        Response.Redirect(this.table.ListActionPath);
    }

    protected void FormView_ItemInserted(object sender, FormViewInsertedEventArgs e)
    {
      if (e.Exception == null ¦¦ e.ExceptionHandled)
        Response.Redirect(this.table.ListActionPath);
    }
  }
}
```

The FormView_ItemCommand event handler in the Insert page template serves the same function the method with this name performs in the Edit page template—redirecting the user back to the List page when she clicks *Cancel*. The FormView_ItemInserted event handler also does that when a new entity has been successfully saved in the database.

Creating a New Page Template

Dynamic Data does not limit the set of page actions and page templates. You can easily define a new action and create a new page template to handle it. As an example, consider the action of deleting an entity instance. The default page templates support deletion directly in the List and Details pages. When you click the Delete link on one of these pages, a JavaScript prompt window is displayed, asking you to confirm the deletion. Although this approach works, it definitely has a Windows-like feel to it. A more traditional way to do this in a web application is to take the user to a separate page where she can review the entity she is about to delete and confirm the action.

Listing 6.9 shows the page template that implements the Delete page action. It is almost identical to the built-in Details page template. Just like the other page templates, this ASPX file needs to be placed in the DynamicData\PageTemplates folder of the web application project, in a file called Delete.aspx.

LISTING 6.9 Delete Page Template (Markup)

```
<%@ Page Language="C#" MasterPageFile="~/Site.master" CodeBehind="Delete.aspx.cs"
  Inherits="WebApplication.DynamicData.PageTemplates.Delete" %>

<asp:Content ContentPlaceHolderID="main" runat="server">
  <asp:DynamicDataManager runat="server">
    <DataControls>
      <asp:DataControlReference ControlID="formView" />
    </DataControls>
  </asp:DynamicDataManager>

  <h2>Are you sure you want to delete this from table <%= table.DisplayName %>?</h2>

  <asp:UpdatePanel runat="server">
    <ContentTemplate>
      <asp:ValidationSummary runat="server" HeaderText="List of validation errors"/>
      <asp:DynamicValidator runat="server" ControlToValidate="formView"
        Display="None"/>

      <asp:FormView ID="formView" runat="server" DataSourceID="dataSource"
        OnItemDeleted="FormView_ItemDeleted">
        <ItemTemplate>
          <asp:DynamicEntity runat="server" />
          <div class="DDFormActions">
            <asp:Button runat="server" CommandName="Delete" Text="Delete"/>
            <asp:DynamicHyperLink runat="server" Action="List" Text="Back to list"/>
          </div>
        </ItemTemplate>
      </asp:FormView>
```

```
            <asp:EntityDataSource ID="dataSource" runat="server" EnableDelete="true" />
            <asp:QueryExtender TargetControlID="dataSource" runat="server">
              <asp:DynamicRouteExpression />
            </asp:QueryExtender>
          </ContentTemplate>
        </asp:UpdatePanel>
</asp:Content>
```

The only substantial difference between this new Delete template and the built-in Details template is the set of button and link controls. The new Delete template uses a `Button` control instead of a `LinkButton` to make confirmation of deletion visually different from merely requesting it. It also does not have an Edit link the Details page template uses to take users to the Edit page.

Although they might seem unnecessary, the `ValidationSummary` and `DynamicValidator` controls still play an important role in the Delete page template. If the user tries to delete a Customer who placed one or more orders, a database error will occur due to a foreign key constraint violation. As discussed in Chapter 8, database errors can be presented to the Dynamic Data as instances of the `ValidationException` class. The `DynamicValidator` control at the top of the page automatically displays unhandled `ValidationException` errors in the `ValidationSummary` instead of generating a yellow screen of death.

After implementing the new Delete page template, you also need to modify the *existing* templates to redirect the user to a new dynamic page generated by the new template instead of displaying the JavaScript prompt. In both List and Details page templates, replace the following `LinkButton`:

```
<asp:LinkButton runat="server" CommandName="Delete" Text="Delete"
OnClientClick='return confirm("Are you sure you want to delete this
item?");'/>
```

with the following `DynamicHyperLink` control:

```
<asp:DynamicHyperLink runat="server" Action="Delete" Text="Delete" />
```

And because the Details page will no longer delete the records, you can remove the `EnableDelete` property from its `EntityDataSource` control in page markup and remove the `ItemDeleted` event handler from the `FormView` control in the code-behind.

Figure 6.7 shows an example of the dynamically generated Delete page for the Product entity type. The entity itself (labels and field values) looks similar to the dynamically generated Details page, which is a great example of how page templates allow you to implement different actions and data access logic while reusing the common presentation logic encapsulated by the entity templates.

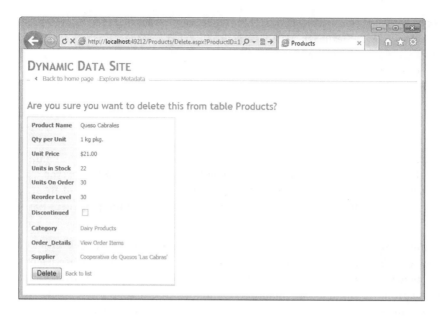

FIGURE 6.7 Dynamic Delete page.

Custom Page Templates

The page templates discussed so far are *dynamic*, meaning they can generate web pages for any entity type in your data model. Thanks to the rich metadata information provided by Dynamic Data in the form of a `MetaTable` object, a single generic page template can handle a particular type of action, such as List or Details, for any entity type. The generated web pages vary depending on the properties of the entity type, but the variations are limited to the order of fields on the form, their labels, and data entry controls. When the user interface cannot be implemented by creating a custom entity template, developers can create *custom* page templates to implement unique functionality required for a particular entity type.

Consider the Orders table in the Northwind sample database. It stores order header information, such as Order Date, Customer, Shipper, and so on. However, the order items are stored in a separate table called Order Details. In the sample data model, these tables are represented by the `Order` and `Order_Detail` classes, respectively. Intuitively, an `Order_Detail` instance is *a part of* the parent Order instance and cannot be entered independently. This is different from how the Order and Customer instances relate to each other: An Order is *associated with* a Customer and can be entered independently. Unfortunately, Dynamic Data cannot distinguish between these types of relationships automatically and has to assume that the `Order_Detail` is an independent entity type. As a result, the default experience for viewing orders is rather cumbersome because it requires users to switch between the Order details page and the Order_Detail List page shown in Figure 6.8.

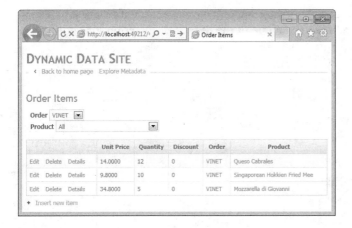

FIGURE 6.8 Default Order Details List page.

Ideally, users should be able to see an entire order on a single page, similar to that shown in Figure 6.9. In a Dynamic Data web application, this can be accomplished by creating a custom Details page template for the Order entity type.

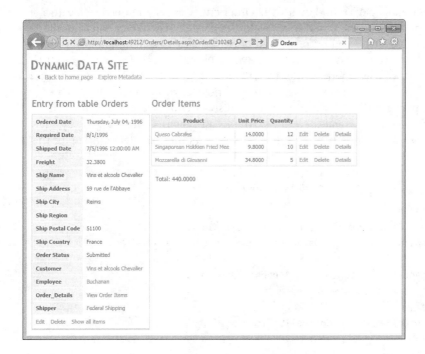

FIGURE 6.9 Custom Order Details page.

Dynamic Data looks for custom page templates under `DynamicData\CustomPages`, in a subfolder with the name that matches the name of the `MetaTable` describing its entity type. Here is how the folder structure looks:

```
DynamicData
    \CustomPages
        \{Table1}
            {Template1}.aspx
            {Template2}.aspx
            . . .
        \{Table2}
            {Template1}.aspx
            {Template2}.aspx
            . . .

        . . .

    \PageTemplates
        {Template1}.aspx
        {Template2}.aspx
        . . .
```

To create a custom Details page template for the Order entity type, you need to create a subfolder called `Orders` (note the plural form, as in the name of the table). Begin implementing the custom page by copying the default `Details.aspx` page template from the `PageTemplates` folder to the newly created `CustomPages\Orders` folder. This gives you the `FormView` control that will display the Order information along with the `EntityDataSource` and `QueryExtender` controls it needs to be able to get the data from the database. The second part of the page needs a `GridView` control to display Order Details plus its own `EntityDataSource` and `QueryExtender` controls. Finally, a `Literal` control to display the order total calculated in the code-behind. Listing 6.10 shows the complete markup of the new page.

LISTING 6.10 Custom Order Details Page Template (Markup)

```
<%@ Page Language="C#"
  MasterPageFile="~/Site.master" CodeBehind="Details.aspx.cs"
  Inherits="WebApplication.DynamicData.CustomPages.Orders.Details" %>

<asp:Content ContentPlaceHolderID="main" runat="Server">
  <asp:DynamicDataManager runat="server">
    <DataControls>
      <asp:DataControlReference ControlID="formView" />
    </DataControls>
  </asp:DynamicDataManager>

  <table>
  <tr valign="top">
    <td>
```

```asp
      <h2>Entry from table <%= ordersTable.DisplayName %></h2>
      <asp:FormView runat="server" ID="formView" DataSourceID="formDataSource">
        <ItemTemplate>
          <asp:DynamicEntity runat="server" />
          <div class="DDFormActions">
            <asp:DynamicHyperLink runat="server" Action="Edit" Text="Edit" />
            <asp:DynamicHyperLink runat="server" Action="Delete" Text="Delete" />
            <asp:DynamicHyperLink runat="server" Action="List" Text="List"/>
          </div>
        </ItemTemplate>
      </asp:FormView>

      <asp:EntityDataSource ID="formDataSource" runat="server"/>
      <asp:QueryExtender TargetControlID="formDataSource" runat="server">
        <asp:DynamicRouteExpression />
      </asp:QueryExtender>
</td>

<td>
      <h2><%= itemsTable.DisplayName %></h2>
      <asp:GridView ID="gridView" runat="server" DataSourceID="gridDataSource"
        AutogenerateColumns="false" AllowSorting="True">
        <Columns>
          <asp:DynamicField DataField="Product" />
          <asp:DynamicField DataField="UnitPrice"/>
          <asp:DynamicField DataField="Quantity"/>
          <asp:TemplateField>
            <ItemTemplate>
              <asp:DynamicHyperLink runat="server" Action="Edit" Text="Edit" />
              <asp:DynamicHyperLink runat="server" Action="Delete" Text="Delete" />
              <asp:DynamicHyperLink runat="server" Action="Details" Text="Details"/>
            </ItemTemplate>
          </asp:TemplateField>
        </Columns>
      </asp:GridView>

      <asp:EntityDataSource ID="gridDataSource" runat="server"
        ConnectionString="name=NorthwindEntities"
        DefaultContainerName="NorthwindEntities"
        EntitySetName="Order_Details" Include="Product"
        OnSelected="GridDataSource_Selected" />
      <asp:QueryExtender TargetControlID="gridDataSource" runat="server">
        <asp:DynamicRouteExpression />
      </asp:QueryExtender>
```

LISTING 6.10 Continued

```
    Total: <asp:Literal ID="totalLiteral" runat="server"/>
  </td>
 </tr>
 </table>
</asp:Content>
```

Note that unlike in the generic List page template, the GridView in this custom page does not rely on the DynamicDataManager control for initialization. The main reason is that the DynamicDataManager determines which MetaTable to associate with its target controls based on the information in the URL route. In this case, the URL route contains the table name Orders, but you need to associate the GridView control with the Order Details table and need to do this in the code-behind, as shown in Listing 6.11.

You also do not want to rely on the DynamicDataManager to initialize the GridView control because we need a specific set of columns to display the order details. You could display them all by assigning the DefaultAutoFieldGenerator to the ColumnsGenerator property of the GridView control; however, this would also include the Order column, which you can see on the default List page of the Order Details table back in Figure 6.8. Because the entire Order will be already displayed on the new page, including this column would be redundant. Although you could hide it by manipulating the entity metadata, it is important to remember that this custom page template does not have to be dynamic. This task is much easier to accomplish by specifying the required Columns explicitly in the page markup, as the DynamicField instances for the Product, UnitPrice, and Quantity properties we want to display.

Another important difference here is that initialization of the gridDataSource instance of the EntityDataSource control is performed directly in markup, with ConnectionString, DefaultContainerName, EntitySetName, and Include properties being "hard-coded" for the purposes of this custom page, where you know exactly which entity it needs to query and don't need to make the code dynamic. However, this code continues to rely on the DynamicRouteExpression in the second QueryExtender control, which conveniently limits the set of Order Details instances retrieved from the database based on the OrderID column value extracted from the page request URL.

LISTING 6.11 Custom Order Details Page Template (Code-Behind)

```
using System;
using System.Collections.Generic;
using System.Data.Objects;
using System.Linq;
using System.Web.DynamicData;
using System.Web.UI.WebControls;
using DataModel;
```

```
namespace WebApplication.DynamicData.CustomPages.Orders
{
  public partial class Details : System.Web.UI.Page
  {
    protected MetaTable ordersTable;
    protected MetaTable itemsTable;

    protected void Page_Init(object sender, EventArgs e)
    {
      this.ordersTable = DynamicDataRouteHandler.GetRequestMetaTable(this.Context);
      this.Title = this.ordersTable.DisplayName;
      this.formDataSource.Include = this.ordersTable.ForeignKeyColumnsNames;

      this.itemsTable = Global.DefaultModel.GetTable(typeof(Order_Detail));
      this.gridView.SetMetaTable(this.itemsTable);
    }

    protected void GridDataSource_Selected(object sender,
      EntityDataSourceSelectedEventArgs e)
    {
      IEnumerable<Order_Detail> orderItems = e.Results.Cast<Order_Detail>();
      decimal totalAmount = orderItems.Sum(item => item.UnitPrice * item.Quantity);
      this.totalLiteral.Text = totalAmount.ToString();
    }
  }
}
```

The Page_Init event handler performs the remaining initialization steps, similar to how this is done in the dynamic page templates. The first part of this method still relies on the GetRequestMetaTable method of the DynamicDataRouteHandler class to retrieve the *Orders* MetaTable using information in the URL route. This was simply carried over from the dynamic Details page template. On the other hand, the *Order Details* MetaTable has to be obtained directly from the default MetaModel object registered in the Global.asax. This MetaTable object (itemsTable) is then associated with the GridView control to provide the DynamicField instances access to the metadata information they need to instantiate appropriate field templates.

The GridDataSource_Selected method handles the Selected event of the EntityDataSource control that retrieves instances from the Order Details table. It calculates the total order amount as a sum of UnitPrice values multiplied by the Quantity of the individual order items. The result is then displayed in the Literal control on the page.

URL Routing

Dynamic Data web applications rely on the general-purpose URL routing capabilities built into ASP.NET. Routes are typically configured at the application start time, in the `Application_Start` event handler located in the `Global.asax` file.

```
RouteTable.Routes.Add(new DynamicDataRoute("{table}/{action}.aspx"));
```

As discussed in the beginning of this chapter, {table} and {action} are placeholders for the two route parameters that have special meaning in ASP.NET Dynamic Data. The first parameter supplies the name of the table whose data needs to be displayed by a dynamic page, and the second determines what kind of page needs to be displayed, or perhaps more precisely, *how* the table data needs to be presented to the user. Dynamic Data expects the table parameter to match the name of one of the `MetaTable` objects that describe entity types registered in the global `MetaModel`, whereas the action parameter provides the information necessary to find the appropriate page template to handle the request. The route definition just shown allows Dynamic Data to determine that the following page request URL applies to the table called Products and the page template called List:

```
http://localhost/Products/List.aspx
```

Action Route Parameter

Routes do not have to include the action parameter as a part of the URL itself. Instead, it can be specified by explicitly setting the `Action` property of the `DynamicDataRoute` class as shown here:

```
RouteTable.Routes.Add(new DynamicDataRoute("{table}")
{
    Action = PageAction.List
});
```

Given this route definition, the URL for displaying a list of products will not include the name of the page template at all and look like this instead:

```
http://localhost/Products
```

Table Route Parameter

Similarly, the table parameter does not have to come from the URL either; it can be specified using the `Table` property of the `DynamicDataRoute` class. Notice how in the following example, the route definition does not include any parameters and simply hard-codes the URL to `"Product"` (singular), which does not match the plural name of the table.

```
RouteTable.Routes.Add(new DynamicDataRoute("Product")
{
  Action = PageAction.Details,
  Table = "Products"
});
```

Based on this route definition, the Dynamic Data web application can use the following URL:

```
http://localhost/Product?ProductID=1
```

instead of the more verbose and less user-friendly:

```
http://localhost/Products/Details.aspx?ProductID=1
```

URL Parameters Versus Query Parameters

URL parameters are an alternative to the Query parameters used by traditional ASP.NET WebForms applications. Whereas the traditional query parameters require both names and values to be present in the query string, the URL parameters allow web applications to determine parameter names automatically, based on the position of their values in the URL. Consider the following route, which replaces the ProductID query parameter with a positional URL parameter:

```
RouteTable.Routes.Add(new DynamicDataRoute("Product/{ProductID}")
{
  Action = PageAction.Details,
  Table = "Products"
});
```

This route definition allows the web application to implement the product catalog without query parameters and support URLs similar to that shown below. This not only makes the URLs shorter and easier for users to read, but also makes it easier for the search engines to index dynamic pages, which is very important for public-facing web sites:

```
http://localhost:49212/Product/3
```

Dynamic Data still supports traditional Query parameters, which you can activate by registering a route that does not include any URL parameters and does not specify parameter values explicitly:

```
RouteTable.Routes.Add(new DynamicDataRoute("Dynamic"));
```

The route registered just shown makes Dynamic Data use URLs that look like this instead:

```
http://localhost/Dynamic?Table=Products&Action=List
```

Dynamic Hyperlinks

Routes have a dual purpose. In addition to helping the ASP.NET runtime determine which ASPX page will be used to handle a particular incoming request, they also determine how hyperlinks pointing to the dynamic pages will be generated. There are several different methods for generating hyperlinks in ASP.NET web applications. One of them involves the DynamicHyperLink control supplied by Dynamic Data. This control inherits from the ASP.NET HyperLink control and allows you to generate hyperlinks to dynamic pages. In the following example, the name of the table and the required action are explicitly specified.

```
<asp:DynamicHyperLink runat="server"
  ContextTypeName="DataModel.NorthwindEntities"
  TableName="Products" Action="List" Text="Show all" />
```

The TableName property specifies the name of the MetaTable describing the target entity, and the ContextTypeName specifies the name of the context class where the target entity is defined. Depending on how the routing is configured, this control generates different URLs without you having to modify any of its markup. Table 6.1 shows examples of the different route definitions and URLs this control would generate based on them.

TABLE 6.1   Examples of URLs Generated by DynamicHyperLink

Route Definition	URL Example
new DynamicDataRoute("{table}/{action}.aspx")	http://localhost/Products/List.aspx
new DynamicDataRoute("{table}/{action}")	http://localhost/Products/List
new DynamicDataRoute("{table}") { Action = PageAction.List });	http://localhost/Products

The DynamicHyperLink control can also be databound to an entity instance, in which case it can automatically determine the ContextTypeName and the TableName and will generate URLs that include names and values of its primary key columns in the query portion of the address. The Details page template discussed earlier takes advantage of this functionality by including the DynamicHyperLink controls as part of the ItemTemplate in the FormView control as shown in the following extract:

```
<asp:FormView runat="server" ID="formView" DataSourceID="dataSource">
  <ItemTemplate>
    <asp:DynamicEntity runat="server" />
    <div class="DDFormActions">
      <asp:DynamicHyperLink runat="server" Action="Edit" Text="Edit" />
      <asp:DynamicHyperLink runat="server" Action="Delete" Text="Delete" />
      <asp:DynamicHyperLink runat="server" Action="List" Text="Show all"/>
```

```
        </div>
      </ItemTemplate>
    </asp:FormView>
```

Notice how the `DynamicHyperLink` controls in this example do not have the `ContextTypeName` and `TableName` properties specified. The `FormView` control databinds its `ItemTemplate` to the entity instance provided by the associated `EntityDataSource` control. The controls locate the `MetaTable` object based on the entity type and generate URLs that look like this:

```
http://localhost/Products/Edit.aspx?ProductID=1
http://localhost/Products/Delete.aspx?ProductID=1
http://localhost/Products/List.aspx?ProductID=1
```

Dynamic hyperlinks can be also generated with the help of the `RouteUrl` markup expression. This is a special syntax that ASP.NET parser recognizes and uses to generate a dynamic URL based on parameter values you specify:

```
<asp:HyperLink runat="server" Text="Show all"
  NavigateUrl="<%$RouteUrl:table=Products, action=List%>" />
```

Under the hood, both the `RouteUrl` markup expression and the `DynamicHyperLink` control rely on the low-level API the ASP.NET provides for routing. The next code sample illustrates how they work by creating a dynamic hyperlink programmatically. It creates a `RouteValueDictionary` to hold the `Table` and `Action` parameter values and then calls the `GetVirtualPath` method of the global `Routes` collection to generate the URL in a form of a virtual path:

```
HyperLink hyperLink = // ...

RequestContext context =
  DynamicDataRouteHandler.GetRequestContext(HttpContext.Current);

RouteValueDictionary routeValues = new RouteValueDictionary();
routeValues["table"] = "Products";
routeValues["action"] = "List";

VirtualPathData pathData = RouteTable.Routes.GetVirtualPath(
  context, routeValues);

hyperLink.NavigateUrl = pathData.VirtualPath;
```

Route Evaluation and Constraints

Although you will probably never need to write code that creates dynamic hyperlinks programmatically, it is important to understand how they are generated by the ASP.NET runtime. In particular, notice the Routes *collection* is used to generate a dynamic URL and not a single particular route object. This is significant because the Routes collection evaluates routes one by one, in the order they were registered, looking for the route matching the supplied set of parameter values. As soon as the match is found, the further evaluation is stopped, and the matching route is used to generate the URL.

A similar evaluation process occurs when the ASP.NET runtime needs to find a page template to handle an incoming web request. It starts with the route that was registered first and goes down the list until it finds the first match. All other routes that were registered after the first match are ignored.

Keeping in mind how the route evaluation process works, register the most specific routes first, leaving the more generic routes until the end. For example, if you had registered the following two routes in this order, your web application would always ignore the second route when generating dynamic hyperlinks:

```
RouteTable.Routes.Add(new DynamicDataRoute("{table}/{action}.aspx"));
RouteTable.Routes.Add(new DynamicDataRoute("{table}")
{
    Action = PageAction.List
});
```

In other words, a Product list hyperlink would always be presented to users as http://localhost/Products/List.aspx and never as http://localhost/Products. However, when handling incoming requests, the second URL would not match the first route, "fall through," and still get picked up by the second route.

Changing the order of route registrations gives you a fair amount of control over the URL resolution process. However, when it is insufficient, you can use route constraints to make it more specific. Route constraints are defined in the Constraints dictionary of a route object as pairs of two string values, where first is a parameter name, and second is a regular expression pattern that the parameter value must match. The following example defines a route where the table parameter value can be either Products or Orders:

```
RouteTable.Routes.Add(new DynamicDataRoute("{table}")
{
    Action = PageAction.List,
    Constraints = new RouteValueDictionary(){{"table","Products|Orders"}}
});
RouteTable.Routes.Add(new DynamicDataRoute("{table}/{action}.aspx"));
```

Based on the route definitions in this last example, only the Products and Orders tables will have the List URLs generated as http://localhost/Products or http://localhost/Orders. All other tables will use the second route and have URLs similar to http://localhost/Suppliers/List.aspx.

ViewName Route Parameter

In the examples of URL routing discussed so far, the action parameter has always matched the name of the page template configured to handle it, such as the Details.aspx page template, which handled the Details page action, and the List.aspx page template, which handled the List action. Having a page template implement a single action makes it focused and easy to maintain. Compared to a traditional ASP.NET WebForms approach (where a single page often tries to support all three item-level actions—Insert, Edit, and Details), single-action page templates are usually simpler. However, you are not limited to having one-to-one relationships between actions and page templates.

If this makes sense in your application, you can have a single page template handle multiple actions. Visual Studio project templates for Dynamic Data web applications include an example of such a page template called ListDetails.aspx. This template combines a GridView control similar to the one in the List page template and a FormView control that displays details of the row currently selected in the grid. This page template can be registered to handle both List and Details actions as shown in this example:

```
RouteTable.Routes.Add(new DynamicDataRoute("{table}")
{
  Action = PageAction.List,
  ViewName = "ListDetails"
});

RouteTable.Routes.Add(new DynamicDataRoute("{table}")
{
  Action = PageAction.Details,
  ViewName = "ListDetails"
});
```

It is actually the ViewName property of the DynamicDataRoute class that determines the name of the page template that will be used to handle the request. If the ViewName was not provided by the route definition, Dynamic Data will assume it to be the same as the Action parameter. Separation of Action from ViewName allows Dynamic Data web applications to change implementation of page templates without breaking the navigation in existing ASPX pages.

Page Template Lookup Rules

Figure 6.10 summarizes the algorithm Dynamic Data uses to find an appropriate page template and handle an incoming web request. Most of the power and flexibility in this process comes from the ASP.NET routing.

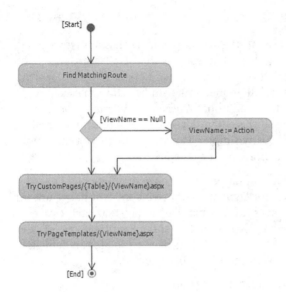

FIGURE 6.10 Page template lookup algorithm.

A Dynamic Data web application first uses the registered URL routes to determine the Table and the Action names. When the matching route is found, unless it provides an explicit ViewName, the Action name is used instead to identify the name of the page template.

Having determined both Table and ViewName from the matching route, Dynamic Data first tries to find a matching *custom* page template in a subfolder with the name of the table inside of the DynamicData\CustomPages. If a custom template exists, it is immediately used to handle the incoming web request.

If a matching custom page template does not exist, Dynamic Data then tries to find a dynamic page template in the DynamicData\PageTemplates folder of the web application. If neither custom nor dynamic page template with the matching ViewName can be found, an HTTP error 404 (Resource cannot be found) is returned back to the user.

Summary

Page templates are responsible for generating web pages that perform CRUD and other generic actions. A single set of page templates can be reused to implement operations for multiple entity types. Out of the box, Dynamic Data web application projects come with page templates for inserting, editing, displaying, and searching for entities of any type. New dynamic page templates can be created to support additional action types, such as deleting an entity.

A page template implements most of the data access and some of the presentation logic required by a dynamic page. Dynamic Data relies on the information provided by ASP.NET routing to determine which page template to use and for which entity type it needs to generate a web page. Dynamic page templates typically rely on special controls, such as `DynamicEntity` and `DynamicFilter` to generate user interface based on metadata information describing the entity type. When dynamically generated user interface is not sufficient, custom page templates can be used to create a unique user interface required for a particular entity type. Page templates do not replace the regular, custom ASP.NET web pages that still need to be used for screens such as home page, login, dashboards, and so on.

Compared to the traditional multi-purpose WebForms pages, which tend to be verbose and have a large number of simple controls, Dynamic Data page templates are typically much smaller and rely on a number of advanced controls, such as `DynamicEntity`, `DynamicFilter`, and `QueryExtender`. By their nature, dynamic controls are much more abstract than the traditional `TextBox` and `DropDownList` and therefore can be harder to understand for developers who are new to Dynamic Data.

Dynamic page templates work well for applications that need to display a large number of similar-looking pages, which tends to be the case for internal enterprise applications. *Custom* page templates, on the other hand, are better suited when unique functionality is required for a particular entity type, such as when implementing a public-facing web site.

CHAPTER 7

Metadata API

All components of Dynamic Data applications, including field templates, entity templates, filter templates, URL routes, and page templates, rely on the Metadata API to implement functionality appropriate for each particular element and combine them in complete websites. This chapter discusses the fundamental parts of the Metadata API you need to understand in order to work with Dynamic Data effectively.

Metadata Classes at a Glance

The Metadata API in Dynamic Data consists of three major classes shown in Figure 7.1: MetaModel, MetaTable, and MetaColumn. The MetaModel class defines the data model as a collection of tables. A single instance of the MetaModel represents an entire data model class, such as the NorthwindEntities. Each MetaTable instance describes a complete entity class like Product and contains one or more MetaColumn instances that describe their properties, like ProductID, ProductName, UnitsInStock, and UnitPrice.

FIGURE 7.1 Metadata API at a glance.

At the highest level, the Metadata API represents a *meta model*—metadata information specific to Dynamic Data. This information is most relevant to Dynamic Data web applications and is exposed using APIs (classes, properties, and methods) designed specifically for this purpose. However, presenting *all* information required by Dynamic Data applications in special APIs would mean recreating `System.Reflection` and `System.ComponentModel` APIs, which are well designed and well known, even if not very easy to use. Instead, Dynamic Data tries to strike a balance between creating an API relevant to dynamic web applications and reusing the existing .NET framework APIs.

The next level down includes the metadata information provided by the *data model*. The data access frameworks, such as LINQ to SQL and Entity Framework, provide metadata information you could use to discover entity classes and access their data. Dynamic Data wraps these APIs in a framework-agnostic *provider model* defined in the `System.Web.DynamicData.Providers` namespace. The provider model is also available through the Metadata API. However, this is an advanced topic that requires special attention. You can find a detailed discussion of this subject in Chapter 13, "Building Dynamic List Pages."

At the lowest level of abstraction is metadata information provided by the .NET runtime. The `Type` class in the `System` namespace provides information about classes, properties, methods, and attributes; it is an incredibly powerful but low-level tool. The `TypeDescriptor` class in the `System.ComponentModel` namespace works at a slightly higher level and has built-in understanding of data annotations. However, using these APIs directly in a

Dynamic Data application would require a lot of tedious coding, cause errors, and significantly reduce developer productivity.

The sheer size of the Metadata API (look at the number of properties in the MetaTable and MetaColumn classes) can be overwhelming at first. Sections in this chapter call out when a particular component of the Metadata API fits into one of the broad categories just discussed. Of course, trying to shoehorn a complex API into a simple classification does not work in all cases, but hopefully it will help you understand it as you are reading this chapter.

Metadata Explorer

The sample solution accompanying this book includes a simple metadata explorer that allows you to examine the metadata using web browser. Its source code is located in the MetaDataExplorer folder of the Dynamic Data web application and includes interactive pages representing the MetaModel, MetaTable, and MetaColumn classes. You can access the metadata explorer from any dynamically generated page, such as the Products/List.aspx, by clicking the Explore Metadata link at the top of the page.

Due to the nature of the subject, discussion of the metadata API can get very abstract. You might find it helpful to have the metadata explorer running on your computer as you are reading this chapter to help you visualize the objects and their relationships. This tool is also helpful when you need to change the data model using Entity Designer or by applying data annotation attributes and see the effect these changes have on the metadata provided by Dynamic Data. Figure 7.2 shows a page describing a MetaTable object for the Product entity generated by the metadata explorer.

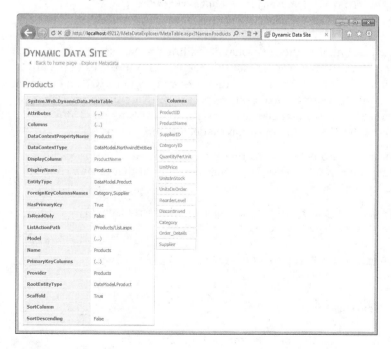

FIGURE 7.2 Metadata explorer.

The MetaModel Class

The MetaModel class serves as a root access point for Dynamic Data components to find information about the tables. In particular, the dynamic URL routing functionality relies on the MetaModel to determine if the incoming request is valid and route it to the appropriate page template. Although multiple instances are supported, a typical Dynamic Data application contains a single MetaModel, created and initialized in the Global.asax as shown in the following example:

```
public class Global : HttpApplication
{
  public static readonly MetaModel DefaultModel = new MetaModel();
  void Application_Start(object sender, EventArgs e)
  {
    DefaultModel.RegisterContext(typeof(NorthwindEntities));
  }
}
```

Data Model Registration

The MetaModel instance is initially empty and requires a call to one of the RegisterContext methods to populate it with MetaTable objects:

```
public void RegisterContext(Type contextType);
public void RegisterContext(Func<object> contextFactory);
public void RegisterContext(DataModelProvider dataModelProvider);
```

In the simplest case, you can initialize the MetaModel by calling the RegisterContext method that takes a type object such as typeof(NorthwindEntities) in the example just shown. MetaModel has built-in support for Entity Framework and LINQ to SQL and expects a type derived from ObjectContext or DataContext, respectively. Using this type, Dynamic Data creates a new instance of the context class whenever a context is required at run time. Any context class registered this way must have a default constructor.

If your context class doesn't have a default constructor or if you need to perform additional initialization steps, you can use the RegisterContext method that takes a context factory *delegate* as a parameter:

```
public static readonly MetaModel DefaultModel = new MetaModel();
void Application_Start(object sender, EventArgs e)
{
  DefaultModel.RegisterContext(this.CreateContext);
}

private object CreateContext()
{
  NorthwindEntities context = new NorthwindEntities();
```

```
    context.ContextOptions.LazyLoadingEnabled = true;
    return context;
}
```

Notice that this example is a bit contrived because you would normally want to rely on the Entity Framework designer, which allows you to choose the default lazy loading option and generate this initialization code as part of the `NorthwindEntities` constructor. However, it doesn't hurt to explicitly do this in a Dynamic Data application, which benefits from lazy loading if you share the data model with other developers, who prefer to have it turned off by default.

When your application uses a LINQ-enabled data access framework other than Entity Framework or LINQ to SQL, you need to use the `RegisterContext` method that takes a `DataModelProvider` instance instead of the context class. A `DataModelProvider` is an object that can extract metadata from a data model and present it to the Dynamic Data metadata API in a format it can consume. Internally, Dynamic Data implements a separate `DataModelProvider` for each Entity Framework and LINQ to SQL and gives you the ability to create your own provider to support third-party frameworks, such as SubSonic, LightSpeed, and LinqConnect.

In addition to the three overloads of the `RegisterContext` method discussed here, `MetaModel` class also includes a second set of similar methods with two parameters each, where the second parameter is a `ContextConfiguration` object. You will most commonly use these methods during the initial development stages of your application to make all tables in your model visible by default:

```
public static readonly MetaModel DefaultModel = new MetaModel();
void Application_Start(object sender, EventArgs e)
{
    var configuration = new ContextConfiguration();
    configuration.ScaffoldAllTables = true;
    DefaultModel.RegisterContext(typeof(NorthwindEntities), configuration);
}
```

It is probably not a good idea to leave this code in a production application, where you normally want to limit user interface to only those tables you actually want your users to access to prevent confusion and accidental data corruption.

Accessing MetaTable Objects

When the `RegisterContext` method is called, the `MetaModel` uses a data model provider to obtain information about tables the data model supports and creates `MetaTable` objects to represent them. When the registration is complete, you can access the tables using a number of different properties and methods:

```
public ReadOnlyCollection<MetaTable> Tables { get; }
public List<MetaTable> VisibleTables { get; }
```

If you need to access the list of all tables, you can use the `Tables` property. It is a read-only collection of `MetaTable` instances, which you can iterate through using a `foreach` loop or interrogate using LINQ to Objects. If you are interested only in tables that will be visible to the current user, you can use the `VisibleTables` property.

Keep in mind that iterating through the list of tables at runtime can be costly, so if you need a particular table, use one of the methods the `MetaModel` class provides for that purpose instead:

```
public MetaTable GetTable(string uniqueTableName);
public MetaTable GetTable(Type entityType);
```

The `GetTable` method that takes a string that contains a table name is the most efficient way to retrieve a specific table from the `MetaModel`. This method retrieves the `MetaTable` from the dictionary of table names and objects that `MetaModel` maintains internally. You typically use one of these methods when building custom pages that don't rely on dynamic data URL routing:

```
MetaTable table = Global.DefaultModel.GetTable("Products");
MetaTable table = Global.DefaultModel.GetTable(typeof(Product));
```

Although using the `GetTable` overload that takes an entity `Type` is more elegant (because it allows you to avoid using hard-coded literals or string constants to specify the table name), it is actually less efficient as it iterates through the entire list of tables to find the one with a matching type. Although the performance impact of a single table lookup might not be noticeable, keep in mind that it quickly increases as your data model becomes more complex and as the number of users accessing your application increases.

The GetTable methods throws an ArgumentException if you specify a name or type of a table that does not belong to the current MetaModel. In the unlikely scenario your code expects to find non-existent tables, you can use the TryGetTable methods instead:

```
public bool TryGetTable(string uniqueTableName, out MetaTable table);
public bool TryGetTable(Type entityType, out MetaTable table);
```

The TryGetTable methods return a Boolean value that indicates whether or not the table was found. The MetaTable itself is returned via the second output parameter. It will be null if the method returns false. This follows a common .NET pattern and mimics the TryGetValue method of the generic Dictionary class:

```
MetaTable table;
if (Global.DefaultModel.TryGetTable("Products", out table))
{
    // use the table here …
}
```

Global Model Registration

By default, when a new MetaModel instance is created, it is registered globally, making it available through the Default property of the MetaModel class as well as its GetModel method. Both of them are static, thus making the model available to any page or control in your web application:

```
public static MetaModel Default { get; }
public static MetaModel GetModel(Type contextType);
```

The Default property gives you an application-independent way to access the default model, which you would normally get to via the DefaultModel property of the Global class defined in Global.asax.cs. In other words, in a typical application, the following lines of code produce the same result:

```
MetaModel model = Global.DefaultModel;
MetaModel model = MetaModel.Default;
```

When multiple data contexts have been registered with Dynamic Data, you can also use the static GetModel method of the MetaModel class to retrieve a globally registered MetaModel using its context type:

```
MetaModel model = MetaModel.GetModel(typeof(NorthwindEntities));
```

When using Dynamic Data in a large web application that interacts with multiple databases and has multiple models, you might want to avoid global registration to reduce chances of having different parts of the application affecting each other. For this purpose, MetaModel class provides an overloaded constructor that takes a Boolean value as a parameter. Passing false to this constructor prevents the model from being globally registered:

```
public MetaModel(bool registerGlobally);
```

Scaffolding Support

Several properties of the MetaModel class are not related to metadata, but instead provide support for dynamic scaffolding of the different template types used by Dynamic Data applications:

```
public IFieldTemplateFactory FieldTemplateFactory { get; set; }
public EntityTemplateFactory EntityTemplateFactory { get; set; }
public FilterFactory FilterFactory { get; set; }
```

The FieldTemplateFactory property gets or sets an object responsible for creating field templates. The EntityTemplateFactory is responsible for creating entity templates, and the FilterFactory is responsible for filter templates. All three of these properties are writeable, allowing you to replace the built-in factories when stock functionality is insufficient.

One particular example of when such a replacement would be beneficial is the limitation of the built-in filter factory, which supports only Boolean, ForeignKey, and Enumeration filters. However, this topic deserves a lot of attention and will be revisited in Chapter 13.

```
public string DynamicDataFolderVirtualPath { get; set; }
```

The DynamicDataFolderVirtualPath property determines where the template factories look for templates. By default, this property is set to "~/DynamicData" but can be changed to a different location if needed.

The MetaTable Class

The main purpose of the MetaTable class is to help page templates generate user interface for different entities in the data model. A single MetaTable instance describes an entire entity class, including its type, properties, attributes, presentation, data access logic, and security permissions.

Entity Definition

Each table in the model is identified by a name, which you can access using the Name property of the MetaTable class:

```
public string Name { get; }
```

Table name usually matches the name of the object context property you would normally use to query the data. In the NorthwindEntities context class, you use the Products property to retrieve instances of the Product entity class from the Products database table. The MetaTable instance describing the Product entity would have the name Products, the same as the name of the NorthwindEntities property.

You can access the list of table columns using the `Columns` property of the `MetaTable` class:

```
public ReadOnlyCollection<MetaColumn> Columns { get; }
public MetaColumn GetColumn(string columnName);
public bool TryGetColumn(string columnName, out MetaColumn column);
```

The `Columns` property returns a collection of read-only `MetaColumn` objects, which are discussed in detail later in this chapter. When you need to get a particular table column, the most effective way to do it at run time is by calling the `GetColumn` or the `TryGetColumn` methods, which take advantage of the internal dictionary of columns that the `MetaTable` class maintains. This is much faster than a typical `foreach` loop, which is always a good thing in a web application where CPU is a precious resource. As you would expect, the `GetColumn` method throws an exception if a column with the specified name cannot be found, and the `TryGetColumn` method returns `false` and does not throw an exception:

```
public TableProvider Provider { get; }
```

The individual column objects are created by the `MetaTable` using definitions returned by a *table provider*, which extracts information from the underlying data access framework. Although normally you should be able to get everything you need directly through the `MetaTable` and `MetaColumn` objects, you have the option of accessing the original provider, which was used to create and configure the table using the `Provider` property of the `MetaTable` class:

```
public Type EntityType { get; }
```

The `EntityType` property of the `MetaTable` class returns a `Type` object that describes the entity class, such as Product. The `Type` class provides access to the .NET runtime metadata describing the entity class, including its properties, methods, events, and so on. Compared to the `MetaTable` class itself, the information available through the `Type` class is very low-level, and you will rarely need to use it in Dynamic Data applications:

```
public Type RootEntityType { get; }
```

The `RootEntityType` property, on the other hand, returns a `Type` object that describes the *root* base class of the entity. There is no example of this in the NorthwindEntities data model here, and diving into this topic would exceed the scope of this book, but you can imagine a CRM system that derives entity classes Prospect and Customer from a common base class called Contact. In this scenario, the `MetaTable` describing the Customer entity would return `typeof(Customer)` as the `EntityType` and `typeof(Contact)` as the `RootEntityType`.

NOTE

When working with derived entity classes, remember that context class generated by the data model does not have a separate property for querying Customers and another one for querying Prospects. This changes how Dynamic Data determines the names for the `MetaTable` instances describing these entities. For a base class like Contact, the `MetaTable` name wil be Contacts, plural. However, for a derived class like Prospect, the `MetaTable` name will be Prospect, singular.

Data Annotations

Entity classes used by Entity Framework and LINQ to SQL can be decorated with a number of different .NET attributes. Some of these attributes have special meaning for Dynamic Data and are represented as distinct properties in the `MetaTable` class:

```
public virtual bool Scaffold { get; }
```

The `Scaffold` property of the `MetaTable` class determines whether the table will be visible (or scaffolded) in the pages generated by Dynamic Data. This includes not only the default main page that simply displays a list of all tables, but also the pages that might include hyperlinks to particular tables. For example, if the Suppliers table is not scaffolded, you will not be able to navigate to it from the Product details page:

```
using System.ComponentModel.DataAnnotations;

[ScaffoldTable(false)]
partial class Supplier {   }
```

By default, the `Scaffold` property value is determined by the value of the `ScaffoldAllTables` property of the `ContextConfiuration` object used to register the context. However, it can be also modified by applying the `ScaffoldTableAttribute` to a specific entity class as just shown:

```
public virtual bool IsReadOnly { get; }
```

The `IsReadOnly` property of the `MetaTable` class determines whether users are allowed to modify it. The page templates created by Dynamic Data projects in Visual Studio use this property to hide links that would normally allow users to insert, modify, and delete the table rows:

```
using System.ComponentModel;

[ReadOnly(true)]
partial class Supplier {   }
```

By default, the `IsReadOnly` property returns `true` for tables that don't have a primary key, which could be the case if the MetaTable represents an entity class that was created for a database view, for which the Entity Framework and LINQ to SQL cannot automatically determine the primary key columns. You can also apply the `ReadOnlyAttribute` to the entity class as just shown to explicitly specify this value based on your needs:

```
public virtual string DisplayName { get; }
```

The `DisplayName` property of the `MetaTable` class determines the text Dynamic Data page templates display when a human-readable name of the table is required on a dynamically generated web page. By default, the `DisplayName` property returns the same value as the `Name` property. If, however, the table name is not user-friendly, such as the Order_Details table in the Northwind database, it can be changed by applying the DisplayNameAttribute to the entity class as shown here:

```
using System.ComponentModel;

[DisplayName("Order Items")]
partial class Order_Detail { }
```

Last, the MetaTable class has a set of three properties that determine how the actual data retrieved from the database table needs to be displayed by the user interface elements generated by Dynamic Data:

```
public virtual MetaColumn DisplayColumn { get; }
public virtual MetaColumn SortColumn { get;
public virtual bool SortDescending { get; }
```

The DisplayColumn property returns a MetaColumn object that represents the property whose value would allow a user to identify a particular entity instance or table row. For the Supplier entity class in the Northwind database scenario, this would normally be the CompanyName property; for the Product entity class, it would be the ProductName. The read-only ForeignKey field template uses the DisplayColumn to provide text for a hyperlink it generates, so that contact name of a Supplier is displayed on the Product details page.

The SortColumn property returns a MetaColumn that should be used to sort the items retrieved from the database by default, and the SortDescending property indicates whether the rows should be sorted in ascending or descending order of the SortColumn values. The ForeignKey_Edit field template uses these properties to sort the items in the drop-down list it generates, making the Suppliers appear in the order of their CompanyName:

```
using System.ComponentModel.DataAnnotations;

[DisplayColumn("CompanyName", "CompanyName", false)]
partial class Supplier { }
```

By default, MetaTable uses a heuristic algorithm to guess the right display column. All three of these properties, DisplayColumn, SortColumn, and SortDescending, can also be specified explicitly by applying the DisplayColumnAttribute to the entity class as just shown. Its constructor takes the name of the display column, the name of the sort column, and a Boolean value that indicates whether default sorting should be performed in descending order.

> **NOTE**
>
> A single display column is often insufficient to provide a meaningful text that identifies rows of a non-trivial entity. Consider a Customer entity where instead of the combined ContactName as we have in the Northwind sample database, you have separate properties called FirstName, LastName, and MiddleName. You would probably want to use a combination of two or three of these properties as a display value.
>
> A straightforward solution to this problem would be to define a custom property called FullName, as just shown and specify it as the display column for the entity class by applying the DisplayColumnAttribute:
>
> ```
> [DisplayColumn("FullName")]
> partial class Customer
> {
>   public string FullName
>   {
>     get { return LastName + ", " + FirstName + " " + MiddleName; }
>   }
> }
> ```
>
> Unfortunately, this approach does not work out of the box due to a limitation of the Entity Framework data model provider in Dynamic Data. As a workaround, you can override the ToString method in your entity class to return the required display string.
>
> ```
> partial class Customer
> {
>   public override ToString()
>   {
>     return LastName + ", " + FirstName + " " + MiddleName;
>   }
> }
> ```
>
> When it comes to populating drop-down lists and generating links to pages, the value returned by the ToString method takes precedence over the column specified in the DisplayColumnAttribute and returned by the DisplayColumn property of the MetaTable class.
>
> Chapter 13, "Building Dynamic List Pages," discusses the Dynamic Data provider model in detail and offers a better solution for this problem.

```
public AttributeCollection Attributes { get; }
```

All attributes of the entity can be also accessed through the Attributes property of the MetaTable class. This includes the built-in attributes from the System.ComponentModel and System.ComponentModel.DataAnnotations namespaces discussed in this book as well as any custom attributes you might have created in your application.

Data Access Support

In addition to the metadata information, the MetaTable class also plays an important role in implementing data access logic in Dynamic Data web applications:

```
public Type DataContextType { get; }
public string DataContextPropertyName { get; }
```

The DataContextType property of the MetaTable class returns a Type object that represents the data context class generated by the data model. This class is typically derived from the ObjectContext base class in Entity Framework and the DataContext class in LINQ to SQL. The DataContextPropertyName property returns the name of the property you would use to query the table rows, such as the Products property in the NorthwindEntities object context. At run time, this information is used by the DynamicDataManager control in page templates to configure the EntityDataSource and LinqDataSource controls responsible for retrieving entity data and saving changes to the database.

> **NOTE**
>
> It is significant that DataContextType is a property of the MetaTable class and not the MetaModel. A single MetaModel instance can have tables from different data contexts registered by separate calls to the RegisterContext method. If different contexts have the tables with the same name, your code needs to distinguish them by passing the context type to the GetTable method of the MetaModel class, along with the table name.

As you might recall from our discussion of the RegisterContext method of the MetaModel class, if the object context requires additional initialization tasks, you can provide a factory method when registering it, instead of simply giving it the type:

```
public virtual object CreateContext();
```

The CreateContext method of the MetaTable class is responsible for creating the context object, either by creating an instance of the registered type or by calling the context factory method, if that's how the context was registered with the MetaModel:

```
public IQueryable GetQuery();
public virtual IQueryable GetQuery(object context);
```

The MetaTable class also provides two overloaded GetQuery methods that can be used to query any table dynamically. This is how the ForeignKey_Edit field template as well as the ForeignKey filter template populate their drop-down list controls. These methods return a LINQ IQueryable object that you can use to retrieve rows from the database. Chapter 14, "Implementing Security," discusses how the GetQuery method can be overridden to implement row-level security.

Presentation Logic Support

Support for presentation logic is, by far, the biggest part of the public interface exposed by the MetaTable class. Here are the important members to consider:

```
public virtual IEnumerable<MetaColumn> GetScaffoldColumns(
    DataBoundControlMode mode, ContainerType containerType);
```

The GetScaffoldColumns method is responsible for returning the list of columns that will be displayed by the default page templates. The containerType parameter specifies whether the columns are needed for a single item view or a list. The mode parameter specifies whether the current entity is displayed in ReadOnly, Insert, or Edit mode.

```
public virtual IEnumerable<MetaColumn> GetFilteredColumns();
```

The GetFilteredColumns method is used by the QueryableFilterRepeater control, which generates the filter controls in the List and ListDetails page templates.

```
public string GetActionPath(string action);
public string GetActionPath(string action, IList<object> primaryKeyValues);
public string GetActionPath(string action, object row);
public string GetActionPath(string action,
    RouteValueDictionary routeValues);
```

The GetActionPath method is used whenever a hyperlink is needed to a dynamically generated page, which includes the DynamicHyperLink control as well as the read-only ForeignKey field template. In the simplest form, this method takes a single action parameter, which can be any string, but typically comes from one of the strings defined in the static PageAction class—Insert, Edit, Details, or List. The remaining overloads of the GetActionPath method are used to specify additional parameter values in the query string. This could be limited to just the primary key values of a particular row when generating a link to a single-item page or any column values when generating a link to a prefiltered list page.

```
public IList<object> GetPrimaryKeyValues(object row);
```

The primary key values can be extracted from a row (an entity instance) using the GetPrimaryKeyValues method. This is how the GetActionPath overload that takes a row object works.

```
public IDictionary<string, object> GetColumnValuesFromRoute(
    HttpContext context);
public DataKey GetDataKeyFromRoute();
```

When a user clicks one of the dynamic hyperlinks, page templates typically have to extract column values from the request query string. This is done with the help of the GetColumnValuesFromRoute method, which is used by the list page template and the GetDataKeyFromRoute method, which does the same thing for single-item templates.

```
public virtual string GetDisplayString(object row);
```

When a human-readable string representing a row or an entity is needed, you can use the GetDisplayString method. This is how the ForeignKey field and filter templates set the Text property of the ListItem objects for their DropDownList controls. This method takes into account the DisplayColumn of the MetaTable to locate the column whose value will serve as the display string.

```
public string GetPrimaryKeyString(IList<object> primaryKeyValues);
public string GetPrimaryKeyString(object row);
```

If you need a string that can be used to uniquely identify an entity and enable retrieving it from database later, you can use one of the GetPrimaryKeyString overloads. This is how the ForeignKey field and filter templates generate the Value property of the ListItem objects in their DropDownList controls.

Security Support

Last, but not least, the MetaTable class includes a set of virtual methods that can be used to implement table-level authorization. The default implementation of these methods returns true, making all tables accessible for all users, as long as these tables are scaffolded. Chapter 14 discusses how Dynamic Data applications can take advantage of this extensibility mechanism to implement role-based UI trimming:

```
public virtual bool CanDelete(IPrincipal principal);
public virtual bool CanInsert(IPrincipal principal);
public virtual bool CanRead(IPrincipal principal);
public virtual bool CanUpdate(IPrincipal principal);
```

The MetaColumn Class

The MetaColumn class describes a single property of an entity class. In the Northwind data model, where the Product entity class represents the Products database table, Dynamic Data creates a separate instance of the MetaColumn class for each property the Product entity class defines, including primitive properties, like ProductID, ProductName, CategoryID, and SupplierID as well as navigation properties like Category and Supplier.

The navigation properties of entity classes are represented by the MetaForeignKeyColumn and MetaChildrenColumn classes derived from the MetaColumn class. These classes are discussed later in this chapter; this section focuses on the common properties of all meta columns and their specialized descendants.

Property Definition

A .NET property is defined by its name, type, and accessibility of its getter and setter.

```
public string Name { get; }
```

The Name property of the MetaColumn class returns the name of the entity property. It is a raw, internal string that can be used to identify the column but might not be appropriate for display to end users.

```
public Type ColumnType { get; }
public TypeCode TypeCode { get; }
```

The ColumnType property returns a Type object that represents the .NET type of the entity property. For the ProductName property of the Product entity, this would be a typeof(string). The TypeCode property, on the other hand, returns one of the members of the TypeCode enumeration, and for the ProductName column, this would be TypeCode.String.

```
public bool IsBinaryData { get; }
public bool IsFloatingPoint { get; }
public bool IsInteger { get; }
public bool IsLongString { get; }
public bool IsString { get; }
```

A set of convenience properties is also available to determine a higher-level group of the property's data types. For example, the IsFloatingPoint property returns true for Float, Double, and Decimal columns; the IsInteger property works similarly for Byte, Int16, Int32, and Int64 columns. The IsLongString property returns true if the MaxLength of the string exceeds one billion characters (1,073,741,819 to be exact). In practical terms, this means memo columns, TEXT and NTEXT in Microsoft SQL Server, and determines whether a MultilineText field template will be used for this column by default.

```
public int MaxLength { get; }
```

For binary and string columns, the MaxLength property returns the maximum length allowed for the column values in the data model. For example, the ProductName column of the Products table is limited to 40 characters, and the MaxLength property would return 40 by default.

```
using System.ComponentModel.DataAnnotations;

[MetadataType(typeof(Product.Metadata))]
partial class Product
{
    public class Metadata
    {
```

```
    [StringLength(32)]
    public object ProductName { get; set; }
  }
}
```

However, the MaxLength property can also be changed by applying the StringLengthAttribute to the entity property in code, as just shown.

```
public virtual bool IsReadOnly { get; }
```

The IsReadOnly property of the MetaColumn class returns true if the entity property value cannot be set by users. A property can be read-only if its setter is not accessible or doesn't exist. The latter option does not apply to entity classes generated by Entity Framework and LINQ to SQL, where a property must have a setter for the framework to be able to set its value based on information retrieved from the database. Both of these frameworks, however, support lower visibility (protected or internal) for property setters.

In addition to changing definition of the entity property in the model, you can also make it read-only by applying the EditableAttribute defined in the System.ComponentModel.DataAnnotations namespace.

```
using System.ComponentModel.DataAnnotations;

[MetadataType(typeof(Product.Metadata))]
partial class Product
{
  public class Metadata
  {
    [Editable(false)]
    public object ProductName { get; set; }
  }
}
```

You can also achieve the same effect and make a property read-only for Dynamic Data purposes by applying the ReadOnlyAttribute defined in the System.ComponentModel namespace. However, the EditableAttribute also allows providing additional metadata information to allow editing separately for Insert and Update modes.

```
public PropertyInfo EntityTypeProperty { get; }
```

The EntityTypeProperty of the MetaColumn class returns an instance of the PropertyInfo class defined in the System.Reflection namespace. PropertyInfo contains a low-level .NET metadata describing the property. It also allows you to dynamically get or set the value of the entity property by calling the GetValue and SetValue methods of the PropertyInfo class.

```
public ColumnProvider Provider { get; }
```

The `Provider` property of the `MetaColumn` class returns the original `ColumnProvider` that was used to create the current `MetaColumn` instance from the information extracted from the data model by the metadata provider. Though you should not need to access the underlying column provider directly, it is accessible through this property.

Property Kind

In addition to the name and type of the entity property, Dynamic Data also needs to know what kind of property is it, or in other words, if the property plays a special role in the entity class.

```
public bool IsPrimaryKey { get; }
```

The `IsPrimaryKey` property of the `MetaColumn` class returns `true` for entity properties that are a part of the entity's primary key. With surrogate primary keys being prevalent in database design today, most entity classes have a single property in their primary keys. However, compound primary keys are also supported. Primary key columns can be accessed quickly using the `PrimaryKeyColumns` property of the `MetaTable` class.

> **NOTE**
>
> An entity class must have a primary key for Entity Framework and LINQ to SQL to be able to update rows in its database table. When reverse-engineering an existing database into a data model, Visual Studio can automatically determine the primary keys for tables but not views. If your data model must include views, you might have to edit the model manually to provide the missing information about primary keys.

```
public bool IsForeignKeyComponent { get; }
```

The `IsForeignKeyComponent` property of the `MetaColumn` class returns `true` for those primitive properties that are a part of one or more navigation foreign key properties. For example, the SupplierID property of the Product entity is a component of a foreign key represented by the `Supplier` navigation property and the `IsForeignKeyComponent` property of the `MetaColumn` object describing the SupplierID property returns `true`.

The foreign key component properties have a special meaning in Dynamic Data applications because they should not be presented to the users under normal circumstances. It would not be very helpful to have a `TextBox` for entering `SupplierID` values in raw integer form. Instead, the navigation property, `Supplier` in this case, is presented as a `DropDownList`, or another appropriate control, with which users can choose a supplier instead of having to enter their IDs.

```
public bool IsGenerated { get; }
```

The `IsGenerated` property of the `MetaColumn` class returns `true` for those properties whose values are automatically generated by the database server. With Microsoft SQL Server, this includes `IDENTITY` columns for which the server generates an incremental value for each new row, ROWVERSION columns for which the server generates incremental values with every insert and update, as well as the computed columns defined at the database table level.

Dynamic Data always chooses a read-only field template to display values of generated columns, regardless of whether the entity itself is displayed in Insert or Edit mode.

```
public bool IsCustomProperty { get; }
```

The IsCustomProperty of the MetaColumn class returns true for properties defined by developers in code as opposed to the normal properties defined in the data model itself. Out of the box, custom properties cannot be used for sorting or filtering purposes. The framework also cannot verify that they are persisted in the database correctly. Because of these reasons, Dynamic Data makes a safe bet and does not create filter or field controls for custom properties by default; although it is possible to change this behavior by applying UIHintAttribute and FilterUIHintAttribute to the property in code.

> **NOTE**
>
> As of .NET version 4.0, service pack 1, the Dynamic Data provider for Entity Framework does not support custom properties, and you will not find MetaColumn objects describing them. This is why it is impossible to use custom properties as display columns. As mentioned earlier, this problem can be solved by extending the metadata provider, which is discussed in Chapter 13.

Data Annotations

A large number of the MetaColumn public interface is dedicated to data annotations—the .NET attributes that can be applied by developers to the entity properties in code.

```
public AttributeCollection Attributes { get; }
```

All attributes applied to a particular entity property can be accessed through the Attributes property of the MetaColumn class. Similar to the Attributes property of the MetaTable class, this property also includes the built-in attributes from the System.ComponentModel and System.ComponentModel.DataAnnotations namespaces as well as any custom attributes that you might have created in your application.

Although it is possible to get all data annotations directly through the Attributes collection, doing so would require scanning it repeatedly, which would quickly drain the precious CPU resources of your web server. Instead, Dynamic Data class scans the attributes only once, when the MetaColumn object is created, and stores their values in fields of the object for instantaneous access later.

Scaffolding Support
Several data annotations and MetaColumn properties play an important role in the scaffolding process, where Dynamic Data determines whether a particular column needs to be

represented by a field or filter control on a page and how the template for that control is selected.

```
public virtual bool Scaffold { get; set; }
```

The Scaffold property of the MetaColumn class determines whether Dynamic Data will generate a field template for the entity property it represents. By default, Scaffold returns false for automatically generated, custom, and primitive properties that are a part of a foreign key. You can change the default value of this property by applying the ScaffoldColumnAttribute or the DisplayAttribute with the AutoGenerateField property value specified.

```
public virtual string UIHint { get; }
```

The UIHint property of the MetaColumn class returns the name of a field template that Dynamic Data tries first when generating a control for the entity property. The UIHint property returns a blank string unless you apply the UIHintAttribute to the entity property in code.

```
public DataTypeAttribute DataTypeAttribute { get; }
```

The DataTypeAttribute property returns the DataTypeAttribute that was applied to the entity property in code. The UIHint and data type take precedence over the more generic template names based on .NET types that Dynamic Data tries when searching for an appropriate field template.

```
public string FilterUIHint { get; }
```

The FilterUIHint property is similar to the UIHint but specifies the name of a *filter* template. It also returns a blank string by default and can be specified by applying the FilterUIHintAttribute to the entity property. Dynamic Data uses filter hints when generating filter controls, typically as part of a QueryableFilterRepeater in the List page template.

```
public bool AllowInitialValue { get; }
```

The AllowInitialValue property of the MetaColumn determines whether the entity property can have a value entered in Insert mode. The AllowInitialValue returns false for generated and read-only properties. You can also override it by applying the EditableAttribute to the entity property in code with the AllowInitialValue specified.

Business Logic Support
Several properties of the MetaColumn class provide support for business logic based on data annotations. This number is surprisingly small, as it covers only three of the attributes discussed in Chapter 3, "Field Templates."

```
public object DefaultValue { get; }
```

The `DefaultValue` property of the `MetaColumn` class returns a value used by default for the entity property in Insert mode. It can be specified in code by applying the `DefaultValueAttribute` to the entity property in code.

NOTE

Dynamic Data, or more specifically the EntityDataSource, does not create a new entity instance when generating an insert page. This is significant, because even though the Entity Framework designer allows you to define default property values in the model, the stock code generators produce entity classes where the default values are assigned in code and entity properties do not have the `DefaultValueAttribute`.

This results in inconsistent behavior when an entity instance is created in code as opposed to the Dynamic Data UI. Although it is straightforward to apply the `DefaultValueAttribute` manually, doing so would be prone to errors in large data models. Instead, consider switching to T4-based text templates for generating entity classes and modifying them to automatically generate the `DefaultValueAttribute`.

```
public bool IsRequired { get; }
```

The `IsRequired` property of the `MetaColumn` returns true if the entity property must have a value. By default, this property returns True for non-nullable entity properties. You can also set it by applying the `RequiredAttribute` to the entity property in code.

Display Support

Several properties of the `MetaColumn` define textual labels describing the entity property that are or can be displayed to the end users.

```
public virtual string DisplayName { get; }
```

The `DisplayName` property returns a string that serves as a label for the entity property on dynamically generated single-item pages, such as Insert, Edit, and Details.

```
public virtual string ShortDisplayName { get; }
```

The `ShortDisplayName` returns a string used in a header of a grid column that displays the entity property values on a dynamically generated List page.

```
public virtual string Prompt { get; }
```

The `Prompt` property returns a string that could be used as a watermark in Edit and Insert mode field templates. None of the field templates supplied with Dynamic Data project templates take advantage of this property. However, you could easily implement support for it with the `TextBoxWatermarkExtender` from the AJAX control toolkit.

All three of these properties—`DisplayName`, `ShortDisplayName`, and `Prompt`—can be specified in code by applying the `DisplayAttribute` to the entity property.

```
public virtual string Description { get; }
```

The Description property of the MetaColumn class returns the description specified in code by applying the DescriptionAttribute to the entity property. The built-in field templates Dynamic Data provides do not currently utilize this property. However, you can easily modify them and use this property to generate a tooltip for the data controls in field templates.

Formatting Options

The last remaining data annotation properties worth mentioning are the ones related to formatting options that can be specified by applying the DisplayFormatAttribute to the entity property. These properties are used by the DynamicControl and DynamicField controls to implement flexible and consistent formatting of field values.

```
public string DataFormatString { get; }
```

The DataFormatString property returns a string that contains a .NET format string, such as "{0:C}", that will be used to convert field value to a string by calling the Format method of the String class. Although including the parameter number 0 might seem unnecessary, knowing that there is only one field value to format, it is required for the format string to work properly.

```
public bool ApplyFormatInEditMode { get; }
```

The ApplyFormatInEditMode property determines whether Dynamic Data will use the DataFormatString not only in Read-only mode and on List and Details pages, but also in Edit mode as well.

```
public string NullDisplayText { get; }
```

The NullDisplayText property specifies the text Dynamic Data will display when the field value is null.

```
public bool ConvertEmptyStringToNull { get; }
```

The ConvertEmptyStringToNull property determines whether NullDisplayText will be used for empty strings as well.

```
public bool HtmlEncode { get; }
```

The HtmlEncode property determines whether any special characters that might be a part of the field value will be encoded using HTML escape sequences. This property is true by default, making the dynamically generated pages immune against HTML injection attacks. You should only consider changing it when your application allows users to enter formatted text in HTML form and performs thorough cleansing of the values entered by users to remove dangerous HTML tags, such as <script>, before saving them in the database.

The MetaForeignKeyColumn Class

The MetaForeignKeyColumn class is a specialized descendant of the MetaColumn class that represents many-to-one and one-to-one navigation properties, such as the Supplier property of the Product entity in the Northwind data model. These "foreign key" columns in the Dynamic Data metadata API have additional attributes that you can access through this class.

```
public MetaTable ParentTable { get; }
```

The ParentTable property returns a MetaTable object describing the parent entity referenced by the foreign key. In case of the Supplier property of the Product entity, the ParentTable property returns the MetaTable object describing the Supplier entity. This property serves an important role in implementing filtering and navigation functionality. In particular, it is used by the ForeignKey field and filter templates to retrieve the rows from the parent table for display in a drop-down list.

```
public ReadOnlyCollection<string> ForeignKeyNames { get; }
```

The ForeignKeyNames property of the MetaForeignKeyColumn class returns a collection of the primitive entity properties that form the foreign key. For the Supplier property of the Product entity, this property returns a collection with a single column name—SupplierID. The collection returned by this property has multiple items only if the parent table has a compound primary key and the foreign key includes multiple primitive properties.

Presentation Logic

The remaining properties and methods of the MetaForeignKeyColumn class provide support for implementing presentation logic in Dynamic Data applications.

```
public bool IsPrimaryKeyInThisTable { get; }
```

The IsPrimaryKeyInThisTable property of the MetaForeignKeyColumn class returns true if any of the primitive components of the foreign key is a member of the primary key of the entity itself. For example, the *Order_Detail* entity in the Northwind data model has a compound primary key that consists of OrderID and ProductID properties. The Order navigation property is represented by a MetaForeignKeyColumn whose IsPrimaryKeyInThisTable returns true because OrderID is a part of the primary key of the Order_Detail entity.

> **NOTE**
> Dynamic Data does not allow editing primary key values by default and uses the IsPrimaryKeyInThisTableProperty property to display read-only field templates for foreign key columns that are a part of a primary key in Edit mode.

```
public IList<object> GetForeignKeyValues(object row);
```

The GetForeignKeyValues method of the MetaForeignKeyColumn class returns a list values of the primitive entity properties that form the foreign key of a given row or entity instance. Using the Products table of the Northwind database as an example, the product called "Chai" has a SupplierID equal to 1; calling the GetForeignKeyValues method for this row returns a list with a single Int32 value (1). The order of values returned by this method matches the order of column names returned by the ForeignKeyNames property.

```
public string GetForeignKeyPath(string action, object row);
public string GetForeignKeyPath(string action, object row, string path);
```

The GetForeignKeyPath methods of the MetaForeignKeyColumn class extract the list of foreign key values from the specified row by calling the GetForeignKeyValues method and then pass it to the GetActionPath method of the ParentTable. The action parameter is typically specified using one of the values defined in the PageAction static class. The row parameter is an instance of the entity that contains the foreign key. And path can be specified when additional query parameters need to be specified in the query string.

Similar to the GetActionPath method of the MetaTable class, the GetForeignKeyPath methods are used when a hyperlink is needed to navigate from a child entity to a parent entity. This is how the read-only ForeignKey field template generates the URL of its hyperlink.

```
public string GetForeignKeyString(object row);
```

The GetForeignKeyString method calls the GetForeignKeyValues method to obtain values of the primitive foreign key columns and converts them to a string where individual values are separated by commas. For the Supplier foreign key of the Product entity, this would return a single SupplierID value, such as "1" for the "Chai" product.

This method serves as a counterpart for the GetPrimaryKeyString method of the MetaColumn class discussed earlier. The ForeignKey_Edit field template uses the GetPrimaryKeyString method to generate values for the drop-down list items representing rows from the parent table. To select the current value of the foreign key property in the drop-down list, it calls the GetForeignKeyString method.

```
public void ExtractForeignKey(IDictionary dictionary, string value);
```

The ExtractForeignKey method is the opposite of the GetForeignKeyString. It takes a comma-separated list of foreign key-Edit values and extracts them into a dictionary. Field templates use this method to implement data-binding logic, extract a current foreign key value from their web controls, and pass it to a data source control. In particular, if the "Exotic Liquids" is selected as a supplier for the "Chai" product, the ExtractForeignKey method will receive a string that contains ID of the supplier - "1" and add value 1 with key "SupplierID" to the dictionary.

The MetaChildrenColumn Class

The `MetaChildrenColumn` class is another specialized descendant of the `MetaColumn` class that represents one-to-many and many-to-many navigation properties. In one-to-many relationships, `MetaChildrenColumn` is the opposite of the `MetaForeignKeyColumn`. For example, the Supplier entity of the Northwind data model has a one-to-many property called Products, which returns all products a particular supplier offers.

```
public MetaTable ChildTable { get; }
```

The `ChildTable` property of the `MetaChildrenColumn` class returns a `MetaTable` object describing the child entity referenced by the navigation property. For the Products property of the Supplier entity, the child entity is Product and the `ChildTable` property of the `MetaChildrenColumn` object would return the Products `MetaTable`.

```
public bool IsManyToMany { get; }
```

The `IsManyToMany` property returns `true` if the column represents a many-to-many relationship and `false` if the relationship is one-to-many. In the Northwind data model, the Employee entity has a many-to-many relationship with Territory, and the `MetaChildrenColumn` instance describing the Territories column has the `IsManyToMany` property set to `true`.

> **NOTE**
>
> LINQ to SQL does not support many-to-many associations natively. The `IsManyToMany` property is always false for columns describing LINQ to SQL data models.

```
public MetaColumn ColumnInOtherTable { get; }
```

The `ColumnInOtherTable` property of the `MetaChildrenColumn` class returns a `MetaColumn` object that represents the opposite end of the association. For the Products property of the Supplier entity, this property returns a `MetaColumn` that represents the `Supplier` property of the Product entity.

This property can return a `MetaForeignKeyColumn` object if the children column represents a one-to-many navigation property, such as the Products property of the Supplier entity, whose counterpart is the Supplier property of the Product entity. It can also return a `MetaChildrenColumn` object if the children column represents a many-to-many navigation property, such as the `Territories` property of the Employee entity, whose counterpart is the `Employees` property of the Territory entity. This property can also return `null` if the navigation property represents a one-way association, or in other words, when the children navigation property doesn't have a counterpart on the other side.

```
public string GetChildrenPath(string action, object row);
public string GetChildrenPath(string action, object row, string path);
```

The GetChildrenPath methods of the MetaChildrenColumn class are used when a hyperlink is needed to navigate from a parent entity to its children. They retrieve the primary key values from the specified row and pass them to the GetActionPath method of the ChildTable. The generated URL contains the route to the child table, including name of the page template based on the specified action and primary key names and values in the query. This is how the Children field template generates a hyperlink that takes the user from the parent entity to the List page of the child entity, filtered by the parent's primary key.

Summary

Dynamic Data metadata API provides the information web applications need to generate pages dynamically. The MetaModel class serves as the entry point for registering data models and accessing the metadata. The MetaTable class describes a single entity as a collection of attributes, such as DisplayName and SortColumn and a collection of MetaColumn objects that describe the entity properties. The MetaColumn class describes primitive entity properties and has two descendant classes—MetaForeignKeyColumn, which describes many-to-one and one-to-one navigation properties, and MetaChildrenColumn, which describes one-to-many and many-to-many navigation properties.

The metadata API in Dynamic Data relies on metadata providers, which are special classes designed to extract metadata information from the underlying data access framework and present it to the meta model classes in a uniform format. Dynamic Data ships with built-in providers for Entity Framework and LINQ to SQL and allows creating custom providers for other data access frameworks.

PART II

Dynamic Data in Real-World Applications

IN THIS PART

Implementing Entity Validation

V alidation of entities is one of the key aspects of business logic. The .NET Framework introduced a new validation framework in Service Pack 1 of version 3.5, at the same time the first version of Dynamic Data was released. This framework is implemented in the `System.ComponentModel.DataAnnotations` namespace and contains a set of attributes and classes for validating objects and their properties.

The Data Annotations namespace is defined in a separate assembly called `System.ComponentModel.DataAnnotations`, installed in the global assembly cache. This assembly is referenced by default when you create a new Dynamic Data project in Visual Studio. If, however, your entity classes are located in a separate project, make sure it references this assembly as well.

Validation Framework

At the core of the validation framework is an abstract base class called `ValidationAttribute`. It defines a virtual method called `IsValid`, which takes an object to validate and returns `true` if it is valid and false if it is not. Concrete descendants of this class, such as the `RequiredAttribute`, override the `IsValid` method to perform the actual validation.

The validation attributes are applied to the things they validate, such as properties, fields, or entire classes. Consider the following example that defines a simple Product entity class with a *required* property called `ProductName`:

```
public class Product
{
    [Required]
    public string ProductName { get; set; }
}
```

The .NET runtime does not invoke the validation attributes automatically. Some code in your application must detect them and invoke the validation logic explicitly. As you might recall from the discussion in Chapter 3, "Field Templates," and Chapter 6, "Page Templates," the DynamicValidator is responsible for doing this in ASP.NET Dynamic Data applications, when this control is used in field templates and its ColumnName property specifies the name of the entity property to which validation attributes might have been applied.

The Data Annotations namespace also provides a helper class, called Validator that uses .NET reflection to validate any object based on the validation attributes applied to its class and individual properties. Here is how to validate an instance of the Product entity class we just defined:

```
var product = new Product();
var context = new ValidationContext(product, null, null);
Validator.ValidateObject(product, context, true);
```

The ValidationContext object contains information about the object being validated. The ValidateObject method passes it to each validation attribute along with the property value to validate. ValidationContext allows implementation of sophisticated validation logic that is not limited to a single property value. Following is the constructor used in the preceding example to create this object:

```
ValidationContext(object instance, IServiceProvider serviceProvider,
    IDictionary<object, object> items)
```

The first parameter, instance, is the object being validated. The second, serviceProvider, and third, items, parameters of the constructor are used in advanced scenarios, some of which will be discussed later. For simple cases, they can be null.

The ValidateObject method of the Validator class takes the object to validate as its first parameter and throws a ValidationException for the first validation attribute whose IsValid method returns false. The actual signature of the ValidateObject method is shown here:

```
void ValidateObject(object instance, ValidationContext validationContext,
    bool validateAllProperties)
```

Despite what its name implies, the validateAllProperties parameter of the ValidateObject method actually determines whether all validation *attributes* will be evaluated or only the instances of the RequiredAttribute. You want to specify true in most circumstances.

> **NOTE**
>
> Validation attributes applied to properties and fields are evaluated before the attributes applied to the class. However, you should not rely on the order of validation within these two groups. The .NET Framework does not guarantee that the order of properties or attributes returned by the reflection APIs will match the order of their appearance in the source code. Even though, in many cases, the order of validation appears to match the order of attributes, there will be exceptions. If the order of validation rules is important, instead of attributes, you need to rely on coded validation discussed in the *Imperative Validation* section of this chapter.

If you want to validate an object without throwing a `ValidationException`, you can call the `TryValidateObject` method of the `Validator` class instead:

```
bool TryValidateObject(object instance, ValidationContext validationContext,
   ICollection<ValidationResult> validationResults, bool validateAllProperties)
```

This method returns a `Boolean` value that indicates whether or not the object is valid and populates the collection you supply in the `validationResults` parameter with a separate `ValidationResult` object for each error detected.

Validation Error Messages

In addition to performing the validation itself, the validation attributes are responsible for generating error messages if the validation fails. Each concrete validation attribute, such as `RequiredAttribute`, discussed so far, provides a default error message. For instance, with the following definition of the ProductName property, the `RequiredAttribute` generates an error message "The ProductName field is required."

```
[Required]
public string ProductName { get; set; }
```

Obviously, this error message is very technical and might not be appropriate for business users. You can replace the internal name of the field in the error message with its human-readable form by applying the `DisplayAttribute` as shown here:

```
[Required]
[Display(Name = "Product Name")]
public string ProductName { get; set; }
```

With this updated definition, the `RequiredAttribute` generates the error message as "The Product Name field is required," which in many instances will be acceptable for display. However, if this is still not enough, you can completely replace the error message by specifying the `ErrorMessage` property in the validation attribute explicitly:

```
[Required(ErrorMessage = "Product Name cannot be empty")]
public string ProductName { get; set; }
```

Both the Validator class and the DynamicValidator control rely on the DisplayAttribute and the ErrorMessage property of validation attributes when generating error messages. If you chose to specify error messages explicitly, keep in mind that you might still need to specify the DisplayAttribute for properties displayed in any dynamically generated pages of your application.

In web applications with localization requirement, display names and error messages cannot be hard-coded as string literals in the entity model. Data annotation attributes support the traditional .NET approach to localization based on assembly resources. You can define display names and error messages as string resources in a RESX file, typically located in the same assembly where the entity classes themselves reside. Visual Studio automatically generates a resource helper class based on the contents of the RESX file. For each string resource, this class has a static property with the matching name, which looks similar to the following pseudo-code:

```
public class Resources
{
  public static string ProductNameDisplayName { get; }
  public static string ProductNameRequiredErrorMessage { get; }
}
```

For a data annotation attribute to retrieve a string from resources, you need to specify the type of the resource class and the name of the property that returns it. For the DisplayAttribute, specify the type via its ResourceType property and the Name property, which normally contains the actual string value but now specifies the name of the resource property that returns it:

```
[Display(ResourceType = typeof(Resources), Name = "ProductNameDisplayName")]
public string ProductName { get; set; }
```

> **NOTE**
>
> Data annotation attributes use reflection to access string resources through a helper class such the one just shown and assume that the class as well as its static properties have public visibility. By default, visibility of the generated resource class is internal, which results in a runtime error in Dynamic Data pages. You can change this using the Visual Studio resource designer.

Validation attributes also rely on the helper classes to retrieve error messages from string resources. The base class, ValidationAttribute, defines two properties that allow you to specify this information—ErrorMessageResourceType and ErrorMessageResourceName. Here is how to change the RequiredAttribute applied to the ProductName property to retrieve the error message using the `ProductNameRequiredErrorMessage` property of the Resources class:

```
[Required(ErrorMessageResourceType = typeof(Resources),
   ErrorMessageResourceName = "ProductNameRequiredErrorMessage")]
public object ProductName { get; set; }
```

Validation in Entity Framework

As of version 4, the Entity Framework offers only limited support for validation attributes and requires additional work from developers. On one hand, the Entity Data Model designer does not allow you to specify data annotations for entity classes and their properties, and on the other, the `ObjectContext` class does not validate entities before they are saved.

> **NOTE**
>
> In version 4.1, the Entity Framework introduced support for validating entities when they are saved. Unfortunately, it also introduced an entirely new API, which is not 100% compatible with Dynamic Data at this time. The differences will not be fully reconciled until the 4.5 release of the .NET Framework comes out. If you choose to use the interim release, you need to make some of the same changes discussed in this chapter.

Specifying Validation Attributes for Entity Classes

Because the Entity Data Model designer generates the entity classes in the `.Designer.cs` file automatically, you cannot simply apply the validation attributes directly to the classes and properties; they will get overwritten next time you update the entity model. Instead, rely on the `partial` class syntax in C# and Visual Basic to extend the generated classes. The code that follows shows an excerpt of the Product entity class as if it has been generated by the Entity Framework and therefore does not have the `RequiredAttribute` applied to its `ProductName` property:

```
public partial class Product
{
   public string ProductName { get; set; }
}
```

Notice that the class is declared as `partial`. This allows a separate file to extend the generated class and apply the `MetadataTypeAttribute` to specify an alternative type that will supply validation attributes and other data annotations for the generated class:

```
using System.ComponentModel.DataAnnotations;

[MetadataType(typeof(Metadata))]
public partial class Product
{
```

```
    private abstract class Metadata
    {
      [Required]
      public object ProductName { get; set; }
    }
}
```

From a validation standpoint, placing any .NET attributes on fields or properties of the metadata class has the same effect as placing them on their counterparts in the real class. Only the name of the field or property matters from the matching prospective, so the metadata class could declare ProductName as a field of type object even though it is a property of type string in the real class. However, if the metadata class has a property or field that *does not* have a property with the same name in the real class, you get an InvalidOperationException whenever you try to access its attributes for the first time, such as when passing an object to the ValidateObject method of the Validator class.

> **NOTE**
>
> The compiler does not issue an error when a partial class contains only one definition, which makes it easy to create partial classes that do not match their generated coun- terparts. You could mistype the name of the class itself or place it in a different name- space. If you notice that additional metadata attributes you applied in the metadata type seem to have no effect on the Dynamic Data pages, double-check that all partial class definitions match, or better yet, create an automated test to verify it, as you learn about later in this chapter.

> **NOTE**
>
> Notice that the Metadata class was made abstract, private, and *nested* intentionally. The metadata classes are never instantiated by the application. In addition to violating object-oriented design principles, making metadata classes public unnecessarily pollutes the IntelliSense information in Visual Studio. This becomes more and more noticeable as the number of metadata classes in your application grows.

To eliminate the confusion of having a different type specified for a property as well as to avoid mistakes caused by incorrect property names in the metadata classes, you can use metadata *interfaces* instead. Here is the same partial Product class extended with a meta- data interface instead of a metadata class:

```
using System.ComponentModel.DataAnnotations;

internal interface IProduct
{
  [Required]
  string ProductName { get; set; }
}
```

```
[MetadataType(typeof(IProduct))]
public partial class Product : IProduct
{
}
```

Notice that the Product class not only implements the IProduct interface, but also specifies it as the metadata type. Unlike the untyped metadata class in the previous example, the metadata interface has to declare the ProductName property of type string for it to match its actual implementation in the real Product class. Should they ever get out of sync, you get an immediate compiler error as opposed to an InvalidOperationException at runtime.

NOTE

Neither of the two approaches to metadata types discussed here is perfect. The nested classes approach results in the best encapsulation; there are no additional types that are introduced at the assembly level. This helps to reduce confusion and makes metadata classes impossible to misuse. The interfaces approach makes maintaining the metadata types easier but results in additional interface types introduced in the data model assembly. The interfaces can be declared as internal, but they will still be visible and possible to misuse in the data model assembly itself. In the end, the decision on whether to use nested classes or interfaces for data annotations will probably depend on your personal taste.

Registering Metadata Provider with TypeDescriptor

If you try to compile and run the following code in a console application separate from a Dynamic Data web application, you might be surprised to find that the RequiredAttribute applied to the ProductName property of the Product class using the metadata class is completely ignored, and the ValidateObject method does not throw the ValidationException, as you would expect:

```
var product = new Product();
var context = new ValidationContext(product, null, null);
Validator.ValidateObject(product, context, true);
```

Behind the scenes, the Validator uses TypeDescriptor, a static class from the System.ComponentModel namespace, to determine the list of attributes applied to each property of the object it needs to validate. The MetadataTypeAttribute applied to the Product class actually does not have any effect *unless it has been configured* for a specific object or its entire class. Dynamic Data does this automatically for all entity classes during context registration, but to perform validation in other types of applications, you need to do this explicitly by calling TypeDescriptor's static AddProviderTransparent method and passing it an instance of the AssociatedMetadataTypeTypeDescriptionProvider class as shown here:

```
TypeDescriptor.AddProviderTransparent(
  new AssociatedMetadataTypeTypeDescriptionProvider(typeof(Product)),
  typeof(Product));
```

Because this code needs to run only once, you can place it in the static constructor of the Product entity class itself, where it will be in close proximity to the `MetadataType` attribute the extended class still needs. Here is a complete version of the Product class extended using the same metadata interface used in the previous example:

```
using System.ComponentModel;
using System.ComponentModel.DataAnnotations;

[MetadataType(typeof(IProduct))]
public partial class Product : IProduct
{
  static Product()
  {
    TypeDescriptor.AddProviderTransparent(
      new AssociatedMetadataTypeTypeDescriptionProvider(typeof(Product)),
      typeof(Product));
  }
}
```

Validating Entities Before Saving

Although Dynamic Data takes care of validating the individual properties of entities when they are created and modified through the dynamic web pages, this approach does not protect you against errors when the entities are manipulated programmatically. Imagine a console application that runs at a scheduled interval to import Products from flat files this imaginary company, Northwind Traders, receives from suppliers. Because you have already created the NorthwindEntities data model for the website itself, it would be beneficial to reuse it in the import application, as it would allow you to reuse the business logic it implements.

Suppose that even though the database schema allows you to store NULL values in the UnitPrice column of the Products table, you decide that from the *business* point of view, each product requires a UnitPrice before you can start offering it on the Northwind Trader's website. Based on this decision, you could go ahead and modify the Product entity metadata to apply the `RequiredAttribute` to the `UnitPrice` property as shown here:

```
[MetadataType(typeof(Product.Metadata))]
partial class Product
{
  static Product()
  {
    TypeDescriptor.AddProviderTransparent(
      new AssociatedMetadataTypeTypeDescriptionProvider(typeof(Product)),
      typeof(Product));
```

```
    }

    private abstract class Metadata
    {
      [Required]
      public object ProductName { get; set; }

      [Required]
      public object UnitPrice { get; set; }
    }
}
```

The following is pseudo-code from the imaginary import application, which creates a new Product entity in the Northwind database. This code actually compiles and runs without error; however, in a real application, the product name would not be hard-coded but loaded form an import file instead:

```
using (NorthwindEntities context = new NorthwindEntities())
{
    var product = new Product();
    product.ProductName = "Test Product";
    product.UnitPrice = null;
    context.Products.AddObject(product);
    context.SaveChanges();
}
```

Because this code does not validate the new Product instance explicitly, the RequiredAttribute, newly added to the UnitPrice property, will have no effect, and an invalid product record will be created in the database without the unit price. Although you could fix the problem in this particular case, having to call the static ValidateObject method every time you create or modify an entity instance is repetitive and prone to errors.

In most scenarios, it is logical to assume that when a developer saves entities to the database, he wants them to be valid, so having to validate them explicitly simply increases the volume of code without adding any new logic to it. Based on this assumption, you can override the SaveChanges method of the Entity Framework's ObjectContext to perform validation for all entities before they are submitted to the database. Listing 8.1 shows how this can be done.

LISTING 8.1 Overriding SaveChanges Method to Implement Validation

```
using System.Collections.Generic;
using System.ComponentModel.DataAnnotations;
using System.Data;
using System.Data.Objects;
using System.Linq;
```

```
namespace Unleashed.EntityFramework
{
  public class UnleashedObjectContext : ObjectContext
  {
    private const EntityState ChangedEntityStates =
      EntityState.Added | EntityState.Modified | EntityState.Deleted;

    public override int SaveChanges(SaveOptions options)
    {
      IEnumerable<ObjectStateEntry> stateEntries = this.ObjectStateManager
        .GetObjectStateEntries(ChangedEntityStates)
        .Where(stateEntry => !stateEntry.IsRelationship);

      foreach (ObjectStateEntry stateEntry in stateEntries)
        this.BeforeSaveChanges(stateEntry);

      return base.SaveChanges(options);
    }

    private void BeforeSaveChanges(ObjectStateEntry stateEntry)
    {
      if (stateEntry.State != EntityState.Deleted)
        this.Validate(stateEntry);
    }

    private void Validate(ObjectStateEntry stateEntry)
    {
      object entity = stateEntry.Entity;
      var context = new ValidationContext(entity, null, null);
      Validator.ValidateObject(entity, context, true);
    }
  }
}
```

First, the overridden SaveChanges method gets a list of state entries for all changed entities from the ObjectStateManager that keeps track of all entities in the ObjectContext. For each of the changed state entries, it calls the BeforeSaveChanges method responsible for performing all entity-specific actions that need to occur before the changes are saved to the database. As we continue expanding Entity Framework capabilities to solve real-world business problems, this method will grow. At this point, however, it is only responsible for validation of the changed entities. The Validate method extracts the actual entity from an ObjectStateEntry and calls the familiar ValidateObject method of the Validator class. If the entity object is invalid, the ValidateObject method throws a

`ValidationException`, preventing the `SaveChanges` method from saving the changes to the database.

> **NOTE**
>
> The `BeforeSaveChanges` method intentionally *excludes* deleted entities from validation because most rules would not be applicable and cause unnecessary errors. Chapter 9, "Implementing Business Logic," includes a detailed discussion of this topic.

Customizing Entity Framework Code Generation

The `UnleashedObjectContext` class shown in Listing 8.1 is available with the sample project accompanying this book. It is defined in a separate assembly called `Unleashed.EntityFramework` and includes a substantial amount of general-purpose code that any Entity Framework application could reuse. Although you could simply copy its code, you might want to have the Entity Framework context class, such as the NorthwindEntities in the ongoing example, *inherit* from it instead. This helps to keep the infrastructure code out of the application, which was beneficial even with the sample entity model discussed in this book.

With the database-first and model-first approaches to Entity Framework model development, the NorthwindEntities class is generated by the Entity Designer. By default, it inherits from the `ObjectContext`. You cannot change its declaration directly because any modifications would be lost next time the code is regenerated. Instead, you need to change the code generator itself. This section shows how you can replace the built-in Entity Framework code with a *text template* that can be customized to change how the code is generated.

> **NOTE**
>
> Customizing the code generated by Entity Framework can solve other common problems as well. For instance, Chapter 9 relies on this approach to provide information about default values of entity properties to Dynamic Data.

Replacing Built-in Code Generator with Text Template

To replace the built-in code generator the Entity Designer uses, right-click the design surface and select Add Code Generation Item from the context menu. In the Add New Item Dialog (see Figure 8.1), choose the ADO.NET Entity Object Generator and give it a name matching the name of the EDMX file.

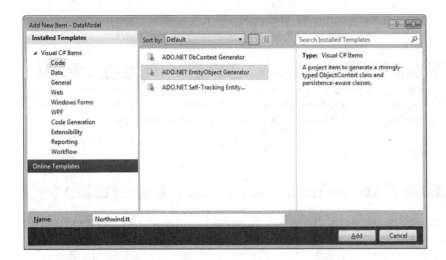

FIGURE 8.1   Add New Code Generation Item dialog.

When you click Add in the Add New Code Generation Item dialog, Visual Studio adds a new *text template* (.TT file) to the project and associate it with the EDMX file. Figure 8.2 shows how this looks in Solution Explorer. Notice that the context and entity classes are now generated in the Northwind.cs under the TT file instead of the default Northwind.Designer.cs under the EDMX.

FIGURE 8.2   Text template in Solution Explorer.

Customizing Text Template to Change Context Base Class

Text templates use ASP.NET-like syntax to generate any code at design time in Visual Studio. This particular text template generates Entity Framework context and entity classes identical to the ones produced by the default code generator. However, unlike the latter, text templates come with complete source code that be customized to fit the unique needs of your project.

NOTE

Complete discussion of text template is outside the scope of this book. You can find detailed information on this topic at http://www.olegsych.com/2007/12/text-template-transformation-toolkit.

You can modify TT files using any text editor, such as the one that comes with Visual Studio. To accomplish the immediate goal of changing the base class of the generated `NorthwindEntities`, search for the word `ObjectContext` in the template and replace it with `UnleashedObjectContext`, as shown in Figure 8.3. When you save the TT file, the `Northwind.cs` under it is automatically regenerated and the `NorthwindEntities` class will inherit from the new base class.

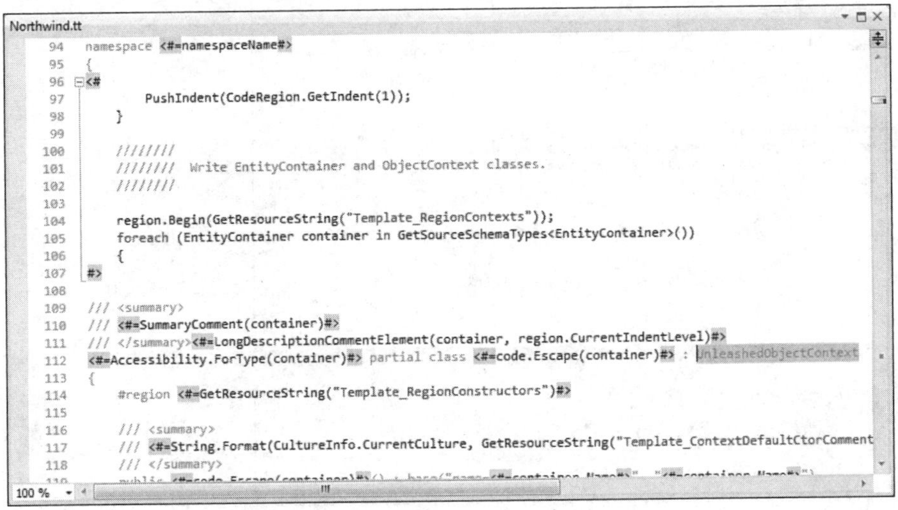

FIGURE 8.3 Changing context base class in the text template.

NOTE

Visual Studio does not offer color syntax highlighting and IntelliSense for TT files. You can download one of several third-party add-ons that provide these capabilities. Figure 8.3 shows the Devart T4 Editor available for download at http://www.devart.com/t4-editor.

Customizing Text Template to Generate Static Constructors

The Entity Framework text template in the sample solution has been further customized to automatically generate static constructors for every entity type as discussed in the *Registering Metadata Provider with TypeDescriptor* section. The following code is now a part of the generated classes and does not need to be hand-coded:

```
static Product()
{
  TypeDescriptor.AddProviderTransparent(
    new AssociatedMetadataTypeTypeDescriptionProvider(typeof(Product)),
    typeof(Product));
}
```

Figure 8.4 shows where the text template was modified. Notice the `WriteStaticConstructor` method call that was added to the template code responsible for generation of entity type declarations. This method is implemented in the end of this method in the Northwind.tt file in the sample solution.

```
Northwind.tt                                                                    ▾ □ ×
    298      ////////
    297      //////// Write EntityType classes.
    298      ////////
    299      region.Begin(GetResourceString("Template_RegionEntities"));
    300      foreach (EntityType entity in GetSourceSchemaTypes<EntityType>().OrderBy(e => e.Name))
    301      {
    302  #>
    303
    304  /// <summary>
    305  /// <#=SummaryComment(entity)#>
    306  /// </summary><#=LongDescriptionCommentElement(entity, region.CurrentIndentLevel)#>
    307  [EdmEntityTypeAttribute(NamespaceName="<#=entity.NamespaceName#>", Name="<#=entity.Name#>")]
    308  [Serializable()]
    309  [DataContractAttribute(IsReference=true)]
    310  <#
    311          foreach (EntityType subType in ItemCollection.GetItems<EntityType>().Where(b => b.Ba
    312          {
    313  #>
    314  [KnownTypeAttribute(typeof(<#=MultiSchemaEscape(subType, code)#>))]
    315  <#
    316          }
    317  #>
    318  <#=Accessibility.ForType(entity)#> <#=code.SpaceAfter(code.AbstractOption(entity))#>partial
    319  {
    320  <#
    321          if (!entity.Abstract)
    322          {
    323              WriteStaticConstructor(entity, code);
    324              WriteFactoryMethod(entity, code);
    325          }
100 %  ▾
```

FIGURE 8.4   Generating static constructor in the text template.

Automated Testing

Due to its importance and relatively low rate of change, business logic in general and the validation logic in particular are good candidates for automated testing. Encapsulating the business logic in the context and entity classes partially generated by the Entity Framework enables focused testing directly at the business level. Unlike testing through the user interface, which depends on a particular presentation layer, such as the ASP.NET WebForms, and often requires manual testing or use of specialized tools, testing at the business level can be done through the application's internal APIs with general-purpose frameworks, such as NUnit or the Visual Studio unit-testing framework.

Automated testing is one of the most powerful tools you can use to improve and maintain the quality of your application. However, like many expensive and powerful tools, automated testing is difficult to apply *cost-effectively*. Many teams and individual developers have tried automated testing only to find that the significant increase in effort required to implement and maintain the tests does not justify the perceived quality improvements. In many instances, these attempts fail because developers try to apply the "best practices" intended to tackle algorithmic complexity of some of the largest software applications and frameworks. These practices do not scale down to the needs of the majority of the information systems where the biggest challenge is the size of the domain (the number of tables in the database, the number of human workflows, and so on) and not the complexity of its individual algorithms.

Although the topic of automated testing is simply too big to cover in detail here, this section presents a practical approach you can use to get started. To reinforce the importance of automated testing of business logic and to prove its practical value on application development projects, the code examples in the remainder of this chapter demonstrate validation logic in the form of automated tests.

Creating a Unit Test

To start implementing automated tests on your project, you need to create a test project first. In most circumstances, you want your automated tests to be in separate assemblies to avoid having them deployed in production environment. This example uses the Visual Studio unit-testing framework, available in all editions, except Express. Visual Studio provides a special project template, which you can choose using the Add New Project dialog shown in Figure 8.5. By convention, the test project has the same name as the project it tests, followed by the .Tests suffix. In this case, the project under test is *DataModel*, which is where the NorthwindEntities context class is defined along with the entity classes, so the test project is called DataModel.Tests.

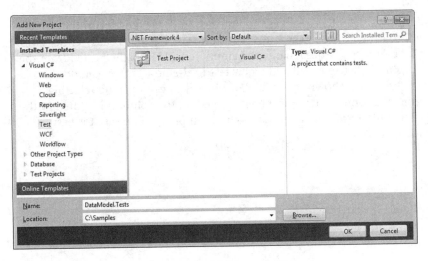

FIGURE 8.5 Adding a new test project to the solution.

When the new test project is created, you need to change it to add a reference to the project under test, DataModel in this example. Another change you might want to make is changing its root namespace to match the root namespace of the project under test. Although for regular projects, it is a good idea to have the root namespace of the project match the name of the assembly, for test projects such as the DateModel.Tests, changing the root namespace to DataModel helps you avoid having to add extra using statements to each file in the test project. The root namespace option can be changed using the project properties window in Visual Studio.

The new test project is created with a single empty test file in it—UnitTest1.cs. A test file contains a class, marked by the TestClassAttribute defined in the Microsoft.VisualStudio.TestTools.UnitTesting namespace. A *test class* can define one or more public methods marked with the TestMethodAttribute. These methods are the actual *tests*. In other words, a single test file can have multiple tests in it.

```
using Microsoft.VisualStudio.TestTools.UnitTesting;

namespace DataModel
{
    [TestClass]
    public class UnitTest1
    {
        [TestMethod]
        public void TestMethod1()
        {
        }
    }
}
```

Also by convention, each test file, as well as the test class in it, is named with the name of the class under test followed by the Test suffix, so a test class for the Product entity class is called ProductTest. You can either rename the empty test file initially created from the project template or simply delete it and add a new test to the project. You can do that with the Add New Test dialog shown in Figure 8.6, which you can open by selecting Add New Test from the context menu of the test project in the Solution Explorer. In the Add New Test dialog, unless you know the specific test template you need, it is best to start with the Basic Unit Test.

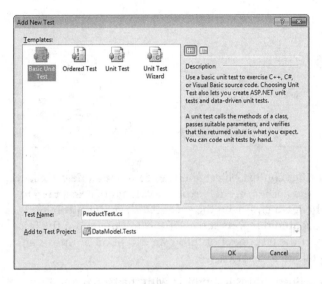

FIGURE 8.6 Adding a new unit test to the project.

You can now create your first test, or test method, to verify that the UnitPrice property of the Product entity is required at the same time the entity instance is saved to the database. Listing 8.2 shows the complete implementation of this test. As you can see, the test method is called UnitPrice_IsRequired, with an underscore serving as a separator between the name of the property under test and the description of the test itself. Because you could have multiple tests for the same property, using underscores helps to organize the test methods in logical groups.

LISTING 8.2 Testing Required UnitPrice Property of the Product Entity

```
using System.ComponentModel.DataAnnotations;
using System.Transactions;
using Microsoft.VisualStudio.TestTools.UnitTesting;

namespace DataModel
{
  [TestClass]
  public class ProductTest
  {
    [TestMethod]
    [ExpectedException(typeof(ValidationException))]
    public void UnitPrice_IsRequired()
    {
      using (new TransactionScope())
      using (NorthwindEntities context = new NorthwindEntities())
      {
        var product = new Product();
```

LISTING 8.2 Continued

```
        product.UnitPrice = null;
        context.Products.AddObject(product);
        context.SaveChanges();
      }
    }
  }
}
```

The test creates a new NorthwindEntities context object and tries to submit a new Product instance to the database without a valid UnitPrice. You expect a ValidationException to be thrown by the SaveChanges method, which is why the ExpectedException attribute was applied to the test method. Visual Studio reports success if this test method if the test does throws the expected exception. If the test does not throw an exception or throws an exception of an unexpected type, a failure is reported.

You can run this and all other tests defined in this test project with the help of the Test View window shown in Figure 8.7. You can find it under Test⯈ Windows in the main menu of Visual Studio.

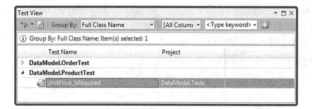

FIGURE 8.7 Running tests using the Test View window.

The results of test execution are shown in the Test Results window (see Figure 8.8).

FIGURE 8.8 Examining execution results in the Test Results window.

Test Isolation

Poor encapsulation can cause tests that previously completed successfully to fail. It is one of the most common reasons developers abandon automated tests. Notice that in the test shown in Listing 8.2, a TransactionScope around the NorthwindEntities context was used. As you recall from Chapter 2, "Entity Framework," a TransactionScope groups multiple data access operations in a single database transaction. If its Complete method is called before the TransactionScope object is disposed, all changes are committed to the database. However, if the TransactionScope object is disposed without calling Complete, all changes are rolled back. This test method takes advantage of this behavior and wraps all database changes in an anonymous TransactionScope, which is always rolled back to ensure that no junk data was left in the database by the previous test runs.

It is important to ensure that tests can run repeatedly and independently of each other in order to be effective quality improvement measures. If tests report false errors because data they expect to be in the database is missing or was changed by other tests, developers will stop running them and eventually stop maintaining them. Do not assume that any test data is already available in the database. If you are testing the Order entity, do not assume that particular Customer or Product entities are readily available. Instead, *create* them in your test and let the TransactionScope rollback the changes at the end of the test. It is fine to rely on seed data that must be available in any valid database for your application and implemented in your database deployment script; so, if you have a table that contains all 50 U.S. states your application uses to verify address information, you can probably assume that Florida is there:

Testing Validation of Different Properties

Testing validation logic of different properties presents another challenge—how do you distinguish a ValidationException thrown by one property from another? The ExpectedExceptionAttribute simply asserts that an exception of a certain type is thrown but cannot distinguish an exception thrown for the UnitPrice property from an exception thrown for the ProductName property. To verify validation exceptions down to the property level, you could modify the test, catch the validation exceptions, and examine the member names explicitly:

```
[TestMethod]
public void UnitPrice_IsRequired()
{
  using (new TransactionScope())
  using (var context = new NorthwindEntities())
  {
    var product = new Product();
    product.UnitPrice = null;
    context.Products.AddObject(product);
    try
    {
      context.SaveChanges();
      Assert.Fail();
    }
    catch (ValidationException e)
    {
      Assert.IsNotNull(e.ValidationResult.MemberNames);
```

```
        Assert.IsTrue(e.ValidationResult.MemberNames.Contains("UnitPrice"));
    }
  }
}
```

Unfortunately, you would also need to ensure that an exception is indeed thrown and that it is of the expected type. This requires almost a dozen lines of code to do what the ExpectedExceptionAttribute did in just one and makes automated tests verbose, discouraging developers from doing it.

Luckily, the Visual Studio unit-testing framework supports custom assertion attributes, and you can create one specifically to verify ValidationException instances. Instead of using the try/catch block, you can replace the ExpectedExceptionAttribute in the original version of the UnitPrice_IsRequired test method with the custom ExpectedValidationExceptionAttribute, shown in Listing 8.3, and implement the same test logic:

```
[TestMethod]
[ExpectedValidationException(MemberName = "UnitPrice")]
public void UnitPrice_IsRequired()
```

LISTING 8.3 ExpectedValidationExceptionAttribute

```
using System;
using System.Collections.Generic;
using System.ComponentModel.DataAnnotations;
using System.Linq;
using Microsoft.VisualStudio.TestTools.UnitTesting;

namespace DataModel
{
  [AttributeUsage(AttributeTargets.Method, AllowMultiple = false, Inherited = true)]
  public class ExpectedValidationExceptionAttribute: ExpectedExceptionBaseAttribute
  {
    public string MemberName { get; set; }

    protected override void Verify(Exception exception)
    {
      this.RethrowIfAssertException(exception);

      IEnumerable<string> memberNames = null;

      var validationException = exception as ValidationException;
      if (validationException != null)
        memberNames = validationException.ValidationResult.MemberNames;
```

```
        if (memberNames != null && memberNames.Contains(this.MemberName))
          return;

        string message = "ValidationException was expected";
        message += " with member name " + this.MemberName;
        message += ". Instead " + exception.GetType().FullName + " was thrown";
        if (memberNames != null && memberNames.Any())
          message += " with member name(s) " + string.Join(", ", memberNames);
        message += ".";
        throw new AssertFailedException(message);
    }
  }
}
```

The custom assertion attribute inherits from the base class,
ExpectedExceptionBaseAttribute, provided by the Visual Studio unit-testing framework
in the Microsoft.VisualStudio.TestTools.UnitTesting namespace. It defines a
property called MemberName, which specifies the name of the property for which a
ValidationException is expected. The ExpectedValidationExceptionAttribute also overrides the Verify method, which takes the actual exception that was thrown by the test
method and throws the AssertFailedException if the actual exception is not a
ValidationException or if it specifies an unexpected MemberName.

Integration Testing Versus Unit Testing

Developers familiar with automated testing will quickly point out that tests created with
the approach described here are *integration* tests and not *unit* tests. Testing purists
frequently frown upon the idea of testing the business and data access logic together like
this, citing poor precision, performance, and reliability of tests and their results. By design,
the integration tests are less precise than unit tests because they exercise multiple units of
code and might not allow you to differentiate between test failures caused by data access
errors and those caused by business logic errors. Because integration tests access an exter-
nal database, they are slower than unit tests that access only objects in memory. When
implemented incorrectly, the integration tests might be dependent on shared test data,
which leads to incorrect or unrepeatable test execution results.

In theory, testing the business logic with pure unit tests, separately from the data access
logic, improves test precision, performance, and reliability. With this approach, the data
access logic needs to be replaced with test doubles, such as stubs or mocks, allowing you
to differentiate business logic errors from data access errors. However, by making tests
more precise, you also reduce the test coverage. The unit tests of the business logic alone
will not let you know when something breaks due to a problem in the data access layer,
which is a much more common problem in applications created with object-relational
mappers like the Entity Framework. The rulebook answer to this problem is that you
should create unit tests for your data access *in addition* to the unit tests for the business
logic. In practice, the resulting volume and complexity of automated tests created with

the pure unit testing approach quickly grows out of control, often exceeding the size of the business logic itself by a factor of five or more. Many development teams try and quickly abandon the idea of automated testing because they cannot justify the effort required to implement and maintain the unit tests that, due to their narrow focus, do not significantly reduce the effort required perform the traditional system testing manually.

By starting with integration tests that exercise both business and data access logic, you immediately begin receiving benefits of automated testing with a minimal investment of effort. You know when your business logic fails either due to algorithmic errors or due to configuration errors in the O/R mapping. As long as you create data required for your tests programmatically, just as you would do in a unit test, the TransactionScope solves the problem of keeping the database, a shared test environment, clean and ready for repeated and reliable test execution. If developers on your team have local database environments, you will be able run hundreds of integration tests per minute.

With the integration-first approach, you still have the option of introducing unit testing for business logic *when* or *if* you discover that the number of tests has grown to the point where running the entire suite takes too long. By then, the sheer number of the integration tests will serve as proof of success of automated testing on this project. You will also have a good understanding of which integration tests are critical enough to be refactored into unit tests to be executed by every developer locally and which can be left as-is for your automated build to run on the server.

Declarative Validation

The System.ComponentModel.DataAnnotations namespace offers a number of validation attributes discussed in this section. By placing validation attributes on the individual properties of entity classes, you can implement business logic declaratively. Aside from being one of the quickest methods, declarative implementation of the business logic keeps it at the highest level of abstraction—as close to the conceptual level in the Entity Data Model designer as possible, helping the entity classes to stay easy to understand and maintain.

RequiredAttribute

The RequiredAttribute ensures that a value is not null and if the value is of type string, it ensures that it is not empty as well:

```
[Required]
public object ProductName { get; set; }
```

Using the property definition just given, you can create the following test to verify that a ValidationException will be thrown by the SaveChanges method if a valid ProductName has not been specified for a new Product instance:

```
[TestMethod]
[ExpectedValidationException(MemberName = "ProductName")]
public void ProductName_IsRequired()
```

```
{
  using (new TransactionScope())
  using (var context = new NorthwindEntities())
  {
    var product = new Product();
    product.ProductName = string.Empty;
    context.Products.AddObject(product);
    context.SaveChanges();
  }
}
```

NOTE

In dynamically generated web pages, the `RequiredAttribute` is typically enforced by the `RequiredFieldValidator` controls created by the field templates.

From a business point of view, requiring each product to have a name probably means that that it should not be empty. Unlike the *not null* constraint you can use in the database column definition, the `RequiredAttribute` has additional logic for strings that not only ensures that a string value is not null, but also that it does not contain only white-space characters. If a non-null, blank string were a valid product name, you could modify the property definition to set the `AllowEmptyStrings` property of the `RequiredAttribute` to true:

```
[Required(AllowEmptyStrings = true)]
public object ProductName { get; set; }
```

With this new definition of the `ProductName` property, the `RequiredAttribute` prevents null values but is happy to accept empty strings as product names. The test method just shown would now fail because `ValidationException` will not be thrown for the `ProductName` property.

NOTE

All other validation attributes discussed throughout the remainder of this section treat `null` values as valid. If a property cannot be `null`, you have to place a `RequiredAttribute` on it to prevent `null` values in addition to any other validation attributes it might need.

RangeAttribute

The `RangeAttribute` verifies that a value falls within a particular range, or more specifically, that the value is greater than or equal to the minimum value and less than or equal to the maximum value. In the Product entity, unless you are paying your customers to take merchandise off your hands, the `UnitPrice` property cannot be less than zero. You can implement this business rule by applying the `RangeAttribute` to it as shown here:

```
[Required]
[Range(0, int.MaxValue)]
public object UnitPrice { get; set; }
```

The following test verifies the implementation of the new business rule:

```
[TestMethod]
[ExpectedValidationException(MemberName = "UnitPrice")]
public void UnitPrice_MustBeGreaterThanZero()
{
    using (new TransactionScope())
    using (var context = new NorthwindEntities())
    {
        var product = new Product();
        product.UnitPrice = -1;
        context.Products.AddObject(product);
        context.SaveChanges();
    }
}
```

> **NOTE**
>
> In dynamically generated web pages, the RequiredAttribute is typically enforced by
> the RangeValidator controls created by the field templates.

The RangeAttribute offers two strongly typed constructors that take range values of
Double and Int32 types. These constructors should be sufficient for most numeric data
types, including the Decimal type used by the UnitPrice property. In addition to the
numeric values, the Range attribute can also validate values of any type that can be
converted from string and implements the IComparable interface such as the DateTime.
The following RangeAttribute verifies that values of the BirthDate property of the
Employee entity fall between 1/1/1900 and 12/31/2050:

```
[Range(typeof(DateTime), "1/1/1900", "12/31/2050")]
public object BirthDate { get; set; }
```

The following test method verifies the RangeAttribute applied to the BirthDate property
by trying to set it to year 74, which could be a problem if user interface code fails to add
century to a two-digit year entered by the user:

```
[TestMethod]
[ExpectedValidationException(MemberName = "BirthDate")]
public void BirthDate_Between1900And2050()
{
    using (new TransactionScope())
    using (var context = new NorthwindEntities())
    {
```

```
    var employee = new Employee();
    employee.BirthDate = new DateTime(74, 1, 1);
    context.Employees.AddObject(employee);
    context.SaveChanges();
  }
}
```

StringLengthAttribute

SQL Server allows you to specify the maximum length of values that can be stored in columns of string types such as CHAR and VARCHAR. However, the errors it reports when encountering values that are too long to be stored in the underlying database column without data truncation do not include the actual column name. This makes debugging of truncation errors unnecessarily difficult. Fortunately, the StringLengthAttribute can be used to validate the string length before the data is sent to the database server. Here is how you can extend the ProductName property of the Product entity class:

```
[Required]
[StringLength(40, MinimumLength = 2]
public object ProductName;
```

The StringLengthAttribute allows you to specify both minimum and maximum length that a string value can have. The *maximum* length is required and specified as the first argument of the constructor. The *minimum* length is optional and has to be specified explicitly by including the name of the MinimumLength property in the constructor.

The following test method verifies how the StringLengthAttribute works by initializing the ProductName property with a string that consists of 41 characters—one character too long. As you would expect from a validation attribute, this code throws a ValidationException, which unlike the low-level SqlException includes the display name of the column that caused the problem:

```
[TestMethod]
[ExpectedValidationException(MemberName = "ProductName")]
public void ProductName_MustBe40CharactersOrLess()
{
  using (new TransactionScope())
  using (var context = new NorthwindEntities())
  {
    var product = new Product();
    product.ProductName = new String('T', 41);
    context.Products.AddObject(product);
    context.SaveChanges();
  }
}
```

> **NOTE**
>
> In dynamically generated web pages, the `StringLengthAttribute` is enforced by the `DynamicValidator` controls created by the field templates. Some field templates also set the `MaxLength` property of the `TextBox` controls to limit the number of characters users can enter.

One downside to using the `StringLengthAttribute` is that it duplicates information about the size of the column. Normally, this information is stored in a single place in your application—the Entity Data Model. When it is duplicated in a hand-written `StringLengthAttribute`, you need to remember to update it in addition to the EMDX if the actual size of the database column changes. It would be a good idea to change the text template to have this attribute automatically as discussed in the "Customizing Entity Framework Code Generation" section earlier in this chapter.

RegularExpressionAttribute

The `RegularExpresionAttribute` can be used to ensure that string values match a particular pattern, such as a phone number or a URL. Here is how you can ensure that the `HomePage` property of the Supplier entity contains a valid URL:

```
[RegularExpression(
  @"(?i)(http|https)://[a-z0-9\-\.]+\.(com|org|net|mil|edu)")]
public object HomePage { get; set; }
```

The `RegularExpressionAttribute` constructor takes a string that contains a regular expression pattern that the values are expected to match. In this example, the pattern expects the URL to start with either *http* or *https*, followed by a "://," followed by a sequence of alpha-numeric symbols, dashes, and periods and one of five predefined top-level domains (.com, .org, and so on).

> **NOTE**
>
> Detailed discussion of regular expressions would take another book of this size. Please visit the following web page to learn more:
> http://msdn.microsoft.com/en-us/library/hs600312.aspx.

> **NOTE**
>
> In dynamically generated web pages, the `RegularExpressionAttribute` is typically enforced by the `RegularExpressionValidator` controls created by the field templates.

Due to the power and inherent complexity of regular expressions, it is a good idea to invest more effort in testing them. In particular, you might want to write both positive and negative tests to ensure not only that your regular expression rejects invalid values, but also that it accepts the valid ones:

```
[TestMethod]
public void HomePage_AcceptsValidUrl()
{
  using (new TransactionScope())
  using (var context = new NorthwindEntities())
  {
    var supplier = new Supplier();
    supplier.CompanyName = "Test Supplier";
    supplier.HomePage = "http://www.contoso.com";
    context.Suppliers.AddObject(supplier);
    context.SaveChanges();
  }
}


[TestMethod]
[ExpectedValidationException(MemberName = "HomePage")]
public void HomePage_RejectsInvalidUrl()
{
  using (new TransactionScope())
  using (var context = new NorthwindEntities())
  {
    var supplier = new Supplier();
    supplier.CompanyName = "Test Supplier";
    supplier.HomePage = "invalid://url";
    context.Suppliers.AddObject(supplier);
    context.SaveChanges();
  }
}
```

Unlike with most other validation attributes that manage to generate reasonably good error messages by default, the RegularExpressionAttribute cannot decipher the original intent and simply includes the entire regular expression pattern in the error message. You definitely don't want to display those error messages to the business users. As discussed in the *Validation Error Messages* section of this chapter, you can specify an alternative error message by setting the ErrorMessage property in the attribute constructor, for example:

```
[RegularExpression(
  @"(?i)(http|https)://[a-z0-9\-\.]+\.(com|org|net|mil|edu)",
  ErrorMessage = "Home Page must be a valid URL")]
public object HomePage { get; set; }
```

EnumDataTypeAttribute

Consider the OrderStatus enumerated type (or *enum* for short) defined in the sample project for the Order entity:

```
public enum OrderStatus: byte
{
    Draft = 0,
    Submitted = 1,
    Paid = 2,
    Fulfilled = 3
}
```

Due to the limitations in the current version of the Entity Framework, the OrderStatus property of the Order entity class is actually of type Byte and allows values other than the 0, 1, 2, and 3 defined in the enum. Even without the limitation, you could cast any value of a compatible numeric type, such as 10 of type Byte in this case, to the enum type, OrderStatus, and store it a variable or property of the enum type.

> **NOTE**
>
> The .NET Framework specifically allows variables of an enum type to store values that are not defined in the enum. This allows class library developers to add new items to existing enum types without breaking binary compatibility with applications that were compiled with the original version of a class library.

The EnumDataTypeAttribute verifies that a value is actually defined in the specified enumerated type. You can apply it to the OrderStatus property of the Order class to ensure that only values defined in the OrderStatus enum can be stored in it:

```
[EnumDataType(typeof(OrderStatus))]
public object OrderStatus { get; set; }
```

You can verify that this attribute works by writing the following test. It sets the OrderStatus property with the value 10, which is *not defined* in the OrderStatus enum. As expected, the validation code in the SaveChanges method detects this error and throws the ValidationException:

```
[TestMethod]
[ExpectedValidationException(MemberName = "OrderStatus")]
public void OrderStatus_RejectsInvalidValues()
{
    using (new TransactionScope())
    using (var context = new NorthwindEntities())
    {
        var order = CreateOrder();
        order.OrderStatus = 10;
        context.Orders.AddObject(order);
```

```
    context.SaveChanges();
  }
}
```

The `EnumDataTypeAttribute` supports not only the integral data types, such as `Byte` used in this example, but also enum and string data types. For properties of enum types, the `EnumDataTypeAttribute` ensures that the enum value is actually defined in the enum type. For `string` properties, the `EnumDataTypeAttribute` parses the enum value from the string and then checks if the enum type defines it. Keep in mind that it uses case-sensitive logic for string parsing, which might not be appropriate for validating string values entered by the users directly.

DataTypeAttribute

Although the `DataTypeAttribute` inherits from the `ValidationAttribute` class, it does not perform any actual validation. Its `IsValid` method only checks the attribute's own parameters. Dynamic Data uses the `DataTypeAttribute` when looking for a field template appropriate for a given property. For example, the `HomePage` property of the Supplier entity stores URLs, and by applying the `DataTypeAttribute` as shown next, you can make Dynamic Data use the URL field template, which generates a hyperlink:

```
[DataType(DataType.Url)]
public object HomePage { get; set; }
```

The `DataTypeAttribute` can help you to implement client-side validation in Dynamic Data web applications if you provide appropriate Edit mode field templates for the different values of the `DataType` enumeration, such as `Currency`, `Time`, or `PhoneNumber`. For details, please see Chapter 3.

Imperative Validation

The simple declarative validation discussed so far is a good first step but is rarely sufficient. Most enterprise applications require more complex validation logic that can span multiple properties, multiple entities, and require custom code.

CustomValidationAttribute

The `CustomValidationAttribute` allows you to specify a static method that will be invoked to validate a particular property. As an example, suppose that at Northwind Traders, all orders are entered electronically, directly into the system, so the `OrderDate` property of the Order entity should never be in the past. You cannot express this condition using the `RangeAttribute` because today's date is not a constant and cannot be specified in an attribute. Here is how you could accomplish this task with the `CustomValidationAttribute`:

```
[Display(Name = "Order Date")]
[CustomValidation(typeof(Order), "ValidateOrderDate")]
public object OrderDate { get; set; }
```

The first parameter of the CustomValidationAttribute constructor specifies the type of
class that implements the custom validation method, and the second specifies the name
of the method itself. Here is the definition of the ValidateOrderDate method taken from
the Order class:

```
public static ValidationResult ValidateOrderDate(
    DateTime? orderDate, ValidationContext context)
{
    if (orderDate != null && orderDate.Value < DateTime.Today)
    {
        return new ValidationResult(
            string.Format("{0} cannot be in the past", context.DisplayName),
            new string[] { context.MemberName });
    }

    return ValidationResult.Success;
}
```

A validation method must be static and must return a ValidationResult. As its first parameter, the validation method takes the value that needs to be validated, such as the value
of the OrderDate property. The type of the first method parameter must either have the
same type as the property, Nullable<DateTime> in this example, or be of type object.
The validation method can also have an optional second parameter of type
ValidationContext, which provides additional information about the property being
validated.

ValidationResult
If the value is correct, the validation method should return ValidationResult.Success, a
special constant for null, defined to make validation methods easier to understand. If the
value is invalid, the method should return an instance of the ValidationResult class with
detailed information about the error. The Validator class will use the information in the
ValidationResult to initialize the ValidationException it will throw when the errors are
detected.

The ErrorMessage property of the ValidationResult contains the error message that is
reported by the exception. This property is initialized by the *first* argument of the
ValidationResult constructor. This same error message is displayed to the users by the
DynamicValidator controls in Dynamic Data web applications. Notice how in this validation method, the DisplayName property of the ValidationContext object is used instead of
hard-coding the property name in the error message. The DisplayName is initialized with
the display name specified in the DisplayAttribute applied to the entity property or the
name of the property itself if no display name was specified explicitly.

The MemberNames property of the ValidationResult contains the names of the property or properties that have invalid values. It is initialized by the *second* argument of the ValidationResult constructor. The member names are used by the DynamicValidator controls in Dynamic Data web application to determine if their associated column is valid. This helps to report validation errors coming from custom validation code consistently with the errors coming from the validation attributes applied declaratively. You can also avoid hard-coding the property name here and rely on the MemberName property of the ValidationContext object, which has the name of the property being validated, OrderDate in this example.

Following is a test you can use to verify the initial implementation of the ValidateOrderDate validation method. Notice how it tries to create an order with a date that was five days ago. The error is detected by the ValidateOrderDate method, and a ValidationException is thrown by the SaveChanges method:

```
[TestMethod]
[ExpectedValidationException(MemberName = "OrderDate")]
public void OrderDate_CannotBeInThePast()
{
  using (new TransactionScope())
  using (var context = new NorthwindEntities())
  {
    var order = CreateOrder();
    order.OrderDate = DateTime.Today.AddDays(-5);
    context.Orders.AddObject(order);
    context.SaveChanges();
  }
}
```

Handling Null Values

When creating validation methods for nullable properties, check to see if the value is null *before* performing additional checks. If null values are valid according to your business rules, the method must return ValidationResult.Success. Otherwise, you need to decide if you want to rely on the RequiredAttribute or implement this logic in the custom validation method itself. Relying on the RequiredAttribute, as in the previous example, makes the CustomValidationAttribute behave consistently with the declarative validation attributes.

Placing the entire validation logic for a given property in a single validation method is typically more verbose; however, it might be easier to follow, especially as the validation rules get more and more complicated. Here is how you could rewrite this custom validation method to verify that the OrderDate is not in the past *and* that it is not null, making a separate RequiredAttribute unnecessary:

```
public static ValidationResult ValidateOrderDate(
  DateTime? orderDate, ValidationContext context)
{
  if (orderDate == null)
```

```
        {
            return new ValidationResult(
                string.Format("{0} is required", context.DisplayName),
                new string[] { context.MemberName });
        }

        if (orderDate.Value < DateTime.Today)
        {
            return new ValidationResult(
                string.Format("{0} cannot be in the past", context.DisplayName),
                new string[] { context.MemberName });
        }

        return ValidationResult.Success;
    }
```

Each of these two approaches of handling null values in custom validation methods has its own advantages. You are in the best position to decide what makes sense on your project; however, you might want to consider starting with the RequiredAttribute as it offers the easiest and smallest solution for the simple scenarios. You can always change your mind later *if* you need to.

Class-Level Validation Methods

You might have noticed that the VerifyOrderDate method actually creates a problem for orders that have already been placed. Imagine that a customer placed an order on Monday night, and on Tuesday morning, an employee ships the order and needs to change its status to Fulfilled. Because the OrderDate is already in the past, the application will not allow the employee to change the order.

The flaw in the original implementation of the VerifyOrderDate is that the value of OrderDate is checked separately from other properties of the Order entity. You still want to make sure that new orders are not submitted with a date in the past, but you also want to allow employees to update the order status later. One possible way to solve this problem is to check the OrderDate property only when the OrderStatus is null, which should be the case for the newly created Order entities before they are marked Submitted.

To perform a validation check that involves more than one property, change the VerifyOrderDate method so that instead of the OrderDate property value, it validates the entire Order entity instance. Begin by moving the CustomValidationAttribute from the OrderDate property to the Metadata class inside of the Order entity:

```
[CustomValidation(typeof(Order), "ValidateOrderDate")]
private abstract class Metadata
{
    [Required]
    [Display(Name = "Order Date")]
    public object OrderDate { get; set; }
}
```

You could also have placed the CustomValidationAttribute on the Order class itself to achieve the same effect. It is largely a matter of personal preference. Placing data annotation attributes on the private Metadata class helps keep the entity class clean and prevents unnecessary details from leaking into help files you might be generating from the documentation comments using tools like Sandcastle.

Here is the updated version of the validation method itself:

```
public static ValidationResult ValidateOrderDate(
  Order order, ValidationContext context)
{
  if (order.OrderStatus == null)
  {
    if (order.OrderDate != null &&
        order.OrderDate.Value < DateTime.Today)
    {
      return new ValidationResult(
        "Order Date cannot be in the past",
        new string[] { "OrderDate" });
    }
  }

  return ValidationResult.Success;
}
```

The new version of the validation method takes an Order as its first parameter and uses this instance to access values of the OrderStatus and OrderDate properties. Unfortunately, now that the method is validating the Order entity, you can no longer use DisplayName and MemberName properties of the ValidationContext object to generate the ValidationResult. For simplicity, they are hard-coded in this example, although it would have been better to either use string constants or resources.

The ValidationContext object the custom validation methods receive as a second parameter has a property called ObjectInstance, which allows you to access the entity instance even in *property* validation methods. Although this works fine in the programmatic tests, when a property validation method is invoked during a web page post-back by DynamicValidator controls, the original entity instance does not exist, and all you have is a property value. In other words, if you need to access multiple entity properties to perform validation, you have to use *class-level* validation methods.

Validating Multiple Rules

You can use multiple validation methods and multiple instances of the
`CustomValidationAttribute` to implement different validation rules. However, if some of
the validation rules are related, it might be easier to implement them together in a single
method. Continuing this example of validating orders, suppose the Northwind Traders
Company allows customers to specify a date they want to have their orders delivered;
however, the orders cannot be delivered in fewer than three days. Validation of the
`RequiredDate` property of the Order entity is closely related to the validation of the
`OrderDate` property because both properties must be validated when the order is
submitted.

The `System.ComponentModel.DataAnnotations` namespace defines a special interface,
`IValidatableObject` that you can implement in entity classes to validate multiple rules at
once. The interface defines a single method called `Validate`, which takes a
`ValidationContext` object as a parameter and returns a collection of `ValidationResult`
objects:

```
public interface IValidatableObject
{
   IEnumerable<ValidationResult> Validate(
     ValidationContext validationContext);
}
```

Notice how similar this method is to the custom validation methods created earlier.
Because `Validate` is an *instance* method, it does not need a separate parameter to receive
the object to validate, and because it can validate multiple rules, it returns an `IEnumerable`
instead of a single `ValidationResult`. Listing 8.4 shows how you implement it in the
`Order` entity class to verify the rules related to both `OrderDate` and `RequiredDate`
properties.

LISTING 8.4 Implementing IValidatableObject Interface

```
using System;
using System.Collections.Generic;
using System.ComponentModel;
using System.ComponentModel.DataAnnotations;

partial class Order : IValidatableObject
{
  public IEnumerable<ValidationResult> Validate(
    ValidationContext validationContext)
  {
    var results = new List<ValidationResult>();
    if (this.OrderStatus != null)
    {
      if (this.OrderDate == null)
```

```
      {
        results.Add(
          new ValidationResult("Order Date is required", new[] { "OrderDate" }));
      }
      else
      {
        if (this.OrderDate.Value < DateTime.Today)
        {
          results.Add(
            new ValidationResult("Order Date cannot be in the past",
              new[] { "OrderDate" }));
        }

        if (this.RequiredDate != null &&
          this.RequiredDate <= this.OrderDate.Value.AddDays(3))
        {
          results.Add(
            new ValidationResult(
              "Required Date must be greater than Order Date + 3 days",
              new[] { "RequiredDate" }));
        }
      }
    }

    return results;
  }
}
```

As you can see, the method performs a number of checks and returns zero or more
ValidationResult objects in a List.

> **NOTE**
>
> You can also take advantage of the C# iterators, which allow using the yield return
> statement and eliminate the need to maintain a list of ValidationResult objects. You
> can find more details on iterators at http://msdn.microsoft.com/
> en-us/library/dscyy5s0.aspx.

When validating an object that implements the IValidatableObject interface, the
Validator class calls its Validate method *after* invoking any validation attributes that
might have been applied to the class or its properties.

Reporting Multiple Errors

As you recall from Listing 8.1, the Validate method of the UnleashedObjectContext class calls the static ValidateObject method of the Validator class to validate all new and modified entity objects. This method throws a ValidationException for the first validation error it encounters. Even though the Validate method of the Order class might report two errors at the same time (one for the OrderDate and one for the RequiredDate properties), only the first one is reported through the exception.

Although reporting a single error at a time might not be a problem in simple pages, like the Order entry form in the sample application, as the number of fields on the form increases, fixing one error only to get another is not very user friendly. Figure 8.9 illustrates the problem.

FIGURE 8.9 First of multiple errors reported in a Dynamic Data web page.

This is not a problem with the built-in validation attributes such as the RequiredAttribute or the CustomValidationAttribute applied to individual properties because they are invoked directly by separate DynamicValidator controls inside the field templates on the web page. In other words, all *property-level* validation attributes are evaluated independently, and all errors are reported to the user at the same time. However, *class-level* CustomValidationAttribute instances and the Validate method of the IValidatableObject interface are invoked only by the ValidateObject method called in the SaveChanges method of the UnleashedObjectContext class, and only the first error is reported.

IDynamicValidatorException Interface

Dynamic Data defines a special interface, IDynamicValidatorException, that allows exception classes to supply information about multiple errors that might have occurred during a single operation. This interface defines a single property, InnerExceptions, which returns a dictionary of entity property names and exceptions encountered for these properties.

```
public interface IDynamicValidatorException
{
    IDictionary<string, Exception> InnerExceptions { get; }
}
```

The built-in `EntityDataSource` control takes advantage of this interface when reporting errors that occur when it tries to assign field values received from the form controls to the properties of entity objects. The Entity Framework implements its own, limited, validation based on the rules embedded directly in the entity data model (EDMX), such as preventing assignment of a `null` value to an entity property that does not allow it. When these errors are detected, the `EntityDataSource` control collects all errors for a given entity object and throws the `EntityDataSourceValidationException`, which implements the `IDynamicValidatorException` interface. In the presentation layer, the `DynamicValidator` controls check all exceptions thrown by the data source control, and if a particular exception implements the `IDynamicValidatorException` interface, the validator controls use its `InnerExceptions` dictionary to find exceptions that apply to the entity properties they validate.

Unfortunately, the `IDynamicValidatorException` is defined in the `System.Web.Extensions` assembly and where the `EntityDataSourceValidationException` is defined in the `System.Web.Entity`. This is not a problem for web applications; however, for other types of applications, using these types means taking a dependency on ASP.NET, which is only included in the full version of the .NET framework and *not* in the client profile.

Modifying ObjectContext to Report Multiple Errors

To avoid adding a dependency on the presentation framework to the business layer of the application, you can use another built-in exception type - `AggregateException`. The .NET Framework version 4 introduced this class in the `System` namespace to support reporting of multiple errors in the Parallel Task Library (TPL). `AggregateException` also defines a property called `InnerExceptions`, although it stores a `ReadOnlyCollection` of Exception objects instead of a `Dictionary`. Here is how declaration of this class looks in simplified form:

```
public class AggregateException : Exception
{
    public ReadOnlyCollection<Exception> InnerExceptions { get; }
}
```

Here is a new version of the `Validate` method of the `UnleashedObjectContext` class that reports multiple validation errors in a single `AggregateException`:

```
private void Validate(ObjectStateEntry stateEntry)
{
    object entity = stateEntry.Entity;
    var context = new ValidationContext(entity, null, null);
    var results = new List<ValidationResult>();
```

```
    if (!Validator.TryValidateObject(entity, context, results, true))
      ThrowValidationException(entity, results);
}
```

The new version calls the `TryValidateObject` method of the static `Validator` class. Unlike the `ValidateObject` method used previously, which throws a single `ValidationException` for the *first* error it detects, the `TryValidateObject` method invokes *all* validation attributes and implementations of the `IValidatableObject` interface. The `TryValidateObject` method collects the errors in the list of `ValidationResult` objects it receives as the third parameter and returns `false` if any errors were detected.

The `ThrowValidationException` method (shown next) uses the validation results to create a list of `ValidationException` objects. If multiple validation results were reported, it throws the `AggregateException`. Otherwise, it throws the `ValidationException` to mimic the simple behavior implemented earlier:

```
protected static void ThrowValidationException(
    object entity, IEnumerable<ValidationResult> results)
{
    var exceptions = new List<ValidationException>();
    foreach (ValidationResult result in results)
      exceptions.Add(new ValidationException(result, null, entity));

    if (exceptions.Count == 1)
      throw exceptions[0];

    throw new AggregateException(exceptions);
}
```

NOTE

The `AggregateException` does not inherit from the `ValidationException` class. Now that the `SaveChanges` method can throw two different exception types, many of the automated tests written so far will fail because they only expect the `ValidationException`. To make them pass, change the `ExpectedValidationExceptionAttribute` to support both types of validation exceptions. You can find the updated implementation of this attribute in the source code accompanying this book.

Extending DynamicValidator to Support AggregateException

As discussed in Chapter 3 and Chapter 6, Dynamic Data relies on the `DynamicValidator` control for exception handling. When used in a field template, this control is responsible for evaluating the validation attributes applied to the entity property the template instance represents. In field and page templates, this control also handles any exceptions Entity Framework may throw. Here is the part of this class that implements exception handling:

```
public class DynamicValidator : BaseValidator
{
    protected virtual Exception ValidationException { get; set; }
    protected virtual void ValidateException(Exception exception);
}
```

The control calls the ValidateException method whenever the EntityDataSource fires its Exception event. The method receives an Exception object and determines whether it represents an error condition expected by the DynamicValidator control. If it does, the ValidateException method assigns the exception object to the ValidationException property. If this property is not null during page validation, the DynamicValidator uses it to display the exception's error message.

Out of the box, DynamicValidator supports only ValidationException and exception types, like EntityDataSourceValidationException, that implement the IDynamicValidatorException interface. Because AggregateException used in this example does not implement this interface, the DynamicValidator controls simply ignore it and let the ASP.NET runtime from generate a yellow page of death. To handle AggregateException and other types of expected exceptions your business layer may throw, you need to subclass the DynamicValidator control and override its ValidateException method.

When overriding the ValidateException method, remember that a single web page can contain a number of dynamic validators. The validators created by field templates are associated with specific entity properties (for these controls, the Column property defined in the DynamicValidator base class returns a MetaColumn object describing their entity property). These validators should report only the exceptions related to their respective entity properties. However, the validator at the top of the page is not associated with any particular entity property (its Column property is null) and should report only the exceptions related to the entire entity.

The ValidationException class used in this example allows you to determine if an error is related to a particular entity property by examining its ValidationResult. The MemberNames property of the ValidationResult can be empty if the error is not related to any particular entity property or contain multiple property names depending on how the validation logic was implemented by the entity class.

For complete details on how to extend the DynamicValidator control and implement support for AggregateException that contains multiple ValidationException instances, please refer to the UnleashedValidator control in the sample solution accompanying this book. Figure 8.10 shows how multiple validation errors are reported in the sample web application where all field and page templates have been modified to use the UnleashedValidator control instead of the built-in DynamicValidator.

FIGURE 8.10 Multiple errors correctly reported on a Dynamic Data web page.

Validating Entity State Changes

Sometimes validating current state of an entity is insufficient. Consider the Order entity and its OrderStatus property, which indicates whether an order has been submitted, paid, or fulfilled. It would be bad if someone could change the status of a fulfilled order back to paid and receive a second product free. Here is a code example that illustrates the problem:

```
using (var context = new NorthwindEntities())
{
   var order = CreateOrder();
   order.OrderStatus = (byte)OrderStatus.Fulfilled;
   context.Orders.AddObject(order);
   context.SaveChanges();
   order.OrderStatus = (byte)OrderStatus.Paid;
   context.SaveChanges();
}
```

The current implementation of the validation logic in the Order class has no knowledge of the previous state of the entity and cannot distinguish a valid order, for which a payment had just been processed, from a rogue order that was tampered with.

Accessing Original Property Values with ObjectStateManager

As discussed in Chapter 2, the Entity Framework keeps track of all changes made to entities in order to support optimistic concurrency. Each ObjectContext, such as the NorthwindEntities in these examples, has an ObjectStateManager, which uses ObjectStateEntry objects to keep track of both *current* and *original* property values for each entity. Here is how you can take advantage of this capability and compare the current value of the OrderStatus property with the original:

```
using (var context = new NorthwindEntities())
{
   var order = CreateOrder();
   order.OrderStatus = (byte)OrderStatus.Fulfilled;
   context.Orders.AddObject(order);
   context.SaveChanges();
   order.OrderStatus = (byte)OrderStatus.Paid;
   var stateEntry = context.ObjectStateManager.GetObjectStateEntry(order);
   byte originalStatus = (byte)stateEntry.OriginalValues["OrderStatus"];
   if (originalStatus == (byte)OrderStatus.Fulfilled &&
       order.OrderStatus != (byte)OrderStatus.Fulfilled)
   {
      // We have a problem
   }
   context.SaveChanges();
}
```

In this new version, the code first calls the GetObjectStateEntry method of the
ObjectStateManager to retrieve an ObjectStateEntry, which allows accessing original
property values of the entity via its OriginalValues property. This property returns an
object of type DbDataRecord defined in the System.Data namespace by the ADO.NET
framework. You can use its indexer to access the original property values by name. Having
retrieved the original value of the OrderStatus property, you can compare it against the
current value in the entity object itself.

Accessing Original Property Values in Validation Methods

Out of the box, validation methods, whether they are defined by applying the
CustomValidationAttribute or implementing the IValidatableObject interface, do
not have access to the ObjectStateEntry, the ObjectStateManager, or even the
ObjectContext for that matter. To access the original property values inside the validation
methods, this information needs to be supplied to them by the Validate method of the
UnleashedObjectContext class. Luckily, ValidationContext (which all validation methods
can receive as a parameter) defines the Items property of type IDictionary<object,
object> *specifically* for that purpose.

Here is how the Validate method in the UnleashedObjectContext was modified to create
the Items dictionary and place an ObjectStateEntry instance in it for the validation
methods to find:

```
private void Validate(ObjectStateEntry stateEntry)
{
   object entity = stateEntry.Entity;

   var items = new Dictionary<object, object>();
   items[typeof(ObjectStateEntry)] = stateEntry;
```

8

```
      var context = new ValidationContext(entity, null, items);

      var results = new List<ValidationResult>();
      if (!Validator.TryValidateObject(entity, context, results, true))
      {
        ThrowValidationException(entity, results);
      }
    }
```

Notice the ObjectStateEntry instance is stored in the dictionary using its own type as the key. This is not a strict requirement; you simply need a well-known value to serve as the key so that validation methods can find it in the dictionary. Using the type itself simply avoids having to define an extra constant just for this purpose. The dictionary is passed to the ValidationContext constructor as the third parameter.

Having changed the validation infrastructure to store the ObjectStateEntry instances in the ValidationContext, you can now implement a validation method in the Order class that takes advantage of it:

```
    [MetadataType(typeof(Order.Metadata))]
    partial class Order
    {
      private abstract class Metadata
      {
        [CustomValidation(typeof(Order), "ValidateOrderStatus")]
        public object OrderStatus { get; set; }
      }

      public static ValidationResult ValidateOrderStatus(
        byte? newStatus, ValidationContext context)
      {
        var stateEntry = (ObjectStateEntry)
         context.Items[typeof(ObjectStateEntry)];
        if (stateEntry.State == EntityState.Modified)
        {
          byte? oldStatus = (byte?)stateEntry.OriginalValues["OrderStatus"];
          if (oldStatus == (byte?)DataModel.OrderStatus.Fulfilled &&
              newStatus != (byte?)DataModel.OrderStatus.Fulfilled)
          {
            return new ValidationResult(
              "Status of fulfilled orders should not be modified",
              new string[] { "OrderStatus" });
          }
        }
        return ValidationResult.Success;
      }
```

}

In this example, a custom validation method called ValidateOrderStatus is associated with the OrderStatus property in the metadata class. The validation method first retrieves the ObjectStateEntry instance that contains the Order entity being validated from the Items dictionary of the ValidationContext object. It then checks the current State of the entity and only performs the validation if the entity is Modified. Because the entity state could also be Added, Deleted, Detached, or Unchanged, you only want to check the OrderStatus property when it is appropriate based on your business rules. You also want to access the OriginalValues property only when the original values are actually available; the property throws the InvalidOperationException when the entity state is Added.

Handling DBNull Values

The OriginalValues property of the ObjectStateEntry class returns an object of type DbDataRecord, which is shared by the Entity Framework with classic ADO.NET. Unfortunately, this means that the original null values are returned as objects of type DBNull and the code has to be prepared to handle them accordingly. In particular, this means that you cannot simply cast the original OrderStatus value to type Nullable<Byte> because DBNull values cannot be converted to this type and throw an InvalidCastException.

One workaround for this problem is to store OrderStatus values in variables of type Object and to use the static Object.Equals method to compare them. Because it takes the object type into account, you can safely compare values of type DBNull and Nullable<Byte> for equality. Here is a new version of the ValidateOrderStatus method, which now correctly handles the scenario where the original value of the OrderStatus is DBNull:

```
public static ValidationResult ValidateOrderStatus(
  byte? newStatus, ValidationContext context)
{
  var stateEntry = (ObjectStateEntry)
    context.Items[typeof(ObjectStateEntry)];
  if (stateEntry.State == EntityState.Modified)
  {
    object oldStatus = stateEntry.OriginalValues["OrderStatus"];
    if (object.Equals(oldStatus, (byte)DataModel.OrderStatus.Fulfilled)
     && !object.Equals(newStatus, (byte)DataModel.OrderStatus.Fulfilled))
    {
      return new ValidationResult(
        "Status of fulfilled orders should not be modified",
        new string[] { "OrderStatus" });
    }
  }
  return ValidationResult.Success;
}
```

Although this approach works, accessing values in the weakly typed object form prevents you from taking advantage of the additional validation that compiler could provide for the values in their original (Nullable<Byte>) form. The DbDataRecord object returns values of type DBNull because this class was designed in ADO.NET version 1, which did not support nullable types that were added to the .NET Framework in version 2. Luckily, with lambda expressions and extension methods introduced in version 3 of the .NET Framework, you can bring the DbDataRecord class into the twenty-first century.

Listing 8.5 shows a static class called DbDataRecordExtensions that defines an extension method called Get for the DbDataRecord class. This class is available in the Unleashed.EntityFramework project of the sample solution accompanying this book.

LISTING 8.5 DbDataRecord Extensions Methods

```
using System;
using System.Data.Common;
using System.Linq.Expressions;

namespace Unleashed.EntityFramework
{
  public static class DbDataRecordExtensions
  {
    public static T Get<T>(this DbDataRecord record, Expression<Func<T>> property)
    {
      string propertyName = ((MemberExpression)property.Body).Member.Name;
      object value = record[propertyName];
      if (value == DBNull.Value)
        return default(T);
      else
        return (T)value;
    }
  }
}
```

The first parameter of the Get method is declared with the keyword this, which allows you to call this static method as if it were an instance method of the DbDataRecord class. The second parameter is a lambda expression that you can use instead of hard-coding the property name as a string. Here's how to change the ValidateOrderStatus method to take advantage of this:

```
    public static ValidationResult ValidateOrderStatus(
      byte? newStatus, ValidationContext context)
    {
      var stateEntry = (ObjectStateEntry)
        context.Items[typeof(ObjectStateEntry)];
      if (stateEntry.State == EntityState.Modified)
      {
```

```
    var order = (Order)stateEntry.Entity;
    byte? oldStatus = stateEntry.OriginalValues
      .Get(() => order.OrderStatus);
    if (oldStatus == (byte)DataModel.OrderStatus.Fulfilled)
     && newStatus != (byte)DataModel.OrderStatus.Fulfilled))
    {
      return new ValidationResult(
        "Status of fulfilled orders should not be modified",
        new string[] { "OrderStatus" });
    }
  }
  return ValidationResult.Success;
}
```

Here, the Get extension method uses the () => order.OrderStatus lambda expression to determine the name of the property, OrderStatus, which it passes to the indexer of the DbDataRecord object to retrieve the original property values. If the original value is DBNull, the Get method returns a default value of the property type—a value that an uninitialized variable of that type would have if you tried to access it. In case of the OrderStatus property, whose type is Nullable<Byte>, the default value is null; for a non-nullable type, such as Byte, the default value would have been 0. If, however, the original value retrieved from the DbDataRecord object is not DBNull, the Get method returns the actual value after casting it to the type of the property itself.

The Get extension method offers several advantages. On one hand, it allows you to avoid having to write special logic to handle DBNull values. On the other hand, it allows you to specify properties as strongly-typed lambda expressions as opposed to hard-coded string literals or constants. They are not only easier to write (with the help from IntelliSense in the Visual Studio editor), but if you ever need to rename the property, the compiler ensures that all references are properly updated.

Summary

The System.ComponentModel.DataAnnotations namespace offers a robust validation framework, which allows implementing validation rules declaratively by placing data annotation attributes, or imperatively, by writing code.

The validation framework is fully integrated in Dynamic Data web applications; a helper class, Validator, can be used to integrate validation with other frameworks as well. Version 4.0 of Entity Framework does not support the validation framework out of the box, and additional steps are necessary to extend object context classes to automatically validate entity objects before they are submitted to the database.

Automated testing allows you to improve the quality of your applications without significant additional effort. With integration tests, you begin reaping the benefits of automated testing almost immediately. However, care should be taken to isolate tests and make sure that they can run repeatedly and independently of each other. `TransactionScope` is the simplest way to isolate integration tests that access the database.

A number of built-in validation attributes is included in the framework out of the box, including attributes for performing required, string length, range, enum, and regular expression checks. Additional validation attributes can be implemented by inheriting from the `ValidationAttribute` class.

Imperative validation logic can be implemented by placing `CustomValidationAttribute` on individual properties or entire classes and implementing special validation methods that return `ValidationResult` objects. Classes can also implement the `IValidatableObject` interface to validate multiple rules and return multiple validation results.

CHAPTER 9

Implementing Business Logic

Business logic, also known as *domain logic*, is code that implements a developer's interpretation of a business domain where the application is intended to solve one or more problems and address opportunities. Because a particular business domain can be described from different points of view, there are different definitions of what constitutes the business logic. This chapter discusses implementation of logic related to real-life *entities*, such as Customers, Products, and Orders, as well as *rules* that determine how these entities interact with each other.

The entities and rules are not directly related to any particular software application; instead, they describe the business itself. Similar to how a retailer could be selling products from a brick-and-mortar store directly to customers, accept orders by phone, allow customers to pick products up, or provide a website where customers submit orders that will be shipped to them by mail, different software applications can implement the same business logic as well. A sales clerk at a physical store could use a Windows-based point-of-sale application to sell a product, and a customer could use a Web-based application to place the order online. In both instances, the order needs to be checked to make sure that the product is in stock, order total must be calculated, product inventory needs to be updated, out-of-stock products need to be reordered, and so on.

In part due to the common need to support the same business services through different applications and in part due to their relative stability, there is a wide agreement in the software development industry that separating the business logic from its presentation is beneficial as it allows reusing the business logic in multiple applications. Separation of business logic from presentation is especially important in ASP.NET Dynamic Data applications. Because virtually the entire user interface of a web application can be generated dynamically, embedding the business logic directly in the web pages of the application is not only less attractive but also more cumbersome. To take advantage of the productivity improvements Dynamic Data offers, you as a web developer need to know how to implement business logic *outside* of the web pages.

Entity Design

Entities are abstractions of things in the business domain. They are implemented as classes in the application and as tables in the database. Although some similarities exist (class properties are similar to table columns for instance), the object-oriented and relational models are very different. The ADO.NET Entity Framework, LINQ to SQL, and other frameworks attempt to bridge the gap between these two radically different ways of representing information by implementing object-relational mapping.

Good entity design requires application of both object-oriented and relational design principles. It would be foolish to try addressing both of these vast topics in this chapter, or even in this book. It is assumed that you already know how to create a class that represents a real-world object or person and use encapsulation and abstraction principles to expose its key attributes as properties. It is also assumed that you know how to create a table to store this information in the database and use normalization techniques to reduce duplication. With these assumptions in mind, this section focuses on practical application of the object-oriented and relational design principles and some of the common pitfalls developers encounter with the Entity Framework.

Measure Impact of Inheritance on Query Performance

Inheritance is one of the most powerful concepts in object-oriented design, allowing a much higher level of reuse and encapsulation than the relational model provides. With the Entity Framework supporting *table-per-type*, *table-per-concrete type*, and *table-per-hierarchy* methods of mapping class hierarchies to database tables, using inheritance in your entity model becomes a very attractive option.

Beware! Although the Entity Framework makes LINQ queries over type hierarchies look deceptively simple, there are significant performance costs associated with the use of inheritance in your conceptual model. Consider the conceptual model shown in Figure 9.1, where you have an abstract base class called User and two concrete classes inheriting from it—Customer and Employee. The Entity Framework allows you to select both Customer and Employee entities by writing a simple LINQ query like this:

```
var users = from u in context.Users
            select u;
```

You can also select all entities of a particular type by using the OfType LINQ extension method, such as the next query, which returns all entities of Customer type:

```
var customers = from c in context.Users.OfType<Customer>()
                select c;
```

Although these LINQ queries work with all three types of inheritance mapping, it is important that you understand how each type of mapping is implemented at the database level, how each type of LINQ queries are translated into SQL, and how they affect the performance of your application. If you are considering using inheritance in your entity model, carefully review the tradeoffs described in this section and measure the impact of inheritance on the performance of *your* system by profiling it. Do not assume that simple LINQ queries will be fast.

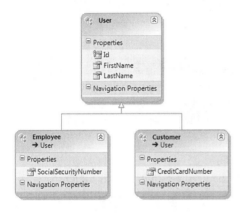

FIGURE 9.1 Conceptual model with inheritance hierarchy.

Table-per-Concrete Type Mapping

With *table-per-concrete type* mapping, each concrete class in the inheritance hierarchy gets its own table. The Employees and Customers tables in the database diagram shown in Figure 9.2 include columns for storing not only the concrete types, Employee and Customer, respectively, but also the abstract base type, User. Notice how both of these tables include the FirstName and LastName columns.

FIGURE 9.2 Table-per-concrete type mapping.

Because database designers most commonly use this type of entity modeling, table-per-concrete type looks like a good way to extract the commonality into a base class. However, although this type of mapping offers good performance for queries against specific concrete types, it has a significant performance penalty for querying across all base types because it relies on the UNION operator to combine results of multiple queries. Table 9.1 shows the examples.

TABLE 9.1 SQL Generated with Table-per-Concrete Type Mapping

LINQ	SQL
from u in context.Users select u;	SELECT * FROM Employees UNION ALL SELECT * FROM Customers
from c in context.Users.OfType<Customer>() select c;	SELECT * FROM Customers

> **NOTE**
>
> Examples of SQL queries generated by the Entity Framework in this section show pseudo-code, which was significantly modified to reduce size and make it easy to compare with LINQ code. The Entity Framework does not generate SELECT * SQL statements.

Whereas in plain SQL, the UNION statement has to be used explicitly, with LINQ to Entities, the query looks as if it spans only one table, making it easy to write queries that will perform poorly due to excessive unions.

Table-per-Type Mapping

With *table-per-type* mapping, each class, regardless of whether it is concrete or abstract, gets its own table in the database. Figure 9.3 shows an example of this type of mapping. As you can see, the User class is mapped to the Users table, with Employee and Customer classes mapped to the Users_Employee and Users_Customer tables, respectively.

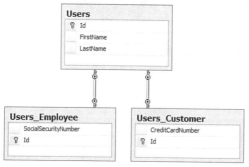

FIGURE 9.3 Table-per-type mapping.

With table-per-type of mapping, iterating over the entities of the base class User requires an outer join with all other tables in the hierarchy because Entity Framework has to instantiate entities of appropriate type, Customer and Employee. Querying for instances of a derived type Customer will be more efficient as it results in an inner join of the tables where its data is stored.

TABLE 9.2 SQL Generated with Table-per-Type Mapping

LINQ	SQL
from u in context.Users select u;	SELECT * FROM Users LEFT OUTER JOIN Users_Customer ON Users.Id = Users_Customer.Id LEFT OUTER JOIN Users_Employee ON Users.Id = Users_Employee.Id
from c in context.Users.OfType<Customer>() select c;	SELECT * FROM Users JOIN Users_Customer ON Users.Id = Users_Customer.Id
from u in context.Users select new { u.FirstName, u.LastName };	SELECT FirstName, LastName FROM Users

Again, the complexity of the actual SQL statement is hidden from the developer writing the LINQ query, making it easy to write queries that are inefficient due to excessive joins. It is possible to optimize these queries with the help of projections, which can reduce or eliminate joins from the generated SQL; however, as a developer you need to understand what is going on.

Table-Per-Hierarchy Mapping

With *table-per-hierarchy* mapping, all classes in a given hierarchy are mapped to the same database table, with a particular column storing a discriminator value that determines the entity type. Figure 9.4 shows a table called Users, which stores both Customer and Employee entities, using the UserType column to distinguish between them.

FIGURE 9.4 Table-per-hierarchy mapping.

The table-per-hierarchy mapping offers a good performance tradeoff between queries across the base types and the queries across the derived types. The SQL generated with this mapping approach is also much closer to the original LINQ code developers write. As you can see in the second example of Table 9.3, the OfType extension method is translated into a straightforward WHERE clause.

TABLE 9.3 SQL Generated with Table-per-Hierarchy Mapping

LINQ	SQL
from u in context.Users select u;	SELECT * FROM Users
from c in context.Users.OfType<Customer>() select c;	SELECT * FROM Users WHERE UserType = 'C'

This approach is also made attractive by Microsoft SQL Server's support of *Sparse Columns*—a storage optimization option for tables with large numbers of nullable columns, which can help storing entities of different types more effective. However, with a small number of types in a hierarchy, the discriminator column might not be selective enough, and the query optimizer might choose to perform a full table scan for each query even if an index covering this column exists. This approach also violates the third form of database normalization, which requires each column to represent a fact about the key, making it unpopular with database designers.

NOTE

Each of the three O/R Mapping approaches discussed here have different trade-offs, making them appropriate for different scenarios. *Theoretically*, the table-per-type mapping should work better for shallow hierarchies of significantly different classes, and the table-per-hierarchy mapping should work better for deep hierarchies of classes with small differences. The table-per-concrete type mapping should work better in queries that retrieve objects of leaf types, and the other types of mapping should work better for queries that retrieve information from base classes. However, the only *reliable* way to determine the best mapping type is through measurement of *actual* results.

Performance tuning and optimization are best left for later stages of application development, when sufficient information and functionality is available to simulate real-world usage scenarios. However, if you are certain you will need to use class inheritance in your entity model, consider starting with the table-per-hierarchy mapping because it offers the best combination of simplicity and performance.

Keep the Conceptual and Storage Models as Close as Possible

Although being able to fine-tune the object-oriented (conceptual) and the relational (storage) models of your application seems like a good idea, this optimization comes at the cost of a significant increase in effort to maintain the two models and mappings between them. Because the Entity Framework allows this flexibility, it cannot automatically update both models based on a change in one. For instance, if you want to change the name of a particular column in the database, you also have to rename the corresponding property in the conceptual model. The same goes for renaming or deleting tables, changing relationships between them, and so on—all of these common changes have to be done in both models separately.

Regardless of the approach you choose to developing your entity model—database-first, model-first, or code-first—you want to minimize the amount of work you spend on the secondary model. In other words, if you start by developing the database model first, you want to spend the least amount of work on maintaining your conceptual model and application classes. Likewise, if you start by developing the application classes first, you want to spend as little time as possible tweaking the database tables the Entity Framework generates for you.

The best way to keep the conceptual and storage models in sync over the life of the application is to reduce the differences between them. Ideally, you want to be able to regenerate your entire secondary model without having to make any tweaks manually. This could require introducing some of the database principles in the class design or taking object-oriented principles into account when designing the tables. For instance, you might want to sacrifice some of the normalization rules or break some of your DBA's favorite naming conventions to make the generated classes easier to use in a .NET language.

This advice might feel counter-intuitive and go against the selling points of the O/R mapping frameworks in general and the Entity Framework in particular. It is based on the lessons learned in real-world projects and realization that additional flexibility rarely justifies the added cost of troubleshooting problems caused by modeling mistakes and confusion caused by the differences between the models. Unless your project has an unlimited budget, you want to avoid paying this price until it becomes a true necessity.

Default Property Values

Setting default values of entity properties presents a surprising challenge in the Dynamic Data applications. Although the Entity Framework allows you to specify default values directly in the model, the Dynamic Data metadata API ignores this information. Figure 9.5 shows an example of setting zero as the default value of the UnitsInStock property of the Product entity in the Properties window of Visual Studio.

FIGURE 9.5 Setting default property value with Entity Designer.

Based on this information from the conceptual model, the Entity Designer generates special initialization code that assigns the default value to the backing field of the entity property. Here is how the code looks if you open the generated NorthwindEntities.cs:

```
[EdmScalarPropertyAttribute(EntityKeyProperty=false, IsNullable=true)]
[DataMemberAttribute()]
public Nullable<global::System.Int16> UnitsInStock
{
    get { return _UnitsInStock; }
    set
    {
        OnUnitsInStockChanging(value);
        ReportPropertyChanging("UnitsInStock");
        _UnitsInStock = StructuralObject.SetValidValue(value);
        ReportPropertyChanged("UnitsInStock");
        OnUnitsInStockChanged();
    }
}
private Nullable<global::System.Int16> _UnitsInStock = 0;
```

This works great when a new entity is created explicitly, such as in the following unit test, but unfortunately, it has no effect in Dynamic Data insert pages:

```
[TestMethod]
public void UnitsInStock_IsZeroByDefault()
{
    var product = new Product();
    Assert.AreEqual((short)0, product.UnitsInStock);
}
```

The Dynamic Data insert page template does not actually create a new entity instance. Instead, the individual field templates set the initial value of their data controls in Insert mode based on the DefaultValue property of the MetaColumn class describing their respective properties. As you recall from Chapter 7, "Metadata API," to determine the default property value, the MetaColumn class checks if a DefaultValueAttribute was applied to the property. In other words, the Entity Framework initializes the default property values in code, but Dynamic Data expects this information to be provided via data annotation attributes, forcing you to maintain property default values in two separate places.

NOTE

The current version of the Dynamic Data provider for Entity Framework ignores the default property values defined in the model. Another possible solution for this problem is to create a custom model provider. More on this in Chapter 13, "Building Dynamic List Pages."

If you are using the database-first or the model-first approach with Entity Framework, the best solution is to customize the code generator so that it not only generates the initialization code for the backing field, but also applies DefaultValueAttribute to entity properties. As discussed in Chapter 8, "Implementing Entity Validation," the built-in code generator in the sample DataModel project accompanying this book has already been replaced with a text template (Northwind.tt). Figure 9.6 shows how this text template was modified to automatically generate a DefaultValueAttribute for each property that has a default value defined in the model.

FIGURE 9.6   Entity Framework text template modified to generate DefaultValueAttribute.

You can locate the part of the text template responsible for generating declarations of primitive properties, such as the UnitsInStock, by searching for the WritePrimitiveTypeProperty method. Notice that in Northwind.tt, the DefaultValueAttribute instances are generated by a helper method with the same name. You can find the complete implementation of this method in the source code accompanying the book. Here is how the modified text template generates the UnitsInStock property:

```
[EdmScalarPropertyAttribute(EntityKeyProperty=false, IsNullable=true)]
[DataMemberAttribute(), DefaultValue(typeof(global::System.Int16), "0")]
public Nullable<global::System.Int16> UnitsInStock
{
    get
    {
        return _UnitsInStock;
    }
    set
    {
```

```
            OnUnitsInStockChanging(value);
            ReportPropertyChanging("UnitsInStock");
            _UnitsInStock = StructuralObject.SetValidValue(value);
            ReportPropertyChanged("UnitsInStock");
            OnUnitsInStockChanged();
        }
    }
    private Nullable<global::System.Int16> _UnitsInStock = 0;
```

> **NOTE**
>
> When writing code by hand, you would typically and rely on the compiler to choose a
> DefaultValueAttribute constructor that matches the type of default value directly,
> such as the DefaultValueAttribute(Int16) for the UnitsInStock property.
> However, generating this code programmatically is challenging. To keep implementation
> simple, the text template in this sample always generates the
> DefaultValueAttribute(Type, String) overload.

Property Interaction Rules

Information systems commonly have a requirement to track information regarding important changes in the state of an entity. In the case of the Northwind Traders web application, you might need to keep track of when each particular order was submitted in the SubmittedDate property of the Order entity. Here is a test that illustrates the expected behavior:

```
[TestMethod]
public void OrderStatus_SetsSubmittedDate()
{
    using (new TransactionScope())
    using (var context = new NorthwindEntities())
    {
        var order = new Order();
        order.OrderDate = DateTime.Today;
        order.OrderStatus = (int)OrderStatus.Submitted;
        context.Orders.AddObject(order);
        context.SaveChanges();
        Assert.IsNotNull(order.SubmittedDate);
        Assert.AreEqual(DateTime.Today, order.SubmittedDate.Value.Date);
    }
}
```

This type of logic is an example of business rules that define interaction between different properties of a single entity. This particular rule could have been defined as "Set SubmittedDate to date and time when the OrderStatus changes from Draft to Submitted."

OnPropertyChanging Partial Methods

The Entity Framework generates a *partial* OnPropertyChanging method for each property, such as the OnOrderStatusChanging method for the OrderStatus property shown here:

```
partial void OnOrderStatusChanging(byte? value);
```

When implemented by a developer, this method receives the new value of the entity property as the parameter and can access the original value through the entity property itself. At first, it looks like an ideal place to implement the code to set the SubmittedDate when the new value of OrderStatus property is Submitted. Unfortunately, this approach does not work in web pages that rely on the EntityDataSource control, such as the page templates in our Dynamic Data web application.

The data source control does not keep the entity object alive between page requests, nor does it serialize the object to the server- or client-side state storage. Instead, it puts the original values of its properties in a hash table and stores the hash table in the ViewState when the page is first rendered. During the post-back, when the data source control needs to save changes, instead of reloading the original entity from the database, it simply creates a brand-new entity object, applies the *original* values from the ViewState, and calls the AcceptChanges method of its ObjectStateEntry. Then it makes a second pass to apply the *current* values of the entity properties received from data entry controls on the page. In other words, *every* OnPropertyChanging partial method is called when *any* property of the entity changes.

To put this in a specific example, imagine changing the shipping address on an already submitted order. Even though the OrderStatus property itself does not change, the OnOrderStatusChanging method will still be called as if the OrderStatus changed from null to Submitted. Therefore, if we try to set the SubmittedDate in the OnOrderStatusChanging method, it would always store the date of the last change made to the order.

ISavableObject Interface

Instead of implementing the partial OnPropertyChanging methods, rely on the ObjectStateEntry class and explicitly compare the original property values it stores with the current values of the entity properties. This approach is similar to the approach discussed in Chapter 8 to implement validation rules based on property value changes. In fact, you could have implemented this logic in a custom validation method, but mixing the interaction logic, which *changes* property values, with the validation logic, which *veri-fies* them, is not a good idea. You have no control over the order in which the validation methods are called and might end up with validation code for a particular property executing *before* the code that changes it, leaving the entity in an invalid state.

Instead, change the ObjectContext class in your project so that it notifies the entity objects before they are saved and allows the entity objects to execute property interaction rules before the validation is performed. For example, the Unleashed.EntityFramework assembly in the sample solution accompanying this book defines an interface called ISavableObject (for consistency with the built-in IValidatableObject interface), that entity classes can implement when they require property interaction logic.

```
interface ISavableObject
{
    void BeforeSave(ObjectStateEntry stateEntry);
}
```

In the Order entity class, you can now implement this interface and have the BeforeSave method get the original value of the OrderStatus property from the ObjectStateEntry, compare it to the current value in the OrderStatus property itself, and set the SubmittedDate property with the system date and time.

```
partial class Order : ISavableObject
{
    public void BeforeSave(ObjectStateEntry stateEntry)
    {
        byte? oldStatus = (byte)DataModel.OrderStatus.Draft;
        if (stateEntry.State == EntityState.Modified)
            oldStatus = stateEntry.OriginalValues.Get(() => this.OrderStatus);

        if (this.OrderStatus == (byte)DataModel.OrderStatus.Submitted &&
            oldStatus == (byte)DataModel.OrderStatus.Draft)
        {
            this.SubmittedDate = DateTime.Now;
        }
    }
}
```

The UnleashedObjectContext class calls the BeforeSave method of each entity object that implements the ISavableObject interface.

```
partial class UnleashedObjectContext
{
    private void BeforeSaveChanges(ObjectStateEntry stateEntry)
    {
        var savable = stateEntry.Entity as ISavableObject;
        if (savable != null)
            savable.BeforeSave(stateEntry);

        if (stateEntry.State != EntityState.Deleted)
            this.Validate(stateEntry);
    }
}
```

As discussed in Chapter 8, the overridden SaveChanges method of the UnleashedObjectContext class calls the BeforeSaveChanges method for every added, modified, or deleted entity before submitting changes to the database. This method receives an ObjectStateEntry that stores both current and original property values of an entity. It checks if the entity implements the ISavableObject interface, calls its BeforeSave method.

When your object context class inherits from the UnleashedObjectContext or has an equivalent functionality, property interaction rules are automatically invoked when an entity object is saved to the database. In other words, whenever a web page changes an Order entity through the NorthwindEntities context, the SubmittedDate is updated automatically based on the value of the OrderStatus property. No changes are required in the web page itself, whether it is a custom page created for editing Order entities or the dynamic Edit page template.

> **NOTE**
>
> The ISavableObject interface and its BeforeSave method work a lot like the UPDATE triggers in Microsoft SQL Server and other relational database management systems. Although you could have indeed implemented this logic in a database trigger, working at the entity level gives you more flexibility and better tools for implementing business rules. You still have the option of using triggers as an optimization step (see *Business Rules in the Database* later in this chapter).

Entity Interaction Rules

Complex interaction rules might not be limited by a single entity object or even a single entity type. For example, when an order is fulfilled, the system needs to update the product inventory to decrement the number of items in stock by the number of items shipped to the customer. In the Northwind sample, this means that when the OrderStatus property of the Order entity changes to Fulfilled, values of the Quantity property of the Order_Detail entities need to be subtracted from the UnitsInStock properties of the corresponding Product entities. In other words, the fulfillment business rule spans three classes, Order, Order_Detail, and Product, and fits into the category of *entity interaction rules*.

There are several different approaches you can take when implementing entity interaction rules with Entity Framework, including (but not limited to):

- ▶ Implementing Entity Interaction Rules as BeforeSave Methods
- ▶ Implementing Entity Interaction Rules as Entity Methods
- ▶ Implementing Entity Interaction Rules as Context Methods

This section discusses these approaches and some of the trade-offs you must take into consideration when choosing how to implement entity interaction rules in your application.

Implementing Entity Interaction Rules in BeforeSave Methods

You can use the BeforeSave "trigger" methods to implement not only property interaction rules, but entity interaction rules as well. For instance, you could change the BeforeSave method of the Order entity class to detect if the OrderStatus property changed from Paid to Fulfilled and update the UnitsInStock property of all Product entities purchased in this Order. The code example that follows illustrates how the implementation could look:

```
partial class Order : ISavableObject
{
   public void BeforeSave(ObjectStateEntry stateEntry)
   {
       byte? oldStatus = (byte)DataModel.OrderStatus.Draft;
       if (stateEntry.State == EntityState.Modified)
          oldStatus = stateEntry.OriginalValues.Get(() => this.OrderStatus);

       if (this.OrderStatus == (byte)DataModel.OrderStatus.Submitted &&
           oldStatus == (byte)DataModel.OrderStatus.Draft)
       {
          this.ShippedDate = DateTime.Now;
          foreach (Order_Detail orderItem in this.Order_Details)
             orderItem.Product.UnitsInStock -= orderItem.Quantity;
       }
   }
}
```

Although this approach is viable for trivial scenarios such as in this example, it quickly becomes overwhelmingly difficult to maintain as the number of rules and their complexity increases. One of the reasons this happens is because the code is *guessing* what the presentation layer is trying to accomplish. When only the OrderStatus property is changing from Paid to Fulfilled, it is easy to see what is going on, but what if another property of the Order entity changes as well? For example, you could have another business rule tied to the ShipVia property of the Order entity to calculate the shipping fee (the Freight property) depending on the shipping option selected by the customer. If the OrderStatus changes to Fulfilled *at the same time* with the ShipVia property, does it mean an employee has chosen a different shipper to expedite the customer's order at no additional cost *or* that the customer stopped by to pick up the order from our physical store and you need to refund the shipping fee? It is impossible to answer this question in the *business* layer of the application because it depends on how the *presentation* layer is implemented.

Implementing complex business rules, such as order fulfillment, in BeforeSave methods (or database triggers for that matter) leads you down the path where you begin thinking about all possible permutations of property changes and what they might mean. Not only does it become difficult to analyze rules upfront, it is just as difficult for someone to learn and maintain the business rules implemented as a mass of if statements later on.

Implementing Entity Interaction Rules as Entity Methods

Alternatively, you can implement a complex business rule as a method in one of the entity classes. For instance, you could implement the order fulfillment rule as the Fulfill method of the Order entity class shown here:

```
partial class Order
{
  public void Fulfill()
  {
    this.OrderStatus = (byte)DataModel.OrderStatus.Fulfilled;
    this.ShippedDate = DateTime.Now;
    foreach (Order_Detail orderItem in this.Order_Details)
      orderItem.Product.UnitsInStock -= orderItem.Quantity;
  }
}
```

Similar to the code previously implemented in the BeforeSave method, the Fulfill method updates the ShippedDate property with the current date and time, iterates through all child Order_Detail objects, and subtracts their Quantity from the UnitsInStock property of their Products. However, instead of comparing the OrderStatus property with its original value, the Fulfill method itself sets it to Fulfilled.

Note that just like in the previous example, the Fulfill method relies on the lazy loading of related entity objects provided by the Entity Framework. Although it makes implementation of entity interaction rules easy, lazy loading might not be efficient because it results in multiple database calls to retrieve all Order_Detail entities first, followed by their respective Product entities, retrieved one at a time in the foreach loop.

Lazy loading functionality in Entity Framework was designed for *desktop* applications, where the initial response that users can see is more important than total duration of the operation. The ObjectContext can also be a long-living object in a desktop application, automatically caching previously loaded entities in memory and improving performance of subsequent operations. However, in web applications, where a new ObjectContext is created for each page request and users do not see anything until all data access is complete and the entire page is generated, lazy loading can significantly affect performance for all users of the system. To avoid the performance hit caused by loading the individual Product entities separately, take advantage of the Include method of the ObjectQuery class and load all Order_Detail and Product entities with the order in a single database query.

6

```
var order = context.Orders
  .Include("Order_Details")
  .Include("Order_Details.Product")
  .First(o => o.OrderID == orderId);
order.Fulfill();
```

You need to place code like this, however, in every page that needs to execute the Fulfill business rule, spilling the *data access logic* into the *presentation layer*, which is, in most circumstances, not a good idea. One of the reasons to avoid it is that the Entity Framework 4 forces you to hard-code the names of the entity classes and their properties as string literals, which are fragile and prone to typos. Even if you address this problem with string constants, it still means hard-coding the knowledge of all entities and relationships necessary for a particular business rule in the presentation layer, possibly in multiple places where the same method is called.

Implementing Entity Interaction Rules as Context Methods

When performance is important and data access logic needs to be encapsulated, it can be beneficial to implement business rules in methods of the *object context class* instead of the entity class. Here is how to reimplement the order fulfillment business rule in the NorthwindEntities class:

```
public partial class NorthwindEntities
{
  public void FulfillOrder(int orderId)
  {
    Order order = this.Orders
      .Include("Order_Details").Include("Order_Details.Product")
      .First(o => o.OrderID == orderId);
    order.OrderStatus = (byte)DataModel.OrderStatus.Fulfilled;
    order.ShippedDate = DateTime.Now;
    foreach (Order_Detail orderItem in order.Order_Details)
      orderItem.Product.UnitsInStock -= orderItem.Quantity;
  }
}
```

The FulfillOrder method takes OrderID as a parameter and retrieves the Order entity, all of its Order_Detail objects, and the related Product entities in a single roundtrip to the database. When all entities are loaded in the context, the code performs the same steps implemented in the Fulfill method earlier—update OrderStatus and ShippedDate and decrement UnitsInStock.

This version of the FulfillOrder method assumes that the caller does not already have the Order instance loaded from the database, so taking its *primary key* value as a parameter is the best option. However, if the Order instance is already loaded, you can change or perhaps create an overloaded version of the FulfillOrder method so that it takes an *entity instance* as a parameter instead. The code sample that follows shows an example of a possible implementation. As you can see, instead of querying the Order entity set, you can query the Order_Details entity set and reduce the number of Include calls to one:

```
public partial class NorthwindEntities
{
  public void FulfillOrder(Order order)
  {
    order.OrderStatus = (byte)DataModel.OrderStatus.Fulfilled;
    order.ShippedDate = DateTime.Now;
    IQueryable<Order_Detail> orderItems = this.Order_Details
      .Include("Product")
      .Where(od => od.OrderID == order.OrderID);
    foreach (Order_Detail orderItem in orderItems)
      orderItem.Product.UnitsInStock -= orderItem.Quantity;
  }
}
```

Although the second version of the FulfillOrder feels more "object-oriented" in that it takes an Order object as a parameter instead of a primitive primary key value, your choice of design approach should be driven by the concrete scenarios you need to implement. If the orders will be marked as fulfilled one at a time from an ASP.NET web page, the calling code only has the primary key value stored in the ViewState of the page, and the first version of the FulfillOrder method will work best. The more elegant second version of the FulfillOrder method might work better only in a scenario where *multiple* orders have already been loaded from the database and the overhead of making an additional database call to retrieve the order instance will not be incurred. In other words, the second style of methods works better for implementing granular business rules that are a part of a larger business process.

NOTE

Implementing entity interaction rules in object context methods and removing dependency on lazy loading helps improve not only *performance*, but also *correctness* of the application. Unless the code reliant on lazy loading explicitly checks that it is enabled, the lazy loading option could be accidentally or intentionally turned off, making an order appear empty when, in fact, its items and products simply have not been loaded from the database.

On the downside, implementing business rules as context methods can feel awkward depending on where you think the method belongs. For instance, if you feel strongly that fulfillment is the behavior of the Order class, moving the Fulfill method to the NorthwindEntities class would mean breaking its encapsulation.

Implementing business rules as *context* methods works well with simple entity models where the amount of business logic is small. As the size and complexity of the model grows, the number of business rule methods reaches the point where maintaining them in a single class becomes problematic. When that happens, you can start extracting methods into separate classes to group them by entity type to which they apply (*table modules*) or business process they implement (*services*). However, it is best to avoid making this design decision too early in the development of the application. Without having a solid understanding of the business domain and required functionality, the premature architecural decisions are often wrong and lead to unnecessary complexity and increased cost.

Validation Rules

As a form of business logic, validation rules are susceptible to many of the same potential problems. As the number of validation rules increases, complexity of the code grows rapidly and, if you are not careful, can have a significant impact on performance of the application as well as your ability to maintain it. Just like with the business logic in general, it helps to keep the validation rules simple and well encapsulated.

To help understand validation rules, they can be separated in two large categories:

▸ Persistence validation

▸ Transition validation

Rules in the *persistence* category determine conditions that an entity must meet to be successfully saved in the database. Most often, validation rules in this category apply to properties entered directly by the users of the application. For instance, a shipping address (ShipAddress, ShipCity, ShipRegion, and other properties) is required for an Order to be accepted by the Northwind Traders.

Transition rules, on the other hand, determine conditions that allow an entity to change from one state to another. For instance, if the Northwind Traders Company requires customers to pre-pay their orders, an Order entity must have OrderStatus of Paid before it can change to Fulfilled. The OrderStatus property is different from the other properties of the Order entity in that it determines its current *state*.

Entity states might not only have different transition rules; they often have different persistence rules as well. For instance, when saving an Order in Submitted state, you may want to validate that you have enough Products in stock for all items in the order; however, this rule does not apply to Fulfilled orders because you might keep them in your system for years after the boxes have left the warehouse.

Validation Rule Design

To find a reasonable compromise between code reuse, complexity, and performance, without having to do a lot of refactoring later, try the following rules of thumb when designing validation logic in your application:

- ▶ Implement persistence validation rules with data annotations

- ▶ Make state properties of entities read-only

- ▶ Implement state transitions and validation in business rule methods

- ▶ Implement state-specific persistence validation in separate validation methods

Implement Persistence Validation Rules with Data Annotations

The validation framework discussed in Chapter 8 offers a great way to implement persistence validation rules by applying pre-built validation attributes or writing custom validation methods for individual properties or entire entities. You can quickly apply the RequiredAttribute to the shipping address properties of the Order entity to ensure that the order is valid before saving it to the database.

Make State Properties of Entities Read-Only

You do not want the users of your application (neither the customers nor the employees) to edit the OrderStatus property directly, even if they initiate the state transition. Customers will submit orders by clicking a Submit button on a check-out page, and a background process handling credit card payments will mark the orders as paid. The best way to ensure that state properties of an entity cannot be changed through the user interface of the application is to make them read-only.

With Entity Framework, you can use the Entity Designer to make the setter of the OrderStatus property internal, as shown in Figure 9.7.

FIGURE 9.7 Changing visibility of entity property setter.

In the code generated by the Entity Designer, the OrderStatus property now looks similar to the following pseudo-code:

```
property byte OrderStatus { get; internal set; }
```

Changing visibility of a property setter to internal makes the property read-only outside of the assembly where its class is defined. As a result, the presentation layer, the WebApplication project in our sample, can continue using a read-only property for display and filtering purposes. However, only the business logic layer, the DataModel project in our sample, can change its value.

> **NOTE**
>
> Making state properties of entities read-only does not offer bulletproof protection against malicious code. For instance, in a full-trust application, this particular security block can be circumvented using Reflection. However, combined with other security measures, some of which are discussed in Chapter 14, "Implementing Security," this approach helps to *improve* security of a well-written application.

Implement State Transitions and Validation in Business Rule Methods

When state properties cannot be modified outside of the business layer, validation of state transition can be separated from validation of entity persistence. You can validate state transitions in the business rule methods, leaving the responsibility for persistence validation to the entities.

For example, because the OrderStatus property is now read-only, you do not need to worry about somebody (a user) or something (incorrect code) changing it from Fulfilled back to Paid when validating the Order entity. To ensure that an order can be fulfilled only once, you can have the FulfillOrder method check that the current OrderStatus is Paid:

```
public partial class NorthwindEntities
{
  public void FulfillOrder(int orderId)
  {
    Order order = this.Orders
      .Include("Order_Details").Include("Order_Details.Product")
      .First(o => o.OrderID == orderId);

    if (order.OrderStatus != (byte)DataModel.OrderStatus.Paid)
    {
      throw new ValidationException(
        new ValidationResult(
          "Order status must be Paid for the order to be fulfilled",
          new[] { "OrderStatus" }),
        null, order.OrderStatus);
    }

    order.OrderStatus = (byte)DataModel.OrderStatus.Fulfilled;
    order.ShippedDate = DateTime.Now;
    foreach (Order_Detail orderItem in order.Order_Details)
      orderItem.Product.UnitsInStock -= orderItem.Quantity;
  }
}
```

Business rule methods should report *expected* error conditions consistently with the regular validation errors reported when entities are saved to the database. Notice how in the example just shown, the FulfillOrder method throws a ValidationException if the OrderStatus property of the order has an unexpected value. This is important because you want to reuse the existing infrastructure for error handling already implemented in the Dynamic Data web pages.

It is equally as important to ensure that *unexpected* error conditions are *not* reported as ValidationException instances. If something unexpected happens, you want the application to fail fast, log detailed information on the server, and display a generic error message to the user without revealing any potentially exploitable technical information about the system. For instance, if the orderId is incorrect and there is no matching order in the database, the LINQ extension method First throws an InvalidOperationException saying, "Sequence contains no elements." This error should not occur under normal circumstances and needs to be investigated by developers, so wrapping it in a ValidationException would only make the problem harder to notice.

NOTE

You can read about the Fail Fast approach in an article written by Jim Shore for IEEE and available online at http://martinfowler.com/ieeeSoftware/failFast.pdf. Although it might seem counterintuitive at first, this approach significantly improves quality of applications by allowing developers to discover expected error conditions quickly and implement appropriate logic for handling them in a way that not only looks pretty, but also makes sense from the business standpoint.

Whether or not an error condition is expected during normal execution of the application depends on the perspective of the developer designing on the business layer. For instance, the FulfillOrder method just shown, which takes an OrderID as a parameter, treats an invalid order status value as an *expected* error condition based on an assumption that this method will be called from an Order web page where the user could click a Fulfill button more than once. This could happen if the user's network connection is interrupted after the initial Order page is displayed and she clicks the browser's Back button to fulfill the order again.

However, the overloaded version of the FulfillOrder method shown next, which takes an Order parameter, assumes that the caller is responsible for checking the current order status before trying to fulfill it. If the order is not Paid when the method is called, it throws the InvalidOperationException to indicate that there is a bug in the calling code.

```
public partial class NorthwindEntities
{
  public void FulfillOrder(Order order)
  {
    if (order.OrderStatus != (byte)DataModel.OrderStatus.Paid)
    {
      throw new InvalidOperationException(
        "Order status must be Paid for the order to be fulfilled");
    }

    order.OrderStatus = (byte)DataModel.OrderStatus.Fulfilled;
    order.ShippedDate = DateTime.Now;
    IQueryable<Order_Detail> orderItems = this.Order_Details
      .Include("Product")
      .Where(od => od.OrderID == order.OrderID);
    foreach (Order_Detail orderItem in orderItems)
      orderItem.Product.UnitsInStock -= orderItem.Quantity;
  }
}
```

A simple rule of thumb to decide which type of exception a business rule method should throw is to think about who is responsible for solving the problem. If the error is caused by something the *user* did and needs to correct *in the application,* throw a ValidationException. If the error is caused by something a *developer* did and needs to correct *in the code* calling the business rule method, throw an InvalidOperationException or an ArgumentException, if the error is associated with a specific method parameter.

> **NOTE**
>
> Trying to design a comprehensive set of validation checks to a business rule method upfront is not only challenging, but also counterproductive as it often leads to analysis paralysis and over-engineering. Instead, it is normal and desirable to add validation checks to the business rule methods as you continue to learn the business domain and discover new error conditions your application needs to handle gracefully. As long as you continue to create new and maintain existing automated tests that cover most of the business logic in your Entity Framework context and entity classes, the risk of introducing breaking changes remains low throughout the lifetime of your project.

Implement State-Specific Persistence Validation in Separate Validation Methods

When persistence validation rules differ significantly between entity states, you can simplify implementation of the validation logic by creating a separate validation method for each distinct entity state. As an example, consider validation rules for the Order entity.

When the OrderStatus is Draft, the Order entity object represents a shopping cart of a customer shopping on the Northwind Trader's website. A draft order might be empty; it does not have to have a shipping address or an order date, but for the sake of this example, let's say that a draft order needs to be associated with a customer because that is how the system retrieves the shopping cart for returning users.

On the other hand, when the OrderStatus is Submitted, the system has to ensure that OrderDate, RequiredDate, and other properties are valid, as well as check that all items in the order have a sufficient number of units in stock. These validation rules are simply not applicable to orders in other states. In particular, for draft orders, you don't care if the items are in stock because you don't know how many items the customer is going to order. On the other hand, for fulfilled orders, the items have already been shipped from the warehouse, and it doesn't make sense to check the current inventory.

Because the declarative validation framework in the DataAnnotations namespace does not support conditional validation, you need to implement state-specific validation rules in validation methods. Although you could create a separate custom validation method for each property, many validation rules apply only to a given entity state, so the same conditional logic will be repeated in multiple validation methods. To reduce code duplication, group validation rules in a smaller number of *state-specific* methods.

Listing 9.1 shows an example of implementing state-specific validation rules for the Order entity. In this implementation, the Order class has a separate validation method for each value of the OrderStatus property—ValidateDraftOrder, ValidateSubmittedOrder, ValidatePaidOrder, and ValidateFufilledOrder—that are called from a switch statement by the main Validate method. With this approach, the validation rules for Submitted orders, which are quite different from the validation rules for Draft orders, are implemented in two different methods and do not conflict with each other.

LISTING 9.1 Partial Order Class with State-Specific Validation Methods

```
partial class Order : IValidatableObject
{
  public IEnumerable<ValidationResult> Validate(ValidationContext context)
  {
    switch ((DataModel.OrderStatus?)this.OrderStatus)
    {
      case null:
      case DataModel.OrderStatus.Draft:
        return this.ValidateDraftOrder(context);

      case DataModel.OrderStatus.Submitted:
        return this.ValidateSubmittedOrder(context);

      case DataModel.OrderStatus.Paid:
        return this.ValidatePaidOrder(context);

      case DataModel.OrderStatus.Fulfilled:
        return this.ValidateFulfilledOrder(context);

      default:
        Debug.Fail("Unexpected OrderStatus value");
        return new ValidationResult[0];
    }
  }

  private IEnumerable<ValidationResult> ValidateDraftOrder(ValidationContext c)
  {
    if (this.Customer == null && string.IsNullOrEmpty(this.CustomerID))
      yield return new ValidationResult(
        "The Customer is required", new[] { "Customer" });
  }

  private IEnumerable<ValidationResult> ValidateSubmittedOrder(ValidationContext c)
  {
    if (this.OrderDate == null)
      yield return new ValidationResult(
        "The Order Date is required", new[] { "OrderDate" });
```

```
    if (this.OrderDate.Value < DateTime.Today)
      yield return new ValidationResult(
        "The Order Date cannot be in the past", new [] { "OrderDate" });

    if (this.RequiredDate != null &&
        this.RequiredDate <= this.OrderDate.Value.AddDays(3))
      yield return new ValidationResult(
        "The Required Date must be greater than Order Date + 3 days",
        new[] { "RequiredDate" });

    Product product = this.Order_Details
      .Where(item => item.Product.UnitsInStock < item.Quantity)
      .Select(item => item.Product).FirstOrDefault();
    if (product != null)
      yield return new ValidationResult(product.ProductName + " is out of stock");
  }

  private IEnumerable<ValidationResult> ValidatePaidOrder(ValidationContext c)
  {
    // Validation logic specific to paid orders
    return new ValidationResult[0];
  }

  private IEnumerable<ValidationResult> ValidateFulfilledOrder(ValidationContext c)
  {
    // Validation logic specific to fulfilled orders
    return new ValidationResult[0];
  }
}
```

Validation rules that are shared by all states of an entity can be implemented either declaratively by applying validation attributes or in the main Validate method of the entity class. For complex entities that need to support large number of validation rules, you might want to consider using the Strategy pattern (*Design Patterns: Elements of Reusable Object-Oriented Software* by Eric Gamma, Richard Helm, Ralph Johnson, and John Vlissides) and moving validation rules specific to a particular state to a separate validation class. However, for simple entities, where the number of rules is relatively small, a simple switch statement showed in this example can do the same job without the overhead of introducing separate validation classes.

Validation of Related Entities

It might be challenging to determine the right place to implement validation logic that requires information from related entities. And although it might seem that the Order_Detail entity should be responsible for validating its Quantity property against the

Product's UnitsInStock, it doesn't work because an Order_Detail object might not change when the order is submitted. Instead, it is better to validate all Order_Detail objects in a particular order at once when the order status changes to Submitted. Not only does this approach allow you to validate the unchanged Order_Detail objects, it is usually more efficient from the database access standpoint as well. Here is an extract from the ValidateSubmittedOrder method in Listing 9.1 that performs this validation:

```
Product product = this.Order_Details
    .Where(item => item.Product.UnitsInStock < item.Quantity)
    .Select(item => item.Product).FirstOrDefault();
if (product != null)
    yield return new ValidationResult(product.ProductName + " is out of
    stock");
```

To check for out-of-stock products in an order, the ValidateSubmittedOrder method iterates over all Order_Detail objects of the order, comparing their Quantity with the number of UnitsInStock of the product. If any order item does not have enough product units available, a ValidationResult is returned to indicate an error.

This code relies on the *lazy loading*, which is enabled by default in the NorthwindEntities class, to access Product entity objects. As you recall from our previous discussion, lazy loading makes writing code easier at the cost of performance. Here is how we could rewrite the Order validation logic to determine if it has any out-of-stock items in a single database request (remember that *context* is the ValidationContext object passed to the ValidateSubmittedOrder method as a parameter):

```
var entities = (NorthwindEntities)context.Items[typeof(ObjectContext)];
string productName = entities.Order_Details
    .Where(item => item.OrderID == this.OrderID
                && item.Product.UnitsInStock < item.Quantity)
    .Select(item => item.Product.ProductName).FirstOrDefault();
if (productName != null)
    yield return new ValidationResult(productName + " is out of stock");
```

Although the new LINQ query looks similar to the previous version, the key difference is that this new version uses the Order_Details property of the NorthwindEntities class, which returns an IQueryable<Order_Detail> instead of the Order_Details property of the Order class, which returns an IEnumerable<Order_Detail>. As a result, instead of using LINQ to Objects and iterating over the lazy-loaded Order_Detail collection in memory of the application, you now use LINQ to Entities to send a single request the database server, query the Order_Details and Products tables, and return the name of the first out-of-stock product.

The ValidateSubmittedOrder method retrieves an instance of the NorthwindEntities object context from the ValidationContext object. As discussed in Chapter 8, the ValidationContext allows the UnleashedObjectContext to pass the ObjectStateEntry object that stores the entity itself to the validation methods. To make the NorthwindEntities object context available as well, the Validate method of the UnleashedObjectContext class was further extended as shown in Listing 9.2.

LISTING 9.2 Making ObjectContext Available to Validation Methods

```
public partial class UnleashedObjectContext
{
  private void Validate(ObjectStateEntry stateEntry)
  {
    object entity = stateEntry.Entity;

    var items = new Dictionary<object, object>();
    items[typeof(ObjectStateEntry)] = stateEntry;
    items[typeof(ObjectContext)] = this;

    var context = new ValidationContext(entity, null, items);

    var results = new List<ValidationResult>();
    if (!Validator.TryValidateObject(entity, context, results, true))
      ThrowValidationException(entity, results);
  }
}
```

Entity Deletion Rules

Because persistence validation rules are designed to ensure that entities are *saved* in a valid state, most of them are not applicable and should not be evaluated when entities are *deleted*. For example, suppose you have a requirement to prevent deletion of orders after they have been submitted. Even though you implemented a custom validation method that requires the OrderDate not to be in the past, from deletion standpoint, you only care about the value of the OrderStatus property. Evaluating the validation rules for the OrderDate and other properties would prevent deletion of an entity that should have otherwise been allowed.

Because persistence validation rules are not applicable to entity deletion, the BeforeSaveChanges method of the UnleashedObjectContext class validates only added and modified entities. On the other hand, the ISavableObject interface is not bound by the same constraints as the validation logic. The UnleashedObjectContext class calls the BeforeSave method of all entities, including the deleted ones, which allows you to implement validation of entity deletion without introducing conflicts with the validation of entity persistence. Here is how you can implement the BeforeSave method in the Order class to allow deleting only Draft orders:

```
partial class Order: ISavableObject
{
  public void BeforeSave(ObjectStateEntry stateEntry)
  {
    if (stateEntry.State == EntityState.Deleted &&
        this.OrderStatus != (byte)DataModel.OrderStatus.Draft)
```

```
        throw new ValidationException("Only draft orders can be deleted");
    }
}
```

As you recall from the previous discussion, a good rule of thumb when designing validation logic is to implement persistence validation with data annotations and transition
validation with business rule methods. From the validation standpoint, deletion is an odd
ball because it can fit in either of these two categories depending on your point of view. It
may be helpful, however, to treat entity deletion as a form of state transition. From this
point of view, the BeforeSave method becomes a special business rule method that can be
used to implement property interaction rules and validation of deletion.

Reusing Entity Validation in Business Rule Methods

Would it be possible or beneficial to reuse the *entity* validation rules in business rule
methods? For instance, you have already implemented validation rules to prevent submitting orders for out-of-stock items. Should the FulfillOrder method also check that all
items are in stock before updating the product inventory? Invoking entity validation rules
from a business rule method is certainly possible and *could be* a good idea.

As discussed in Chapter 8, the UnleashedObjectContext class was extended to perform
validation of all entities before they are saved in the database. It defines a method called
Validate (see Listing 9.2), which takes an ObjectStateEntry as a parameter and validates
a single entity object. To make invoking validation rules in business rule methods more
clean and convenient, UnleashedObjectContext also provides an overloaded version of
this method (shown next) that takes an entity object as a parameter. This method retrieves
its ObjectStateEntry from the ObjectStateManager, and calls the main Validate method.

```
public partial class UnleashedObjectContext
{
    protected void Validate(object entity)
    {
        ObjectStateEntry stateEntry =
            this.ObjectStateManager.GetObjectStateEntry(entity);
        this.Validate(stateEntry);
    }
}
```

With the new Validate method, you *could* modify the FulfillOrder business rule method
to check the order before trying to fulfill it and ensure that it is valid according to all
property- and entity-level validation attributes and coded rules implemented for the Order
entity class.

```
public partial class NorthwindEntities
{
    public void FulfillOrder(Order order)
    {
```

```
this.Validate(order);

if (order.OrderStatus != (byte)DataModel.OrderStatus.Paid)
{
  throw new InvalidOperationException(
    "Order status must be Paid for the order to be fulfilled");
}

order.OrderStatus = (byte)DataModel.OrderStatus.Fulfilled;
order.ShippedDate = DateTime.Now;
IQueryable<Order_Detail> orderItems = this.Order_Details
  .Include("Product")
  .Where(od => od.OrderID == order.OrderID);
foreach (Order_Detail orderItem in orderItems)
  orderItem.Product.UnitsInStock -= orderItem.Quantity;
  }
}
```

Remember that all modified entities go through the mandatory validation before they are persisted in the database in the SaveChanges method that was overidden in the UnleashedObjectContext. Although you could also call the Validate method at the end of FulfillOrder as well to check the modified Order and Product entities, doing so would most likely result in the same validation rules executed two times without any additional changes made to the entities in between. In other words, forcing validation of entity objects *at the end* of business rule methods is usually redundant and can lead to unnecessary performance problems if validation rules require access to related entities that have to be retrieved from the database.

Forcing validation of entity objects *in the beginning* of business rule methods can also be redundant. If a business rule method, such as the overload of FulfillOrder that takes OrderID as a parameter, is responsible for retrieving an entity object from the database, you can often assume that the entity object is still valid because it already passed all validation rules last time it was saved to the database. In the FulfillOrder(Order) method, the calling code could have changed the Order entity, making its explicit validation potentially worthwhile. However, in the FulfillOrder(Int32) method, you can safely assume that the Order entity retrieved from the database is still valid, making the explicit revalidation unnecessary.

Although reusing entity- and property-level validation rules in business rule methods helps to improve correctness of your application and its data integrity, it comes at the cost of additional resources required to perform the extra checks. It is usually *not* a good idea to do this in production code. However, you can benefit from the additional validation in business rule methods during active development and testing of your application by *conditionally compiling it*. Here is how you could change the FulfillOrder method to validate the Order object only in the *Debug* configuration of the DataModel project, which defines the DEBUG compiler symbol.

```
public void FulfillOrder(Order order)
{
  #if DEBUG
    this.Validate(order);
  #endif
  // ...
}
```

You can use the Debug version of the business layer during the initial active development and testing of your application, when finding problems faster is more important than squeezing every bit of performance from the application. When the testing is finished and you are ready to deploy the application to the production environment, it should be safe to assume that the interaction between the presentation and business logic was implemented correctly. At this point, you can deploy the Release version of the business layer, which does not have the additional validation checks and will work faster.

If you do choose to perform additional validation in the release version of the application, it is a good idea to verify that it has no significant effect on the application performance. Remember that CPU and RAM resources of web servers can be increased easily, but additional database access can be costly and limits the application's ability to scale.

Saving Changes

When implementing business rule methods, such as the FulfillOrder method of the NorthwindEntities context, you might be wondering if saving changes (by calling the SaveChanges method of the ObjectContext) is a good idea. If the SaveChanges method has to be called anyway, why not simply call it from the FulfillOrder method itself?

A business rule method knows how to retrieve and manipulate a specific set of entities. However, it has no way of saving only those entities it modifies. The SaveChanges method of the ObjectContext class saves *all* changed entities, so calling it in the FulfillOrder method could affect not only the Order and Product entities it modified, but also all other entities that were changed before the method was called. This might produce unexpected side effects further up the call stack, especially when business rule methods can be called from other methods. From the viewpoint of a developer reading the code, it is also easier to understand the code if it is responsible for both creating the ObjectContext and saving changes. Because there is no way to tell if the FulfillOrder method saves changes by reading this code alone, intuitively, you would assume that changes are not saved unless the SaveChanges method is called:

```
using (var context = new NorthwindEntities())
{
  int orderId = // ...
  context.FulfillOrder(orderId);
  context.SaveChanges();
}
```

Saving changes inside of business rule methods also makes maintenance of automated tests more difficult. Although the `TransactionScope`-based approach to enforcing test isolation discussed in Chapter 8 will continue to work, saving changes from a method under test requires additional disk access and makes the test slower. As the number of automated tests increases, their performance becomes more and more important. By keeping saving logic out of business rule methods, you reduce disk access and speed up the tests.

Although there are no hard rules against this, it is usually a good idea to keep the persistence logic out of the business rule methods and entity classes. Instead, it is better to save changes in the business *process* code, which is usually implemented outside of the Entity Framework context and invoked by the user. For example, a web page or a console application is a better place to save changes.

Managing Transactions

Although the `TransactionScope` supports hierarchical transactions and you *could* put one inside of a business rule method, you need to remember that transactions do not apply to changes made in the memory of the application. For instance, you could modify the `FulfillOrder` method to update the Order and Product entities inside of a `TransactionScope`:

```
using (var transaction = new TransactionScope())
{
    order.OrderStatus = (byte)DataModel.OrderStatus.Fulfilled;
    order.ShippedDate = DateTime.Now;
    IQueryable<Order_Detail> orderItems = this.Order_Details
        .Include("Product")
        .Where(od => od.OrderID == order.OrderID);
    foreach (Order_Detail orderItem in orderItems)
        orderItem.Product.UnitsInStock -= orderItem.Quantity;
    transaction.Complete();
}
```

However, remember that the Order and Product entities are not saved to the database here; they are merely modified *in memory*. The `TransactionScope` in this example encompasses only the query that retrieves the Order_Detail and Product entities from the database. Because Microsoft SQL Server and other database servers already execute SQL queries in transactions by default, using an explicit transaction here would only increase complexity without adding any benefits. Instead, it is better to implement transaction logic in the same place as the persistence logic—outside of the business rule methods, as shown in the following example:

```
using (var transaction = new TransactionScope())
using (var context = new NorthwindEntities())
{
    int orderId = // ...
```

```
    context.FulfillOrder(orderId);
    context.SaveChanges();
    transaction.Complete();
}
```

Invoking Business Rules in Web Applications

Out of the box, Dynamic Data does not provide a way to invoke a custom business rule method from a dynamically generated page. Instead, you need to create a custom page or a custom page template and write code to call the method explicitly. Listing 9.3 shows markup of a custom page that displays an Order entity in a read-only `FormView` control, with a Fulfill button that users can click to mark the order as fulfilled.

LISTING 9.3 Custom Order Page with Fulfill Button (Markup)

```
<%@ Page Language="C#"
  MasterPageFile="~/Site.master" CodeBehind="SamplePage.aspx.cs"
  Inherits="WebApplication.Samples.Ch9.EntityMethod.SamplePage" %>

<asp:Content ContentPlaceHolderID="main" runat="server">
  <h2>Entry from table <%= ordersTable.DisplayName %></h2>
  <asp:ValidationSummary runat="server" />
  <unl:UnleashedValidator runat="server" ID="validator"
    ControlToValidate="formView" Display="None"/>
  <asp:FormView runat="server" ID="formView" DataSourceID="dataSource"
    DataKeyNames="OrderID">
    <ItemTemplate>
      <asp:DynamicEntity runat="server" />
      <tr><td colspan="2">
        <asp:Button runat="server" Text="Fulfill" OnClick="FulfillButton_Click" />
      </td></tr>
    </ItemTemplate>
  </asp:FormView>
  <asp:EntityDataSource ID="dataSource" runat="server"
    ConnectionString="name=NorthwindEntities"
    DefaultContainerName="NorthwindEntities" EntitySetName="Orders" />
  <asp:QueryExtender TargetControlID="dataSource" runat="server">
    <asp:DynamicRouteExpression />
  </asp:QueryExtender>
</asp:Content>
```

Most of the code in Listing 9.3 is very similar to the Details page template discussed in Chapter 6, "Page Templates." (In fact, you could have created it as a custom page template for the Order entity.) The only notable difference here is the Fulfill button, which replaced the usual Edit, Delete, and Show All Items links used by the Details page template. Listing 9.4 shows the code-behind.

LISTING 9.4 Custom Order Page with Fulfill Button (Code-Behind)

```
using System;
using System.Collections.Generic;
using System.Linq;
using System.Web.DynamicData;
using DataModel;

namespace WebApplication.Samples.Ch9.ContextMethod
{
  public partial class SamplePage : System.Web.UI.Page
  {
    protected MetaTable ordersTable;

    protected void Page_Init(object sender, EventArgs e)
    {
      this.ordersTable = MetaModel.Default.GetTable(typeof(Order));
      this.formView.SetMetaTable(this.ordersTable);
      this.dataSource.Include = this.ordersTable.ForeignKeyColumnsNames;
    }

    protected void FulfillButton_Click(object sender, EventArgs args)
    {
      using (var context = new NorthwindEntities())
      {
        int orderId = (int)this.formView.DataKey.Value;
        context.FulfillOrder(orderId);
        context.SaveChanges();
        this.Response.Redirect(
          this.ordersTable.GetActionPath(PageAction.Details,
          new List<object>(new object[] { orderId })));
      }
    }
  }
}
```

The FulfillButton_Click method handles the Click event of the Fulfill button. Because the event handler is invoked during a post-back, the original Order entity instance displayed by the page is no longer available. In this example, OrderID is extracted from the DataKey property of the FormView control. Alternatively, if this were a custom page template and the OrderID was available in the URL, you could have obtained it by calling the GetColumnValuesFromRoute method of the MetaTable object discussed in Chapter 7.

If the SaveChanges method completes successfully without any validation or database exceptions thrown, the FulfillButton_Click method redirects the user's browser to the dynamically generated Details page for the current order. The address of this page is determined by calling the GetActionPath method of the MetaTable object describing the Order entity. This is consistent with the pattern used by the default page templates in Dynamic Data applications that have a distinct page per action. If you prefer to display the updated entity in the same page, you could simply call the DataBind method of the FormView control instead.

Error Handling

As discussed in Chapter 8, the EntityDataSource control catches the exceptions that might be thrown by the SaveChanges method of the NorthwindEntities context class and, by the means of its Exception event, notifies the DynamicValidator controls on the page, enabling them to display the expected validation errors. However, the FulfillButton_Click event handler in Listing 9.4 works with a NorthwindEntities context object *directly* and currently does not have any error handling logic. If the business rule or the SaveChanges methods throw a ValidationException, the user will see a yellow page of death generated by the ASP.NET runtime.

As of version 4 of the .NET Framework, there is no way to make the EntityDataSource control execute custom code and reuse the error-handling infrastructure the DynamicValidator controls and the field templates provide for Insert, Update, Delete, and Select operations. You have to write your own code to catch and display expected exceptions. The next example shows a new version of the FulfillButton_Click event handler that displays all error messages in the ValidationSummary control at the top of the page.

```
protected void FulfillButton_Click(object sender, EventArgs args)
{
  using (var context = new NorthwindEntities())
  try
  {
    int orderId = (int)this.formView.DataKey.Value;
    context.FulfillOrder(orderId);
    context.SaveChanges();
    this.Response.Redirect(
      this.ordersTable.GetActionPath(PageAction.Details,
      new List<object>(new object[] { orderId })));
  }
  catch (Exception e)
  {
    if (!this.validator.HandleException(e)) throw;
  }
}
```

The new version of the FulfillButton_Click event handler wraps a try/catch block around the FulfillOrder and SaveChanges method calls, which could throw validation exceptions. The catch block intercepts all exceptions and passes them to the HandleException method of the UnleashedValidator (defined at the top of the page in Listing 9.3). If the HandleException method returns false, the code re-throws the exception.

As discussed in Chapter 8, the UnleashedValidator class inherits from the built-in DynamicValidator and extends error handling to support AggregateException. The HandleException method receives an Exception object as a parameter, iterates over all UnleashedValidator controls on the page, including those in field templates, and attempts to handle the exception by passing it to each validator's ValidateException method. The HandleException returns true if one or more validators on the page were able to handle the exception by setting their ValidationException properties. For complete details, please refer to the UnleashedValidator source code in the Unleashed.DynamicData project accompanying the book.

Figure 9.8 shows an example of an error message displayed because of the ValidationException thrown in the FulfillOrder business rule method.

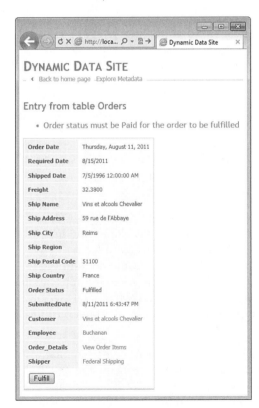

FIGURE 9.8 Validation error from calling a business rule method.

> **NOTE**
>
> The read-only field templates do not include validators by default. With less than ten read-only field templates included in a `Dynamic Data` project out of the box, you can add the `UnleashedValidator` controls to the field templates and improve display of property-specific errors. However, if you choose to do it, make sure the validators are hidden when there are no errors; otherwise, the increase in the size of generated HTML and JavaScript could have a significant impact on performance of *all* read-only pages in the application.

Business Rules in the Database

Some of the business logic discussed in this chapter is similar to what you can do with database stored procedures, triggers, and check constraints. It is indeed possible to implement robust business rules directly at the database level; however, doing so has an immediate impact on performance and scalability of the overall system, which are especially important for high-volume web applications.

A system scales *up* when its performance can be increased by installing faster or additional CPUs and RAM on a single physical computer. On the other hand, a system scales *out* when its performance can be increased by adding more computers. Scaling up is expensive; the cost of both hardware and software grows *exponentially* as the number of CPUs and amount of RAM increases beyond typical commodity levels. In practice, this means that performance you can get out of a database server has a practical limit, sometimes called a glass ceiling, which would require unreasonably high costs to break through. Scaling out is much cheaper, as the cost of adding commodity servers to the system grows only *linearly*. Unfortunately, most relational database management systems that exist today scale up much better than they scale out; in fact, scaling out a database server is nearly impossible without redesigning the system itself.

In general, scalability of an information system can be improved by performing CPU-bound tasks on the application servers (such as a web server in our example) and I/O-bound tasks on the database server. Most of the business rules discussed so far are CPU-bound, or in other words, they only need CPU cycles to execute and do not need to access the database. Therefore, implementing them in the entity classes of the application allows you to scale out the system by adding application servers and leaving the precious resources of the database server available for compiling queries and calculating execution plans.

However, some types of business logic, such as validation of uniqueness or referential integrity, are I/O-bound. They require access to data and can be implemented more efficiently on the database server. Suppose that all products in the Northwind database must have unique names. If you implement this validation logic in the Product entity class, the application would need to send one request to the server to query the Products table for products with a given name, followed by another request to insert a new record. However, if you create a UNIQUE KEY constraint for the Products table in the database, the application only needs to send a single request to insert the new record and can rely on the database server to verify that the ProductName of the new record is unique. Both implementations require the same number of logical operations; however, the database implementation requires fewer server requests, results in less data sent back and forth, and allows the database server to choose the best way to enforce the uniqueness rule.

Integrating Database Validation in Dynamic Data Applications

Here is a T-SQL script you can use to implement validation of the ProductName uniqueness at the database level:

```
ALTER TABLE [dbo].[Products]
    ADD CONSTRAINT [UK_Products]
    UNIQUE (ProductName)
```

Without additional changes, an attempt to create a new Product with a duplicate name through the Dynamic Data web application results in a yellow screen of death, as shown in Figure 9.9.

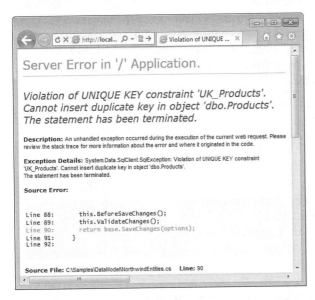

FIGURE 9.9 Default error page generated for database exceptions.

Obviously, a yellow page of death is not acceptable in a production-ready web application, and you need to change it to report the error consistently with other validation results implemented in the application code. In particular, you need to catch the appropriate exceptions and rethrow them wrapped inside of ValidationException instances. Here is how you can override the SaveChanges method of the NorthwindEntities class to do this:

```
public override int SaveChanges(SaveOptions options)
{
  try
  {
    return base.SaveChanges(options);
  }
  catch (UpdateException e)
  {
    HandleSqlException(e);
    throw;
  }
}
```

The new version of the SaveChanges method puts the call to the base method inside of a try/catch block to intercept database errors reported as instances of the UpdateException class by the Entity Framework. The UpdateException itself provides a very generic error message saying that an error has occurred when trying to save changes; however, the underlying database error is still available through its InnerException property used in the HandleSqlException method shown here:

```
private static void HandleSqlException(Exception e)
{
  SqlException error = e.InnerException as SqlException;
  if (error != null)
  {
    if (error.Number == 547)
      HandleReferenceConstraintViolation(error);
    else if (error.Number == 2627)
      HandleUniqueKeyConstraintViolation(error);
  }
}
```

In this example, Microsoft SQL Server is used, so the inner exception will be of type SqlException defined in the System.Data.SqlClient namespace. You can determine what kind of error has occurred by looking at the SQL error Number, which for the violation of a UNIQUE KEY constraint will be 2627 and for a FOREIGN KEY violation will be 547.

The Microsoft SQL Server documentation does not offer a comprehensive list of error numbers and suggests querying the sys.messages view for details. You might find this impractical for finding an error number based on an error type given the list includes more than 8,000 messages for a single language. It is often easier to find a specific error code by triggering the error condition with a SQL script and getting it from the actual error reported by the SQL Server.

If you are using a database platform other than Microsoft SQL Server, you need to rely on the low-level exceptions, error messages, and error codes provided by your database vendor because the current version of the Entity Framework does not allow accessing this information in a generic fashion.

Error codes, such as 547 and 2627 in the previous example, are difficult to under-stand and remember. Just like with any hard-coded literals, it is usually a good idea to use constants that encapsulate them instead. Unfortunately, the .NET SQL Client does not offer ready-to-use constants. In this case, they are left as literals because HandleSqlException method is the only place in the sample application where they are being used. They also appear next to the HandleReferenceConstraintViolation and HandleUniqueKeyConstraintViolation methods, which help to explain their meaning.

When you detect an expected database exception, such as the violation of a UNIQUE KEY constraint, you can wrap it in a ValidationException, which the DynamicValidator controls in the application web pages display to the users. Because different database errors require slightly different handling logic, there is a separate method for each expected type of error, such as the HandleUniqueKeyConstraintViolation method shown here:

```
private static void HandleUniqueKeyConstraintViolation(SqlException error)
{
   throw new ValidationException(error.Message);
}
```

The initial implementation of the unique key violation error handler simply throws a ValidationException with the low-level error message reported by the database. Although this prevents the yellow page of death, the error message is not very helpful and will say something along these lines:

```
Violation of UNIQUE KEY constraint 'UK_Products'. Cannot insert duplicate
key in object 'dbo.Products'.
```

This error message contains technical terms, such as the table name, as opposed to the business terms used by the application user interface. It also does not explain what a "duplicate key" means for Products—is it the Product Name alone, a Product Name from a particular Supplier, or perhaps a Product Name within a particular Category? And last, but not least, it reveals the low-level technical details that can help an attacker access the database directly.

Detailed metadata information about database constraints, such as which columns constitute a particular UNIQUE KEY, is available in the SQL Server database itself. You could extract it with the help of the SQL Server Management Objects API provided in the Microsoft.SqlServer.Smo assembly by the SQL Server client. Knowing the database columns, you could then use the Entity Framework mapping schema to determine the entity properties mapped to these columns and then determine their display names with the help of the TypeDescriptor.

As you can imagine, the metadata-driven approach requires a lot of work. In addition to using the metadata APIs for both SQL Server and Entity Framework, you would have to parse the Entity Framework mapping schema (MSL) in raw XML form because it has no public API at this time. Even if you go through all this trouble, the resulting error message you could generate automatically will probably be very technical, dry, and difficult for business users to understand. Instead, you can display a *custom* error message when a particular database constraint is violated, which is both easier to implement and provides more meaningful messages to the users.

> **NOTE**
>
> Because database error messages are application-specific, the sample solution accompanying this book implements them in the NorthwindEntities class (application) and not in the UnleashedObjectContext base class (infrastructure).

```
static readonly Dictionary<string, ValidationResult> ConstraintErrors =
  new Dictionary<string, ValidationResult>()
  {
    { "UK_Products", new ValidationResult(
      "Product Name must be unique.", new string[] { "ProductName" }) },
    { "FK_Order_Details_Products", new ValidationResult(
      "Product is referenced in one or more Orders and"+
      "cannot be deleted.") }
  };
```

ConstraintErrors is a static dictionary, defined in the NorthwindEntities class to store constraint names and ValidationResult objects that represent their violation errors. A ValidationResult object allows you to not only provide a meaningful error message, but also associate it with a particular property, such as the ProductName, which the DynamicValidator controls can use to display an asterisk next to the offending field

control on the web page. You also need to modify the HandleUniqueKeyConstraint
Violation method, as shown next, to take advantage of the new dictionary:

```
private static void HandleUniqueKeyConstraintViolation(SqlException error)
{
  Match match = Regex.Match(error.Message,
    "Violation of UNIQUE KEY constraint '(?<Constraint>.+?)'",
    RegexOptions.IgnoreCase);
  string constraint = match.Groups["Constraint"].Value;
  ValidationResult validationResult;
  if (ConstraintErrors.TryGetValue(constraint, out validationResult))
    ThrowValidationException(null, new [] { validationResult });
}
```

The new version the HandleUniqueKeyConstraintViolation method uses regular expressions, namely the Regex class from the System.Text.RegularExpressions namespace, to
extract the constraint name from the error message. The regular expression pattern
includes a capture group called Constraint. Having extracted the name of the constraint
from the capture group, the code tries to lookup a ValidationResult object in the
ConstraintErrors dictionary and if the lookup was successful, calls the
ThrowValidationException method. As you might recall from Chapter 8, this method is
defined in the UnleashedObjectContext base class. It takes the entity object as its first
parameter, a list of ValidationResult objects, and throws an appropriate exception, either
a ValidationException or an AggregateException, depending on the number of validation results.

> **NOTE**
>
> Detailed discussion of regular expressions could take hundreds of pages. For addi-
> tional information on this subject, please refer to the following resources:
>
> ▶ http://msdn.microsoft.com/library/hs600312.aspx
> ▶ *Sams Teach Yourself Regular Expressions in 10 Minutes*

Figure 9.10 shows the final version of the UNIQUE KEY error message displayed on the
Product insert page. Notice that a custom error message is now displayed at the top of the
page, and an asterisk indicates that Product Name is the field that caused the error.

9

FIGURE 9.10 Custom error generated for an expected database exception.

Implementing Validation Rules in Triggers

By optimizing LINQ queries and performing validation checks only when they are appropriate in the life cycle of the business entity, such as validating that product inventory is sufficient only when the order status changes from Draft to Submitted, you should be able to reach adequate performance in most validation methods of your application. However, if you find that further optimization is necessary, you can reimplement I/O-bound validation logic in database triggers. Here is a trigger that implements the validation rule for checking product inventory at the database level:

```
CREATE TRIGGER [Order_CheckOutOfStockProducts]
   ON [dbo].[Orders] FOR INSERT, UPDATE AS
BEGIN
   SET NOCOUNT ON;

   DECLARE @productName NVARCHAR(50);
   SELECT @productName = product.ProductName
   FROM [Order Details] AS item
   JOIN inserted ON item.OrderID = inserted.OrderID
   JOIN Products AS product ON item.ProductID = product.ProductID
   WHERE inserted.OrderStatus = 1
      AND product.UnitsInStock < item.Quantity;
```

```
   IF @productName <> null
   BEGIN
      DECLARE @errorMessage NVARCHAR(MAX) = @productName + ' is out of
stock';
      RAISERROR (@errorMessage, 11, 0);
   END;
END;
```

Just like the last version of the Order validation logic that was implemented using LINQ in the application code, this T-SQL code executes a single query, joining the Order Details and the Products tables to find order items for products out of stock. The only notable difference in the query logic is the use of the inserted pseudo-table, which in this trigger provides access to the rows of the Orders table that were inserted or updated. The query sets the @productName variable with the name of an out-of-stock product, and the trigger calls the RAISERROR system function if any such products are found.

The first parameter of RAISERROR is the error message that will be reported to the application. The second parameter, *severity*, indicates the type of error. Severity values between 11 and 16 indicate user errors and throw a SqlException in .NET applications. The third parameter, state, provides additional information about where the error has occurred, and you can simply use zero, if you don't plan to use it.

Custom validation errors implemented this way can be handled similarly to the built-in errors, such as the UNIQUE KEY and FOREIGN KEY constraint violations discussed earlier. All that is needed is to change the HandleSqlException method of the NorthwindEntities class, as shown next, to handle the SqlException instances thrown by RAISERROR:

```
private static void HandleSqlException(Exception e)
{
   SqlException error = e.InnerException as SqlException;
   if (error != null)
   {
      if (error.Number == 547)
         HandleReferenceConstraintViolation(error);
      else if (error.Number == 2627)
         HandleUniqueKeyConstraintViolation(error);
      else if (error.Number >= 50000 && error.Class <= 16)
         throw new ValidationException(error.Message);
   }
}
```

The HandleSqlException method wraps all SqlException instances with error codes 50000 and above and severity levels 16 and below in ValidationException instances. These error codes and severity levels distinguish the *user errors* reported by calling RAISERROR from *informational messages* and *system errors*. Informational messages have severity level 10 or lower and do not throw a SqlException. System errors have severity level 17 or higher, and although they also throw SqlException, system errors are not expected during normal execution of the application and thus should not be reported as validation errors.

NOTE

Triggers and stored procedures described here are more challenging with the *code-first* approach to development of the entity model. The database management functionality built into the Entity Framework does not support triggers and stored procedures directly, requiring you to manage their source code separately and making database deployment more complex. The *database-first* and *model-first* approaches, on the other hand, rely on SQL scripts for database deployment and do not have this problem.

Implementing Business Rules in Stored Procedures

Similar to validation rules, it is possible to optimize business rule methods by re-implementing them in SQL stored procedures. Listing 9.5 shows a stored procedure, which is a T-SQL equivalent of the FulfillOrder business rule method implemented earlier.

LISTING 9.5 FulfillOrder Stored Procedure

```
CREATE PROCEDURE [dbo].[FulfillOrder]
  @orderId int
AS
BEGIN
  UPDATE Orders SET
    OrderStatus = 3,
    ShippedDate = GETDATE()
  WHERE OrderID = @orderId
    AND OrderStatus = 2;

  IF @@ROWCOUNT = 0
  BEGIN
    RAISERROR ('Order status must be Paid for the order to be fulfilled', 11, 0);
    RETURN;
  END;

  UPDATE Products SET
    UnitsInStock = UnitsInStock - od.Quantity
  FROM Products AS p
  JOIN [Order Details] AS od ON p.ProductID = od.ProductID
  WHERE od.OrderID = @orderId;
END
```

The T-SQL version of the FulfillOrder is slightly more efficient as it checks the current order status as part of the UPDATE statement that changes it. The @@ROWCOUNT system variable indicates the actual number of rows affected by the previous statement, allowing this code to determine if the UPDATE statement was successful. Note that unlike throwing an exception in the .NET code, calling RAISERROR in T-SQL does not interrupt the execution of the stored procedure unless it is done from within a TRY block. This is why the FulfillOrder method has a RETURN statement right after RAISERROR; otherwise, the second UPDATE statement, which modifies the UnitsInStock column of the Product table, would be executed even for unpaid orders.

After creating the FulfillOrder stored procedure, you need to import its definition in the NorthwindEntities entity model. As you recall from a discussion in Chapter 2, "Entity Framework," this requires two steps. First, you need to use the Entity Designer to update the model from the database and create a definition of the stored procedure in the *storage model* of the EDMX. Second, you need to use the Model Browser to create a function import in the *conceptual model*, which generates a new method in the NorthwindEntities class when the EDMX file is saved.

Because additional code is required to handle database errors, you do not want the stored procedure method to be called directly by the presentation layer. Instead, you want the function import to have a different name—SqlFulfillOrder—and have *internal* access so that only the FulfillOrder method can call it and not the web application. Here is how the FulfillOrder method will look after the optimization:

```
public void FulfillOrder(int orderId)
{
  try
  {
    this.SqlFulfillOrder(orderId);
  }
  catch (EntityCommandExecutionException e)
  {
    HandleSqlException(e);
    throw;
  }
}
```

Note that the SqlFulfillOrder is called within a try/catch block because Entity Framework reports database errors that occur when calling stored procedures as instances of the EntityCommandExecutionException class. Because the code calling the FulfillOrder method expects only ValidationException, the FulfillOrder method catches the EntityCommandExecutionException instances and passes them to the HandleSqlException method created earlier. In other words, the exception handling code implemented here allows the order status validation now implemented in the T-SQL to continue throwing ValidationException as if it was still implemented in the .NET code.

Side Effects of Stored Procedures

The performance improvement of reimplementing business rule methods as stored procedures comes at a cost of introducing several undesirable side effects in your business layer design:

▶ Stored procedures persist changes to the database, unlike the business rule methods, which typically modify entity objects in memory and assume that the SaveChanges method of the ObjectContext will be called separately.

▶ Stored procedures bypass any validation or business rules you implemented in entity classes, executing only those implemented in the stored procedure itself or in the database triggers. For instance, the RangeAttribute applied to the UnitsInStock property of the Product entity class to prevent negative values is ignored.

▶ Stored procedures ignore state of any entities that were modified in the object context but not saved to the database yet. For instance, the code calling the FulfillOrder method might have changed status of the order to Paid, but in the database it is still stored as Submitted, causing an error in the stored procedure.

▶ Stored procedures don't automatically refresh entities in the object context. For instance, the FulfillOrder stored procedure might have changed the UnitsInStock in a particular *row* in the Products table in the database, but the *entity object* that represents this row in the application code remains the same, which could lead to optimistic concurrency errors later.

In web applications, where ObjectContext instances are created and destroyed for each incoming request, you might be able to accept the risk of having these side effects. However, they present a significant problem in desktop and console applications, where ObjectContext instances can have a longer life span. If other types of applications reuse your business logic layer, such as the DataModel assembly in this book's sample, you need to consider the decision to implement business rules as stored procedures very carefully. In many instances, the problems caused by the side effects and overhead of the workarounds you might be forced to implement are not worth the performance improvement you gain by using stored procedures in the first place.

Summary

O/R mapping frameworks, such as the Entity Framework and LINQ to SQL, provide a solid foundation for implementing business logic in your applications. Although good entity design requires solid understanding of both object-oriented and relational design principles, it allows you to create classes that represent real-world entities from your business domain and their interaction rules. Encapsulation of entities and rules in the business layer of the application is essential in Dynamic Data applications that can generate significant portions of the user interface dynamically and cannot have the business logic embedded in the presentation layer.

Although your first choice in implementing business rules should be application code, I/O-bound logic can be optimized to work at the database level. The database servers already validate uniqueness and referential integrity; custom validation and business rules can be implemented in database triggers and stored procedures as well. With a small upfront investment in integration of database error handling, this optimization can be done as needed without affecting the rest of the application.

CHAPTER 10

Building Custom Forms

Dynamic Data offers two different, complementary approaches for implementing user interface. On one hand, you can use data annotation attributes, such as Display and UIHint, to modify the metadata describing entity types in your data model. The *dynamic* entity and page templates use this metadata information to generate functional pages for displaying, inserting, and editing the entity instances at runtime. On the other hand, you can accomplish the same task by using the Dynamic Data components to build *custom* field, entity, and page templates as well as custom pages.

Custom user interfaces work well for the majority of information systems, where the challenge is to provide a good experience for users working with a relatively small number of entity types. On the other side of this spectrum are specialized applications, such as document management systems, where the challenge is to support a large number of entity types with acceptable experience. This is a different type of complexity, and a metadata-focused approach becomes more appropriate as it results in smaller codebase and maintenance effort.

Although the metadata-focused approach to user interface has unique advantages, it is significantly more complex and difficult to understand. Not only does a developer need to understand how the Dynamic Data components interpret the built-in metadata, but they also have to understand the custom attributes and templates built by other developers on their team. The template-focused approach, on the other hand, is much closer to the traditional ASP.NET architecture of pages and user controls. It is also easier to understand because it produces concrete UI elements for specific entity types as opposed to abstract templates that can handle any entity type.

It is ironic that when faced with the choice of implementation approach, most ASP.NET developers new to Dynamic Data tend to err on the side of metadata and neglect the use of templates. We can only speculate as to why this tendency exists. Metadata indeed plays an important role in Dynamic Data applications. For some tasks, such as specifying display names of entity types and their properties, the use of data annotation attributes is required. When you know that field labels can be specified in the metadata, it seems logical to specify the order of fields on the form in the metadata as well, even though the form layout has nothing to do with the business logic and it could be easily implemented with custom entity or page templates. Continuing this line of thought leads you down the path of trying to use metadata to control all presentation aspects of all entities.

This and subsequent chapters discuss common challenges that arise in real-world web application projects and how they can be addressed with Dynamic Data components. This chapter starts with concrete, template-based solutions that are easier to understand and implement. Chapter 11, "Building Dynamic Forms," shows how these specific solutions can be generalized to take advantage of metadata and generate user interface dynamically.

Multimode Entity Templates

As discussed in Chapter 4, "Entity Templates," entity templates are primarily responsible for implementing form layouts. Out of the box, Dynamic Data provides *dynamic* entity templates for displaying entities as a single column of labels and controls in Read-only, Insert, and Edit modes. Dynamic Data also allows you to define *custom* templates that are not limited to the single-column layout.

Custom Templates

Listing 10.1 shows the markup of the custom Edit mode entity template, Customers_Edit.ascx, created for the Customer entity type in Chapter 4, Instead of a single column of labels and controls, this entity template relies on the HTML `fieldset` control to group the address fields together, with the customer ID and name displayed above it. Another template, `Customers.ascx`, replicates the same Customer form layout in Read-only mode. If you were to compare the markup for these two custom templates, the only difference between them is the `Mode` attribute of the `DynamicControl` instances they use. The Edit-mode entity template sets it to `Edit`, and the read-only entity template leaves it as `ReadOnly`.

LISTING 10.1 Edit-Mode Customer Entity Template (Markup)

```
<%@ Control Language="C#" CodeBehind="Customers_Edit.ascx.cs"
  Inherits="WebApplication.DynamicData.EntityTemplates.CustomerEditEntityTemplate"%>
```

```
<label>ID:</label>
<asp:DynamicControl runat="server" DataField="CustomerID" Mode="Edit"/>
<label>Name:</label>
<asp:DynamicControl runat="server" DataField="ContactName" Mode="Edit"/>
<fieldset><legend>Address</legend>
  <label>Street:</label>
  <asp:DynamicControl runat="server" DataField="Address" Mode="Edit"/><br />
  <label>City:</label>
  <asp:DynamicControl runat="server" DataField="City" Mode="Edit"/>
  <label>State:</label>
  <asp:DynamicControl runat="server" DataField="Region" Mode="Edit"/>
  <label>Zip:</label>
  <asp:DynamicControl runat="server" DataField="PostalCode" Mode="Edit"/>
</fieldset>
```

This way of implementing a custom form layout is not ideal. Each of the two custom templates recreates the same layout, essentially duplicating the implementation and increasing the cost of ongoing maintenance. Though this might not be a big deal for a template as simple as the one in this example, the problem becomes more and more apparent as the complexity and the number of the custom entity templates grows.

Because in this and a majority of other scenarios the Mode of the DynamicControl instances match the mode of the entity template itself, you could set it programmatically, inside of the Init event handler for individual controls. This would allow the Customers entity template to support all three modes—Read-only, Edit, and Insert—making the Customers_Edit.ascx entity template unnecessary. Listing 10.2 shows the new version of this *multimode* entity template.

LISTING 10.2   Multimode Customer Entity Template (Markup)

```
<%@ Control Language="C#" CodeBehind="Customers.ascx.cs"
  Inherits="WebApplication.DynamicData.EntityTemplates.CustomerEntityTemplate" %>

<label>ID:</label>
<asp:DynamicControl runat="server" DataField="CustomerID"
  OnInit="DynamicControl_Init"/>
<label>Name:</label>
<asp:DynamicControl runat="server" DataField="ContactName"
  OnInit="DynamicControl_Init"/>
<fieldset><legend>Address</legend>
  <label>Street:</label>
  <asp:DynamicControl runat="server" DataField="Address"
    OnInit="DynamicControl_Init"/><br />
  <label>City:</label>
  <asp:DynamicControl runat="server" DataField="City"
    OnInit="DynamicControl_Init"/>
```

LISTING 10.2 Continued

```
  <label>State:</label>
  <asp:DynamicControl runat="server" DataField="Region"
    OnInit="DynamicControl_Init"/>
  <label>Zip:</label>
  <asp:DynamicControl runat="server" DataField="PostalCode"
    OnInit="DynamicControl_Init"/>
</fieldset>
```

Notice how instead of specifying the Mode property for each DynamicControl in the markup, a method called DynamicControl_Init is used to handle the Init events of all DynamicControl instances. Listing 10.3 shows the code-behind where this method is defined. The DynamicControl_Init method relies on its first argument, sender, to determine which DynamicControl instance needs to be initialized. It then sets the Mode property of this control with the value of the Mode property of the entity template itself.

LISTING 10.3 Multimode Customer Entity Template (Code-Behind)

```
using System;
using System.Web.DynamicData;

namespace WebApplication.DynamicData.EntityTemplates
{
  public partial class CustomerEntityTemplate : EntityTemplateUserControl
  {
    protected void InitDynamicControl(object sender, EventArgs e)
    {
      var dynamicControl = (DynamicControl)sender;
      dynamicControl.Mode = this.Mode;
    }
  }
}
```

The new *multimode* Customers entity template is slightly more complex than the old, Edit mode entity template that did not require any logic in the code-behind. However, this approach eliminates the duplication of markup that existed with two separate mode-specific templates, making creation and maintenance of custom entity templates much more attractive. There is just one problem—it does not work, not right away.

Dynamic Templates

Unfortunately, the algorithm illustrated in Figure 5.4 that Dynamic Data uses to look up entity templates chose the *dynamic* Edit mode template, Default_Edit.ascx, even though a *custom* multimode entity template might exist for the Customer entity. It turns out that the dynamic entity templates suffer from the same code duplication problem as the initial version of the Customer entity templates, and you can solve it using the exact same approach. Listing 10.4 shows the markup of the dynamic Edit mode template.

LISTING 10.4 Edit-Mode Dynamic Entity Template (Markup)

```
<%@ Control Language="C#" CodeBehind="Default_Edit.ascx.cs"
  Inherits="WebApplication.DynamicData.EntityTemplates.DefaultEditEntityTemplate" %>
<table class="DDDetailsTable">
  <asp:EntityTemplate runat="server" ID="entityTemplate">
    <ItemTemplate>
      <tr>
        <td class="DDLightHeader">
          <asp:Label runat="server" OnInit="Label_Init"
            OnPreRender="Label_PreRender"/>
        </td>
        <td>
          <asp:DynamicControl runat="server" ID="DynamicControl" Mode="Edit"
            OnInit="DynamicControl_Init" />
        </td>
      </tr>
    </ItemTemplate>
  </asp:EntityTemplate>
</table>
```

As you can see, the Default_Edit entity template hardcodes the Edit value for the Mode property of the DynamicControl instances. The Default_Insert entity template hardcodes the Insert value, and the Default (Read-only) template leaves the default, ReadOnly value. Aside from this, there are no other significant differences between the three dynamic templates, and you can replace them with the single multimode template shown in Listing 10.5.

LISTING 10.5 Multimode Dynamic Entity Template (Markup)

```
<%@ Control Language="C#" CodeBehind="Default.ascx.cs"
  Inherits="WebApplication.DynamicData.EntityTemplates.DefaultEntityTemplate" %>
<table class="DDDetailsTable">
  <asp:EntityTemplate runat="server" ID="entityTemplate">
    <ItemTemplate>
      <tr>
        <td class="DDLightHeader">
          <asp:Label runat="server" OnInit="Label_Init"
            OnPreRender="Label_PreRender" />
        </td>
        <td>
          <asp:DynamicControl runat="server" ID="dynamicControl"
```

10

LISTING 10.5 Continued

```
            OnInit="DynamicControl_Init" />
        </td>
      </tr>
    </ItemTemplate>
  </asp:EntityTemplate>
</table>
```

Notice how this new version is nearly identical to the previous one shown in Listing 10.4. The hardcoded Mode property was removed from the DynamicControl, but the DynamicControl_Init event handler was already in place because the dynamic entity templates already need to initialize another property of the DynamicControl instances programmatically, the DataField property.

Listing 10.6 shows the code-behind of the dynamic multimode entity template. Bold font indicates the only significant difference between this new implementation and the code-behind of the original Default_Edit and Default_Insert entity templates.

LISTING 10.6 Multimode Dynamic Entity Template (Code-Behind)

```csharp
using System;
using System.Collections.Generic;
using System.Web.DynamicData;
using System.Web.UI.WebControls;

namespace WebApplication.DynamicData.EntityTemplates
{
  public partial class DefaultEntityTemplate : EntityTemplateUserControl
  {
    private MetaColumn currentColumn;

    protected override void OnLoad(EventArgs e)
    {
      IEnumerable<MetaColumn> scaffoldColumns = this.Table.GetScaffoldColumns(
        this.Mode, this.ContainerType);
      foreach (MetaColumn column in scaffoldColumns)
      {
        this.currentColumn = column;
        NamingContainer container = new NamingContainer();
        this.entityTemplate.ItemTemplate.InstantiateIn(container);
        this.entityTemplate.Controls.Add(container);
      }
    }

    protected void Label_Init(object sender, EventArgs e)
    {
```

```
      Label label = (Label)sender;
      label.Text = this.currentColumn.DisplayName;
    }

    protected void Label_PreRender(object sender, EventArgs e)
    {
      Label label = (Label)sender;
      DynamicControl dynamicControl =
        (DynamicControl)label.FindControl("dynamicControl");
      FieldTemplateUserControl fieldTemplate =
        dynamicControl.FieldTemplate as FieldTemplateUserControl;
      if (fieldTemplate != null && fieldTemplate.DataControl != null)
      {
        label.AssociatedControlID =
          fieldTemplate.DataControl.GetUniqueIDRelativeTo(label);
      }
    }

    protected void DynamicControl_Init(object sender, EventArgs e)
    {
      DynamicControl dynamicControl = (DynamicControl)sender;
      dynamicControl.DataField = this.currentColumn.Name;
      dynamicControl.Mode = this.Mode;
    }
  }
}
```

As you can see, the only change needed is to make in the original Edit mode dynamic template to support multiple modes is add a single line to initializing the Mode property of the DynamicControl instances programmatically, based on the Mode property provided by the EntityTemplateUserControl base class. Everything else in the code-behind was already in place.

Now that there is only one dynamic multimode template, Dynamic Data uses the custom entity template, Customers.ascx, in Edit mode before falling back to the dynamic template, Default.ascx. This allows you to implement custom form layouts in a single place by implementing multimode entity templates. However, this approach still allows you to build mode-specific templates, such as Customers_Edit.ascx, in case you need to fine-tune the appearance of the entity form in different modes.

Creating Dynamic Label Control

There is one flaw in this last implementation of the custom multimode entity template, Customers.ascx: Display names of the columns are hard-coded in the markup of the template. This presents a problem because the same display names also must be specified in the entity metadata for the validation error messages that can be displayed to the users to include human-readable property names instead of their internal, PascalCased, values. Listing 10.7 shows an example of how the display names can be specified by applying the `DisplayAttribute` to entity properties.

LISTING 10.7 Customer Entity Data Annotations

```
using System.ComponentModel.DataAnnotations;

namespace DataModel
{
  [MetadataType(typeof(Customer.Metadata))]
  partial class Customer
  {
    public abstract class Metadata
    {
      [Display(Name = "Name")]
      public object ContactName { get; set; }

      [Display(Name = "ID")]
      public object CustomerID { get; set; }
    }
  }
}
```

With the current implementations, the display names specified with data annotations match the names hard-coded in the template markup. However, in real-world applications, it is common for the terminology to change as developers continue learning the business domain. When a display name for a particular property changes, it needs to be updated in all places where it is hard-coded. Dynamic entity templates solve this problem by generating the labels from column metadata, so the display names can be specified only once in the data model. However, using the same approach in custom entity templates is problematic because the built-in `Label` control cannot be directly associated with a particular `MetaColumn`.

This problem can be solved by a simple control, `UnleashedLabel`, included in the sample `Unleashed.DynamicData` project accompanying this book. This control inherits from the `Label` class and, similar to `DynamicControl` and `DynamicHyperLink`, defines a property called `DataField` to hold the name of the entity property whose display name needs to be rendered by the template. You can specify the `DataField` in template markup and the control would find the corresponding `MetaColumn` and render its `DisplayName` at runtime. So instead of hard-coding the customer name like this:

```
<label>Name</label>
```

you can implement it in the template markup as shown here:

```
<unl:UnleashedLabel runat="server" DataField="ContactName"/>
```

> **NOTE**
>
> Although the name DynamicLabel would be more appropriate for this particular control, it is called *UnleashedLabel*. To avoid confusion and clearly distinguish them from the built-in controls provided by Dynamic Data, you will see the *Unleashed* prefix used for all new and extended controls created in this book.

Listing 10.8 shows the source code of this control with some of the error-handling logic removed to make it easier to read. You can find the complete source code of this control in the Unleashed.DynamicData project of the solution accompanying this book.

LISTING 10.8 UnleashedLabel Implementation

```
using System;
using System.ComponentModel;
using System.Web.DynamicData;
using System.Web.UI.WebControls;

namespace Unleashed.DynamicData
{
  public class UnleashedLabel : Label
  {
    [DefaultValue("")]
    public string DataField
    {
      get
      {
        object obj = this.ViewState["DataField"];
        return obj != null ? (string)obj : string.Empty;
      }
      set
      {
        this.ViewState["DataField"] = value;
      }
    }

    protected override void OnInit(EventArgs e)
    {
      base.OnInit(e);
      MetaTable table = this.FindMetaTable();
      MetaColumn column = table.GetColumn(this.DataField);
      this.Text = column.DisplayName;
    }

    protected override void OnPreRender(EventArgs e)
    {
```

LISTING 10.8 Continued

```
    base.OnPreRender(e);
    var fieldTemplate = this.FindFieldTemplate(this.DataField)
      as FieldTemplateUserControl;
    if (fieldTemplate != null && fieldTemplate.DataControl != null)
    {
      this.AssociatedControlID =
        fieldTemplate.DataControl.GetUniqueIDRelativeTo(this);
    }
  }
}
}
```

Most of the work in UnleashedLabel is done by the OnInit method. It uses the
FindMetaTable extension method defined in the DynamicDataExtensions class to find the
MetaTable object associated with the FormView or GridView hosting this control. As you
recall from Chapter 7, "Metadata API," all page templates in Dynamic Data have to associate a MetaTable object with their databound controls either with the help of a
DynamicDataManager control or explicitly in code-behind. The UnleashedLabel control
takes advantage of this fact similar to how the DynamicControl does.

Having obtained the MetaTable object, the OnInit method calls its GetColumn method to
find the MetaColumn object describing the entity property based on the DataField property
supplied in markup. After the MetaColumn object has been retrieved, its DisplayName property value is then used to initialize the Text property of the label.

Aside from having to find the MetaColumn object programmatically, the OnInit method in
UnleashedLabel performs the same function as the Label_Init event handler in the
dynamic entity template shown in Listing 10.6; it initializes the label text based on the
display name of the entity property. Likewise, the OnPreRender method is very similar to
the Label_PreRender event handler in that it associates the label with the data control
generated by the field template. The only significant difference here is that this code relies
on the FindFieldTemplate extension method defined in the DynamicDataExtensions class
to find the field template instead of accessing the corresponding DynamicControl directly.

NOTE

To use this control in markup, you could register it in the various pages and user
controls individually. However, because the sample solution uses it pervasively, it
makes sense to register it globally by adding the following line to the
System.Web/Pages/Controls section of the Web.config file:

```
<add tagPrefix="unl"
  assembly="Unleashed.DynamicData"
  namespace="Unleashed.DynamicData "/>
```

Extending DynamicControl

Up until now, you had to specify the Init event handler for every instance of
DynamicControl in each multimode entity template. For custom templates, especially the
more complex ones, this is not only tedious and error prone, it also increases the size of
template markup, making it less readable.

To make implementation of custom multimode templates even easier, the
UnleashedControl (in the sample Unleashed.DynamicData project) extends the built-in
DynamicControl to set its own Mode property based on the mode of the parent entity
template. Instead of the following markup

```
<asp:DynamicControl runat="server" DataField="ContactName"
  OnInit="DynamicControl_Init"/>
```

you would simply write

```
<unl:UnleashedControl runat="server" DataField="ContactName"/>
```

and not have to worry about specifying the Init event handler. Listing 10.9 includes the
complete source code of the UnleashedControl.

LISTING 10.9 UnleashedControl Implementation

```
using System;
using System.Web.DynamicData;
using System.Web.UI.WebControls;

namespace Unleashed.DynamicData
{
  public class UnleashedControl : DynamicControl
  {
    protected override void OnInit(EventArgs e)
    {
      if (this.Mode == DataBoundControlMode.ReadOnly)
      {
        var entityTemplate = this.TemplateControl as EntityTemplateUserControl;
        if (entityTemplate != null)
          this.Mode = entityTemplate.Mode;
      }

      base.OnInit(e);
    }
  }
}
```

10

As you can see, all work in the UnleashedControl is done by its only method called OnInit. In the base class, DynamicControl, this virtual method is responsible for finding an appropriate field template and instantiating it inside of the dynamic control. This overridden method performs the additional initialization steps before calling the inherited version.

First, it checks to see if the Mode property is different from the default value ReadOnly; you do not want to silently overwrite the value specified by the developer in template markup. If the mode has not been specified explicitly, the code probes the TemplateControl property to find the parent entity template, an instance of the EntityTemplateUserControl class. If the parent entity template was found, the code initializes the Mode property of the dynamic control based on the Mode property of the parent entity template.

With the UnleashedControl and UnleashedLabel controls, you can modify the custom multimode template for the Customer entity to look similar to what is shown in Listing 10.10. This new version no longer requires additional initialization logic in the code behind and does not hardcode display names of the properties in template markup. At this point, it has no plumbing that would unnecessarily obscure the intent of the markup—it only contains logic defining the form layout and does not duplicate any information from the entity metadata.

LISTING 10.10 Customer Entity Template with Extended Controls (Markup)

```
<%@ Control Language="C#" CodeBehind="Customers.ascx.cs"
  Inherits="WebApplication.DynamicData.EntityTemplates.CustomerEntityTemplate" %>

<unl:UnleashedLabel runat="server" DataField="CustomerID" />
<unl:UnleashedControl runat="server" DataField="CustomerID" />
<unl:UnleashedLabel runat="server" DataField="ContactName" />
<unl:UnleashedControl runat="server" DataField="ContactName" />
<fieldset>
  <legend>Address</legend>
  <unl:UnleashedLabel runat="server" DataField="Address" />
  <unl:UnleashedControl runat="server" DataField="Address" />
  <br />
  <unl:UnleashedLabel runat="server" DataField="City" />
  <unl:UnleashedControl runat="server" DataField="City" />
  <unl:UnleashedLabel runat="server" DataField="Region" />
  <unl:UnleashedControl runat="server" DataField="Region" />
  <unl:UnleashedLabel runat="server" DataField="PostalCode" />
  <unl:UnleashedControl runat="server" DataField="PostalCode" />
</fieldset>
```

Configuring Field Templates

When creating custom entity templates, you have a good control over placement of the field templates. You can arrange `DynamicControl` instances using HTML `table` or `div` tags and CSS if that is what you prefer. However, there is no obvious way to control appearance of controls within the field templates. Take a look at Figure 10.1, which shows a web page generated by the custom entity template for the Customer entity.

FIGURE 10.1   Web page with default address field template.

Notice how the Address text box cuts off a long string even though there is plenty of space available on the right side of the control. Had this page been built with traditional ASP.NET controls, you could have easily changed the `Columns` property of the address `TextBox` control and made it wider. How do you configure a field template instantiated by a `DynamicControl`?

Specifying a Field Template Explicitly

You can choose a specific field template to be created by a `DynamicControl` by setting its `UIHint` property. In this example, you might want to try using the `MultilineText` field template for the Address property as it creates a wider `TextBox` in `Edit` mode:

```
<asp:DynamicControl runat="server" DataField="Address"
   UIHint= "MultilineText"/>
```

The `UIHint` property is usually assigned in page or template markup. However, it can be initialized programmatically as well, by handling the `Init` event of the `DynamicControl` as shown next:

```
protected void DynamicControl_Init(object sender, EventArgs e)
{
   var dynamicControl = (DynamicControl)sender;
   dynamicControl.UIHint = "MultilineText";
}
```

10

Figure 10.2. shows how the Customer edit page looks with the `MultilineText` field template used for the `Address` property.

FIGURE 10.2 Web page with multiline address field template.

Unfortunately, the attempt to use the `MultilineText` template does not give the right solution. The `TextBox` control generated by this field template is simply too big. With several rows of empty space, it not only takes too much real estate, but can also mislead the users into thinking that they can put the entire address, including city, state, and zip code, into the same field.

Configuring Field Templates Declaratively

`DynamicControl` also allows you to configure the field template it instantiates. You can set any public property of the field template by specifying *custom attributes* for its parent `DynamicControl`.

First, you need to modify the appropriate field template to define a property you want to assign. In this example, the `Text_Edit` field template is used for the `Address` property of the Customer entity by default. The new property will be called Columns and allow you to set the `Columns` property of the `TextBox` control created by this template. Following is an extract from `Text_Edit.ascx.cs` that defines this property:

```
public partial class Text_EditField : FieldTemplateUserControl
{
    public int Columns { get; set; }
}
```

There are several different ways to initialize the `Columns` property of the `TextBox` control created by this field template. The simplest approach is to use an ASP.NET data binding expression and modify the markup file, `Text_Edit.ascx`, as shown here:

```
<asp:TextBox ID="textBox" runat="server" Text='<%# FieldValueEditString %>'
    Columns='<%# Columns %>'/>
```

With these changes made, you can now change the custom Customer entity template to specify the Columns value for the Address field:

```
<unl:UnleashedControl runat="server" DataField="Address" Columns="65"/>
```

NOTE

This example is using the UnleashedControl created earlier in this chapter. However, this technique works just as well with the built-in DynamicControl provided by Dynamic Data.

Figure 10.3 shows the web page generated by the Customer entity template with these changes implemented. Notice how much wider the Address text box is now, allowing the entire address value to be displayed without cutting it off.

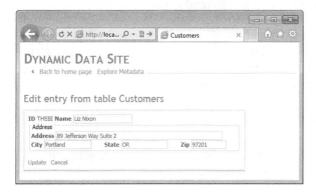

FIGURE 10.3 Web page with configured Address field template.

Although the layout of the Customer form is still far from perfect, with this approach you can continue working on the Text_Edit field template to expose the properties necessary to configure the TextBox size to meet your requirements and personal taste. This could include the Width property of the TextBox control or perhaps the CssClass or Style properties. Essentially, this is the same process you would follow to design and implement a traditional UserControl that encapsulates a TextBox and needs to provide sufficient means to configure its appearance.

Configuring Field Templates Programmatically

You can also configure the field templates and their data controls programmatically. Instead of specifying custom attributes for DynamicControl as discussed in the previous

10

section, you could have used the following method to handle the `Load` event of the `Address` control in this custom Customer entity template:

```
protected void Address_Load(object source, EventArgs e)
{
    var addressControl = (DynamicControl)source;
    var template = (FieldTemplateUserControl)addressControl.FieldTemplate;
    var addressTextBox = (TextBox)template.DataControl;
        addressTextBox.Columns = 65;
}
```

Given an instance of the `DynamicControl`, you can access the field template it creates via its `FieldTemplate` property. Unfortunately, this property is of type `Control`, so you must downcast the value it returns to the `FieldTemplateUserControl` class to access the `DataControl` property, which returns the actual `TextBox` that displays the address. Having located the actual data control, you can programmatically configure any of its properties, such as the `Columns` property used in this example.

The declarative and programmatic approaches of configuring field templates have different tradeoffs. The declarative approach requires you to modify each field template to expose the properties you need to configure in entity templates. However, when the properties are defined, their use in template markup is more concise. Unfortunately, neither Visual Studio nor ASP.NET runtime warns you if you mistype or try setting a non-existent field template property as a custom attribute of `DynamicControl`. Custom attributes that do not match field template properties are silently ignored.

The programmatic approach requires no changes to the field templates but more code for each customization. It also has negative impact on the page size by unnecessarily increasing the size of field template's `ViewState`. Finally, by accessing the data control directly instead of a specific property exposed by the field template, you might be breaking its internal assumptions, which can have unexpected side effects when the implementation of the field template changes.

Creating Custom Field Templates

Suppose you have a requirement to allow users entering Customer information to select State values from a drop-down list. In the sample data model, State values are stored as strings in the Region column of the Customers table. Based on this information, Dynamic Data chooses the `Text_Edit` field template for this column and displays a simple `TextBox` control, which is not what you need. Although the `ForeignKey_Edit` field template looks promising, as it creates a `DropDownList` control, it requires a foreign key column referencing a lookup table, which you do not have in the data model.

When functionality of the available built-in field templates is not sufficient, you can create a *custom* field template to meet your requirements. In the sample project, a custom field template called `State_Edit` was added to the `DynamicData\FieldTemplates` of the

web application project. Figure 10.4 shows an example of the Customer edit page generated with the new field template; Listing 10.11 shows its markup.

FIGURE 10.4 Web page with a custom State field template.

LISTING 10.11 State_Edit Field Template (Markup)

```
<%@ Control Language="C#" CodeBehind="State_Edit.ascx.cs"
  Inherits="WebApplication.DynamicData.FieldTemplates.StateEditField" %>

<asp:DropDownList ID="dropDownList" runat="server" />

<asp:RequiredFieldValidator runat="server" ID="requiredFieldValidator"
  ControlToValidate="dropDownList" Enabled="false" />
<asp:DynamicValidator runat="server" ID="dynamicValidator"
  ControlToValidate="dropDownList" />
```

Although this custom field template is built specifically for the Region column, it is still
important to follow the pattern used by the generic field templates and create the
RequiredFieldValidator and DynamicValidator controls to validate values selected by
the users in the DropDownList. You want to keep the business logic out of custom
templates as much as possible. On one hand, this makes implementation of the user
interface easier—simply place the appropriate validators in template markup and let
Dynamic Data take care of the rest. On the other hand, consolidating the business logic
in the data model with data annotations and custom code implemented in your entity
classes helps to keep it maintainable and testable.

As you would expect, most of the heavy lifting in the State_Edit field template is done
in its code-behind, which is shown in Listing 10.12.

LISTING 10.12 State_Edit Field Template (Code-Behind)

```
using System;
using System.Collections.Specialized;
using System.Web.DynamicData;
```

LISTING 10.12 Continued

```
using System.Web.UI;
using System.Web.UI.WebControls;

namespace WebApplication.DynamicData.FieldTemplates
{
  public partial class StateEditField : FieldTemplateUserControl
  {
    public override Control DataControl
    {
      get { return this.dropDownList; }
    }

    private static readonly string[] states = new string[]
    {
      "AL", "AK", "AZ", "AR", "CA", "CO", "CT", "DE", "FL", "GA",
      "HI", "ID", "IL", "IN", "IA", "KS", "KY", "LA", "ME", "MD",
      "MA", "MI", "MN", "MS", "MO", "MT", "NE", "NV", "NH", "NJ",
      "NM", "NY", "NC", "ND", "OH", "OK", "OR", "PA", "RI", "SC",
      "SD", "TN", "TX", "UT", "VT", "VA", "WA", "WV", "WI", "WY"
    };

    protected override void OnInit(EventArgs e)
    {
      base.OnInit(e);

      this.dropDownList.Items.Add(new ListItem(string.Empty));
      foreach (string state in states)
        this.dropDownList.Items.Add(new ListItem(state));

      this.SetUpValidator(this.requiredFieldValidator);
      this.SetUpValidator(this.dynamicValidator);
    }

    protected override void OnDataBinding(EventArgs e)
    {
      base.OnDataBinding(e);
      if (this.dropDownList.Items.FindByValue(this.FieldValueEditString) != null)
        this.dropDownList.SelectedValue = this.FieldValueEditString;
    }

    protected override void ExtractValues(IOrderedDictionary dictionary)
    {
      dictionary[this.Column.Name] =
        this.ConvertEditedValue(this.dropDownList.SelectedValue);
```

```
      }
    }
}
```

The `OnInit` method populates the list of items in the `DropDownList` control using a static array of U.S. state abbreviations and initializes the validators by calling the `SetUpValidator` method provided by the `FieldTemplateUserControl` base class. The `OnDataBinding` method provides the initial selection for the `DropDownList` based on the state value previously stored in the database, and the `ExtractValues` method returns the new value selected by the user to the data source control when it is time to save the customer entity in the database.

```
<unl:UnleashedControl runat="server" DataField="Region" UIHint="State" />
```

With the new custom field template created, you can now modify the Customer entity template as just shown to use it for the `Region` property instead of the default field template.

> **NOTE**
>
> Value of the `UIHint` property of the `DynamicControl` class should not include the `_Edit` suffix used in the name of the field template. As explained in Chapter 4, Dynamic Data automatically adds this suffix to the `UIHint` value when looking for the field template, and had you set `UIHint` to `State_Edit`, it would be looking for a field template called `State_Edit_Edit`.

Implementing Interaction Between Field Templates

Unfortunately, as you start using the new `State` field template, you soon discover that it does not work well for international customers. Northwind Traders does business with customers in Europe also, but only United States and Canada use states, or more appropriately, regions, in their mailing addresses. Moreover, for the United States and Canada, you also need the users to see only the regions appropriate for a particular country. In other words, the field template for the Region property of the Customer entity must somehow work together with the field template for the `Country` property to provide the required user experience.

You can start tackling this problem by renaming the custom field template from `State_Edit` to `Region_Edit` to more accurately reflect that it is being used not only for customers in the U.S., but in other countries as well. Because the list of regions is no longer static, you cannot pretend to know all possible regions in all countries and need to go back to using a `TextBox` as a data entry control. However, to keep data entry easy for the most common countries, you can use the `AutoCompleteExtender` from the AJAX

10

control toolkit to suggest a list of well-known regions to users based on the countries they enter.

```
<asp:TextBox ID="textBox" runat="server" Text="<%# FieldValueEditString %>"/>
<ajax:AutoCompleteExtender ID="autoCompleteExtender" runat="server"
    TargetControlID="textBox" ServicePath="/RegionCompletionService.svc"
    ServiceMethod="GetCompletionList" />
```

The `AutoCompleteExtender` requires a web service method to get the list of suggested values. This web service, shown in Listing 10.13, defines a single method, `GetCompletionList`, that will be called by the client-side JavaScript code generated by the `AutoCompleteExtender` based on the `ServicePath` and `ServiceMethod` attributes. Although the method name itself is configured in markup, the names and the order of the parameters have to match exactly what the `AutoCompleteExtender` implementation expects. In particular, the `prefixText` parameter receives the current value user entered in the Region text box, the *count* specifies the number of matching items that should be returned, and the `contextKey` will be the value user entered in the Country field.

LISTING 10.13 RegionCompletionService Implementation

```
using System;
using System.Collections.Generic;
using System.Linq;
using System.ServiceModel;

namespace WebApplication
{
  [ServiceContract]
  public class RegionCompletionService
  {
    private static readonly Dictionary<string, string[]> regionsByCountry =
      new Dictionary<string, string[]>(StringComparer.InvariantCultureIgnoreCase)
      {
        { "Canada",
          new[] {
            "ON", "QC", "NS", "NB", "MB", "BC", "PE", "SK", "AB", "NL",
            "NT", "UT", "NU"
          }
        },
        { "USA",
          new[] {
            "AL", "AK", "AZ", "AR", "CA", "CO", "CT", "DE", "FL", "GA",
            "HI", "ID", "IL", "IN", "IA", "KS", "KY", "LA", "ME", "MD",
            "MA", "MI", "MN", "MS", "MO", "MT", "NE", "NV", "NH", "NJ",
```

```
            "NM", "NY", "NC", "ND", "OH", "OK", "OR", "PA", "RI", "SC",
            "SD", "TN", "TX", "UT", "VT", "VA", "WA", "WV", "WI", "WY"
        }
      }
   };

   [OperationContract]
   public string[] GetCompletionList(
     string prefixText, int count, string contextKey)
   {
     var country = contextKey ?? string.Empty;
     string[] regions;
     if (regionsByCountry.TryGetValue(country, out regions))
     {
       var ignoreCase = StringComparison.InvariantCultureIgnoreCase;
       return regions
         .Where(r => r.StartsWith(prefixText, ignoreCase))
         .Take(count)
         .ToArray();
     }
     return new string[0];
   }
  }
}
```

The RegionCompletionService uses a `Dictionary` object to store a list of regions for each known country. The `GetCompletionList` method performs lookup in the dictionary to find an array of regions for the given country and returns only those regions that start with the prefix entered by the user. Both dictionary lookup and the prefix filtering are implemented to ignore case.

With WCF, implementing a service is only half the battle; endpoint configuration is crucial to allow the client code (which in this case is JavaScript) to call the service successfully. In the sample project, this is done by specifying the `WebScriptServiceHostFactory` in the `@ServiceHost` directive of the .SVC file, which takes care of configuring the HTTP endpoint based on the location of the SVC file and accepting JSON-formatted method calls generated by the `AutoCompleteExtender`.

LISTING 10.14 RegionCompletionService.svc

```
<%@ ServiceHost Language="C#" Debug="true"
  Service="WebApplication.RegionCompletionService"
  CodeBehind="RegionCompletionService.svc.cs"
  Factory="System.ServiceModel.Activation.WebScriptServiceHostFactory" %>
```

10

Accessing Initial Field Values of Other Columns

The next and biggest challenge is to figure out how to get the current value of the Country property inside of the Region_Edit field template. The most reliable way to do this is by getting it from the actual field template instantiated for the Country property.

> **NOTE**
>
> At first thought, the Row property of the FieldTemplateUserControl (the base class of the custom field template) looks as if it could be used to access other property values. Logically one would expect this property to return the entity instance, which is being edited by the field template. This is indeed the case with LINQ to SQL. Entity Framework, or more specifically the EntityDataSource control, wraps the actual entity instance inside of an EntityDataSourceWrapper object. The code example that follows shows how to implement a strongly-typed property that returns the Customer instance inside of the custom field template:
>
> ```
> private Customer Customer
> {
>   get
>   {
>     Customer customer = this.Row as Customer;
>     if (customer == null)
>     {
>       var typeDescriptor = (ICustomTypeDescriptor)this.Row;
>       if (typeDescriptor != null)
>         customer = (Customer)typeDescriptor.GetPropertyOwner(null);
>     }
>     return customer;
>   }
> }
> ```
>
> This code works with both LINQ to SQL and Entity Framework, but unfortunately, there are still two problems with this approach. The Row property of the FieldTemplateUserControl class is only available during the data binding stage of the ASP.NET page lifecycle. During post-backs, which is when you would want to check for a modified Country property value, accessing this property throws an InvalidOperationException. Moreover, this property returns null when the field template is instantiated in Insert mode, making it impossible to determine the default value of the Country property.

The FieldTemplateUserControl base class provides a method called FindOtherFieldTemplate that takes the name of the entity property as a parameter and returns the field template that was instantiated for it. The earliest stage in the field template's lifecycle when it can call this method is the Load. Although it is technically possible to call it during the Init stage, the result would depend on the order in which the field templates are created, and the method returns null if the other field template has not been created yet. This example shows how this can implemented by overriding the OnLoad of the field template:

```
private FieldTemplateUserControl countryFieldTemplate;
protected override void OnLoad(EventArgs e)
{
  base.OnLoad(e);
  this.countryFieldTemplate = this.FindOtherFieldTemplate("Country");
}
```

Having located the field template instance of the Country property, you can use it to access the property value and store the country name in the ContextKey of the AutoCompleteExtender, which will pass it to the GetCompletionList of the RegionCompletionService. This needs to be done during the Data Binding stage of the field template lifecycle when the Customer entity instance has already been retrieved from the database during the Load stage. The next code example shows how this can be implemented in the overridden OnDataBinding method:

```
protected override void OnDataBinding(EventArgs e)
{
  base.OnDataBinding(e);
  string country = this.countryFieldTemplate.FieldValueEditString;
  this.autoCompleteExtender.ContextKey = country;
}
```

Accessing Modified Field Values of Other Columns

At this point, the Region field template can display the list of regions appropriate for the current country when the web page is first rendered for an existing Customer entity instance. However, when the field template is used in Insert mode and the customer entity does not exist, the country name has not been entered yet, and the list of regions will be empty. The list will also not be updated when user changes the Country value from its initial value. So the last challenge is to figure out how to reload the list of regions as the Country property value changes.

Just like in a traditional ASP.NET application, you can use post-backs and event handlers to implement code that reacts to user input. The custom Region field template needs to respond to the change made by the user in the Country field template, which requires accessing the TextBox control it instantiates. The next example shows an extract from the Region_Edit field template that accomplishes this task:

```
protected override void OnLoad(EventArgs e)
{
  base.OnLoad(e);
  var countryFieldTemplate = this.FindOtherFieldTemplate("Country");
  var countryTextBox = (TextBox)countryFieldTemplate.DataControl;
  countryTextBox.AutoPostBack = true;
```

10

```
        countryTextBox.TextChanged += CountryTextBox_TextChanged;
    }

    private void CountryTextBox_TextChanged(object sender, EventArgs e)
    {
        var countryTextBox = (TextBox)sender;
        this.autoCompleteExtender.ContextKey = countryTextBox.Text;
    }
```

The overridden OnLoad method retrieves the TextBox control created by the countryFieldTemplate through its DataControl property. It then assigns the CountryTextBox_TextChanged method as an event handler to its TextChanged event. This event handler is where you can access the current Country value from the text box and store it in the ContextKey of the AutoCompleteExtender. Note that by default, changing a value in a TextBox control does not trigger a post-back. For the list of regions to be updated immediately, as the user modifies the Country field value, the OnLoad method explicitly sets the AutoPostBack property of the country TextBox control to true. This triggers a post-back when the user tabs out or clicks away from the text box after changing the Country value.

Initial Implementation of the Region_Edit Field Template

Figure 10.5 shows a web page generated after the Customer entity template was modified to use the Region field template.

FIGURE 10.5 Web page with custom Region field template.

The complete code-behind file of the Region_Edit field template is shown in Listing 10.15.

LISTING 10.15 Initial Implementation of the Region_Edit Field Template (Code-Behind)

```
using System;
using System.Collections.Specialized;
using System.Web.DynamicData;
using System.Web.UI;

namespace WebApplication.DynamicData.FieldTemplates
{
```

```csharp
public partial class RegionEditField : FieldTemplateUserControl
{
  private FieldTemplateUserControl countryFieldTemplate;

  public override Control DataControl
  {
    get { return this.textBox; }
  }

  protected override void OnInit(EventArgs e)
  {
    base.OnInit(e);
    this.textBox.ToolTip = this.Column.Description;
    this.SetUpValidator(this.requiredFieldValidator);
    this.SetUpValidator(this.dynamicValidator);
  }

  protected override void OnLoad(EventArgs e)
  {
    base.OnLoad(e);
    this.countryFieldTemplate = this.FindOtherFieldTemplate("Country");
    var countryTextBox = (TextBox)this.countryFieldTemplate.DataControl;
    countryTextBox.AutoPostBack = true;
    countryTextBox.TextChanged += CountryTextBox_TextChanged;
  }

  protected override void OnDataBinding(EventArgs e)
  {
    base.OnDataBinding(e);
    string country = this.countryFieldTemplate.FieldValueEditString;
    this.autoCompleteExtender.ContextKey = country;
  }

  protected override void ExtractValues(IOrderedDictionary dictionary)
  {
    dictionary[this.Column.Name] = this.ConvertEditedValue(this.textBox.Text);
  }

  private void CountryTextBox_TextChanged(object sender, EventArgs args)
  {
    var countryTextBox = (TextBox)sender;
    this.autoCompleteExtender.ContextKey = countryTextBox.Text;
  }
}
```

10

Improving Encapsulation of Field Templates

Although the current implementation of the Region field template satisfies your immediate requirements, it also suffers from a serious problem. By accessing the DataControl of the Country field template directly and casting it down to the TextBox type, the Region field template assumes that the Country field template will always use a TextBox as its data control. Although this assumption is correct today, it easily breaks as soon as you decide to change what is really an internal implementation of how the Country property is presented on the web page. You could decide to create a custom field template with a DropDownList so that users can pick a country instead of typing its name. You could also decide to change the Text_Edit field template to use a third-party control instead of the built-in TextBox. Any number of changes like this breaks the Region_Edit field template.

As the number of dynamic and custom field templates increases, improving encapsulation helps to keep their maintenance simple. The need to access the current field value and detect its changes is a common problem. You can solve it by introducing an extended base class for field templates that provides a common way to access this information without having to take a dependency on the specific implementation details of a particular template. In the sample solution accompanying this book, this new base class is called UnleashedFieldTemplate; you can see its complete source code in Listing 10.16.

LISTING 10.16 UnleashedFieldTemplate Base Class

```
using System;
using System.Collections.Specialized;
using System.ComponentModel;
using System.Web.DynamicData;
using System.Web.UI;
using System.Web.UI.WebControls;

namespace Unleashed.DynamicData
{
  public class UnleashedFieldTemplate : FieldTemplateUserControl
  {
    private static readonly object FieldValueChangedEvent = new object();

    public virtual bool AutoPostBack { get; set; }

    public override object FieldValue
    {
      get { return base.FieldValue; }
      set
      {
        if (base.FieldValue != value)
        {
          base.FieldValue = value;
          this.OnFieldValueChanged(EventArgs.Empty);
```

```csharp
      }
    }
  }

  protected override object GetColumnValue(MetaColumn column)
  {
    try
    {
      return base.GetColumnValue(column);
    }
    catch (InvalidOperationException)
    {
      return this.ExtractFieldValue();
    }
  }

  public event EventHandler FieldValueChanged
  {
    add { this.Events.AddHandler(FieldValueChangedEvent, value); }
    remove { this.Events.RemoveHandler(FieldValueChangedEvent, value); }
  }

  protected new UnleashedFieldTemplate FindOtherFieldTemplate(string columnName)
  {
    return (UnleashedFieldTemplate)base.FindOtherFieldTemplate(columnName);
  }

  protected virtual void OnFieldValueChanged(EventArgs e)
  {
    var eventHandler = (EventHandler)this.Events[FieldValueChangedEvent];
    if (eventHandler != null)
      eventHandler(this, e);
  }

  private object ExtractFieldValue()
  {
    var dictionary = new OrderedDictionary();
    this.ExtractValues(dictionary);
    if (this.Column is MetaForeignKeyColumn)
    {
      var values = new object[dictionary.Count];
      dictionary.Values.CopyTo(values, 0);
      return string.Join(",", values);
    }

TypeConverter converter =
```

LISTING 10.16 Continued

```
        TypeDescriptor.GetConverter(this.Column.ColumnType);
        return converter.ConvertFrom(dictionary[this.Column.Name]);
    }
  }
}
```

FieldValue Property

The built-in `FieldTemplateUserControl` base class already provides a property called `FieldValue`. However, it is available only during the data binding stage of the page life-cycle, and it throws an `InvalidOperationException` if you try accessing it during post-back. This limitation also affects the `FieldValueString` and `FieldValueEditString` properties that return a formatted version of the `FieldValue`. Luckily, the `FieldValue` property is declared as virtual, and the `UnleashedFieldTemplate` overrides it to remove this limitation.

The overridden `FieldValue` property getter calls the inherited getter, which invokes the `GetColumnValue` method to do the actual work. This method is overridden in the `UnleashedFieldTemplate` class to catch the `InvalidOpertationException` and call the `ExtractFieldValue` method, which is discussed shortly, to retrieve the current field value from the template's data control. The overridden setter of the `FieldValue` property checks if the new field value is different from the old one and calls the `OnFieldValueChanged` method to raise the `FieldValueChanged` event if that is the case.

ExtractFieldValue Method

The `ExtractFieldValue` method calls the `ExtractValues` method, which is defined as virtual in the `FieldTemplateUserControl` class specifically for extracting the current field value from the template's data control. The `ExtractValues` method is already implemented in all appropriate Edit mode field templates that come with Dynamic Data projects, and you can simply call it here instead of reinventing the wheel. It takes an `OrderedDictionary` as a parameter and populates it with column names and values. Because a particular data control might store a field value in a different format, such as a `TextBox` storing a numeric value as a string, the `ExtractFieldValue` method uses a `TypeConverter` to convert the extracted field value to the actual type of the column.

The `ExtractFieldValue` method has a special logic for handling foreign key columns. At the time of data binding, a foreign key column is a navigation property, so the `FieldValue` property returns an actual target entity instance, such as a `Customer` instance. At post-back time, however, there are no entity instances, and you can only get the values of the underlying primitive columns, such as a CustomerID. If the foreign key consists of multiple primitive columns, the `ExtractFieldValue` method returns a coma-separated list of their values, which is also how the built-in `ForeignKey_Edit` field template stores them in the `ListItem` instances of its `DropDownList` control.

FieldValueChanged Event

The `OnFieldValueChanged` method is responsible for invoking the `FieldValueChanged` event handlers, if any have been assigned, when the `FieldValue` property changes. Following the standard .NET event implementation pattern, this method is declared as virtual. This allows the descendants to handle the event by overriding the method, which is more efficient than assigning an event handler.

> **NOTE**
>
> The `FieldValueChanged` event explicitly defines the add and remove blocks to take advantage of the `Events` collection inherited from the ASP.NET `Control` class. This collection is optimized for storing infrequently assigned event handlers and allows you to store event handlers in a hash table instead taking space for each event in every instance of the control. The `FieldValueChangedEvent` object is used as a hash key to store and retrieve the `FieldValueChanged` event handlers, if any.

AutoPostBack Property

The `AutoPostBack` property of the field template encapsulates the `AutoPostBack` property of the data entry controls. Consumers, such as the custom `Region` field template, typically set it when they need to receive immediate notifications about field value changes. Unfortunately, ASP.NET controls do not have a common base class that would allow setting their `AutoPostBack` property generically. The individual field templates are responsible for initializing their data controls based on this property.

Extending Existing Field Templates

To take advantage of the better encapsulation offered by the new `UnleashedFieldTemplate` base class, you need to implement the following changes in each of the existing field templates:

▶ Change the field template to inherit from the `UnleashedFieldTemplate` class.

▶ Set data control's `AutoPostBack` property value with the value from the `AutoPostBack` property of the field template.

▶ Raise the `FieldValueChanged` event when data control's value changes.

▶ Update data control's value when `FieldValue` changes.

With the exception of the last one, these tasks are what the original version of the `Region_Edit` field template had hard-coded. By implementing these changes, you are encapsulating this logic inside of each general-purpose field template and allowing the custom field template to access the information without taking dependencies on the internal implementation details of other templates. Listings 10.17 and 10.18 show the markup and code-behind of the `Text_Edit` field template that has already been extended. The changes (indicated by bold font) are discussed through the remainder of this section.

10

LISTING 10.17 Extended Text_Edit Field Template (Markup)

```
<%@ Control Language="C#" CodeBehind="Text_Edit.ascx.cs"
  Inherits="WebApplication.DynamicData.FieldTemplates.TextEditField" %>

<asp:TextBox ID="textBox" runat="server" Text='<%# FieldValueEditString %>'
  AutoPostBack="<%# AutoPostBack %>" Columns="<%# Columns %>"
  OnTextChanged="TextBox_TextChanged"/>

<asp:RequiredFieldValidator runat="server" ID="requiredFieldValidator"
  ControlToValidate="textBox" Enabled="false" />
<asp:RegularExpressionValidator runat="server" ID="regularExpressionValidator"
  ControlToValidate="textBox" Enabled="false" />
<asp:DynamicValidator runat="server" ID="dynamicValidator"
  ControlToValidate="textBox" />
```

Changing Field Template's Base Class

As the base class of the field template is specified in its code-behind file (Listing 10.18), you need to change it from the built-in `FieldTemplateUserControl` to the new `UnleashedFieldTemplate`.

Setting Data Control's AutoPostBack Property

The `Text_Edit` field template uses a `TextBox` as its data control. The easiest way to initialize its `AutoPostBack` property is with an ASP.NET data binding expression, `<%# AutoPostBack #>`, in template's markup file, as was shown in Listing 10.15. This expression is evaluated during the data binding stage when the page is first generated. It assigns the value of the `AutoPostBack` property provided by the base class, `UnleashedFieldTemplate`, to the `AutoPostBack` property of the `TextBox` control.

Raising the FieldValueChanged Event

The `TextBox` control used by the `Text_Edit` field template offers a `TextChanged` event, which you can use to detect when a user changes its value. In template markup, the `TextBox_TextChanged` method is assigned as an event handler. Its implementation, shown in Listing 10.18, simply calls the `OnFieldValueChanged` method inherited from the `UnleashedFieldTemplate` to raise the `FieldValueChanged` event.

LISTING 10.18 Extended Text_Edit Field Template (Code-Behind)

```
using System;
using System.Collections.Specialized;
using System.Web.UI;

namespace WebApplication.DynamicData.FieldTemplates
{
  public partial class Text_EditField : UnleashedFieldTemplate
  {
```

```csharp
    public override Control DataControl
    {
      get { return this.textBox; }
    }

    public int Columns { get; set; }

    protected void Page_Load(object sender, EventArgs e)
    {
      this.textBox.ToolTip = this.Column.Description;
      if (this.Column.MaxLength < 20)
        this.textBox.Columns = this.Column.MaxLength;

      this.SetUpValidator(this.requiredFieldValidator);
      this.SetUpValidator(this.regularExpressionValidator);
      this.SetUpValidator(this.dynamicValidator);
    }

    protected override void ExtractValues(IOrderedDictionary dictionary)
    {
      dictionary[this.Column.Name] = this.ConvertEditedValue(this.textBox.Text);
    }

    protected override void OnDataBinding(EventArgs e)
    {
      base.OnDataBinding(e);
      if (this.Column.MaxLength > 0)
      {
        this.textBox.MaxLength = Math.Max(
          this.FieldValueEditString.Length, this.Column.MaxLength);
      }
    }

    protected override void OnFieldValueChanged(EventArgs e)
    {
      base.OnFieldValueChanged(e);
      this.textBox.Text = this.FieldValueEditString;
    }

    protected void TextBox_TextChanged(object sender, EventArgs e)
    {
      this.OnFieldValueChanged(e);
    }
  }
}
```

Updating Data Control When FieldValue Changes

Template's `FieldValue` property can also change because of something *outside* of the field template, perhaps another custom field template. You could imagine a custom `ZipCode` field template that in response to the user entering a valid U.S. zip code could look up the name of the city it represents and change the value displayed by the general-purpose `Text_Edit` field template for the `City` field.

The field template (`Text_Edit`) can detect when the `FieldValue` property changes by overriding the `OnFieldValueChanged` method, as shown in Listing 10.18. Notice how this overridden method sets the `Text` property of the `TextBox` control using the `FieldValueEditString` property of the template. As discussed in Chapter 3, "Field Templates," this property returns the `FieldValue` formatted appropriately for Edit mode. This property is used in the template markup to provide the initial value for the `Text` property at the time of data binding, and the overridden `OnFieldValueChanged` method needs to be consistent with this logic.

Taking Advantage of the Extended Field Templates

With the new version of the general-purpose `Text_Edit` field template, you can now modify the custom `Region_Edit` field template shown back in Listing 10.15 so that it no longer depends on the `Country` data control being a `TextBox`. In the next example, its `OnLoad` method was modified to initialize the `AutoPostBack` property of the template and assign its `FieldValueChanged` event:

```
private UnleashedFieldTemplate countryFieldTemplate;

protected override void OnLoad(EventArgs e)
{
    base.OnLoad(e);
    this.countryFieldTemplate = this.FindOtherFieldTemplate("Country");
    this.countryFieldTemplate.AutoPostBack = true;
    this.countryFieldTemplate.FieldValueChanged +=
        CountryFieldTemplate_FieldValueChanged;
}
```

The `FieldValueChanged` event handler, which is shown next, replaces the `TextChanged` event handler from the previous version of the `Region_Edit` field template, which had to extract the current field value directly from the `TextBox` data control. Now that the `FieldValueEditString` property of the `Country` field template became available during post-backs, this method uses it to update the list of regions in the drop-down list. Notice that this is the same way the drop-down list is initially populated in the `OnDataBinding` method when the page is generated for the first time:

```
private void CountryFieldTemplate_FieldValueChanged(
    object sender, EventArgs e)
{
    string country = this.countryFieldTemplate.FieldValueEditString;
    this.PopulateRegionList(country);
}
```

The modified version of the `Region_Edit` field template is now less dependent on how the Country field is implemented in the user interface. You can replace the `Country` field template completely, and as long as the new template inherits from the `UnleashedFieldTemplate` and implements the pattern just discussed, this will not break the `Region_Edit` field template.

Using Entity Templates to Control Field Templates

Although this latest implementation of the `Region_Edit` field template does what it needs to do for the Customers entity template, it has a significant design flaw that limits its reuse. By locating the Country field template directly, it assumes that the name of the field storing the country name is always *Country*. Although this is correct for the Customer, Employee, and Supplier entities in the Northwind data model, this is not the case for the Order entity where the column storing the country name is called *ShipCountry*. Obviously, this would prevent you from being able to use the `Region` field template to build an order entry screen. This assumption also creates another problem–the `Region` field template requires you to *have* the `Country` field on the page. This would prevent you from using this control if you wanted to build a Customer form specific for the U.S. customers only. You can overcome these limitations by moving the logic that determines the country out of the Region field template and placing it in the Customer entity template that hosts it.

Listings 10.19 and 10.20 show the source code (markup and code-behind, respectively) of the final version of the `Region` template. As usual, the significant differences are highlighted in bold. Notice that the newly defined `Country` property has replaced the logic that used to be in the `OnLoad` and `OnDataBinding` methods of the previous version of the `Region` field template shown back in Listing 10.15. Because the `Country` property is public, this field template now relies on its consumer, the Customer entity template in this case, to provide this value instead of hard-coding it.

LISTING 10.19 Final Version of the Region_Edit Field Template (Markup)

```
<%@ Control Language="C#" CodeBehind="Region_Edit.ascx.cs"
  Inherits="WebApplication.DynamicData.FieldTemplates.RegionEditField" %>
<asp:TextBox ID="textBox" runat="server" AutoPostBack="<%# AutoPostBack %>"
  Text="<%# FieldValueEditString %>" OnTextChanged="TextBox_TextChanged" />
<ajax:AutoCompleteExtender ID="autoCompleteExtender" runat="server"
  TargetControlID="textBox" ServicePath="/RegionCompletionService.svc"
  ServiceMethod="GetCompletionList" MinimumPrefixLength="0" />
<asp:RequiredFieldValidator runat="server" ID="requiredFieldValidator"
  ControlToValidate="textBox" Enabled="false" />
<asp:DynamicValidator runat="server" ID="dynamicValidator"
  ControlToValidate="textBox" />
```

10

Compared to the original version of this field template shown in Listing 10.11, the only difference in the final markup of the Region field template is the addition of the AutoPostBack and OnTextChanged attributes to the TextBox control. These changes actually implement the UnleashedFieldTemplate pattern and are not directly related to moving the logic for determining Country field value out of this template.

LISTING 10.20 Final Version of the Region_Edit Field Template (Code-Behind)

```
using System;
using System.Collections.Specialized;
using System.Web.UI;

namespace WebApplication.DynamicData.FieldTemplates
{
  public partial class RegionEditField : UnleashedFieldTemplate
  {
    public string Country
    {
      get { return this.autoCompleteExtender.ContextKey;  }
      set { this.autoCompleteExtender.ContextKey = value; }
    }

    public override Control DataControl
    {
      get { return this.textBox; }
    }

    protected override void OnInit(EventArgs e)
    {
      base.OnInit(e);
      this.textBox.ToolTip = this.Column.Description;
      this.SetUpValidator(this.requiredFieldValidator);
      this.SetUpValidator(this.dynamicValidator);
    }

    protected override void ExtractValues(IOrderedDictionary dictionary)
    {
      dictionary[this.Column.Name] = this.ConvertEditedValue(this.textBox.Text);
    }

    protected void TextBox_TextChanged(object sender, EventArgs e)
    {
      this.OnFieldValueChanged(e);
    }
  }
}
```

Extending DynamicControl (Again)

The UnleashedControl class introduced in the beginning of this chapter takes care of initializing its Mode property based on the mode of the entity template that hosts it. This control can provide several additional properties and methods to make manipulating field templates easier. Listing 10.21 shows the final version of this class. With the exception of the first half of the OnInit method, the rest of its code is new.

LISTING 10.21 Final Version of the UnleashedControl

```
using System;
using System.ComponentModel;
using System.Web.DynamicData;
using System.Web.UI.WebControls;

namespace Unleashed.DynamicData
{
  public class UnleashedControl : DynamicControl
  {
    private static readonly object FieldValueChangedEvent = new object();

    public new UnleashedFieldTemplate FieldTemplate
    {
      get { return (UnleashedFieldTemplate)base.FieldTemplate; }
    }

    [Browsable(false)]
    public object FieldValue
    {
      get { return this.FieldTemplate.FieldValue; }
      set { this.FieldTemplate.FieldValue = value; }
    }

    public event EventHandler FieldValueChanged
    {
      add
      {
        this.Events.AddHandler(FieldValueChangedEvent, value);
        if (this.FieldTemplate != null)
          this.FieldTemplate.FieldValueChanged += value;
      }
      remove
      {
        this.Events.RemoveHandler(FieldValueChangedEvent, value);
        if (this.FieldTemplate != null)
          this.FieldTemplate.FieldValueChanged -= value;
      }
```

10

LISTING 10.21 Continued

```
    }

    protected override void OnInit(EventArgs e)
    {
      if (this.Mode == DataBoundControlMode.ReadOnly)
      {
        EntityTemplateUserControl entityTemplate =
          this.TemplateControl as EntityTemplateUserControl;
        if (entityTemplate != null)
        {
          this.Mode = entityTemplate.Mode;
          this.ValidationGroup = entityTemplate.ValidationGroup;
        }
      }

      base.OnInit(e);

      var eventHandler = (EventHandler)this.Events[FieldValueChangedEvent];
      if (eventHandler != null)
        this.FieldTemplate.FieldValueChanged += eventHandler;
    }
  }
}
```

In the built-in DynamicControl class, the FieldTemplate property returns an object of type Control. The UnleashedControl redefines this property to return a strongly typed instance of the UnleashedFieldTemplate class. This helps to reduce the amount of typecasting in this class as well as in entity templates that need to access the field templates directly.

The FieldValue property provides a convenient way of getting and setting the FieldValue property of the underlying field template programmatically. It is not intended to be used from markup.

The FieldValueChanged event is also a convenience wrapper. It can be used to assign event handlers for the field template's FieldValueChanged event. Unlike the FieldValue property, this event *is* intended for use in markup, although it can be used programmatically as well. To support assigning event handlers from markup, when the field template has not been instantiated yet, the event handlers are stored in the Events list of the UnleashedControl itself. When the field template has been created in the OnInit method, the event handlers, if any, are assigned to the field template's own event.

Taking Advantage of the UnleashedControl in Entity Templates

With the new version of the `UnleashedControl`, you only need to make minimal changes to the Customer entity template. Listing 10.22 shows the final version of the markup file with the changes highlighted with bold font.

LISTING 10.22 Final Version of the Customer Entity Template (Markup)

```
<%@ Control Language="C#" CodeBehind="Customers.ascx.cs"
  Inherits="WebApplication.DynamicData.EntityTemplates.CustomerEntityTemplate" %>

<unl:UnleashedLabel runat="server" DataField="CustomerID" />
<unl:UnleashedControl runat="server" DataField="CustomerID" />
<unl:UnleashedLabel runat="server" DataField="ContactName" />
<unl:UnleashedControl runat="server" DataField="ContactName" />
<fieldset>
  <legend>Address</legend>
  <unl:UnleashedLabel runat="server" DataField="Address" />
  <unl:UnleashedControl runat="server" DataField="Address" Columns="65"/>
  <br />
  <unl:UnleashedLabel runat="server" DataField="City" />
  <unl:UnleashedControl runat="server" DataField="City" />
  <unl:UnleashedLabel runat="server" DataField="Region" />
  <unl:UnleashedControl ID="regionControl" runat="server" DataField="Region"
    UIHint="Region" />
  <unl:UnleashedLabel runat="server" DataField="PostalCode" />
  <unl:UnleashedControl runat="server" DataField="PostalCode" />
  <unl:UnleashedLabel runat="server" DataField="Country" />
  <unl:UnleashedControl ID="countryControl" runat="server" DataField="Country"
    AutoPostBack="True" OnFieldValueChanged="Country_FieldValueChanged" />
</fieldset>
```

As you can see, IDs for both `Country` and `Region` controls are specified to make them easier to work with in the code-behind. The `Country` control also takes advantage of the new capabilities of the `UnleashedControl` to specify the `OnFieldValueChanged` event handler.

The code-behind, shown in Listing 10.23, performs the logic that used to be implemented by the `Region` field template. Now that it no longer has to access the `Country` field template directly, the `UpdateRegionCountry` method gets the current `FieldValue` from the `Country` field template and assigns it to the `Region` template's `Country` property. The `UpdateRegionCountry` method is called twice—the first time during the data binding stage (from the `OnDataBinding` method), when the initial value of the `Country` field is retrieved from the database, and second time during post-backs (from the `Country_FieldValueChanged` method), when this value is modified by the user.

10

LISTING 10.23 Final Version of the Customer Entity Template (Code-Behind)

```
using System;
using System.Web.DynamicData;
using WebApplication.DynamicData.FieldTemplates;

namespace WebApplication.DynamicData.EntityTemplates
{
  public partial class CustomerEntityTemplate : EntityTemplateUserControl
  {
    protected override void OnDataBinding(EventArgs e)
    {
      base.OnDataBinding(e);
      this.UpdateRegionCountry();
    }

    protected void Country_FieldValueChanged(object source, EventArgs e)
    {
      this.UpdateRegionCountry();
    }

    private void UpdateRegionCountry()
    {
      var regionTemplate = (RegionEditField)this.regionControl.FieldTemplate;
      regionTemplate.Country = (string)this.countryControl.FieldValue;
    }
  }
}
```

By extracting the interaction logic from the Region field template into the Customer entity template, you have improved the field template's encapsulation and made it more flexible. Overall, this makes it a better component, allowing you to reuse it in more scenarios, such as when building a custom Order entity template. Although it might seem that implementing the interaction between the Region and Country fields in every custom entity template unnecessarily increases the development effort, the fact that the internal dependency between two field templates has been eliminated makes them much easier to understand and maintain independently of each other.

Placing the interaction code in entity templates also makes it much easier to understand and maintain the entity templates because it makes the interaction between field templates clearly visible. Imagine having to fix a bug in a complex form that has several dozen field templates, many interacting with each other under the covers. In fact, this approach implements the classic Model-View-Controller (MVC) pattern designed to solve common problems that arise in implementations of complex user interfaces. The entity template plays the role of a Controller coordinating the field templates playing the role of Views while the entity instance plays the role of a Model.

> **NOTE**
>
> The MVC *design* pattern should not be confused with the ASP.NET MVC *framework*. The ASP.NET MVC framework is simply one of many possible implementations of the MVC pattern. The MVC framework is neither superior to other implementations, nor is it required to use to reap the benefits of the MVC pattern. Both the MVC framework and the approach described here are simply different tools that you can choose to solve various problems.

Summary

Custom entity templates are ideal for implementing form layout when you want to provide the best possible user interface for a particular entity in your data model. Unfortunately, the entity template lookup rules combined with the built-in implementation of the dynamic entity templates forces you to create at least two versions of each custom template to implement a particular form layout in Edit, Insert, and Read-only modes. By combining the built-in dynamic entity templates in a single, multimode `Default.ascx` template, you enable creation of custom entity templates that support multiple modes as well and significantly reduce the amount of effort required to implement and maintain custom templates in general. A simple custom control, `UnleashedLabel`, can be created to display field labels based on the metadata information and avoid hard-coding it in custom entity templates.

Custom field templates are the best way to implement unique presentation requirements for a particular entity property, such as the `Region` property, one of several properties that store address information. You can configure public properties of both custom and general-purpose field templates declaratively by specifying custom attributes for the `DynamicControl` in template markup and programmatically by handling the `Load` event of the `DynamicControl`.

The best place to implement interaction between field templates, such as the filtering of the list of Regions based on the `Country` value entered by the user, is in custom entity templates. This helps to maximize reuse of field templates and makes it easier to understand and maintain dependencies between field templates in the long term. The built-in implementation of `DynamicControl` and `FieldTemplateUserControl` classes provided by Dynamic Data requires accessing internal implementation details of individual field templates to determine the current field values and detect their changes. With simple extensions of these classes, such as the `UnleashedControl` and `UnleashedFieldTemplate` provided in the sample solution, you can improve encapsulation of the field template and make accessing field values easier.

10

Building Dynamic Forms

The biggest advantage Dynamic Data offers is the dramatic reduction in the amount of code in your application. Consider the number of ASPX files a web application would need to have for the Northwind Traders sample database. If you were using WebForms, you could manually create *two* ASPX files per entity—one multipurpose "form" page for inserting, editing, displaying, and deleting single rows, plus another "list" page for searching for and browsing through all rows. With 11 distinct entity types in the Northwind database, this means that *22* separate ASPX pages would have to be created. With ASP.NET MVC, you typically have separate single-purpose views, requiring *five* ASPX files per entity, increasing the total number of ASPX files to to *55*, more than doubling the number of hand-written ASPX pages with WebForms. With Dynamic Data, which generates code at *run time*, the application can be built with only four ASPX files (page templates), regardless of the number of entity types.

Dynamic Data gives you a working application as soon as the initial version of the entity/data model is available. You can immediately begin sharing it with the business and collecting feedback on functioning web pages as opposed to UML diagrams or screen mockups. With a good set of dynamic templates, you can refine the entity model and solicit additional feedback in rapid successive iterations without the penalty of maintaining the presentation logic. If a particular entity requires a custom user interface that cannot be generated dynamically, you can hand-code it using either the WebForms or the MVC framework, when the entity model is stable.

By helping to postpone the hand-coding of the user interface and making the application size smaller, Dynamic Data

helps your project stay agile, reduces waste, and enables you to focus on the most important aspect of the information system—its domain model. After all, the biggest risk on any
development project is building the wrong thing. If your domain model is wrong, your
application will be wrong, no matter how pretty it looks. This is the most important
reason you might want to master the metadata-driven development of web applications
with Dynamic Data. This chapter focuses on how to do this *effectively*, points out some of
the pitfalls and shortcomings you might encounter, and discusses how to work around
them.

Basic Form Layout

When creating custom forms, you control their layout by explicitly creating table or
other HTML elements. You determine which entity properties appear on the form and
where they are displayed by creating a DynamicControl for each property and placing it in
the required location.

With the default entity template, Dynamic Data generates a single-column form for any
entity type, with labels on the left side and data entry fields on the right side. Unless you
specify otherwise, Dynamic Data uses a heuristic algorithm to display all appropriate
properties it supports. In particular, this list does not include the generated, custom, and
foreign key properties. *Generated properties*, such as properties mapped to identity columns
in a Microsoft SQL Server database, typically contain information not suitable for display
to end users. *Custom properties*, such as a FullName property that could be defined in a
contact entity class to concatenate the FirstName, LastName, and MiddleInitial properties, cannot be used in LINQ filters with Entity Framework and would break list pages.
Foreign key properties, such as a CustomerId, are not only inappropriate for users to see or
edit directly, they are a part of navigation properties, such as *Customer*, which are already
displayed, usually with a ForeignKey field template.

If this default set of properties selected for display by Dynamic Data does not meet your
requirements, you can explicitly show or hide a particular property with the help of the
DisplayAttribute. The code snippet next illustrates how to show the EmployeeID and
hide the Orders properties of the Employee entity:

```
[MetadataType(typeof(Metadata))]
partial class Employee
{
    private abstract class Metadata
    {
        [Display(AutoGenerateField = true)]
        public object EmployeeID { get; set; }

        [Display(AutoGenerateField = false)]
        public object Orders { get; set; }
    }
}
```

The `AutoGenerateField` property affects both single-item forms and list pages generated by Dynamic Data. For list pages, you can also set the `AutoGenerateFilter` property in the `DisplayAttribute` to explicitly specify whether the `QueryableFilterRepeater` control will generate a `DynamicFilter` control instance for this property.

> **NOTE**
>
> `DisplayAttribute` is the main data annotation attribute you use to control the layout and appearance of dynamic forms in version 4.0 or later of ASP.NET Dynamic Data. It was designed to replace several other data annotation attributes, including `DisplayNameAttribute`, `DescriptionAttribute`, `ScaffoldColumnAttribute`, and `ReadOnlyAttribute`, that were used by the original version of Dynamic Data released with ASP.NET 3.5 SP1. These attributes are still supported; however, with rare exceptions, you should consider using the `DisplayAttribute` as it combines multiple annotations into a single, easy-to-discover attribute class.

By default, properties appear on a dynamic form in the order they are defined in the entity model. If this does not match what you need, *ideally* you want to change the order of properties in the entity model. This is easy to do if you are using the code-first approach with Entity Framework. If you are using the model-first approach, you can do this by editing the raw XML in the EDMX file in a text editor. If you are using the database-first approach, you need to reorder columns in the database table and regenerate the model. Controlling order of data entry controls on dynamic forms by reordering properties in the entity model is ideal because it eliminates ambiguity and keeps the model simple. After all, if you had a custom form laid out with an HTML table, you would want to move a particular row to its new location, keeping the order of elements in the markup in sync with their appearance on screen. Same idea applies to controlling order of controls in dynamically generated forms.

However, in the real world, you have to deal with the less than ideal tools and larger than ideal databases. When changing the order of properties in the entity model becomes impractical, you can specify it explicitly by setting the `Order` property of the `DisplayAttribute`. Here is an example that shows how to do this for the `FirstName` and `LastName` properties of the Employee entity:

```
[MetadataType(typeof(Metadata))]
partial class Employee
{
    private abstract class Metadata
    {
        [Display(Order = 110)]
        public object FirstName { get; set; }

        [Display(Order = 120)]
        public object LastName { get; set; }
    }
}
```

When specifying order numbers explicitly, give yourself a little room by starting with appropriate gaps between neighboring properties. In the example just shown, the `FirstName` and `LastName` properties that sit next to each other have a gap of 10 in their order numbers. If you need to insert another property, perhaps the `MiddleInitial`, between them in the future, you will be able to do it without having to renumber all properties. Start with a gap of 100 for larger entities that have 20 or more properties. This allows you to move entire groups of properties without renumbering. When the entity design stabilizes, you can either renumber the properties to have a uniform gap or create a custom entity template and remove order numbers from the metadata entirely.

All properties with an explicit display order are displayed first. Properties that do not have `DisplayAttribute` or don't have the `Order` property specified are displayed at the end of the list. This logic is currently implemented by giving properties a default order of 10,000. Keep this in mind when working with large entities—you don't want your explicit order numbers to exceed this number.

Even though gaps allow you to change the order of properties on dynamic pages without having to renumber all of them, it is still a good idea to have the property order in the actual source file match the order of their order numbers. This makes it easier to understand how the dynamic page will look and make maintaining order numbers simpler.

Configuring Appearance of Labels

In custom forms, the text elements and labels that appear on pages are specified explicitly in their markup. In dynamically generated pages, Dynamic Data uses the internal name of entities and their properties by default. When the internal name does not match what you want to appear on screen, your first choice should be to adjust the internal name in the entity model. For instance, if your entity model has a Customer entity, such as the one from the Northwind Traders sample shown in Figure 11.1, you might have properties such as `ContactName` and `CompanyName` that use PascalCase or another naming convention to concatenate multiple words into a single identifier.

FIGURE 11.1 Customer entity in Entity Designer.

Although business users can easily understand the term ContactName, it is not a proper English word; it would be unprofessional to show it in the application. You already know from the previous chapters in this book that you can easily extend metadata information to specify that Name is the proper display name for the ContactName property. However, before you add a DisplayAttribute to the model, take this opportunity to stop and think about *why* the internal property name does not match its display name. This can be a sign of a mismatch between the domain terminology of your business users and the internal technical terminology you use in the implementation of the app. In this example, you might speculate that you cannot use the term Name because you want to distinguish between the name of the person and the name of his or her company: Thus, technical terms ContactName and CompanyName were chosen to distinguish them. But why is there ambiguity here in the first place? Does your company, Northwind Traders, serve consumers or businesses? If you are a consumer-focused company, you can reinforce this fact in your entity model by renaming the ContactName property to simply Name and changing the CompanyName property to simply Company, making it one of the address properties.

It is very important to keep internal entity and property names accurate. When names displayed on screen do not match expectations of your business users, the first choice should be to change the entity model to match terminology of your business domain. Ideally, you want to propagate these name changes all the way down to the database level and have the names of tables and columns consistent with the names of entities and properties. Refactoring tools in Visual Studio make this task possible today, even with significant amounts of .NET and SQL code. Getting in the habit of applying domain terminology throughout the application helps to reduce the cost of ongoing maintenance and helps the entire development team, including the new members, to understand the application better.

When the internal name of a property *is* consistent with the business terminology but still not appropriate for display to users, you can use data annotations to specify proper names that should be used instead. Of course, you might also have to resort to this approach when renaming properties in your entity model and columns in your database becomes too difficult. You can start by setting the Name property of the DisplayAttribute— Dynamic Data uses this value whenever a display name is required for the entity property, including form labels, grid column headers, and validation error messages. If a single display name is not enough, you can also specify a separate value in the ShortName property of the DisplayAttribute, which is automatically used in grid column headers. The code snippet that follows shows an example of specifying a display name and a short name for the HomePhone property of the Employee entity in the Northwind sample:

```
[MetadataType(typeof(Metadata))]
partial class Employee
{
    private abstract class Metadata
    {
        [Display(Name = "Home Phone", ShortName = "Home #")]
        public object HomePhone { get; set; }
    }
}
```

> **NOTE**
>
> It is not necessary to specify both `ShortName` and `Name` properties of the `DisplayAttribute` if they have the same value. If the `ShortName` is not specified, Dynamic Data automatically uses the `Name` instead.

Prompt Annotation

The `DisplayAttribute` includes several additional properties that can be used to further tune the appearance of the entity property in dynamically generated pages, although not all of them are supported by the Dynamic Data out of the box. In particular, the `Prompt` property of the `DisplayAttribute` could be used to provide a custom string for use in form labels, similar to how the `ShortName` property specifies display name for grid column headers. To implement this, you can simply change the dynamic entity template, `Default.ascx`, to use the prompt string if it was specified and otherwise fall back to using the display name string, as shown next:

```
protected void Label_Init(object sender, EventArgs e)
{
  var label = (Label)sender;
  label.Text = this.currentColumn.Prompt
    ?? this.currentColumn.DisplayName;
}
```

> **NOTE**
>
> Here and in the rest of this chapter, assume dynamic entity templates `Default.ascx`, `Default_Edit.ascx`, and `Default_Insert.ascx` have been combined into a single, multimode template, `Default.ascx`, as discussed in Chapter 10, "Building Custom Forms."

This code first appeared in Listing 10.6 and was discussed in detail in Chapter 10. The `Label_Init` method handles the `Init` event of the `Label` control the entity template generates for each entity property. The `currentColumn` field contains a reference to the `MetaColumn` object describing the current entity property for which a label and a data entry control are being generated. The original version of this code initialized the label `Text` using only the `DisplayName` property of the `MetaColumn` object. The new version just shown first tries to initialize the label text using the `Prompt` before falling back to the `DisplayName`.

11

> **NOTE**
>
> As discussed in Chapter 7, "Metadata API," the `MetaColumn` class encapsulates data annotation attributes applied to the entity property. Although it allows accessing data annotation attributes, using its `Attributes` property, it also provides strongly typed properties to access specific annotations directly. For example, the `DisplayName` and `Prompt` properties of the `MetaColumn` class return values specified in the `Name` and `Prompt` properties of the `DisplayAttribute`, respectively. Using these properties is not only easier, it is also faster due to metadata caching performed by Dynamic Data.

> **NOTE**
>
> The `??` *operator* is a C# null-coalescing operator. It's a powerful shortcut but can be confusing if you are not familiar with it. Here is how a single line of code from the snippet just shown can be replaced with a more verbose, but straightforward, `if` *statement*:
>
> ```
> if (this.currentColumn.Prompt != null)
>    label.Text = this.currentColumn.Prompt;
> else
>    label.Text = this.currentColumn.DisplayName;
> ```

After implementing support for the `Prompt` annotation in the dynamic entity template, you can further refine the definition of the Employee entity and specify a custom string for use with the `HomePhone` property in form labels as shown next. Also the `RequiredAttribute` is added to the HomePhone property to help illustrate the fact that the `Name` annotation is still important because it is used to generate validation error messages.

```
[MetadataType(typeof(Metadata))]
partial class Employee
{
    private abstract class Metadata
    {
        [Required]
        [Display(Name = "Home Phone", ShortName = "Home #",
          Prompt = "Home Phone Number:")]
        public object HomePhone { get; set; }
    }
}
```

Notice how the `Name`, `ShortName`, and `Prompt` annotations look in a dynamically generated UI in Figure 11.2. At the top of the picture, you can see a fragment of a dynamic form where the `Prompt` annotation appears as a label to the left of the phone number text box.

At the bottom of the picture, a fragment of a dynamic grid shows the home phone column where the ShortName annotation appears in the column header. On the right side, you can see the validation error message generated by the RequiredAttribute, which includes the Name annotation.

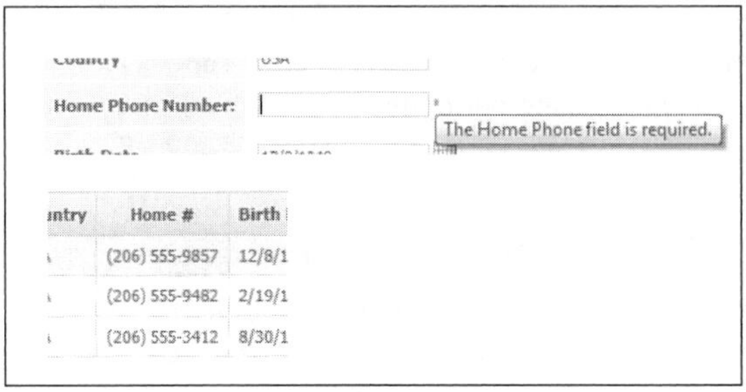

FIGURE 11.2 Name, ShortName, and Prompt annotations in dynamic UI.

Description Annotation

The DisplayAttribute also defines Description property, which most of the built-in field templates supplied by Dynamic Data use to provide a tooltip for their data controls. The Description annotation offers a good way to store documentation describing the entity properties during initial development of the entity model. During active development, descriptions in code help upi remember the intent of different properties; the tooltips in the user interface make discussing them with the business users easier as well. When the entity model design is stable, you refine the descriptions to serve as interactive hints for users during data entry. The code snippet that follows illustrates the last scenario; you can see how it looks in Figure 11.3:

```
[MetadataType(typeof(Metadata))]
partial class Employee
{
    private abstract class Metadata
    {
        [Display(Prompt = "Home Phone Number:",
          Description = "Please enter a 10-digit Phone Number")]
        public object HomePhone { get; set; }
    }
}
```

FIGURE 11.3 Description annotation in Dynamic UI.

In field templates, this annotation is available via the Description property of the MetaColumn class. Field templates typically use it in Load event handlers to set the ToolTip property of their data control, such as a TextBox or a DropDownList. The Boolean_Edit, ForeignKey_Edit, and ManyToMany_Edit field templates do not support the Description annotation out of the box. However, it is easy enough to fix this problem by adding code similar to the following snippet. This example was taken from the Boolean_Edit field template in the source code accompanying this book:

```
protected void Page_Load(object sender, EventArgs e)
{
    this.checkBox.ToolTip = this.Column.Description;
}
```

> **NOTE**
>
> By design, the DisplayAttribute cannot be applied to classes; it contains many properties that simply would not be applicable. To provide a human-readable name for an entity type, you need to use the DisplayNameAttribute, as shown in here:
>
> ```
> [DisplayName("Order Items")]
> partial class Order_Detail
> {
> }
> ```

Configuring Field Templates

After specifying which properties of an entity should appear on a dynamic form, in what order they should appear, and what labels they should display, you might also need to specify which field templates will be used for data entry and how they should be configured.

Making Properties Read-Only

One of the important decisions to make when designing entities in your application is whether a particular property can be modified by the user directly or supplied by the system and displayed to the user in Read-only mode. In a *custom* page or template, you can specify whether an Edit mode or a Read-only field template will be loaded by setting the Mode property of the DynamicControl or DynamicField explicitly in markup:

```
<asp:DynamicControl runat="server" DataField="SubmittedDate" Mode="ReadOnly"/>
```

When the DynamicControl instances are generated *dynamically*, the field template mode needs to come from the model. If you were using a code-first or model-first approach in your entity model, your first choice should be making that property Read-only in the entity model. Here is an example of doing this with a code-first approach:

```
public DateTime SubmittedDate { get; internal set; }
```

Notice that the property setter has internal visibility, which, assuming your entity model is in a separate project, will make it read-only in the Dynamic Data web application. With the model-first approach, you can change property visibility in the Entity Designer and have it generate the property with an internal setter.

Although it is also possible to use the Entity Designer to change property visibility with the database-first approach, you might want to avoid doing this because customization made to the generated entity model by hand quickly becomes difficult to maintain. With the database-first approach, when the EDMX is regenerated every time the database schema changes, your best option is to apply the EditableAttribute to the property in the metadata class. Here is how you can do this for the Order entity:

```
[MetadataType(typeof(Metadata))]
partial class Order
{
    abstract class Metadata
    {
        [Editable(false)]
        public object SubmittedDate { get; set; }
    }
}
```

Whether you make a particular property read-only in the entity model or use the EditableAttribute, Dynamic Data (or more specifically the DynamicControl) uses the metadata information to load a read-only version of the field template, even if the mode of the form itself is Edit or Insert.

The EditableAttribute can be also used to selectively change whether a particular property can be edited in the Insert mode. For instance, if you wanted to allow your customers to enter the RequiredDate for their orders only when submitting the order but prevent them from changing it later, you could specify false as the AllowEdit property of the EditableAttribute, but true as its AllowInitialValue property. Here is an example:

```
[MetadataType(typeof(Metadata))]
partial class Order
{
    abstract class Metadata
    {
        [Editable(false, AllowInitialValue = true)]
        public object RequiredDate { get; set; }
    }
}
```

Overriding Default Field Templates

Dynamic Data chooses an appropriate field template for each property based on its type. If you find yourself in a situation where you need to change the field template Dynamic Data selected, it is best to stop and ask yourself if the property has an appropriate type. For instance, if you have a string property and want to force Dynamic Data to use an integer field template, there is a good chance that the property type is incorrect. The best course of action in that situation would be to correct the problem at the source—in the entity model and the database.

If the property does have an appropriate type, but the .NET type is not specific enough for your needs, your next choice is to apply the DataTypeAttribute to the property in the metadata class. For example, the HomePhone property of the Employee entity is of type string; however, it is very different from another string property, Notes. The first stores phone numbers; the second stores one or more lines of text. Here is how you can clarify this distinction in the entity model by applying the DataTypeAttribute:

```
[MetadataType(typeof(Metadata))]
partial class Employee
{
  private abstract class Metadata
  {
    [DataType(DataType.PhoneNumber)]
    public object HomePhone { get; set; }

    [DataType(DataType.MultilineText)]
    public object Notes { get; set; }
  }
}
```

By applying the DataTypeAttribute, you are giving Dynamic Data a more specific type it can use to choose a more appropriate field template, such as the MultilineText_Edit field template that comes with Dynamic Data out of the box and the PhoneNumber_Edit field template created in Chapter 3, "Field Templates."

> **NOTE**
>
> Applying the DataTypeAttribute to specify MultilineText type for a string property should not be necessary in many circumstances. Dynamic Data is smart enough to automatically recognize properties mapped to database columns of type VARCHAR(MAX) or TEXT as MultilineText. Therefore, treat it with suspicion and remember that it is better to address a mismatch by changing the entity model instead of applying a data annotation attribute.

Configuring Appearance of Values

When building custom forms with Dynamic Data components, you can explicitly control appearance of values by specifying the `DataFormatString`, `NullDisplayText`, and `HtmlEncode` properties of the `DynamicControl` and `DynamicField` controls directly in markup. With the `TextBox`-based field templates, you can also control appearance of values in Edit and Insert mode by setting the `ApplyFormatInEditMode` and `ConvertEmptyStringToNull` properties. Here is an example used in Chapter 3, which covers this topic in detail, to display the `ShippedDate` property of the Order entity in MM/dd/yy format:

```
<asp:DynamicField DataField="ShippedDate" DataFormatString="{0:MM/dd/yy}" />
```

You can also specify these values in the metadata, by applying the `DisplayFormatAttribute` to entity properties as shown here:

```
[MetadataType(typeof(Metadata)]
partial class Order
{
    abstract class Metadata
    {
        [DisplayFormat(DataFormatString = "{0:MM/dd/yy}")]
        public object SubmittedDate { get; set; }
    }
}
```

> **NOTE**
>
> Under the hood, the `DynamicControl` uses properties of the `DisplayFormatAttribute` applied to the column to initialize its own. In other words, if you have a `DataFormatString` annotation specified in the metadata and in markup, the value specified in markup takes precedence, as you would expect.

If you need values of a particular property to appear consistently on multiple pages of your web application, the `DisplayFormatAttribute` works great because it allows you to specify the format string in a single place. However, because this logic falls in to the presentation category, you should use this attribute with caution. You can often avoid using the `DisplayFormatAttribute` and embedding the presentation logic in the business layer by using the `DataTypeAttribute` instead. For `Date`, `Time`, and `Currency` data types, this attribute provides default format strings, which are sufficient in many cases. Here is how you could modify metadata of the `SubmittedDate` property to use the `DataType` annotation instead:

```
[MetadataType(typeof(Metadata)]
partial class Order
```

```
{
  abstract class Metadata
  {
    [DataType(DataType.Date)]
    public object SubmittedDate { get; set; }
  }
}
```

For DataType.Date, the DataTypeAttribute provides a default format string {0:d}, which with English (United States) regional settings is equivalent to the custom format string {0:M/d/yyyy}. If you can live with a four-digit year format for the SubmittedDate, using the DataTypeAttribute instead of the DisplayFormatAttribute is better. It is not only simpler, but also keeps the presentation logic out of the entity model and keeps the metadata at the (higher) business level. Otherwise, using the DisplayFormatAttribute might still be preferrable to embedding this information in multiple custom pages throughout the application.

Enum Properties and Enumeration Templates

In entity design, you often come across the need to have a property with a fixed list of possible values. A common way to present such properties to users is a drop-down list or a group of radio-buttons. Discovering a need for such a control is another opportunity for you to stop and carefully consider how this information should be presented in the entity model.

If the list of possible values for a property will grow over time and the application will not need any special logic for each new value, it is best to make this property a foreign key and store the values in a separate table/entity. Dynamic Data automatically uses the ForeignKey field templates for foreign key properties, and the users see a drop-down list populated with values from the lookup table.

On the other hand, if the list of possible values for a property is fixed and *especially* if the application will have different business rules for different values, it is best to define the list of values as an enumerated type, such as the EmployeeType enum shown in the code in this example:

```
public enum EmployeeType: byte
{
  Fulltime = 0,
  PartTime = 1,
  Temporary = 2
}
```

Because the Entity Framework does not support enumerated types in .NET version 4, you also have to rely on the EnumDataTypeAttribute to associate the enum type with an integral entity property as shown here:

```
[MetadataType(typeof(Metadata))]
partial class Employee
{
    private abstract class Metadata
    {
        [EnumDataType(typeof(EmployeeType))]
        public object EmployeeType { get; set; }
    }
}
```

As you recall from Chapter 3, Dynamic Data automatically uses the *Enumeration* field templates for all properties that have the EnumDataTypeAttribute applied. In Edit mode, the enum items are displayed in a DropDownList control that looks identical to the drop-down list produced by the foreign key template.

There is a wide gray area between these two extremes, and you will often need to make a judgment call on whether a particular property should be an enum or a foreign key. On one hand, using a lookup table and a foreign key is more flexible—you could add new values without recompiling the application—and implementing reports at the database level is easier. On the other hand, using enum properties is much simpler, especially when you need to have business rules attached to different values.

When in doubt, it is best to start with the simplest solution and change it when you have a better understanding of the business domain. With this in mind, start with an enum because this approach reduces the number of entities and relationships in your entity model as well as the number of tables and foreign keys in your database. It also simplifies the application code because there is no need to load lookup values from a table or define special constants. Later, if you discover that business users will want to add new values to the list *regularly*, you can create a lookup entity and introduce a foreign key then.

Extending the Enumeration Field Templates

Unfortunately, Dynamic Data web applications do not support display name annotations for enum items out of the box. For instance, if your enum items need to have compound names, such as PartTime, the built-in Enumeration and Enumeration_Edit field templates display the internal names to the users. Obviously, this looks unprofessional, and you might be tempted to convert the enum property to a foreign key and introduce a lookup table just to store the display names. Luckily, it is easy to solve this problem by extending the built-in templates and taking advantage of the data annotation attributes. This is a small, one-time investment of effort that will provide ongoing savings in cost and complexity over the lifetime of your application.

To specify display names for enum items, you can either create a new or reuse an existing data annotation attribute. As it turns out, the DisplayAttribute can be applied not only to entity properties, but to enum items as well. The following code shows how to modify the definition of the EmployeeType enum to specify display names for all its values:

```
public enum EmployeeType: byte
{
    [Display(Name = "Full-time")] Fulltime = 0,
    [Display(Name = "Part-time")] PartTime = 1,
    [Display(Name = "Temporary")] Temporary = 2
}
```

> **NOTE**
>
> Reusing an existing .NET framework type is always better when it fits your needs because it helps keep the solution smaller and simpler. In this example, reusing the `DisplayAttribute` to provide display names for enum items offers not only consistency with entity properties, but also allows you to take advantage of the built-in localization support and use additional display name properties, such as the `ShortName` and `Description`. However, always be cognizant of the side effects from reusing a type for an unintended purpose. The `AutoGenerateField` and `AutoGenerateFilter` properties of `DisplayAttribute` will not be applicable to enum items, possibly causing confusion for other developers. In this scenario, the benefits of reuse and consistency outweigh the added complexity of creating a new attribute. However, use your own judgment to make similar tradeoffs in your projects.

Having decided on how display names of enum items will be specified in the model, you now need to modify the `Enumeration.ascx` and `Enumeration_Edit.ascx` field templates to access the additional metadata. To make this task easier, as well as to enable reuse of this logic in additional field templates (you might need another field template that displays a list of radio-buttons instead of a drop-down list), the sample solution implements it in a new base class with the two enumeration field templates to inheriting from it.

Listing 11.1 shows the complete source code of the new base class, called `UnleashedEnumerationFieldTemplate` to follow the naming convention established in this book. This class inherits from the `UnleashedFieldTemplate` (a class introduced in Chapter 10) and overrides the `FieldValueString` property and the `PopulateListControl` method inherited from the ultimate base class of field templates—the `FieldTemplateUserControl` provided by Dynamic Data.

As you are reviewing the implementation of this class, notice that the `BuildEnumDictionary` method is responsible for collecting the metadata information describing a given enum type. It uses reflection API to examine each item defined in the enum type, determine its display name, and store the enum names and values in an `OrderedDictionary` object. This specialized collection class was chosen because, on one hand, you need a dictionary to support fast lookup of a display name based on an enum value. On the other hand, you want to preserve the original order of enum items when showing their display names in a drop-down list. The `OrderedDictionary` class from the `System.Collections.Specialized` namespace is the only dictionary class provided by the .NET framework that also preserves the order of its items.

The GetEnumDictionary method is responsible for calling the BuildEnumDictionary method to extract metadata the first time a particular enum type is processed by the application, caching the results to improve performance. This is a common and important pattern when working with metadata. You want to cache the extracted metadata because it requires multiple sequential loops and reflection calls to collect. You definitely want to avoid doing this unnecessarily as it will have a significant negative impact on overall performance of the web application. In a worst-case scenario, where you have a page with a GridView control that displays multiple enumeration columns and a large number of rows, the performance hit might be noticeable even with a *single* user accessing the system. By storing the extracted metadata in a static ConcurrentDictionary object, the UnleashedEnumeraterFieldTemplate ensures that any given enum time is processed only in the application's lifetime, minimizing any performance impact of reflection.

LISTING 11.1 UnleashedEnumerationFieldTemplate Base Class

```
using System;
using System.Collections;
using System.Collections.Concurrent;
using System.Collections.Specialized;
using System.ComponentModel.DataAnnotations;
using System.Linq;
using System.Reflection;
using System.Web.DynamicData;
using System.Web.UI.WebControls;

namespace Unleashed.DynamicData
{
  public class UnleashedEnumerationFieldTemplate : UnleashedFieldTemplate
  {
    private static readonly ConcurrentDictionary<Type, IOrderedDictionary>
      enumCache = new ConcurrentDictionary<Type, IOrderedDictionary>();

    public override string FieldValueString
    {
      get
      {
        object fieldValue = this.FieldValue;
        Type enumType = this.Column.GetEnumType();
        if (fieldValue != null && enumType != null)
        {
          fieldValue = Enum.ToObject(enumType, fieldValue);
          IOrderedDictionary enumDictionary = GetEnumDictionary(enumType);
          var enumName = (string)enumDictionary[fieldValue];
          if (!string.IsNullOrEmpty(enumName))
            return enumName;
```

```
    }

    return base.FieldValueString;
  }
}


protected new void PopulateListControl(ListControl listControl)
{
  Type enumType = this.Column.GetEnumType();
  Type underlyingType = Enum.GetUnderlyingType(enumType);
  IOrderedDictionary enumDictionary = GetEnumDictionary(enumType);
  foreach (DictionaryEntry entry in enumDictionary)
  {
    var enumName = (string)entry.Value;
    object enumValue = Convert.ChangeType(entry.Key, underlyingType);
    listControl.Items.Add(new ListItem(enumName, enumValue.ToString()));
  }
}


private static IOrderedDictionary GetEnumDictionary(Type enumType)
{
  IOrderedDictionary enumDictionary;
  if (!enumCache.TryGetValue(enumType, out enumDictionary))
  {
    enumDictionary = BuildEnumDictionary(enumType);
    enumCache.TryAdd(enumType, enumDictionary);
  }

  return enumDictionary;
}


private static IOrderedDictionary BuildEnumDictionary(Type enumType)
{
  var dictionary = new OrderedDictionary();
  FieldInfo[] enumFields = enumType.GetFields(
    BindingFlags.Static | BindingFlags.GetField | BindingFlags.Public);
  foreach (FieldInfo enumField in enumFields)
  {
    object enumValue = enumField.GetValue(null);
    DisplayAttribute annotation = enumField
      .GetCustomAttributes(typeof(DisplayAttribute), false)
      .OfType<DisplayAttribute>().FirstOrDefault();
    string enumName = annotation != null
      ? annotation.GetName()
      : enumValue.ToString();
    dictionary.Add(enumValue, enumName);
```

LISTING 11.1   Continued

```
    }

    return dictionary;
  }
 }
}
```

Implementation of the overridden `FieldValueString` property getter is straightforward. It calls the `GetEnumDictionary` method to retrieve the dictionary with display names and values of the enum items and uses it to find the display name that matches the current field value. However, it also has to support a couple of edge cases. One of them is when the field value is `null` and you have to call the inherited getter to properly handle formatting options for null values. The other is when the field value does not match any known enum item and you, again, call the inherited getter, which converts it to `string` based on the property's formatting options.

The `PopulateListControl` method uses the `new` keyword because this method is not virtual in the base class, `FieldTemplateUserControl`. However, this should not be a problem because the method will not be called polymorphically. Consistently with its implementation in the base class, the `PopulateListControl` method also converts enum values to their underlying integral equivalents for use in the list items. So instead of a longer "`PartTime`", the value of the enum item will be simply "`1`". This reduces the size of HTML and post-back data used by the page.

To take advantage of the new base class, you need to modify the `Enumeration.ascx.cs` and the `Enumeration_Edit.ascx.cs` code-behind files that come with the enumeration field templates out of the box so that they inherit from `UnleashedEnumerationFieldTemplate` instead of the built-in `FieldTemplateUserControl`. Because `PopulateListControl` is a direct replacement for the inherited method, no further changes are needed in the `Enumeration_Edit` field template. It automatically starts showing the annotation-based display names as illustrated in Figure 11.4.

FIGURE 11.4 Extended Enumeration_Edit Field template.

In addition to inheriting from the `UnleashedEnumerationFieldTemplate` base class, the Enumeration field template also needs to be modified to use the overridden `FieldValueString` instead of the `EnumFieldValueString` property that was defined in this template out of the box. Markup of the modified version of the Enumeration field template is shown in Listing 11.2.

LISTING 11.2 Modified Enumeration Field Template (Markup)

```
<%@ Control Language="C#" CodeBehind="Enumeration.ascx.cs"
  Inherits="WebApplication.DynamicData.FieldTemplates.EnumerationField" %>
<asp:Literal runat="server" ID="literal" Text="<%# FieldValueString %>" />
```

Overall, the implementation of the Enumeration field template becomes much simpler because you are mostly removing unnecessary code. The new version of the code-behind is shown in Listing 11.3.

LISTING 11.3 Modified Enumeration Field Template (Code-Behind)

```
using System.Web.UI;
using Unleashed.DynamicData;

namespace WebApplication.DynamicData.FieldTemplates
{

  public partial class EnumerationField : UnleashedEnumerationFieldTemplate
  {
    public override Control DataControl
    {
      get { return this.literal; }
    }
  }
}
```

Figure 11.5 shows how the modified version of the Enumeration field template looks on a page; as you can see, the display name of the EmployeeType is shown, not its internal (PascalCased) name.

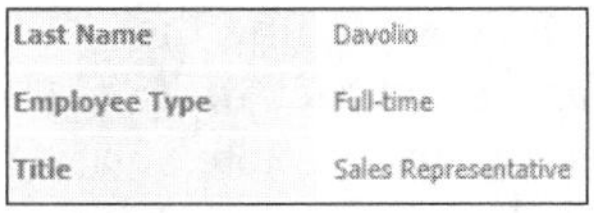

Last Name	Davolio
Employee Type	Full-time
Title	Sales Representative

FIGURE 11.5 Extended Enumeration field template.

Enum types help to reduce complexity of entity models and improve performance of the application. This simple extension to the built-in Enumeration field templates to support display name annotations eliminates one of the most common reasons why developers introduce lookup tables in their applications. This allows you to take full advantage of enums today and prepare for the upcoming 4.5 release of the Entity Framework where you get first class support in both Entity Designer and LINQ to Entities.

Custom Data Types and UI Hints

The `DataType` enumeration does not define all possible business data types you might need in your entity models. For instance, the `Region` property of the Employee entity is of type `string`, a low-level technical type; however, from a business perspective, you could consider it to have a high-level type `state`, which limits its potential values to a list of about 50 states and territories used by the U.S. Postal Service. You can indicate this design in the entity model by applying the `DataTypeAttribute` to the `Region` property and specifying a custom type name instead of a predefined value from the `DataType` enumeration. Here is an example:

```
[MetadataType(typeof(Metadata))]
partial class Employee
{
    private abstract class Metadata
    {
        [DataType("State")]
        public object Region { get; set; }
    }
}
```

> **NOTE**
>
> As you might want to point out, you could also have created an enumerated type to represent the USPS list of states and territories. For the sake of this example, let's continue with the assumption that using a string type makes more sense. As you see shortly, this is not a final design of the `Region` property anyway.

Dynamic Data treats custom data type names as first-class citizens. During field template lookup, it tries to find a template with the name matching the custom type specified in the `DataTypeAttribute` and falls back to the physical type only if it does not find the match. As it happens, a field template called `State_Edit.ascx` was created back in Chapter 10, which displays a drop-down list and allows users to select a valid state. Dynamic Data automatically uses it for the `Region` property of the Employee entity based on the data annotation in the preceding sample code.

City	Seattle
State	WA [▼]
Zip	98122
Country	USA

FIGURE 11.6 Web page generated by State field template.

When you encounter a property that fits one of the types defined in the DataType enumeration or perhaps a custom type unique to your business domain, it is a good idea to go ahead and use the DataTypeAttribute to indicate that decision in the entity model. In some cases, Dynamic Data will already have a built-in field template for this data type. When it does not, you can easily implement a new field template with a matching name, such as the PhoneNumber_Edit field template created in Chapter 3. By applying the DataTypeAttribute during entity design, you are documenting the business purpose of the property as well as some implied expectations of how values of this type will be presented to the users.

By applying the DataTypeAttribute to a property, you are saying that its type is *fundamental* to the business domain. For instance, the PhoneNumber and EmailAddress types are ubiquitous in contact management. However, saying that a particular type is fundamental is a strong statement, and discovering new types is difficult as it requires a solid understanding of the business domain. It is a good idea to postpone defining a new data type until you have at least two, ideally three or more, entity properties with a solid match for the emerging pattern.

What if you already know that a particular property needs a different UI but do not have any other examples that would justify definition of a new "data type?" In this situation, it is better to use the UIHintAttribute and specify the name of a custom field template instead of a data type. Going back to the example of Region property in the Employee entity, you could revise the premature decision to call "State" a data type and use the UIHint annotation instead:

```
[MetadataType(typeof(Metadata))]
partial class Employee
{
    private abstract class Metadata
    {
        [UIHint("State")]
        public object Region { get; set; }
    }
}
```

Although the value specified in both DataType("State") and UIHint("State") annotations is the same, the choice of attribute helps you to convey the design intent and distinguish between a distinct data type and a simple instance of a common data type that needs special user interface.

> **NOTE**
>
> Remember that by using the `UIHintAttribute`, you add *presentation* logic to the *business* layer of your application. Although placing business logic *code* in the code-behind files of a web application clearly is undesirable as it quickly leads to code duplication and makes automated testing difficult, combining presentation and business *models* is not necessarily a bad idea. You could argue that consistently using a `UIHint` instead of a `DataType` annotation helps to clarify your design intent in the model—a tangible benefit. However, every time you use the `UIHint` annotation, more and more of the presentation logic is mixed in with the business logic, making the model more complex. Use this as an opportunity to stop and consider whether creating a custom page or template for the given entity and *separating* the presentation logic from the business model would make the overall design simpler and easier to maintain.

Specifying Field Template Parameters

As discussed in Chapter 10, `DynamicControl` can initialize custom properties of field templates using matching attributes specified in markup. As an example, the built-in `Text_Edit` field template was extended with a custom `Columns` property that can be used to set the `Columns` property of the `TextBox` control it contains. If you had created a custom entity or page template for the Employee entity, you could make the Address text box wider and accommodate longer addresses by using the following markup:

```
<asp:DynamicControl runat="server" DataField="Address" Columns="65"/>
```

The `UIHintAttribute` also supports custom property values. They are exposed for consumption via its `ControlParameters` property, which returns an IDictionary<string, object>, and have to be specified as a sequence of names and values in the `UIHintAttribute` constructor, following the hint and presentation layer parameters. It is easier to explain this with an example; following is how you could specify the `Columns` parameter for the `Address` property in the metadata:

```
[MetadataType(typeof(Metadata))]
partial class Employee
{
    private abstract class Metadata
    {
        [UIHint("Text", "WebForms", "Columns", 65)]
        public object Address { get; set; }
    }
}
```

In this example, "Text" is the hint, the name of a field template; "WebForms" is the name of the presentation layer for which the `UIHint` is intended; and "Columns" is the name of the first control parameter followed by 65, its value. The `UIHintAttribute` constructor has an open-ended array as its last argument, so if you needed to specify additional control parameters, you would simply add more names and values to this list.

> **NOTE**
>
> Specifying "WebForms" as the presentation layer in the UIHintAttribute constructor is only required when you need separate UIHint annotations for different presentation frameworks, such as MVC and WebForms, for the same property. In that case, Dynamic Data picks the UIHint where the presentation layer is specified as "WebForms". Otherwise, it uses the UIHint for "MVC" or the one where the presentation layer is not specified. If you are not planning to use UIHint annotations with multiple platforms, leaving it null might be the best option.

Unfortunately, the built-in DynamicControl does not support custom control parameters specified in the UIHintAttribute the way it supports its own custom attributes specified in markup. However, you can easily work around this limitation by extending the dynamic entity templates. As discussed in Chapter 4, "Entity Templates," and later in Chapter 10, the dynamic entity templates rely on the Init event handler to initialize each DynamicControl it creates. Extending this event handler is the simplest way to implement support for custom parameters. Here is how you can extend the Init event handler implemented in Default.ascx.cs, the code-behind file of the combined entity template created in Chapter 10:

```
protected void DynamicControl_Init(object sender, EventArgs e)
{
  var dynamicControl = (DynamicControl)sender;
  dynamicControl.DataField = this.currentColumn.Name;
  dynamicControl.Mode = this.Mode;
  dynamicControl.ValidationGroup = this.ValidationGroup;

  var hint = this.currentColumn.Attributes.OfType<UIHintAttribute>()
    .FirstOrDefault();
  if (hint != null)
  {
    foreach (KeyValuePair<string, object> p in hint.ControlParameters)
      dynamicControl.SetAttribute(p.Key, p.Value.ToString());
  }
}
```

The new code (indicated by bold font) tries to find a UIHintAttribute applied to the current column (a MetaColumn object describing an entity property for which a field template needs to be created). If the attribute was found, it uses the names and values in the ControlParameters dictionary to set custom attributes for the DynamicControl. The DynamicControl, which has not created the field template yet, takes care of the rest and uses the custom attribute values to set the public properties defined by the field template class, like the `Columns` property defined by the `Text_Edit` field template. Figure 11.7 shows how the Address text box, dynamically configured by this code, is now much wider than text boxes for other string properties.

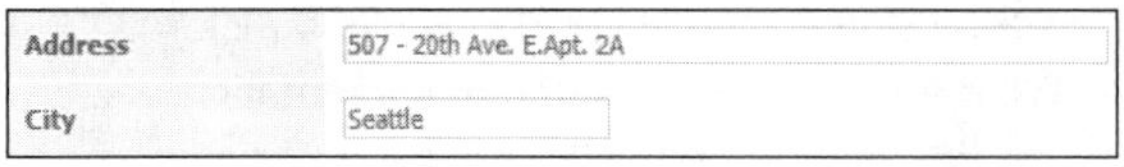

| Address | 507 - 20th Ave. E.Apt. 2A |
| City | Seattle |

FIGURE 11.7 Address TextBox with Columns parameter.

Extending Dynamic Data to Support Control Parameters

Although the current solution allows you to continue evolving the Employee form with metadata, at some point, you might need to create a custom entity or page template. In a custom template, having to specify the `Init` event handler for every `DynamicControl` instance becomes a nuisance you would rather avoid. You also have a problem with the dynamic list pages that display data with the help of `GridView` control because it does not offer an easy way to access the `DynamicControl` instances.

This section shows how the Dynamic Data controls can be extended to implement consistent support for metadata-driven control parameters.

Extending DynamicControl to Support Control Parameters

The `UnleashedControl` was introduced in Chapter 10 to encapsulate some of the functionality necessary to implement field template interaction. You can further extend it to support control parameters. Here is an extract from `UnleashedControl.cs` (without the rest of the implementation reviewed in Chapter 10, which is not relevant to this discussion):

```
protected override void OnInit(EventArgs e)
{
  // ...
  this.Init += this.InitializeControlParameters;
  base.OnInit(e);
  // ...
}

private void InitializeControlParameters(object sender, EventArgs args)
{
  MetaColumn column = this.Column ?? this.Table.GetColumn(this.DataField);
  var hint = column.Attributes.OfType<UIHintAttribute>().FirstOrDefault();
  if (hint != null)
  {
    foreach (KeyValuePair<string, object> p in hint.ControlParameters)
```

```
        this.SetAttribute(p.Key, p.Value.ToString());
    }
}
```

Notice that you cannot implement this logic directly in the overridden OnInit method of the UnleashedControl. On one hand, you do not know which entity property this control represents *before* the inherited OnInit method is called because the Init event handler in the dynamic entity template has not had a chance to initialize the DataField property yet. On the other hand, *after* the inherited OnInit method is finished, the field template has already been created, and calling the SetAttribute method will have no effect. To solve this problem, the custom attributes are set in the InitializeControlParameters method. This method is added as the last handler to the Init event, which fires at the appropriate moment—after the initialization code in the dynamic entity templates but before the field template is created.

Although implementing initialization of field template parameters in the UnleashedControl is a little more involved, it offers a better encapsulation and allows you to simplify the implementation of the default entity template. This becomes more important as you begin implementing additional dynamic entity templates later in this chapter. Consider the final version of the Default.ascx entity template in Listing 11.4.

LISTING 11.4 Final Version of Default Entity Template (Markup)

```
<%@ Control Language="C#" CodeBehind="Default.ascx.cs"
  Inherits="WebApplication.DynamicData.EntityTemplates.DefaultEntityTemplate" %>
<table class="DDDetailsTable">
  <asp:EntityTemplate runat="server" ID="entityTemplate">
    <ItemTemplate>
      <tr>
        <td class="DDLightHeader">
          <unl:UnleashedLabel runat="server" OnInit="Label_Init" />
        </td>
        <td>
          <unl:UnleashedControl runat="server" OnInit="DynamicControl_Init" />
        </td>
      </tr>
    </ItemTemplate>
  </asp:EntityTemplate>
</table>
```

Because the UnleashedControl and UnleashedLabel (also introduced in Chapter 10) controls are designed to work with minimum configuration in both custom and dynamic entity templates, you only need to initialize their respective DataField properties with the name of the entity property for which the controls are being generated. The controls

themselves take care of doing the rest, such as determining the display name of the property to use as a label, initializing the mode of the field template based on the mode of the
entity template, and so on. Listing 11.5 shows the updated code-behind. Notice how the
`Label_Init` and `DynamicControl_Init` methods shrink to a mere one line of code each,
and the `Label_PreRender` method, responsible for associating labels with their data
controls, disappears entirely.

LISTING 11.5 Final Version of Default Entity Template (Code-Behind)

```csharp
using System;
using System.Collections.Generic;
using System.Web.DynamicData;

namespace WebApplication.DynamicData.EntityTemplates
{
  public partial class DefaultEntityTemplate : EntityTemplateUserControl
  {
    private MetaColumn currentColumn;

    protected override void OnLoad(EventArgs e)
    {
      IEnumerable<MetaColumn> scaffoldColumns =
        this.Table.GetScaffoldColumns(this.Mode, this.ContainerType);
      foreach (MetaColumn column in scaffoldColumns)
      {
        this.currentColumn = column;
        var container = new NamingContainer();
        this.entityTemplate.ItemTemplate.InstantiateIn(container);
        this.entityTemplate.Controls.Add(container);
      }
    }

    protected void Label_Init(object sender, EventArgs e)
    {
      ((UnleashedLabel)sender).DataField = this.currentColumn.Name;
    }

    protected void DynamicControl_Init(object sender, EventArgs e)
    {
      ((UnleashedControl)sender).DataField = this.currentColumn.Name;
    }
  }
}
```

Extending DynamicField to Support Control Parameters

The updated `UnleashedControl` allows you to take advantage of metadata-driven control parameters in pages that rely on entity templates and *template controls*, such as the `FormView` or the `ListView`. However, you still have the same limitation in pages that rely on *field controls*, such as the `GridView` or the `DetailsView`. Listing 11.6 shows an example of such a page.

LISTING 11.6 Page with GridView and DynamicField Controls (Markup)

```
<%@ Page Language="C#"
  MasterPageFile="~/Site.master" CodeBehind="SamplePage.aspx.cs"
  Inherits="WebApplication.Samples.Ch11.DynamicField.SamplePage" %>

<asp:Content ContentPlaceHolderID="main" runat="server">
  <asp:GridView ID="gridView" runat="server" DataSourceID="dataSource"
    AutoGenerateEditButton="true" AutoGenerateColumns="false"
    DataKeyNames="EmployeeID">
    <Columns>
      <asp:DynamicField DataField="FirstName" />
      <asp:DynamicField DataField="LastName" />
      <asp:DynamicField DataField="Address" />
      <asp:DynamicField DataField="City" />
      <asp:DynamicField DataField="Region" />
      <asp:DynamicField DataField="Country" />
      <asp:DynamicField DataField="PostalCode" />
    </Columns>
  </asp:GridView>
  <asp:EntityDataSource ID="dataSource" runat="server"
    ConnectionString="name=NorthwindEntities" EntitySetName="Employees"
    DefaultContainerName="NorthwindEntities" EnableUpdate="True" />
</asp:Content>
```

If you build and run this page, notice that the Address text box appears with its default size, ignoring the `Columns` parameter specified in the metadata to make it wider. This is because the `DynamicField` instances used to define grid columns create `DynamicControl` objects, which do not support control parameters defined in metadata. You can solve this problem by extending the `DynamicField` class to override its `CreateDynamicControl` method and return a new `UnleashedControl` instead of the built-in `DynamicControl`. Listing 11.7 shows how the `UnleashedField` class (available the sample solution) does that.

LISTING 11.7 UnleashedField Implementation

```
using System.Web.DynamicData;

namespace Unleashed.DynamicData
{
  public class UnleashedField : DynamicField
  {
    protected override DynamicControl CreateDynamicControl()
    {
      return new UnleashedControl();
    }
  }
}
```

Extending DefaultAutoFieldGenerator to Support Control Parameters

With the UnleashedField class, you can fix the problem in the custom GridView page from Listing 11.6 by simply replacing the DynamicField instances with the extended controls. However, solving the problem in the *dynamic* page templates is a little more involved. As you recall from discussions in Chapter 6, "Page Templates," a special Dynamic Data class, DefaultAutoFieldGenerator, is responsible for automatically generating the DynamicField instances for GridView and DetailsView controls based on a MetaTable object associated with it. Because the DefaultAutoFieldGenerator creates the DynamicField instances, you also need to extend it to have the UnleashedField instances created in dynamic page templates instead. Listing 11.8 shows the UnleashedFieldGenerator class, also available in the sample solution.

LISTING 11.8 UnleashedFieldGenerator Implementation

```
using System.Web.DynamicData;
using System.Web.UI.WebControls;

namespace Unleashed.DynamicData
{
  public class UnleashedFieldGenerator: DefaultAutoFieldGenerator
  {
    public UnleashedFieldGenerator(MetaTable table): base(table)
    {
    }

    protected override DynamicField CreateField(MetaColumn column,
      ContainerType containerType, DataBoundControlMode mode)
    {
      var field = new UnleashedField();
      field.DataField = column.Name;
      if (containerType == ContainerType.List)
```

```
          field.HeaderText = column.ShortDisplayName;
      else
          field.HeaderText = column.Prompt ?? column.DisplayName;
      field.ItemStyle.Wrap = false;
      return field;
    }
  }
}
```

11

The `UnleashedFieldGenerator` provides a parameterized constructor, which is required to specify the `MetaTable` object when the generator is created. It also overrides the `CreateField` method to create and initialize a new instance of the `UnleashedField` control. In particular, it sets the `HeaderText` property of the new field using different values from the column metadata, depending on the context where the new field will be used. If `List` value was passed as the `containerType`, it means that the field will appear in a `GridView` control and the short version of column's display name is used as the header. Otherwise, if `Item` container type was specified, the field will appear in a `DetailsView` control and the *prompt* (if it was specified) or the full display name of the column will be displayed in the label. Finally, wrapping is turned off to prevent validators from appearing on the next line if an error needs to be reported by the field template.

With the `UnleashedFieldGenerator` class, you still have to modify the `List` and `ListDetails` page templates to use it. In custom pages, where you initialize the `ColumnsGenerator` property of `GridView` control explicitly, you can simply change the code to instantiate the `UnleashedFieldGenerator` explicitly. However, in the dynamic page templates that come with the Dynamic Data project in Visual Studio, the `DefaultAutoFieldGenerator` is created by the `DynamicDataManager` during the `InitComplete` event of the `Page`. To replace this logic, you can create your own `Page.InitComplete` event handler as shown in this code snippet:

```
public partial class List : System.Web.UI.Page
{
  protected MetaTable table;
  protected void Page_InitComplete(object sender, EventArgs e)
  {
    this.gridView.ColumnsGenerator = new UnleashedFieldGenerator(this.table);
  }
}
```

Because the `Page_InitComplete` method runs after the event handler the `DynamicDataManager` uses to initialize the `ColumnsGenerator` property of the `GridView`, this code replaces it with the `UnleashedFieldGenerator`. As a result, the `GridView` will be populated with `UnleashedField` instances that have full support for metadata-driven control parameters, and the Address text box, for which the `Columns` parameter was specified in metadata of the Employee entity, will now be wide enough to support longer address values.

Field Template Interaction in Dynamic Forms

Is it possible to implement interaction between field templates in a dynamically generated web page? Yes. In fact you already have all the tools you need. Is it a good idea? Most of the time, it is not. When you discover that two or more data entry controls on a form need to interact with each other, the best course of action is to create a custom entity or page template, where implementing the interaction will be easier and more straightforward. Chapter 10, "Building Custom Forms," discusses how to accomplish this task in detail.

However, you might discover recurring patterns in your entity model, where different properties need the same type of interaction. In Chapter 10, a custom entity template was created for the Customer entity to help users enter address information by suggesting a list of *regions* based on the name of the *country* they entered. In the Northwind sample model, several other entities include address properties, including Customer, Employee, Supplier, and Order. After implementing the same pattern several times for different entities, you might decide that a single, *dynamic* implementation would be beneficial.

NOTE

Remember that falling into the trap of creating a dynamic solution where custom code would be more appropriate is very common. Dynamic is not better than Custom. Don't try to implement a dynamic solution based on just one or two instances of a particular pattern. With such a small number of cases, you will not have a sufficient understanding of the pattern and will not recoup the additional effort required to implement a dynamic solution. Even such a common pattern as the Region/Country properties could have been efficiently implemented with custom code, such as the generic Address entity template discussed in Chapter 4.

The key to implementing field template interaction with metadata is to place the logic of *how* to interact in the field templates and storing the information of *who* to interact with in the metadata. As an example, the Region field template created in Chapter 10 can be modified to provide an auto-completion list for users based on the value in the Country field template. However, because the country property can have different names in different entities—it is called ShipCountry in the Order entity—you do not want to hard-code it in the Region field template itself. Instead, the Country property name can be specified as a control parameter in the UIHintAttribute for the Region property, as shown in this code snippet:

```
[MetadataType(typeof(Metadata))]
partial class Employee
{
  private abstract class Metadata
  {
    [UIHint("Region", "WebForms", "CountryField", "Country")]
    public object Region { get; set; }
```

```
        }
    }
```

Listing 11.9 shows the complete code-behind file of the `Region_Edit` field template, updated to support the `CountryField` parameter. Notice that the template class now has a matching public property, which is automatically initialized by the `UnleashedControl` based on the property metadata.

LISTING 11.9 Region_Edit Field Template Extended with CountryField Parameter

```
using System;
using System.Collections.Specialized;
using System.Web.UI;

namespace WebApplication.DynamicData.FieldTemplates
{
  public partial class RegionEditField : UnleashedFieldTemplate
  {
    private UnleashedFieldTemplate countryTemplate;

    public string Country
    {
      get { return this.autoCompleteExtender.ContextKey;  }
      set { this.autoCompleteExtender.ContextKey = value; }
    }

    public string CountryField { get; set; }

    public override Control DataControl
    {
      get { return this.textBox; }
    }

    protected override void OnInit(EventArgs e)
    {
      base.OnInit(e);
      this.textBox.ToolTip = this.Column.Description;
      this.SetUpValidator(this.requiredFieldValidator);
      this.SetUpValidator(this.dynamicValidator);
    }

    protected override void OnLoad(EventArgs e)
    {
      base.OnLoad(e);

      this.countryTemplate = this.FindOtherFieldTemplate(this.CountryField);
```

LISTING 11.9 Continued

```
    if (this.countryTemplate != null)
    {
      this.countryTemplate.AutoPostBack = true;
      this.countryTemplate.DataBinding += this.CountryFieldValueChanged;
      this.countryTemplate.FieldValueChanged += this.CountryFieldValueChanged;
    }
  }

  protected override void ExtractValues(IOrderedDictionary dictionary)
  {
    dictionary[this.Column.Name] = this.ConvertEditedValue(this.textBox.Text);
  }

  protected void TextBox_TextChanged(object sender, EventArgs e)
  {
    this.OnFieldValueChanged(e);
  }

  private void CountryFieldValueChanged(object sender, EventArgs args)
  {
    this.Country = this.countryTemplate.FieldValueEditString;
  }
 }
}
```

The overridden OnLoad method passes the CountryField property value to the
FindOtherFieldTemplate method provided by the base class, FieldTemplateUserControl,
to find the actual field template that was created for the Country property on the page. If
the country field template was found, its AutoPostBack property is set to true to make
sure that a post-back occurs when the user changes the country value and can update the
auto-completion list accordingly. The code also adds event handlers for the DataBinding
and FieldValueChanged events of the country template.

The DataBinding event fires during initial rendering of the page, when the initial values of
the country and region properties are loaded from the database. The FieldValueChanged
event fires during a post-back, when the user changes the country value on the page. In
both instances, you want to get the current value of the country field and use it to
provide a corresponding list of regions. As you recall from the discussion in Chapter 10,
the Region template uses the AutoCompleteExtender from the AJAX Control Toolkit to call
the RegionCompletionService method that provides the list of regions. The country value
serves as the contextKey in the web service call.

As you can see, very few changes were required in the Region field template to support dynamic interaction with the country property. In fact, it is similar to the initial implementation created in Chapter 10, where the name of the country property was hard-coded. With the knowledge of the property name extracted outside of the field template, it is now generic enough to support any region property in the Northwind entity model and could be reused on other projects.

Fixing the FindOtherFieldTemplate Method

Unfortunately, the FindOtherFieldTemplate method provided by Dynamic Data does not work in the dynamically populated FormView and GridView controls and simply returns null. It is possible that this method was created for the initial release of Dynamic Data in service pack 1 of the .NET Framework 3.5 and has not been updated to work with the entity templates introduced in version 4.0. As a workaround, this method was reimplemented in the UnleashedFieldTemplate base class. Listing 11.10 shows a partial listing of the class, with just the code relevant to the current discussion.

LISTING 11.10 FindOtherFieldTemplate Method in UnleashedFieldTemplate

```
using System;
using System.Collections.Specialized;
using System.ComponentModel;
using System.Web.DynamicData;
using System.Web.UI;
using System.Web.UI.WebControls;

namespace Unleashed.DynamicData
{
  public partial class UnleashedFieldTemplate : FieldTemplateUserControl
  {
    protected new UnleashedFieldTemplate FindOtherFieldTemplate(string columnName)
    {
      var template = (UnleashedFieldTemplate)
        base.FindOtherFieldTemplate(columnName);

      if (template == null && !string.IsNullOrEmpty(columnName))
      {
        Control parent = this.FindParentOfAllFieldTemplates();
        template = (UnleashedFieldTemplate)
          FindControlRecursively(parent, "__" + columnName);
      }

      return template;
    }

    private Control FindParentOfAllFieldTemplates()
```

LISTING 11.10 Continued

```
  {
    Control parent = this.Parent;
    while (parent != null)
    {
      if (parent is GridViewRow ||
          parent is FormViewRow ||
          parent is DetailsViewRow)
        break;
      parent = parent.Parent;
    }

    return parent;
  }

  private static Control FindControlRecursively(Control parent, string id)
  {
    Control control = parent.FindControl(id);
    if (control != null)
      return control;

    foreach (Control child in parent.Controls)
    {
      control = FindControlRecursively(child, id);
      if (control != null &&
          0 == string.Compare(control.ID, id, StringComparison.OrdinalIgnoreCase))
        return control;
    }

    return null;
  }
}
```

The reimplemented FindOtherFieldTemplate method first tries to call the inherited version, which succeeds if this field template was created in a custom page and the built-in logic was sufficient to find the template. If the template was not found, the FindOtherFieldTemplate first locates the ultimate parent of all field templates of the current entity. It does that by calling the FindParentOfAllFieldTemplates method, which walks up the parent chain until it finds a known container, which could be a GridViewRow, a FormViewRow, or a DetailsViewRow, depending on the type of control used to create the UI—a GridView, a FormView, or a DetailsView, respectively. Having located the ultimate parent, the FindOtherFieldTemplate calls the FindControlRecursively method, which traverses the hierarchy of controls recursively until it finds the target field template.

A couple of odd points in the `FindOtherFieldTemplate` method are worth special attention. First, the ID of the target field template is determined by concatenating two underscore characters with the column name. This is how `DynamicControl` generates IDs of field templates in the current version, and the `UnleashedFieldTemplate` is forced to do it explicitly because this API is not publicly accessible. If the implementation changes in a future version of Dynamic Data, this code will be broken. Hopefully, the original `FindOtherFieldTemplate` actually works by then and you can simply remove this workaround instead of fixing it.

The other odd point in the `FindOtherFieldTemplate` method is the additional check performed by the `FindControlRecursively` method to ensure that the ID of the field template actually matches the ID you are looking for. This is done to ignore the false positive matches from the `CheckBoxList` and `RadioButtonList` controls, which override the `FindControl` method and always return self, regardless of the control ID value that was passed in.

Creating Additional Dynamic Entity Templates

The Default entity template gives your forms a plain single-column layout with labels on the left and data controls on the right. You can control display names and order of properties on this form as well as specify which field templates should be loaded for different properties. This is often adequate for simple entities that have a relatively small number of properties. For larger entities, such as the Employee entity, this simplistic approach to form layout can produce a rather long web page with extra space available on the right side. Normally, when this happens, consider creating a custom entity template and specify a more appropriate layout, perhaps with two columns of labels and data controls. However, it is also possible to create a more sophisticated entity template that will do it dynamically based on the metadata.

`DisplayAttribute` defines a property called `GroupName`, which can be used to specify arbitrary strings for grouping controls on a dynamically generated page. For instance, you could use values like "Contact", "Address", and "Organization" to generate HTML `fieldset` controls that display labels and data controls in group boxes similar to Windows applications. Alternatively, you could also use group names such as "Left" and "Right" to assign each of the properties of the Employee entity one of two columns that display side-by-side. Here is a fragment of the Employee metadata class that shows an example of the second approach:

```
[MetadataType(typeof(Metadata))]
partial class Employee
{
  private abstract class Metadata
  {
    [Display(GroupName = "Left", Order = 100)]
    public object FirstName { get; set; }
```

```
        [Display(GroupName = "Left", Order = 110)]
        public object LastName { get; set; }

        [Display(GroupName = "Right", Order = 200)]
        public object Address { get; set; }

        [Display(GroupName = "Right", Order = 210)]
        public object City { get; set; }
    }
}
```

Combined with the other annotations and several common types of form layouts, the GroupName annotation enables you to continue evolving the entity model without having to create custom entity and page templates even for larger entities, where a single-column layout is no longer practical. However, as you might suspect based on this open-ended description, the GroupName annotation is not supported by the Default entity template that comes with the Dynamic Data project template. This section discusses how to implement additional dynamic entity templates and form layouts.

Extending Metadata to Support Entity UI Hints

Implementing multiple form layouts in a single dynamic entity template is usually not a good idea. On one hand, making a single template responsible for more than one layout would quickly make it too complex to maintain. On the other hand, you do not want to risk breaking all existing dynamic forms by adding a new layout. Instead, it is better to use separate entity templates for different layouts.

Specifying a particular entity template is easy when you are creating a custom page. All you need to do is specify a UIHint attribute value for the DynamicEntity control, which serves as the first candidate name when Dynamic Data searches for the matching entity template. Chapter 4 showed how to take advantage of the UIHint attribute to reuse generic templates for different entity types.

```
        <asp:DynamicEntity runat="server" UIHint="Contact" />
```

However, there is no built-in capability in Dynamic Data to specify the UI hint in entity metadata. You can solve this problem by defining your own data annotation, such as the EntityUIHintAttribute in the sample solution, and changing the dynamic page templates to initialize the UIHint property of the DynamicEntity control programmatically. Listing 11.11 shows the definition of the new attribute.

LISTING 11.11 EntityUIHintAttribute Implementation

```
using System;

namespace Unleashed.DataAnnotations
{
```

```
[AttributeUsage(AttributeTargets.Class, AllowMultiple = false)]
public class EntityUIHintAttribute : Attribute
{
  public EntityUIHintAttribute(string entityUIHint)
  {
    this.EntityUIHint = entityUIHint;
  }

  public string EntityUIHint { get; private set; }
}
}
```

This attribute is applied to an entity class or its associated metadata class. Its constructor takes a string that serves as the entity UI hint and stores it in the `EntityUIHint` property, which is accessed by the page templates. Here is how definition of the Employee entity class looks with the new hint applied:

```
[MetadataType(typeof(Metadata))]
partial class Employee
{
  [EntityUIHint("TwoColumn")]
  private abstract class Metadata
  {
    [Display(GroupName = "Left", Order = 100)]
    public object FirstName { get; set; }

    [Display(GroupName = "Left", Order = 110)]
    public object LastName { get; set; }

    [Display(GroupName = "Right", Order = 200)]
    public object Address { get; set; }

    [Display(GroupName = "Right", Order = 210)]
    public object City { get; set; }
  }
}
```

Similar to the field template hint specified with the `UIHintAttribute`, the entity hint is a name of a particular template you want Dynamic Data to use instead of the default. In this example, `TwoColumn` is the name of the new dynamic entity template created shortly to implement a simple two-column form layout.

> **NOTE**
>
> Because the EntityUIHintAttribute is applied to entity classes, it has to be accessible from the project where your EDMX (entity model) is defined. As you can tell by looking at the namespace declaration, this attribute is defined in the Unleashed.DataAnnotations project of the sample solution accompanying this book. It is referenced by the DataModel project, which contains the entity model itself.

Extending Page Templates to Support EntityUIHintAttribute

To support the entity UI hints, you need to extend the built-in page templates that come with Dynamic Data project templates to initialize the UIHint property of the DynamicEntity control programmatically. Similar to other dynamic controls, this task has to be performed in the Init event handler before the control loads the template. You can modify markup of the three built-in page templates—Details, Insert, and Edit, plus the Delete page template created in Chapter 6, to define the Init event handler:

```
<asp:DynamicEntity runat="server" OnInit="DynamicEntity_Init" />
```

Make sure you leave the Mode attribute as is (the Edit and Insert page templates set it to Edit and Insert, respectively). The Init event handler itself is shown next. As you can see, it tries to find the EntityUIHintAttribute in the MetaTable object describing the entity class. If the attribute is found, the code sets the UIHint property of the DynamicEntity control:

```
protected void DynamicEntity_Init(object sender, EventArgs e)
{
  var entityUIHintAttribute = this.table.Attributes
    .OfType<EntityUIHintAttribute>().FirstOrDefault();
  if (entityUIHintAttribute != null)
    ((DynamicEntity)sender).UIHint = entityUIHintAttribute.EntityUIHint;
}
```

UnleashedEntity Control

You can reimplement the DynamicEntity initialization logic in all four of the dynamic page templates. With a small number of page templates, this will not be a big effort. However, it is always a good idea to avoid code dulplication. One of the ways to do it is to create an extended version of the DynamicEntity control, such as the UnleashedEntity in the sample solution. Listing 11.12 shows its source code.

LISTING 11.12 UnleashedEntity Implementation

```csharp
using System;
using System.Linq;
using System.Web.DynamicData;
using Unleashed.DataAnnotations;

namespace Unleashed.DynamicData
{
  public class UnleashedEntity: DynamicEntity
  {
    protected override void OnLoad(EventArgs e)
    {
      this.Load += this.InitializeFromMetadata;
      base.OnLoad(e);
    }

    private void InitializeFromMetadata(object sender, EventArgs e)
    {
      if (string.IsNullOrEmpty(this.UIHint))
      {
        MetaTable table = this.FindMetaTable();
        var attribute = table.Attributes.OfType<EntityUIHintAttribute>()
          .FirstOrDefault();
        if (attribute != null)
          this.UIHint = attribute.EntityUIHint;
      }
    }
  }
}
```

The DynamicEntity control creates the entity template in its OnLoad method; the UnleashedEntity overrides it and relies on the Load event handler called InitializeFromMetadata to initialize the UIHint property. Because the DynamicEntity control does not offer a Table property, the MetaTable object describing the current entity has to be located by calling the FindMetaTable extension method. This method is actually defined in the DynamicDataExtensions class, but calling it with the extension syntax makes the code a lot shorter.

> **NOTE**
>
> Creating the UnleashedEntity control just for the sake of initializing its UIHint might seem excessive compared to other, simpler ways you could encapsulate this functionality. However, there are other reasons to extend this control as well. Recall the capability implemented in the UnleashedControl to inherit its Mode property from the parent entity template. The UnleashedEntity control implements similar logic, which enables using generic templates discussed in Chapter 4 inside of multimode templates from Chapter 10 without having to implement additional initialization. Refer to the source code accompanying this book to see how this was accomplished.

With all four page templates modified to use the UnleashedEntity instead of the DynamicEntity control, you now have support for metadata-driven entity UI hints in your Dynamic Data web application and can begin implementing additional form layouts as in separate dynamic entity templates.

Building a Dynamic Two-Column Entity Template

As you might recall, the idea of the two-column entity template is that you specify the name of the column where you want a particular property to display using the GroupName property of the DisplayAttribute applied to it in the metadata. In the following code snippet, the FirstName and LastName properties need to be in the column called "Left", and the Address and City properties need to be in the column called "Right". The job of the TwoColumn entity template is to define these two columns and instantiate the dynamic controls and their labels in the appropriate column, based on the GroupName annotation:

```
[MetadataType(typeof(Metadata))]
partial class Employee
{
  [EntityUIHint("TwoColumn")]
  private abstract class Metadata
  {
    [Display(GroupName = "Left", Order = 100)]
    public object FirstName { get; set; }

    [Display(GroupName = "Left", Order = 110)]
    public object LastName { get; set; }

    [Display(GroupName = "Right", Order = 200)]
    public object Address { get; set; }

    [Display(GroupName = "Right", Order = 210)]
    public object City { get; set; }
  }
}
```

Markup of the TwoColumn entity template is shown in Listing 11.13. By comparing this markup with the Default entity template back in Listing 11.4, you can see that it has an additional HTML table with two cells, each of them containing a nested table and an ASP.NET PlaceHolder control, where the dynamically instantiated controls will be added, depending on their GroupName annotation.

LISTING 11.13 TwoColumn Entity Template (Markup)

```
<%@ Control Language="C#" CodeBehind="TwoColumn.ascx.cs"
  Inherits="WebApplication.DynamicData.EntityTemplates.TwoColumnEntityTemplate" %>
<asp:EntityTemplate runat="server" ID="entityTemplate">
  <ItemTemplate>
    <tr>
      <td class="DDLightHeader">
        <unl:UnleashedLabel runat="server" OnInit="Label_Init" />
      </td>
      <td>
        <unl:UnleashedControl runat="server" OnInit="DynamicControl_Init" />
      </td>
    </tr>
  </ItemTemplate>
</asp:EntityTemplate>
<table>
  <tr>
    <td style="vertical-align:top">
      <table class=" DDDetailsTable">
        <asp:PlaceHolder runat="server" ID="left" />
      </table>
    </td>
    <td style="vertical-align:top">
      <table class=" DDDetailsTable">
        <asp:PlaceHolder runat="server" ID="right" />
      </table>
    </td>
  </tr>
</table>
```

Listing 11.14 shows the code-behind file of the TwoColumn entity template with the differences from the default entity template shown in bold font. The main difference from the default entity template is located in the OnLoad method of the TwoColumnEntityTemplate. Notice how instead of adding the dynamically created controls to the EntityTemplate itself, it calls the FindGroupPlaceHolder method and adds them to the PlaceHolder control it returns. In other words, the Default entity template uses the EntityTemplate control as both a *template* to create the dynamic controls and a *container* to host them. The TwoColumn template, however, uses the EntityTemplate control only as a template, and the two PlaceHolder controls serve as containers for the generated controls.

LISTING 11.14 TwoColumn Entity Template (Code-Behind)

```
using System;
using System.Collections.Generic;
using System.ComponentModel.DataAnnotations;
using System.Linq;
using System.Web.DynamicData;
using System.Web.UI.WebControls;

namespace WebApplication
{
  public partial class TwoColumnEntityTemplate : EntityTemplateUserControl
  {
    private MetaColumn currentColumn;

    protected override void OnLoad(EventArgs e)
    {
      IEnumerable<MetaColumn> scaffoldColumns =
        this.Table.GetScaffoldColumns(this.Mode, this.ContainerType);
      foreach (MetaColumn column in scaffoldColumns)
      {
        this.currentColumn = column;
        var container = new NamingContainer();
        this.entityTemplate.ItemTemplate.InstantiateIn(container);
        PlaceHolder placeHolder = this.FindGroupPlaceHolder(column);
        placeHolder.Controls.Add(container);
      }
    }

    protected void Label_Init(object sender, EventArgs e)
    {
      ((UnleashedLabel)sender).DataField = this.currentColumn.Name;
    }
```

```
protected void DynamicControl_Init(object sender, EventArgs e)
{
  ((UnleashedControl)sender).DataField = this.currentColumn.Name;
}

private PlaceHolder FindGroupPlaceHolder(MetaColumn column)
{
  PlaceHolder placeHolder = null;
  var display = column.Attributes.OfType<DisplayAttribute>().FirstOrDefault();
  if (display != null && !string.IsNullOrWhiteSpace(display.GroupName))
    placeHolder = (PlaceHolder)this.FindControl(display.GroupName);
  return placeHolder ?? this.left;
}
}
}
```

The FindGroupPlaceHolder method tries to find a DisplayAttribute applied to the entity property described by the MetaColumn object it receives. If the DisplayAttribute is found and has the GroupName property specified, it calls the FindControl method inherited from the ASP.NET's Control base class to find the PlaceHolder with the matching name. If the entity property does not have a GroupName annotation or if the PlaceHolder with the specified name could not be found, the "left" PlaceHolder is returned by default. In other words, unless you specify otherwise, the TwoColumn entity template displays controls on the left side of the page.

Figure 11.8 shows how the Employee details page can look when the EntityUIHintAttribute is applied to the entity class and the GroupName annotation is specified for the appropriate entity properties.

FIGURE 11.8 TwoColumn entity template.

Although it is hard to tell by just looking at the code in the OnLoad method of the TwoColumn entity template, the Order annotation is still as relevant here as it is in the Default (single-column) template. Because the GetScaffoldColumn method returns MetaColumn objects sorted by the Order value, the controls are instantiated and added to the two PlaceHolder controls in the proper order, as specified in the metadata. Keep in mind that both entity templates (single-item forms) and list page templates use the Order annotation to determine order of controls and columns respectively. Dealing with a large number of properties can be still difficult when it comes to the GridView columns.

The approach used to create the TwoColumn entity template can also work for advanced page layouts that have more "zones" than just two, such as the popular "two columns with a footer" layout used by many applications including the Work item Form in Visual Studio Team Explorer. It typically has two columns with small data controls that occupy the top half of the page and a combined footer area contains big data controls, such as multiline text boxes, that need to be much wider than a single column would allow.

To support a more complex form layout, you would simply need to create a new entity template with an appropriate structure of HTML table (or div, if you prefer using CSS) elements and place a PlaceHolder control in locations where you want the data controls to appear and give them appropriate names, such as "Left", "Right", "Bottom", and so on. As long as you use the matching names in the GroupName annotations, the FindGroupPlaceHolder method will be able to find them, no matter how complex the form is.

Summary

The ability to build user interfaces based on metadata is one of the key advantages Dynamic Data offers. It dramatically reduces the amount of presentation code you have to write and maintain over the lifetime of an application and, *when used judiciously*, significantly increases the speed of development. By postponing implementation of the user interface, Dynamic Data allows you to focus on the most important part of the application—its entity model. You can then refine it through short successive iterations, collecting feedback from business users based on actual working applications instead of diagrams, and greatly reduce risk and uncertainty in the project.

Out of the box, Dynamic Data offers robust capabilities for building single-column forms through metadata. The DisplayAttribute allows you to control display names and order of entity properties on forms and in grids. The DisplayFormatAttribute offers configuration options to control appearance of values in both Read-only and Edit mode. The DataTypeAttribute and the UIHintAttribute can be used to override the default rules Dynamic Data uses when selecting a field template for a particular property. The EnumDataTypeAttribute can be applied to an integral property to associate it with a list of predefined values that are presented to the users as a DropDownList control by the Enumeration field template.

This chapter discussed in detail how to overcome some of the limitations of Dynamic Data. The Enumeration field templates can be extended to take advantage of the DisplayAttribute to specify human-readable display name for enum items. Dynamic Data controls can be also extended to support field template parameters specified declaratively with the UIHintAttribute. Although it should be done with great caution, interaction between field templates can be configured through the metadata. Finally, additional dynamic entity templates can be implemented to take advantage of extended data annotations, such as the EntityUIHintAttribute discussed in this chapter.

Building Custom Search Pages

Dynamic Data offers powerful and flexible building blocks for creating list pages and search screens—common features in most enterprise applications. As discussed in Chapter 6, "Page Templates," DynamicField can be used with the standard GridView control to quickly build pages that display data in tabular format. By relying on the same rich set of field templates used by the DynamicControl, the DynamicField allows you to significantly improve code reuse and create field templates for both list and single-item pages. The DynamicFilter along with the QueryExtender controls discussed in Chapter 5, "Filter Templates," can be used to quickly build powerful search screens that rely on an extensible set of filter templates and generate LINQ queries, translated by the Entity Framework to SQL statements and executed directly by the database servers.

Although the data entry pages typically display information about a single entity, read-only pages in general and list pages in particular often need to combine information from several related entities on a single page. For instance, a product search page might need to display and allow users to search for products by the country of origin. In the Northwind Traders sample database, this means combining information from the Product and Supplier entities on the same screen because in this entity model, the product's country is determined by the address of the supplier. In this chapter, you look at extending the capabilities of Dynamic Data to handle some of the common scenarios of working with related entities in list pages and search screens.

Displaying Information from Related Entities

The first example is a page that displays a list of items a customer previously ordered from the Northwind Traders website. For each item, the page displays name of the product, quantity, date of the order, and the order status. You can see how this page will look in Figure 12.1. Of course, in a real-world application, this page might also allow users to reorder items by clicking a link or selecting a check box next to each item. However, to keep the example simple, this particular functionality is not implemented.

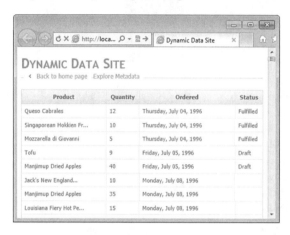

FIGURE 12.1 List page with columns from multiple related entities.

This page displays properties of three related entities: Order_Detail, Product, and Order. As you can see by looking at the Northwind entity model, the Order_Detail entity has two *foreign key* (also known as *navigation*) properties called Product and Order that point to the respective parent entities. On the sample page in the figure, the first column displays the ProductName property of the parent Product entity, and the last two columns display the OrderDate and OrderStatus properties of the parent Order entity.

Consider how this page could be implemented with the built-in controls and field templates provided by Dynamic Data. For the ProductName, you could have used the built-in ForeignKey field template, which would display product names as hyperlinks. However, there is no way to display both OrderDate and OrderStatus using just the field templates that Dynamic Data offers out of the box. The ForeignKey field template can display value of only one property, the one specified in the DisplayColumnAttribute applied to the parent entity class, so you could display either the OrderDate or the OrderStatus, but not both.

To solve this problem, the sample solution includes a new field template called Parent (for consistency with the built-in Children template). This template can be used with foreign key columns and allows you to set the DisplayField attribute to any column from the parent entity to display. Following is an example of using this template with the Order property of the Order_Detail entity to display the OrderDate property of the parent Order entity. Listing 12.4 later in this section shows a complete markup of the sample page.

```
<unl:UnleashedField DataField="Order" UIHint="Parent"
   DisplayField="OrderDate" />
```

12

> **NOTE**
>
> UnleashedField is an extended version of the built-in DynamicField, which was introduced in Chapter 11, "Building Dynamic Forms." For the purposes of this discussion, they are the same.

Listing 12.1 shows the markup of the Parent field template. Notice that unlike the built-in ForeignKey template, which determines the value of the parent column directly and displays it in a HyperLink control, the *Parent* field template uses a nested UnleashedControl, which as you recall inherits from the DynamicControl provided by Dynamic Data. In other words, the Parent field template uses another field template to display the parent property. That field template will be located based on the metadata information describing the parent property. This allows you to reuse the logic already implemented in the numerous built-in and custom field templates for different types of properties, including enumeration, foreign key, and Boolean, which you otherwise would have to reimplement.

LISTING 12.1 Parent Field Template (Markup)

```
<%@ Control Language="C#" CodeBehind="Parent.ascx.cs"
  Inherits="WebApplication.DynamicData.FieldTemplates.ParentFieldTemplate" %>
<unl:DataItemContainer runat="server" ID="container">
  <unl:UnleashedControl runat="server" ID="control" OnInit="Control_Init" />
</unl:DataItemContainer>
```

Field templates rely on ASP.NET data binding to extract values of their columns from the entity object provided by the EntityDataSource control. Although the Parent field template itself is bound to the *child* entity, Order_Detail in this example, the nested field template created by its UnleashedControl, needs to be bound to the *parent* entity, Order or Product. To accomplish this, the Parent field template wraps the UnleashedControl inside of the DataItemContainer, a simple control, shown in Listing 12.2, that implements the IDataItemContainer interface defined by ASP.NET Framework in the System.Web.UI namespace and allows switching the data binding context for its child controls.

LISTING 12.2 DataItemContainer Control

```
using System.Web.UI;

namespace Unleashed.DynamicData
{
  public class DataItemContainer: Control, IDataItemContainer
  {
    public object DataItem { get; internal set; }
```

LISTING 12.2 Continued

```
    public int DataItemIndex { get; internal set; }
    public int DisplayIndex { get; internal set; }
  }
}
```

Code-behind of the Parent field template is shown in Listing 12.3. Notice the public
DisplayField property, which is set as a custom attribute in page markup to specify the
name of the property of the parent entity the template needs to display.

LISTING 12.3 Parent Field Template (Code-Behind)

```
using System;
using System.Web.UI;
using System.Web.DynamicData;

namespace WebApplication.DynamicData.FieldTemplates
{
  public partial class ParentFieldTemplate : UnleashedFieldTemplate
  {
    public override Control DataControl
    {
      get { return this.control.FieldTemplate.DataControl; }
    }

    public string DisplayField { get; set; }

    protected void Control_Init(object sender, EventArgs args)
    {
      this.container.SetMetaTable(this.ForeignKeyColumn.ParentTable);
      this.control.DataField = this.DisplayField;
    }

    protected override void OnDataBinding(EventArgs e)
    {
      this.container.DataItem = this.FieldValue;
      base.OnDataBinding(e);
    }
  }
}
```

The Control_Init method uses the DisplayField property to initialize the DataField
property of the nested UnleashedControl; however, that is only half the information
it needs to locate the MetaColumn describing the parent entity property. The

UnleashedControl also needs the MetaTable object describing the parent entity, which the Control_Init method provides by getting the ParentTable from the ForeignKeyColumn object and associating it with the DataItemContainer.

The overridden OnDataBinding method is responsible for changing the data binding context for the nested field template. During data binding, the FieldValue property of the field template associated with a foreign key property returns the parent entity object, lazy-loading it with the help of Entity Framework if necessary. By storing the parent entity object in the DataItem property of the DataItemContainer, this code ensures that the nested field template is bound to the parent entity object and not to the child entity object as the field template itself.

Putting it all together, Listing 12.4 shows the markup of the sample page implemented using this new field template. This markup should be already familiar to you from the previous chapters. It uses UnleashedField—the class created in Chapter 11 to extend the DynamicField provided by Dynamic Data. However, for the purposes of this discussion, you could have also used DynamicField instances.

LISTING 12.4 List Page with Columns from Multiple Related Entities (Markup)

```
<%@ Page Language="C#"
  MasterPageFile="~/Site.master" CodeBehind="SamplePage.aspx.cs"
  Inherits="WebApplication.Samples.Ch12.ParentFieldTemplate.SamplePage" %>
<asp:Content ContentPlaceHolderID="main" runat="server">
  <asp:GridView runat="server" ID="gridView" DataSourceID="dataSource"
    AutoGenerateColumns="false" AllowSorting="true">
    <Columns>
      <unl:UnleashedField DataField="Product" HeaderText="Product" UIHint="Parent"
        DisplayField="ProductName" SortExpression="Product.ProductName" />
      <unl:UnleashedField DataField="Quantity" HeaderText="Quantity" />
      <unl:UnleashedField DataField="Order" HeaderText="Ordered" UIHint="Parent"
        DisplayField="OrderDate" SortExpression="Order.OrderDate" />
      <unl:UnleashedField DataField="Order" HeaderText="Status" UIHint="Parent"
        DisplayField="OrderStatus" SortExpression="Order.OrderStatus" />
    </Columns>
  </asp:GridView>
  <asp:EntityDataSource runat="server" ID="dataSource"
    ConnectionString="name=NorthwindEntities"
    DefaultContainerName="NorthwindEntities" EntitySetName="Order_Details" />
</asp:Content>
```

Notice that although the Quantity column comes directly from the Order_Detail entity, whose data is loaded by the EntityDataSource control, for the *Product*, *Ordered*, and *Status* columns, the UIHint attribute is set to Parent, the name of the new field template. A custom attribute, DisplayField, is used to specify the property of the parent entity whose value the page needs to display.

The code-behind file, shown in Listing 12.5, performs not only the required step of associating a MetaTable object with the GridView control, but also initializes the Include property of the EntityDataSource control. In dynamic page templates, this step is performed by the DynamicDataManager control. In this sample page, it is required to eagerly load the parent entities, Product and Order, referenced by the foreign key properties of the child Order_Detail entity. Implementation of the Parent field template assumes that the parent entity object is available during data binding. Without eager loading, this would either result in an error, if the lazy loading option was turned off, or multiple queries would be sent to the database to retrieve parent entities individually.

LISTING 12.5 List Page with Columns from Multiple Related Entities (Code-Behind)

```
using System;
using System.Web.DynamicData;

namespace WebApplication.Samples.Ch12.ParentFieldTemplate
{
  public partial class SamplePage : System.Web.UI.Page
  {
    protected override void OnInit(EventArgs e)
    {
      base.OnInit(e);
      MetaTable table = Global.DefaultModel.GetTable(this.dataSource.EntitySetName);
      this.gridView.SetMetaTable(table);
      this.dataSource.Include = table.ForeignKeyColumnsNames;
    }
  }
}
```

As you can see, having the Parent field template at your disposal makes implementing list pages that display information from multiple related entities almost as easy as creating custom pages for a single entity. The Parent field template works equally well in single-item pages built with the FormView control and entity templates or the DetailsView control. However, it can only be used in Read-only mode; trying to edit properties of parent entities at the same time with the child entities would be not only challenging to implement, but also confusing for the application's users.

Column Sorting Across Related Entities

The GridView control allows users to click the column headers to sort the rows in ascending or descending order of the column values. With LINQ-enabled data source controls, this functionality takes advantage of server-side sorting by generating LINQ queries that have an ORDER BY clause when translated to SQL. It turns out you do not have to implement any additional support for this logic in the Parent field template. In a custom page, all that is required is to specify the appropriate value in the SortExpression property of the UnleashedField (this property is actually inherited directly from the DataControlField base class). The following markup snippet illustrates how this was done in the last sample page:

```
<unl:UnleashedField DataField="Product" HeaderText="Product" UIHint="Parent"
    DisplayField="ProductName" SortExpression="Product.ProductName" />
```

With a LINQ-enabled data source, the SortExpression can traverse related entities through the navigation properties. To allow sorting the list of order items by the product name, you simply specify SortExpression of the first column as Product.ProductName, where Product is the name of the navigation property of the Order_Detail entity. What the SortExpression does when the user clicks the Product column in the GridView control on the sample page is very similar the following LINQ query. Of course, setting the SortExpression does not require any custom code and is much more compact:

```
using (var context = new NorthwindEntities())
{
    IQueryable<Order_Detail> query =
        from item in context.Order_Details
        orderby item.Product.ProductName
        select item;
}
```

Building Custom Search Pages

Many similarities exist between the DynamicControl and field templates on one side and the DynamicFilter control and filter templates on the other. As you recall from a discussion in Chapter 10, "Building Custom Forms," the DynamicControl allows you to assemble custom entity forms from field templates based on the type of entity properties. If you need a specific field template for a given property, such as the MultilineText template, you can specify its name in the UIHint attribute of the DynamicControl:

```
<asp:DynamicControl runat="server" DataField="Address"
    UIHint="MultilineText" />
```

If you want to provide additional information to the field template, you can do so by specifying custom attributes directly in markup. The DynamicControl automatically assigns the custom attribute values, such as the Columns attribute shown next, to the matching public properties of the field template:

```
<asp:DynamicControl runat="server" DataField="Address" Columns="65" />
```

When it comes to dynamic filters, the DynamicFilter control also supports the ability to specify the template name explicitly by setting its FilterUIHint attribute in markup. You can take advantage of the Text filter template created in Chapter 5 to create a filter control for the `ProductName` property of the Product entity:

```
<asp:DynamicFilter runat="server" DataField="ProductName"
  FilterUIHint="Text"/>
```

You also want to be able to specify custom attributes in page markup and access them in the filter template. For instance, when configuring the ProductName filter, you might need to make the `TextBox` control wider and allow users to see longer values without scrolling. In page markup, you would want to write something like this:

```
<asp:DynamicFilter runat="server" DataField="ProductName"
  FilterUIHint="Text" Columns="100"/>
```

In the Text filter template, you would want to define a public property called `Columns` and use it to initialize the `TextBox` the template creates, like so:

```
public partial class TextFilter
{
  public int Columns { get; set; }

  protected override void OnInit(EventArgs e)
  {
    base.OnInit(e);
    if (this.Columns > 0)
      this.textBox.Columns = this.Columns;
  }
}
```

Unfortunately, the `DynamicFilter` control does not support use of custom attributes to initialize public properties of the filter templates. So if you wanted to provide the ability to change the size of the `TextBox` control in the Text filter template from a custom page, you couldn't simply specify it in the page markup as just shown. Instead, you would have to stick it in the `FilterUIHintAttribute` applied to the property in the entity model and add code to the filter template to retrieve it dynamically. This is not only more cumbersome, it also forces you to place presentation logic of a specific page in the entity model.

Consider the `Parent` field template that displays values of properties from a related entity. This template uses a `DynamicControl` (yes, an `UnleashedControl` in this example, which is not important for this discussion) to locate and instantiate another field template. A similar *filter* template could allow you to build search pages based on columns from related entities. Perhaps you need to create a page where users can search for Products by the Country of their Suppliers. Here is how you would want to use this filter template in page markup:

```
<asp:DynamicFilter runat="server" DataField="Supplier"
  FilterUIHint="Parent" DisplayField="Country"/>
```

This filter template would also need a nested `DynamicFilter` control to load another filter template, appropriate for the specified `DisplayField`. The following snippet shows how markup of this filter template *could* look:

```
<%@ Control Language="C#" CodeBehind="Parent.ascx.cs"
    Inherits="WebApplication.DynamicData.Filters.ParentFilter" %>
<asp:DynamicFilter ID="filter" runat="server" OnInit="Filter_Init"/>
```

Unfortunately, it is not possible to use the `DynamicFilter` control inside of a filter template like this. Internal implementation of the `DynamicFilter` control relies on the `InitComplete` event of the `Page` class to instantiate the filter template, and by the time the nested `DynamicFilter` is created, this event has already fired, and the nested filter template is never created.

Overcoming Limitations of Dynamic Filters

To be consistent with the capabilities offered by the `DynamicControl`, the `DynamicFilter` control needs to support custom attributes and work inside of other filter templates. These capabilities are important not only for consistency's sake; without them, the `DynamicFilter` control encourages embedding presentation information in the business layer and limits your ability to create advanced filter templates necessary for real-world search pages.

Unfortunately, implementation of the `DynamicFilter` in ASP.NET version 4.0 does not allow you to fix these problems by inheriting from and extending this control. The only way to eliminate them is by completely rewriting this control along with other controls and classes that depend on it. Table 12.1 shows the original controls that come with Dynamic Data and the replacement controls you can find in the source code accompanying this book.

TABLE 12.1 Replacement Filter Classes and Controls

Built-in	Replacement
QueryableFilterUserControl	UnleashedFilterTemplate
DynamicFilter	UnleashedFilter
DynamicFilterExpression	UnleashedFilterExpression
QueryableFilterRepeater	UnleashedFilterRepeater

With the exception of the `UnleashedFilterTemplate`, which inherits from the `QueryableFilterUserControl`, the rest of these classes are not related to the corresponding built-in classes that come with Dynamic Data. However, they are designed to be fully-compatible with their built-in equivalents and allow you to simply change the class names in markup and source files of your application. Figure 12.2 shows a class diagram that provides a high-level overview of the new classes.

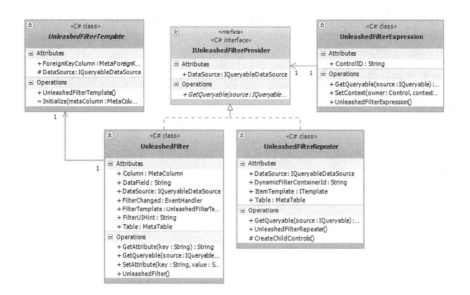

FIGURE 12.2 Unleashed filter classes.

UnleashedFilter

The UnleashedFilter control is a replacement for the built-in DynamicFilter control. It provides properties (DataField, FilterUIHint, and FilterTemplate) events (FilterChanged) and methods (OnFilterChanged) that mimic corresponding members of the DynamicFilter control and should be 100% compatible and familiar to you from a discussion in Chapter 5.

The DataSource property is new. It allows you to get or set the IQueryableDataSource instance with which the filter is associated. In the DynamicFilter, the data source object is stored in a private field; however, in the UnleashedFilter, you need to be able to set it not only from a data source expression, but also from a filter template that has a nested filter control.

The Table and Column properties of the UnleashedFilter are provided for consistency and mimic similar properties of the built-in DynamicControl. You can set the Table property explicitly, but the control can also determine it automatically by retrieving the MetaTable object associated with its DataSource control. Likewise, the Column property can be set directly; however, the control automatically finds the MetaColumn object in the associated MetaTable using the name specified in the DataField property.

Like the DynamicControl, the UnleashedFilter supports specifying custom attributes in page markup and automatically sets matching public properties of the filter template it instantiates. And like the UnleashedControl, the UnleashedFilter automatically initializes public properties of the filter template based on the control parameters specified for the entity property with the FilterUIHintAttribute.

UnleashedFilterRepeater

The UnleashedFilterRepeater control is a replacement for the built-in
QueryableFilterRepeater. As you recall from Chapter 6, this control is used by the List
page template to automatically generate filters for all filterable properties of a given entity
class. It allows you to define an ItemTemplate markup, typically containing a Label and a
DynamicFilter controls that are dynamically instantiated for every filterable property.
QueryableFilterRepeater control is responsible for initializing the DynamicFilter
instances it generates. Because the UnleashedFilter is not related to the built-in
DynamicFilter, the QueryableFilterRepeater cannot initialize it dynamically, which is
why it had to be replaced with the UnleashedFilterRepeater. For compatibility, the
replacement control defines both ItemTemplate and DynamicFilterContainerId properties
that work exactly like they do in the QueryableFilterRepeater.

Similarly to the UnleashedFilter, the UnleashedFilterRepeater class defines DataSource
and Table properties, allowing you to configure it programmatically. It also does not rely
on the Page events, which makes it possible to use inside of other filter templates.

UnleashedFilterExpression

The UnleashedFilterExpression is a replacement for the built-in DynamicFilterExpression.
As you recall from Chapters 5 and 6, this class is used in page markup to associate
DynamicFilter and QueryableFilterRepeater controls with a QueryExtender control.
DynamicFilterExpression is responsible for supplying the filter controls with the
IQueryableDataSource instance (an EntityDataSource or LinqDataSource) received from
the query extender. The DynamicFilterExpression works with the built-in controls and
just like the controls themselves, does not allow extension by inheritance, forcing a
complete replacement.

UnleashedFilterTemplate

The UnleashedFilterTemplate base class is a replacement for the built-in
QueryableFilterUserControl. Unlike the other filter classes, however, the
QueryableFilterUserControl provides a fair amount of utility methods used in the
enumeration and foreign key filter templates. As a compromise between quality of
design and code reuse, the UnleashedFilterTemplate inherits from the
QueryableFilterUserControl and exposes the properties and methods required for
initialization via .NET Reflection.

Using .NET Reflection in a web application is far from ideal. Aside from being fragile in
face of potential future changes in the .NET framework, Reflection requires the web application to run in full-trust mode, which can be a problem in a shared hosting environment. If that is a concern, you might need to reimplement the QueryableFilterUserControl
entirely.

Using Replacement Filter Controls

The beginning of this section discussed several limitations in the implementation of the
build-in DynamicFilter control, including its reliance on the Page events and lack of
support for custom attributes and metadata-driven control parameters. In the next section,

you see how overcoming the first limitation enables you to create an advanced filter template that can filter a query of child entities based on properties of their parents. However, for illustration of the immediate benefits, consider the sample page in Listing 12.6, which shows an example of using the UnleashedFilter control to specify custom attributes.

LISTING 12.6 Product Search Page with Wide ProductName Filter (Markup)

```
<%@ Page Title="" Language="C#"
  MasterPageFile="~/Site.master" CodeBehind="SamplePage.aspx.cs"
  Inherits="WebApplication.Samples.Ch12.UnleashedFilter.SamplePage" %>
<asp:Content ContentPlaceHolderID="main" runat="server">
  <unl:UnleashedFilter runat="server" ID="productNameFilter" FilterUIHint="Text"
    DataField="ProductName" Columns="100"/>
  <asp:GridView runat="server" ID="gridView" DataSourceID="dataSource"
    AutoGenerateColumns="false">
    <Columns>
      <unl:UnleashedField DataField="ProductName"/>
      <unl:UnleashedField DataField="Supplier" HeaderText="Origin"
        UIHint="Parent" DisplayField="Country" />
    </Columns>
  </asp:GridView>
  <asp:EntityDataSource runat="server" ID="dataSource"
  ConnectionString="name=NorthwindEntities" DefaultContainerName="NorthwindEntities"
  EntitySetName="Products"/>
  <asp:QueryExtender runat="server" TargetControlID="dataSource">
    <unl:UnleashedFilterExpression ControlID="productNameFilter"/>
  </asp:QueryExtender>
</asp:Content>
```

This sample page demonstrates how the UnleashedFilter control enables you to set a custom attribute Columns for the UnleashedFilter control in page markup and make the text box generated by the ProductName filter wider. The custom attribute matches the public property called Columns declared by the Text filter template, and the UnleashedFilter takes care of initializing it for you. The Text filter template, located in the DynamicData\Filters folder of the sample web application, has been modified to inherit from the new UnleashedFilterTemplate. Its OnInit method initializes the Columns property of the actual TextBox control where the user enters a product name to search. Figure 12.3 shows how the resulting page looks with the wide ProductName filter text box above the grid.

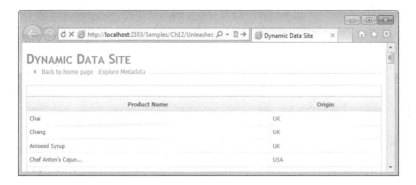

FIGURE 12.3 Product search page with wide product name filter.

Remember that to be compatible with the UnleashedFilter control, all existing filter templates must be modified to inherit from the UnleashedFilterTemplate instead of the built-in QueryableFilterUserControl. The filter templates accompanying this book have been updated; their source code is not listed here to save space.

Although this is not strictly required at this time, you might also want to go ahead and change the dynamic page templates, List and ListDetails, to use the UnleashedFilterRepeater and UnleashedFilter controls instead of the built-in QueryableFilterRepeater and DynamicFilter controls, respectively. Support the UnleashedFilter provides control parameters in the FilterUIHintAttribute is essential to building search pages dynamically, which is discussed in the Chapter 13, "Building Dynamic List Pages."

Filtering Based on Related Entities

Now that the building blocks are in place, let's get back to the original goal of building a page that displays information from multiple entities. The earlier example you used the Parent field template, which allows displaying values from any property of a parent entity in the same GridView or DetailsView with its children. However, when building search screens, you often need to not only *display*, but also allow users to *filter* based on information from related entities. Consider the web page shown in Figure 12.4, which displays a list of products and their countries of origin. Although the product name comes from the ProductName property of the *Product* entity, the country of origin comes from the Country property of the *Supplier* entity. The Supplier and Product entities form a parent-child relationship, connected by the Supplier foreign key property of the Product entity.

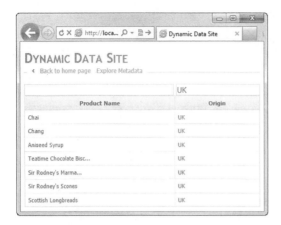

FIGURE 12.4 Product search page filtered by supplier country.

This page displays the Origin column using the UnleashedField and Parent field template with markup shown here:

```
<unl:UnleashedField DataField="Supplier"
   UIHint="Parent" DisplayField="Country"/>
```

To implement the requirement of searching for products by their countries of origin, you would like to use a similar pattern with markup that looks like this:

```
<unl:UnleashedFilter runat="server" DataField="Supplier"
   FilterUIHint="Parent" DisplayField="Country"/>
```

In other words, the Parent *filter* template is also associated with the Supplier property of the Product entity and displays the filter control for the Country property of the parent Supplier entity.

As you can see in Listing 12.7, the approach used in the Parent filter template to locate and instantiate a filter template appropriate for the parent property is also similar to the one used to implement the Parent field template earlier. Its markup defines a nested instance of the UnleashedFilter control that will be responsible for loading another filter template based on the property of the parent entity specified as the DisplayField.

LISTING 12.7 Parent Filter Template (Markup)

```
<%@ Control Language="C#" CodeBehind="Parent.ascx.cs"
  Inherits="WebApplication.DynamicData.Filters.ParentFilter" %>
<unl:UnleashedFilter ID="filter" runat="server" OnInit="Filter_Init"/>
```

Just like with the Parent field template, most of the implementation of the Parent filter template is in its code-behind file. At a high-level, it is responsible for two things—initializing the nested UnleashedFilter control with all information required to load the appropriate filter template for the parent entity property and implementing the query logic required to filter child entities based on the parent property value. In the following two sections, *Initializing Nested Filter Control* and *Implementing Query Logic*, you get a close look at the internals of this filter control. Based on this example, some of the more challenging aspects of advanced filter template design are discussed. However, you can also skip them and continue reading the section *Using the Parent Filter Template* later in the chapter.

Initializing Nested Filter Control

The filter control needs an `IQueryableDataSource` object (an `EntityDataSource` or a `LinqDataSource`), a `MetaTable` describing the target entity, and a name of the target entity property. Listing 12.8 shows the part of ParentFilter implementation responsible for the initialization.

LISTING 12.8 Parent Filter Template (Initialization Logic)

```
using System;
using System.Linq;
using System.Linq.Expressions;
using System.Web.DynamicData;
using System.Web.UI.WebControls;

namespace WebApplication.DynamicData.Filters
{
  public partial class ParentFilter : UnleashedFilterTemplate
  {
    private object dataSourceContext;

    public string DisplayField { get; set; }

    protected void Filter_Init(object sender, EventArgs args)
    {
      this.filter.DataSource = this.DataSource;
      this.filter.Table = this.ForeignKeyColumn.ParentTable;
      this.filter.DataField = this.DisplayField;
      ((EntityDataSource)this.DataSource).ContextCreated +=
        this.DataSourceContextCreated;
      ((EntityDataSource)this.DataSource).Selecting += this.DataSourceSelecting;
    }

    private void DataSourceContextCreated(object sender,
      EntityDataSourceContextCreatedEventArgs e)
    {
      this.dataSourceContext = e.Context;
    }

    private void DataSourceSelecting(object sender,
```

LISTING 12.8 Continued

```
        EntityDataSourceSelectingEventArgs e)
    {
        if (string.IsNullOrEmpty(e.SelectArguments.SortExpression))
        {
            e.SelectArguments.SortExpression = string.Join(",",
                this.ForeignKeyColumn.Table.PrimaryKeyColumns.Select(c => c.Name));
        }
    }
}
}
```

The `Filter_Init` method handles the `Init` event of the nested `UnleashedFilter` control and initializes all required properties. In particular, it sets the `DataSource` property of the `UnleashedFilter` control with the `DataSource` object of the filter template itself. It also sets the `Table` property of the nested `UnleashedFilter` control. Normally, this is not necessary because the `UnleashedFilter` automatically uses the `MetaTable` object associated with the data source control. However, in this case you want the nested `UnleashedFilter` control to be associated with the `MetaTable` object describing the *parent* entity. That is why it is set explicitly, using the `ParentTable` property of the `ForeignKeyColumn` object that represents the foreign key entity property Supplier, with which the filter template is associated.

> **NOTE**
>
> In the Parent *field* template, the `DataItemContainer` provided both the `MetaTable` and entity object. In *filter* templates, which do not rely on data binding to display initial values, this works differently. Instead of data binding, filter templates rely on the `DefaultValue` and `DefaultValues` properties provided by the `QueryableFilterUserControl` base class.

Finally, the `Filter_Init` method sets the `DataField` property of the nested `UnleashedFilter` control. It does that based on the value of the `DisplayField` property of the filter template itself. In this current example, the `DisplayField` property is specified as a custom attribute of the `UnleashedFilter` in page markup, and the control takes care of initializing the property automatically.

The last task performed by the `Filter_Init` method is setting up a couple of event handlers for the data source control. The `DataSourceContextCreated` method handles the `ContextCreated` event. This method saves the `ObjectContext`, a `NorthwindEntities` object in this example, in the `dataSourceContext` private field of the template. This is important for the query logic discussed next that relies on the `join` LINQ operator and requires both queries to come from the same `ObjectContext`.

The `DataSourceSelecting` handles the `Selecting` event of the `EntityDataSource` control to work around some of its limitations. The built-in paging logic in the `EntityDataSource` control relies on the built-in LINQ operators `Skip` and `Take`. The Entity Framework implementation of LINQ requires these operators to be preceeded by an `OrderBy` and, normally, the `EntityDataSource` is responsible for generating it. However, it does not automatically generate the `OrderBy` operator when the query has been modified by a `QueryExtender`, which causes a runtime error. The `DataSourceSelecting` method in the filter template supplies a default sort expression to the `EntityDataSource` control unless it was already supplied by a `GridView` control in response to a user clicking one of the column headers.

Implementing Query Logic

As you might recall from a discussion in Chapter 5, query logic is implemented by overriding the `GetQueryable` method inherited from the `QueryableFilterUserControl` base class. This method receives an `IQueryable` object as a parameter, modifies the query based on the control or controls it displays, and returns the modified query. The built-in filter templates that come with Dynamic Data implement query logic by creating lambda expressions dynamically, using LINQ `Expression` objects. This task can be significantly simplified with Dynamic LINQ, a sample project that comes with Visual Studio and allows manipulating LINQ expressions as simple strings instead of objects. Unfortunately, as you see shortly, Dynamic LINQ cannot help implementing complex logic the Parent filter template requires, and you have to resort to the low-level LINQ `Expression` manipulation.

> **NOTE**
>
> This section walks you through implementation of a specific filter template. However, the general approach of starting with the high-level LINQ query and progressively digging down to deeper levels works well for developing any custom filter template in general. Although you can simply get the Parent control from the book's source code, reading this section will help you learn how to build your own advanced filter templates that require using low-level LINQ expressions.

LINQ Expression Mechanics

Before you jump into the implementation details of query logic for an advanced filter template, like Parent, first figure out how you would implement it without the dynamic filters. Here is a LINQ query you could have written to retrieve all products imported from the UK:

```
using (var context = new NorthwindEntities())
{
  IQueryable<Product> query =
    from p in context.Products
    where p.Supplier.Country == "UK"
    select p;
  // ...
}
```

Notice how much easier it is to filter Product entities based on Supplier entity properties with LINQ than it is with plain SQL. LINQ allows you to traverse the Supplier navigation property and specify filter criteria for the parent entity without having to implement an explicit join. Here is an equivalent query that looks closer to the INNER JOIN SQL statement you would have to create without LINQ:

```
IQueryable<Product> query =
    from p in context.Products
    join s in context.Suppliers.Where(s => s.Country == "UK")
      on p.SupplierID equals s.SupplierID
    select p;
```

Obviously, this query is more verbose and difficult to understand; it is unlikely you would have chosen this approach when implementing custom filtering logic. However, it does offer an important advantage over its predecessor when it comes to building queries dynamically. By using an explicit join operator, this new query helps you to see that you can combine two completely independent queries, context.Products and context.Suppliers.Where(s => s.Country == "UK"), to return a set of child, Product, and entities filtered by search criteria applied to its parent entity, Supplier.

This is exactly how the Parent filter template works to fit into the constraints of the Dynamic Data filtering architecture. The template receives the child query, context.Products, has the nested filter template generate the parent query, context.Suppliers.Where(s => s.Country == "UK"), combines them with a join, and uses a select to return just the child entities.

Unfortunately, Dynamic LINQ does not support the join operator, so you have to implement this logic from ground up with the LINQ expression API. This is, by far, the most complex, error-prone, and time consuming programming task you will encounter when building dynamic web applications. On the bright side, it helps you to gain a new level appreciation of the heavy lifting that the C# and Visual Basic compilers do for you when converting the magically simple LINQ queries to expressions.

To build a LINQ query dynamically, you have to be familiar with the extension method syntax (as opposed to the language-integrated syntax) of building LINQ queries. LINQ expressions are an object model that represents queries built with LINQ extension methods. Because the language-integrated query syntax is a higher-level abstraction on top of the extension methods, it is easier to make a mental jump from the LINQ extension methods to LINQ expressions. Here is the same query, expressed with the LINQ extension method, Join:

```
IQueryable<Product> query = Queryable.Join(
    context.Products,
    context.Suppliers.Where(s => s.Country == "UK"),
    p => p.SupplierID,
    s => s.SupplierID,
    (p, s) => p);
```

To eliminate ambiguity, here the static Join method of the Queryable class is called explicitly, not as an extension method. This is the lowest-level code you can write in C# to create a LINQ query, but it still hides a lot of complexity. As you can see from its declaration shown next, the Join method is *generic*:

```
public static IQueryable<TResult> Join<TOuter, TInner, TKey, TResult>(
    this IQueryable<TOuter> outer,
    IEnumerable<TInner> inner,
    Expression<Func<TOuter, TKey>> outerKeySelector,
    Expression<Func<TInner, TKey>> innerKeySelector,
    Expression<Func<TOuter, TInner, TResult>> resultSelector
)
```

It is a bit overwhelming trying to understand something so abstract. You might find it helpful to look at the Join method with specific parameters, which you can do by writing a sample query in Visual Studio and pointing the mouse cursor at the method name to see the tooltip while stepping over it in debugger. Here is what the debugger displays for this sample query:

```
IQueryable<Product> Queryable.Join<Product, Supplier, int?, Product> (
    IQueryable<Product> outer,
    IEnumerable<Supplier> inner,
    Expression<Func<Product, int?>> outerKeySelector,
    Expression<Func<Supplier, int?>> innerKeySelector,
    Expression<Func<Product, Supplier, Product>> resultSelector)
```

To break it down into smaller pieces, the *outer* parameter is the query that returns child entities, and the *inner* parameter is the query that returns parent entities—in this example, products and suppliers, respectively. When no additional filter criteria is applied to either query, these parameters could be simply context.Products and context.Suppliers, respectively, resulting in a join performed between the two entire tables. From the standpoint of the Parent filter template, you do not need to worry about constructing these parameters with LINQ expression objects. The GetQueryable method receives the first query as its argument, and the nested filter template builds the second query.

The outerKeySelector parameter is a lambda expression that takes a Product entity as a parameter and returns value of its SupplierID property. In the original query, this looks simply like p => p.SupplierID; however, with LINQ expression objects, building the key selector is a little more involved. Here is how you could do it:

```
ParameterExpression parameter = Expression.Parameter(typeof(Product));
MemberExpression property = Expression.Property(parameter, "SupplierID");
LambdaExpression productKeySelector = Expression.Lambda(
    property, parameter);
```

The innerKeySelector parameter is very similar, only it takes a Supplier entity as a parameter and returns value of its SupplierID property. In the original query, it looked like this: s => s.SupplierID. What you don't see, however, is that the compiler automatically converted the int value of the SupplierID property of the Supplier entity to the int? type expected by the Join method for compatibility with the SupplierID property of the Product entity, which is nullable. With LINQ expression objects, this key selector could be built like this:

```
ParameterExpression parameter = Expression.Parameter(typeof(Supplier));
MemberExpression property = Expression.Property(parameter, "SupplierID");
UnaryExpression converted = Expression.Convert(property, typeof(int?));
LambdaExpression supplierKeySelector = Expression.Lambda(
    converted, parameter);
```

Finally, the resultSelector parameter is a lambda expression that takes a Product and a Supplier objects as parameters and returns the Product object. In the original query, the lambda expression looked like this: (p, s) => p. With LINQ expression objects, this lambda can be constructed as such:

```
ParameterExpression product = Expression.Parameter(typeof(Product));
ParameterExpression supplier = Expression.Parameter(typeof(Supplier));
LambdaExpression resultSelector = Expression.Lambda(
    product, product, supplier);
```

> **NOTE**
>
> The order of arguments in the Expression.Lambda method is a little confusing. The body of the lambda expression is specified as the *first* argument, followed by a parameter array (C# keyword params), that specifies parameters of the lambda expression. In other words, the order of arguments is a reverse of what you might intuitively expect. Remembering this and carefully inspecting each expression object in Visual Studio debugger can help you to avoid this gotcha when programming LINQ expressions.

At this point, you know how to provide all arguments to the Queryable.Join method; what is left to do is construct the method call itself. Keep in mind that the Join operator will be translated to SQL by the Entity Framework and executed by the database server. In other words, the Join extension method will not be called by the application itself, and you need to construct it as a MethodCallExpression object. You can accomplish this task with the help of the the Expression.Call factory method, or more specifically, with this particular overload:

```
public static MethodCallExpression Call(
    Type type,
    string methodName,
    Type[] typeArguments,
    params Expression[] arguments
)
```

The *type* parameter represents type, whose method you need to call, Queryable in the example. The methodName parameter is a string containing the name of the method to be called, "Join" in this example. The typeArguments is an array of the type arguments that will be used by the .NET runtime to create a specific implementation of the generic Join method. The *arguments* parameter is an array of Expression objects that represent the arguments that will be passed to the method. With the selectors built earlier, here is how the Join LINQ expression can be created in code:

```
MethodCallExpression joinCall = Expression.Call(
    typeof(Queryable),
    "Join",
    new Type[] {
        typeof(Product),
        typeof(Supplier),
        typeof(int?),
        typeof(Product)
    },
    new Expression[] {
        productQuery.Expression,
        supplierQuery.Expression,
        productKeySelector,
        supplierKeySelector,
        resultSelector
    }
)
```

> **NOTE**
>
> It is easy to confuse typeArguments with arguments. With the dozen or so different overloads that the Expression.Call method defines, this results in compiler errors that make very little sense and do not help to understand the problem. When working with MethodCallExpression objects, remember that in a generic method call, the typeArguments are the things that go between < >, and arguments are the things that go between ( ).

The final step in constructing a LINQ query with expression objects is to convert the LINQ expression to an IQueryable object and replace the original query. Here is how this can be done in the example with products and suppliers:

```
IQueryProvider queryProvider = productQuery.Provider;
productQuery = queryProvider.CreateQuery(joinCall);
```

Here you use the IQueryProvider object returned by the Provider property of the original product query. The IQueryProvider interface defines a CreateQuery method that takes a lambda expression object as a parameter and returns an IQueryable object that represents the new query. By passing a MethodCallExpression to the CreateQuery method of the query provider, you create a new IQueryable (that is, a new LINQ query) that returns results of a join between Product and Supplier queries.

Each LINQ-enabled framework, such as Entity Framework or LINQ to SQL, provides its own implementation of the IQueryProvider, which allows the same code to construct LINQ queries independently of the underlying data access technology.

Query Logic in the Parent Filter Template

Instead of hard-coding type and property names as shown in the previous section, the parent filter template builds the Join query dynamically, relying on the metadata information describing the foreign key column and the child and parent tables it links together. Still, the structure of the code is similar to the specific example just discussed and should be easy for you to follow. Listing 12.9 shows the remaining implementation of the Parent filter template. It includes the overridden GetQueryable method and the helper methods it uses to build the required lambda expressions: BuildChildKeySelector, BuildParentKeySelector, and BuildResultSelector.

For a filter template, it is important to modify the query only if the user actually entered search criteria in its control. As you are reading this code, remember that childQuery is an IQueryable object created by the EntityDataSource control on the page (Product query in the example). Notice how the code creates an empty query for the parent entity (a query that returns *all* Suppliers) by calling the GetQuery method of the MetaTable object describing the parent entity. This empty parent query is passed to the GetQueryable method of the nested filter template. Only if the query it returns is not the same as the original empty query will the Parent filter template generate a Join query. If the nested filter template returned the empty query without any filter criteria for the parent table, or in other words, if the user did not enter any filter criteria for the parent table, adding a Join to the child query is not necessary and would only slow it down.

Calling the GetQuery method of the MetaTable object as opposed to using the corresponding entity set property (such as Suppliers) of the ObjectContext directly is important for consistency with the Dynamic Data architecture. The GetQuery method of the MetaTable class is virtual and can be overridden to implement row-level security as discussed in Chapter 14. It is also important to pass it the same ObjectContext that was collected by the ContextCreated event handler discussed earlier, to ensure that both queries in the join come from the same ObjectContext.

LISTING 12.9 Parent Filter Template (Query Logic)

```
using System;
using System.Linq;
using System.Linq.Expressions;
using System.Web.DynamicData;
using System.Web.UI.WebControls;
```

```csharp
namespace WebApplication.DynamicData.Filters
{
  public partial class ParentFilter : UnleashedFilterTemplate
  {
    public override IQueryable GetQueryable(IQueryable childQuery)
    {
      MetaTable parentTable = this.ForeignKeyColumn.ParentTable;
      IQueryable emptyQuery = parentTable.GetQuery(this.dataSourceContext);
      IQueryable parentQuery = this.filter.FilterTemplate.GetQueryable(emptyQuery);
      if (parentQuery != emptyQuery)
      {
        MetaTable childTable = this.ForeignKeyColumn.Table;
        MetaColumn childColumn = childTable.GetColumn(
          this.ForeignKeyColumn.ForeignKeyNames[0]);
        MetaColumn parentColumn = parentTable.PrimaryKeyColumns[0];

        MethodCallExpression joinCall = Expression.Call(
          typeof(Queryable),
          "Join",
          new Type[] {
            childQuery.ElementType,
            parentQuery.ElementType,
            childColumn.EntityTypeProperty.PropertyType,
            childQuery.ElementType
          },
          new Expression[] {
            childQuery.Expression,
            parentQuery.Expression,
            BuildChildKeySelector(childQuery.ElementType, childColumn.Name),
            BuildParentKeySelector(parentQuery.ElementType, parentColumn.Name,
              childColumn.EntityTypeProperty.PropertyType),
            BuildResultSelector(childQuery.ElementType, parentQuery.ElementType)
          });

        childQuery = childQuery.Provider.CreateQuery(joinCall);
      }

      return childQuery;
    }

    private static LambdaExpression BuildChildKeySelector(
      Type entityType, string propertyName)
    {
      ParameterExpression parameter = Expression.Parameter(entityType, "child");
      MemberExpression property = Expression.Property(parameter, propertyName);
```

LISTING 12.9 Continued

```
      return Expression.Lambda(property, parameter);
    }

    private static LambdaExpression BuildParentKeySelector(
      Type entityType, string propertyName, Type expectedPropertyType)
    {
      ParameterExpression parameter = Expression.Parameter(entityType, "parent");
      MemberExpression property = Expression.Property(parameter, propertyName);
      if (property.Type == expectedPropertyType)
        return Expression.Lambda(property, parameter);

      UnaryExpression convertedProperty = Expression.Convert(property,
        expectedPropertyType);
      return Expression.Lambda(convertedProperty, parameter);
    }

    private static LambdaExpression BuildResultSelector(
      Type childEntityType, Type parentEntityType)
    {
      ParameterExpression child = Expression.Parameter(childEntityType, "child");
      ParameterExpression parent = Expression.Parameter(parentEntityType, "parent");
      return Expression.Lambda(child, child, parent);
    }
  }
}
```

While reading this code, you might have noticed a hard-coded assumption it makes about the number of primitive columns in the foreign key. This implementation of the Parent filter template assumes that the primary key of the parent entity consists of a single column. If your entity model uses compound keys (keys consisting of more than one column), this filtering logic would produce incorrect results. With *static* LINQ queries, compound foreign key values are usually represented with anonymous types, automatically generated by the compiler. With *dynamic* LINQ queries, this requires emitting anonymous types at run time, a large and complex topic that would be difficult to cover in this book.

Compound keys largely have fallen out of favor with database architects over the past decade. Even the Northwind sample database, which is more than ten years old, does not have compound foreign keys. This assumption helps to significantly simplify implementation of the Parent filter template. However, compound keys have some advantages that might be important in your application. If that is your situation, take a closer look at the Dynamic LINQ sample (it is included with this book's source code). The Dynamic LINQ includes APIs for emitting anonymous types, which should help to implement a more sophisticated version of dynamic queries that support compound keys.

Using the Parent Filter Template

With the Parent filter template implementation completed, you can finally create the sample page shown back in Figure 12.4. As you recall, it includes a GridView control with one column showing product names and the other column showing their countries of origin. At the top of the page, you have two dynamic filters, one based on the ProductName property of the Product entity and the other based on the Country property of the parent Supplier entity. Listing 12.10 shows a complete markup of the sample page.

LISTING 12.10 Product Search Page Filtered by Supplier Country (Markup)

```
<%@ Page Title="" Language="C#"
  MasterPageFile="~/Site.master" CodeBehind="SamplePage.aspx.cs"
  Inherits="WebApplication.Samples.Ch12.ParentFilterTemplate.SamplePage" %>
<asp:Content ContentPlaceHolderID="main" runat="server">
  <unl:UnleashedFilter runat="server" ID="productNameFilter" FilterUIHint="Text"
    DataField="ProductName" Columns="100" />
  <unl:UnleashedFilter runat="server" ID="originFilter"
    DataField="Supplier" FilterUIHint="Parent" DisplayField="Country" />
  <asp:GridView runat="server" ID="gridView" DataSourceID="dataSource"
    AutoGenerateColumns="false">
    <Columns>
      <unl:UnleashedField DataField="ProductName" />
      <unl:UnleashedField DataField="Supplier" HeaderText="Origin"
        UIHint="Parent" DisplayField="Country" />
    </Columns>
  </asp:GridView>
  <asp:EntityDataSource runat="server" ID="dataSource"
    ConnectionString="name=NorthwindEntities"
    DefaultContainerName="NorthwindEntities" EntitySetName="Products" />
  <asp:QueryExtender runat="server" TargetControlID="dataSource">
    <unl:UnleashedFilterExpression ControlID="productNameFilter" />
    <unl:UnleashedFilterExpression ControlID="originFilter" />
  </asp:QueryExtender>
</asp:Content>
```

Notice the UnleashedFilter control associated with the Supplier column of the Product entity. Its FilterUIHint is set to "Parent", the name of the new filter template, and the DisplayField custom attribute is set to "Country", the name of the property from the parent Supplier entity for users to filter the list of products by.

Summary

In this chapter, you saw some of the techniques for building custom pages that display information in tabular format and allow users to search for information by filtering and sorting the data. You reviewed some of the limitations of the built-in templates and controls that Dynamic Data provides out of the box and focused on the commonly requested need to display read-only information from several related tables on a single page. Unlike displaying data from a single entity, which Dynamic Data does very well, this type of functionality is not provided out of the box but not difficult to implement.

The UnleashedFilter control created in this chapter along with the UnleashedFilterTemplate base class for filter templates and the supporting UnleashedFilterExpression eliminates the limitations unnecessarily imposed by the built-in DynamicFilter control in version 4.0 of ASP.NET. In particular, by avoiding the Page events, the UnleashedFilter allows you to create advanced filter templates that use nested filter controls to generate powerful queries that span multiple related entities. Similar to the DynamicControl, the UnleashedFilter also accepts custom attributes and automatically initializes the matching public properties of the filter template it creates. Consistently with the extended functionality of the UnleashedControl created earlier in this book, the UnleashedFilter also recognizes control parameters specified in the FilterUIHintAttribute that might be applied to the property in the entity model and uses them to initialize the matching public properties of the filter template as well.

To enable building pages that display and allow filtering by properties from multiple related entities, a field template and a filter template (both called Parent) were created. Both templates are designed for use with foreign key navigation properties, like the Supplier property of the Product entity. In custom pages, you can use these templates explicitly by setting the UIHint or FilterUIHint properties of the UnleashedControl or the UnleashedFilter controls, respectively. Both templates define a property called DisplayField, which specifies the name of the property in the parent entity that you want to display on the page and, in the case of the Parent filter template, allow users to filter by.

CHAPTER 13

Building Dynamic List Pages

Just like when building metadata-driven *forms* in Chapter 11, "Building Dynamic Forms," during development of the metadata-driven list pages the goal is to get the best possible, not perfect, dynamic UI based on the information in the entity model and data annotations you supply.

Dynamic forms and list pages rely on a lot of common metadata. In a typical dynamic form, entity properties appear in a vertical list of labels and controls, and in a dynamic list page, they appear in a horizontal list of GridView columns. The DisplayAttribute is used by both to determine the human-readable display names as well as order of appearance on the page. Using this and other data annotation attributes to configure dynamic list pages is similar to the process and techniques discussed in previous chapters.

There are, however, significant differences between form and list pages. Some of them are fundamental, such as the absence of the equivalent for entity templates. Because DynamicField does not inherit from Control, placing instances of this class in a separate user control without the parent GridView control is impossible. Other differences, such as the algorithms used by Dynamic Data to look up field and filter templates, are the result of the implementation limitations of the built-in components of the framework.

One of these limitations was solved in the previous chapter by introducing the UnleashedFilter control to replace the built-in DynamicFilter. It enables you to specify custom parameters for filter templates directly in the entity model by applying the FilterUIHintAttribute to entity properties.

```
[MetadataType(typeof(Metadata))]
partial class Product
{
  private abstract class Metadata
  {
    [UIHint("Text", null, "Columns", 100)]
    [FilterUIHint("Text", null, "Columns", 100)]
    public object ProductName { get; set; }
  }
}
```

Just like the UnleashedControl, which was extended in Chapter 11 to automatically initialize matching public properties of the field templates based on the control parameters specified in the UIHintAttribute, the UnleashedFilter initializes public properties of the filter templates based on the information specified in the FilterUIHintAttribute, such as the *Columns* property in this example.

This chapter centers discussion on eliminating some of the shortcomings in Dynamic Data that make building metadata-driven list pages more difficult than they really need to be. It also continues the discussion of how to build list pages that display and allow searching information from multiple related entities, this time dynamically. To accomplish these goals, the sample solution extends the metadata information, which was reviewed in Chapter 7, "Metadata API."

Extending Filter Lookup Rules

As you might recall from a discussion in Chapter 3, "Field Templates," Dynamic Data uses a sophisticated algorithm to locate field templates based on the metadata information describing entity properties. It first checks the entity property for presence of the UIHintAttribute, which can specify the name of a field template explicitly. If the property does not have a UI hint, Dynamic Data then checks it for the DataTypeAttribute, which can specify a business-level name of the property type, such as EmailAddress or Date, and look for field templates with the matching name. In the absence of a high-level data type, Dynamic Data uses a low-level type of the entity property, such as String or DateTime, to look for the matching field template. If a direct match is not immediately available, Dynamic Data uses a fallback algorithm to try more and more generic types, such as going from Float to decimal to string.

The lookup algorithm used for *field* templates makes it easier to develop dynamic pages because it significantly reduces the amount of additional data annotation attributes needed in the entity model. Unfortunately, Dynamic Data does not implement the same fallback-based rules for locating *filter* templates. In fact, it hard-codes the lookup rules to the three types of filter templates that come with it out of the box—Boolean, Enumeration, and ForeignKey. For all other types of properties—String, Int32, DateTime, and so on—the filter template name has to be specified explicitly.

When building custom search screens, the overhead of specifying the filter templates is not significant—you simply need to specify the FilterUIHint attribute for any instance of the DynamicFilter (or the UnleashedFilter) control that needs it. The custom page template encapsulates the presentation logic for a particular entity, and having filter templates specified there explicitly is not a problem. However, when building search pages dynamically, you must specify the FilterUIHintAttribute directly in the entity model. Figure 13.1 shows a Product list page, which has a typical selection of built-in filter templates. With only Boolean, Enumeration, and ForeignKey filters supported out of the box, this means having to use the FilterUIHintAttribute *a lot*, not only increasing the amount of code you have to write and maintain, but also forcing you to hardcode the presentation logic in the business layer of the application.

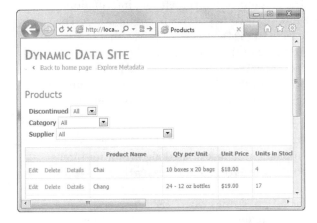

FIGURE 13.1 Product list page with default filter lookup algorithm.

Luckily, Dynamic Data allows replacing the filter lookup algorithm, and it can be brought up to par with the field templates. The MetaModel class defines a property called FilterFactory that stores an object responsible for locating and instantiating the filter templates. However, it is the MetaTable class, with the help of the GetFilteredColumns method, that determines whether a particular MetaColumn is considered filterable, before the filter factory gets involved. In this section, you learn how to extend the built-in FilterFactory, MetaModel, and MetaTable classes to implement a fallback-based algorithm for filter templates that closely mimics the default algorithm used for field templates.

Extending the FilterFactory Class

FilterFactory is a simple class defined in the System.Web.DynamicData namespace. In addition to its constructor, it defines only two public methods—CreateFilterControl and GetFilterVirtualPath:

```
public class FilterFactory
{
  public FilterFactory();
  public virtual QueryableFilterUserControl CreateFilterControl(
    MetaColumn column, string filterUIHint);
  public virtual string GetFilterVirtualPath(
    MetaColumn column, string filterUIHint);
}
```

The GetFilterVirtualPath method is responsible for determining a virtual path to a filter template, such as ~\DynamicData\Filters\Text.ascx, that matches the given MetaColumn object and filterUIHint. The column contains metadata information describing the entity property, and the filter hint comes from the page markup. The CreateFilterControl is invoked by the DynamicFilter (or, in our case, the UnleashedFilter) control to create an instance of the filter template. Internally, the CreateFilterControl calls the GetFilterVirtualPath method and caches its results to improve performance for subsequent lookups of the same column and hint combination. Therefore, you need to override only the GetFilterVirtualPath method and can leave the CreateFilterControl method as is.

Listing 13.1 shows the complete implementation of UnleashedFilterFactory, a class that extends the built-in FilterFactory to implement fallback-based algorithm for filter template lookup. As you can see, it overrides the GetFilterVirtualPath method just discussed; however, most of the heavy lifting is actually done by the GetFilterCandidates method. This method returns an IEnumerable of strings where each item is a *possible* name of the filter template, based on the given MetaColumn and filter hint. The GetFilterVirtualPath method tries the candidate names until it finds an existing .ASCX file in the DynamicData\Filters folder of the project. If none of the candidate names matches an existing filter template, the GetFilterVirtualPath calls the base method, inherited from the FilterFactory, to handle the Boolean, ForeignKey, and Enumeration filter templates it supports.

LISTING 13.1 UnleashedFilterFactory Implementation

```
using System;
using System.Collections.Generic;
using System.Web;
using System.Web.Compilation;
using System.Web.DynamicData;

namespace Unleashed.DynamicData
{
  public class UnleashedFilterFactory : FilterFactory
  {
    private static readonly Dictionary<Type, Type> FallbackTypes =
      new Dictionary<Type, Type>
        {
```

```csharp
    { typeof(float),           typeof(decimal) },
    { typeof(double),          typeof(decimal) },
    { typeof(short),           typeof(int) },
    { typeof(byte),            typeof(int) },
    { typeof(long),            typeof(int) },
    { typeof(char),            typeof(string) },
    { typeof(int),             typeof(string) },
    { typeof(decimal),         typeof(string) },
    { typeof(Guid),            typeof(string) },
    { typeof(DateTime),        typeof(string) },
    { typeof(DateTimeOffset),  typeof(string) },
    { typeof(TimeSpan),        typeof(string) }
  };

private readonly string filtersFolder;

public UnleashedFilterFactory(MetaModel model)
{
  if (model == null) throw new ArgumentNullException("model");
  this.filtersFolder = VirtualPathUtility.Combine(
    model.DynamicDataFolderVirtualPath, "Filters/");
}

public override string GetFilterVirtualPath(
  MetaColumn column, string filterHint)
{
  foreach (string candidate in this.GetFilterCandidates(column, filterHint))
  {
    string path = VirtualPathUtility.Combine(
      this.filtersFolder, candidate + ".ascx");
    if (BuildManager.GetObjectFactory(path, false) != null) return path;
  }
  return base.GetFilterVirtualPath(column, filterHint);
}

private IEnumerable<string> GetFilterCandidates(
  MetaColumn column, string filterHint)
{
  if (!string.IsNullOrEmpty(filterHint))
    yield return filterHint;
  if (!string.IsNullOrEmpty(column.FilterUIHint))
    yield return column.FilterUIHint;
  if (column.DataTypeAttribute != null)
    yield return column.DataTypeAttribute.GetDataTypeName();

  Type currentType = column.ColumnType;
```

LISTING 13.1 Continued

```
      while (currentType != null)
      {
        yield return currentType.FullName;
        yield return currentType.Name;
        if (currentType == typeof(int))
          yield return "Integer";
        if (currentType == typeof(string))
          yield return "Text";
        if (!FallbackTypes.TryGetValue(currentType, out currentType))
          break;
      }
    }
  }
}
```

The GetFilterCandidates method mimics the algorithm implemented by the built-in
FieldTemplateFactory for *field* templates. It first returns the UI hint specified in page
markup, then the UI hint specified in FilterUIHintAttribute that might be applied to
the property in the entity model, and the type name specified in the DataTypeAttribute.
If a matching template has not been found, the GetFilterCandidates method begins a
fallback loop, where it tries the full name of the property type (such as System.Int32), its
short name (such as Int32), and alias (such as Integer, if any) and continues the process
with the next type.

The fallback rules are defined in a static dictionary called FallbackTypes declared in the
beginning of the class. Looking at the initialization code, you can tell that for a property
of type Int16 (short in C#), the fallback type is Int32 (int in C#), and for Int32, the fallback type is String. Take the UnitsInStock property of the Product entity as an example.
This property is of type Int16 and, in absence of the FilterUIHintAttribute and
DataTypeAttribute, the UnleashedFilterFactory tries the sequence of filter template
names shown in Table 13.1 until it finds a matching file in the Filters directory.

TABLE 13.1 Example of Filter Template Lookup for Int16 Column

Iteration 1	Iteration 2	Iteration 3
System.Int16.ascx	System.Int32.ascx	System.String.ascx
Int16.ascx	Int32.ascx	String.ascx
	Integer.ascx	Text.ascx

The diagram in Figure 13.2 summarizes the filter lookup algorithm implemented by the
UnleashedFilterFactory. Similar to the lookup rules for field templates discussed in
Chapter 3, this algorithm assumes that all primitive data types have corresponding filter
templates. The Text filter template created in Chapter 5, "Filter Templates," is similar to
the Text field template in how it can handle all of the primitive data types; however,
that limits it to performing only a simple equality check, leaving out other, more useful

filtering operators, such as "contains" or "starts with" because they are only applicable to strings. Although this is not done in the source code accompanying this book, real-world applications typically have a bigger set of filter templates, implementing additional type-specific filtering operators for numbers and dates in filter templates called Decimal.ascx, Integer.ascx, and DateTime.ascx. This removes the requirement for the Text filter template to support multiple primitive data types and allows you to implement string-specific filtering operators in this control instead.

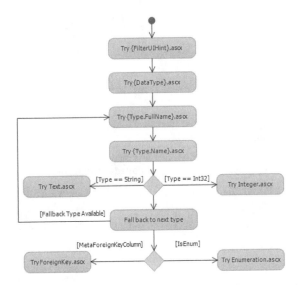

FIGURE 13.2 Unleashed filter lookup algorithm.

Extending the MetaTable Class

The second part of the algorithm that determines which entity properties will have filter templates generated dynamically is implemented in the MetaTable class, which defines a virtual method called GetFilteredColumns that returns an IEnumerable of MetaColumn objects.

```
public class MetaTable
{
    public virtual IEnumerable<MetaColumn> GetFilteredColumns();
}
```

The GetFilteredColumns method is called by the built-in QueryableFilterRepeater control (and by the UnleashedFilterRepeater) to get a list of properties that can be filtered. For each MetaColumn object it returns, the repeater creates a DynamicFilter (or the UnleashedFilter) control, which in turn calls the CreateFilterControl method of the FilterFactory just implemented to locate and create the filter templates.

The default implementation of the GetFilteredColumns method in the MetaTable class assumes that only properties of Boolean, ForeignKey, and Enumeration types can be filtered. Even though the UnleashedFilterFactory already supports other property types, the default implementation of the MetaTable cannot take advantage of it automatically. To work around this shortcoming, the built-in MetaTable has to be extended to override the GetFilteredColumns method. Listing 13.2 shows the complete implementation of the UnleashedMetaTable from the Unleashed.DynamicData project of the sample solution.

LISTING 13.2 UnleashedMetaTable Implementation

```
using System.Collections.Generic;
using System.ComponentModel.DataAnnotations;
using System.Linq;
using System.Web.DynamicData;
using System.Web.DynamicData.ModelProviders;
using System.Web.UI.WebControls;

namespace Unleashed.DynamicData
{
  public class UnleashedMetaTable : MetaTable
  {
    public UnleashedMetaTable(UnleashedMetaModel model, TableProvider provider)
      : base(model, provider)
    {
    }

    public override IEnumerable<MetaColumn> GetFilteredColumns()
    {
      return this.GetScaffoldColumns(
        DataBoundControlMode.ReadOnly, ContainerType.List)
        .Where(column => IsFilterable(column));
    }

    private bool IsFilterable(MetaColumn column)
    {
      if (!string.IsNullOrEmpty(column.FilterUIHint)) return true;

      DisplayAttribute display = column.Attributes.OfType<DisplayAttribute>()
        .FirstOrDefault();
      if (display != null && display.GetAutoGenerateFilter().HasValue)
        return display.GetAutoGenerateFilter().Value;

      if (column.IsCustomProperty) return false;
      if (column is MetaChildrenColumn) return false;
      return true;
    }
  }
}
```

The overridden `GetFilteredColumns` method calls the `GetScaffoldColumns` method of the `MetaTable` to get a list of all properties that can be displayed in a list page in read-only mode. In other words, only columns already displayed in a dynamic `GridView` control are candidates for filtering. This eliminates some low-level properties, such as the generated primary keys and primitive components of foreign keys that are not displayed in list pages by default. From the end-user perspective, it would be strange to see an option to filter a Product page by the ProductID or the SupplierID columns, which are not displayed in the grid.

The initial list of properties returned by the `GetScaffoldColumns` method is further reduced by calling the `IsFilterable` method and leaving only those `MetaColumn` objects for which it returns `true`. This method mimics the rules used by the `GetScaffoldColumns` method itself, only as they apply to filtering of property values, not their display. For instance, if the property has a `FilterUIHintAttribute` applied to it, assume that it is filterable. Likewise, if the property has a `DisplayAttribute` applied with an explicitly specified `AutoGenerateFilter` value, this value determines whether the property is considered filterable (`true` or `false`). All other types of properties, with the exception of custom properties and "children" navigation properties, are considered filterable by default.

Extending the MetaModel Class

The `MetaModel` class serves as a root object for accessing the metadata information in Dynamic Data web applications. Its default implementation creates and exposes the built-in `FilterFactory` and `MetaTable` classes. The `UnleashedMetaModel` extends the built-in class to create the `UnleashedFilterFactory` and `UnleashedMetaTable` instances instead. Listing 13.3 shows a complete implementation of the new class.

LISTING 13.3 Unleashed.DynamicData\UnleashedMetaModel.cs

```
using System;
using System.Web.DynamicData;
using System.Web.DynamicData.ModelProviders;

namespace Unleashed.DynamicData
{
  public class UnleashedMetaModel : MetaModel
  {
    public UnleashedMetaModel()
    {
      this.FilterFactory = new UnleashedFilterFactory(this);
    }

    protected override MetaTable CreateTable(TableProvider provider)
    {
      return new UnleashedMetaTable(this, provider);
    }
  }
}
```

As you can see, implementation of the UnleashedMetaModel class is simple. Its constructor replaces the built-in FilterFactory with a new instance of the UnleashedFilterFactory class, and the CreateTable method is overridden to return a new instance of the UnleashedMetaTable instead of the built-in MetaTable. This ensures that all objects in the Tables collection are of the type UnleashedMetaModel. All that is left to do is modify the Global.asax file of the web application to use the UnleashedMetaModel instead of the built-in MetaModel, as shown in Listing 13.4.

LISTING 13.4 Modifying Global.asax.cs to Use UnleashedMetaModel

```
using System;
using System.Web.DynamicData;
using System.Web.Routing;
using DataModel;

namespace WebApplication
{
  public class Global : System.Web.HttpApplication
  {
    public static UnleashedMetaModel DefaultModel = new UnleashedMetaModel();

    void Application_Start(object sender, EventArgs e)
    {
      var modelConfiguration = new ContextConfiguration{ ScaffoldAllTables = true };
      DefaultModel.RegisterContext(typeof(NorthwindEntities), modelConfiguration);

      RouteTable.Routes.Add(new DynamicDataRoute("{table}/{action}.aspx"));
    }
  }
}
```

Figure 13.3 shows how the Product list page looks with the extended filter lookup algorithm. Comparing it with the original version back in Figure 13.2, you can see that it now has filter controls for textual and numeric properties, such as the ProductName and UnitsInStock. These controls were generated by the Text filter template, which was developed in Chapter 5. Although its immediate capabilities are limited to simple equality checks, thanks to the fallback-based algorithm, the dynamic pages can automatically take advantage of the new filter templates as you implement them, without requiring additional changes in the page template itself.

FIGURE 13.3 Product list page with extended filter lookup algorithm.

Although using this convention-based algorithm to automatically display appropriate filter templates for all entity properties is more consistent with the overall scaffolding functionality of Dynamic Data, it does change its default behavior. Whereas earlier you had to apply a `FilterUIHintAttribute` to *enable* filter generation, you now have to apply the `DisplayAttribute` and set its `AutoGenerateFilter` property to `false` to *disable* it. Here is how to prevent a default filter from being generated for the `ProductName` property of the Product entity:

```
[MetadataType(typeof(Metadata))]
partial class Product
{
  private abstract class Metadata
  {
    [Display(AutoGenerateFilter = false)]
    public object ProductName { get; set; }
  }
}
```

NOTE

The built-in filter scaffolding algorithm is closer to an opt-in model, whereas the replacement implements an opt-out model.

Building Dynamic UI with Custom Properties

Chapter 11 discussed how by automatically generating a reasonably good user interface at run time based on metadata information, Dynamic Data allows you to rapidly evolve the entity model. This approach helps delay implementation of the presentation code while at the same time helping to collect feedback from the business users working with a real application and not just screen mockups or diagrams.

Both Entity Framework and LINQ to SQL enable you to extend entity classes and define custom properties, such as calculated properties or properties that return data from related entities. Custom properties are a powerful tool that allows you to extend the entity model beyond the limits imposed by the current tools for Entity Framework and LINQ to SQL. For instance, you could extend the Product entity class with a custom property called Country that returns the country of the Supplier:

```
partial class Product
{
    public string Country { get { return this.Supplier.Country; } }
}
```

With a custom property defined, you can easily have a Country column automatically generated on a Product list page. Listing 13.5 shows markup of a *custom* page that displays a GridView control with plain-text columns for all public properties of the Product class, including the custom Country property just defined. The only special steps needed are to set the ContextTypeName property of the EntityDataSource control to enable lazy loading, which the property relies on, and set the EnableFlattening property to false, which prevents the data source control from generating special wrappers for each entity object. Entity wrappers are used with the initial release of Entity Framework, which did not support foreign key properties. Today, they are not necessary and only prevent data bound controls, such as the GridView, from accessing custom properties defined in the entity class.

LISTING 13.5 List Page with Plain-Text Columns for Custom Properties

```
<%@Page Language="C#" MasterPageFile="~/Site.master" CodeBehind="SamplePage.aspx.cs"
  Inherits="WebApplication.Samples.Ch13.CustomProperty.SamplePage" %>
<asp:Content ContentPlaceHolderID="main" runat="server">
  <asp:GridView runat="server" DataSourceID="dataSource" />
  <asp:EntityDataSource runat="server" ID="dataSource"
    ContextTypeName="DataModel.NorthwindEntities"
    EntitySetName="Products" EnableFlattening="False" />
</asp:Content>
```

Using custom properties with Dynamic Data can help reduce the need for creating custom pages too early in web application projects. In some cases, custom properties make sense from the entity modeling prospective, making highly normalized entity models more developer-friendly. In others cases, creating a custom property in the business model to implement presentation logic can be a reasonable compromise compared to creating a new custom page, which is almost certainly a bigger investment in terms of effort and code size.

Out of the box, Dynamic Data does not allow you to take advantage of custom entity properties. The next section discusses how to overcome this limitation.

Implementing Support for Custom Properties

The Dynamic Data metadata API discussed in Chapter 7 does support custom properties. In particular, the MetaColumn class has a property called IsCustomProperty, which returns true when the entity property the column represents was not defined in the .EDMX or .DBML file. The trouble, however, is that Dynamic Data does not create MetaColumn objects for custom properties. Figure 13.4 shows a screenshot of the metadata page for the Product entity. Notice that the Country property is missing from the list of columns on the right even though it was already defined in the class.

FIGURE 13.4 Default metadata of the Product entity does not include custom properties.

Chapter 7 briefly touched on the fact that Dynamic Data relies on *metadata providers* to extract the information about entities and properties from the underlying framework, such as the Entity Framework or LINQ to SQL. The reason custom properties are not available through the meta-model API is that the built-in providers do not supply them. By extending the built-in metadata providers, you can help Dynamic Data recognize the custom properties and enable most of the rich template scaffolding for displaying and filtering them. In this section, you see how this can be accomplished.

Model Providers

The provider API is defined in the System.Web.DynamicData.ModelProviders namespace. At the high-level, it consists of the four classes shown in Figure 13.5—DataModelProvider, TableProvider, ColumnProvider, and AssociationProvider. The DataModelProvider class provides the information required to construct a MetaModel object consumed by a Dynamic Data application. For instance, it includes a property called Tables, which returns a collection of TableProvider objects. Each TableProvider encapsulates a single entity class and provides all information necessary to construct a MetaTable object. In particular, it has a property called Columns that returns a collection of ColumnProvider objects that MetaTable uses to construct MetaColumn instances. Unlike the metadata API, where the MetaColumn class has two descendants, MetaForeignKeyColumn and MetaChildrenColumn, that represent navigation properties (such as the Supplier property of the Product entity), the provider API uses a separate class called AssociationProvider.

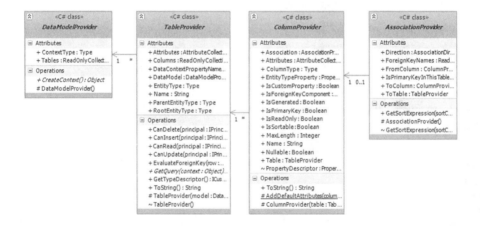

FIGURE 13.5 Metadata providers.

Dynamic Data comes with several built-in model providers, including providers for the Entity Framework and LINQ to SQL. Each model provider includes a set of four classes, each inheriting from the corresponding provider base class and overriding the required virtual methods and properties. Knowledge of the built-in model providers is hard-coded in the MetaModel class, which allows you to register both Entity Framework ObjectContext types and LINQ to SQL DataContext types by calling the same RegisterContext method, which takes Type as a parameter. However, the MetaModel class also defines an overloaded version of the RegisterContext method that takes a DataModelProvider as a parameter and that enables you to create custom providers for other LINQ-enabled frameworks and use them with Dynamic Data.

```
public class MetaModel
{
   public void RegisterContext(Type contextType);
   public void RegisterContext(DataModelProvider dataModelProvider);
}
```

To enable support for custom properties, the Decorator design pattern can be applied to create a set of provider classes that wrap the original Entity Framework provider objects and provide additional metadata information on top of what is available out of the box. In the sample solution, a class called UnleashedColumnProvider encapsulates custom entity properties. The UnleashedTableProvider class wraps a built-in TableProvider object provided by Dynamic Data and returns a Columns collection populated with ColumnProvider objects representing the properties defined in the EDMX file plus the UnleashedColumnProvider objects representing custom properties defined in the partial classes of the entity model. Finally, the UnleashedModelProvider wraps a DataModelProvider, enabling you to replace the limited built-in provider with the extended one, which supports custom properties.

Creating a Custom Property ColumnProvider

The UnleashedColumnProvider class inherits from the built-in ColumnProvider class and encapsulates metadata about a single custom property. As you see shortly, when the chapter gets into the implementation of the UnleashedTableProvider, it relies on the TypeDescriptor API to extract property metadata provided by the .NET run time. As you recall from the discussion in Chapter 7, the TypeDescriptor API is defined in the System.ComponentModel namespace. Both Dynamic Data and the validation framework rely on the TypeDescriptor instead of the low-level .NET Reflection API it extends.

The complete source code of the UnleashedColumnProvider is shown in Listing 13.6. Although most of the members in the ColumnProvider base class are virtual, they don't have to be overridden. Instead, the constructor of the UnleashedColumnProvider class takes a PropertyDescriptor object as its second parameter and initializes the properties, such as the Name and ColumnType. The first parameter of the constructor supplies a TableProvider object, required by the only constructor available in the ColumnProvider base class.

LISTING 13.6 UnleashedColumnProvider Implementation

```
using System.ComponentModel;
using System.Web.DynamicData.ModelProviders;

namespace WebApplication
{
   public sealed class UnleashedColumnProvider: ColumnProvider
   {
      public UnleashedColumnProvider(
         UnleashedTableProvider table, PropertyDescriptor descriptor)
         : base(table)
```

LISTING 13.6 Continued

```
    {
      this.Name = descriptor.Name;
      this.ColumnType = descriptor.PropertyType;
      this.Nullable = this.ColumnType.IsValueType == false ||
        System.Nullable.GetUnderlyingType(this.ColumnType) != null;
      this.IsReadOnly = descriptor.IsReadOnly;
      this.IsCustomProperty = true;
    }
  }
}
```

Extending the TableProvider to Support Custom Properties

The UnleashedTableProvider class inherits from the built-in TableProvider and encapsulates the metadata information describing a single entity type, such as Product. Because on one hand, the Entity Framework and LINQ to SQL model providers are internal and on the other hand they contain quite a bit of logic, you do not want to simply reimplement them. Instead, the UnleashedTableProvider delegates implementation of most of its virtual properties and methods to the *original* TableProvider object it receives as the second parameter in its constructor.

The only property that does not simply return the original value is Columns. Instead, the UnleashedTableProvider constructor takes a collection of ColumnProvider objects returned by the original Columns property and adds to it the UnleashedColumnProvider objects for each custom property defined in the entity class. This combined collection is stored in a private field called *columns* and returned by the overridden Columns property. You can see the complete source code of the UnleashedTableProvider in Listing 13.7 with points worthy of attention shown in bold.

LISTING 13.7 UnleashedTableProvider Implementation

```
using System;
using System.Collections.Generic;
using System.Collections.ObjectModel;
using System.ComponentModel;
using System.Data.Objects.DataClasses;
using System.Linq;
using System.Security.Principal;
using System.Web.DynamicData.ModelProviders;

namespace Unleashed.DynamicData
{
  public sealed class UnleashedTableProvider: TableProvider
  {
```

```csharp
private readonly TableProvider original;
private readonly ReadOnlyCollection<ColumnProvider> columns;

public UnleashedTableProvider(
  UnleashedModelProvider model, TableProvider original)
  : base(model)
{
  this.original = original;

  IEnumerable<PropertyDescriptor> customProperties = TypeDescriptor
    .GetProperties(original.EntityType).Cast<PropertyDescriptor>()
    .Where(p => !p.PropertyType.IsSubclassOf(typeof(EntityReference)))
    .Where(p => this.RootEntityType.IsAssignableFrom(p.ComponentType))
    .Where(p => original.Columns.All(c => c.Name != p.Name));

  this.columns = original.Columns
    .Concat(customProperties.Select(p => new UnleashedColumnProvider(this, p)))
    .ToList().AsReadOnly();
}

public override AttributeCollection Attributes
{
  get { return this.original.Attributes; }
}

public override ReadOnlyCollection<ColumnProvider> Columns
{
  get { return this.columns; }
}

public override string DataContextPropertyName
{
  get { return this.original.DataContextPropertyName; }
}

public override Type EntityType
{
  get { return this.original.EntityType; }
}

public override string Name
{
  get { return this.original.Name; }
}

public override Type ParentEntityType
```

LISTING 13.7 Continued

```
    {
      get { return this.original.ParentEntityType; }
    }

    public override Type RootEntityType
    {
      get { return this.original.RootEntityType; }
    }

    public override bool CanDelete(IPrincipal principal)
    {
      return this.original.CanDelete(principal);
    }

    public override bool CanInsert(IPrincipal principal)
    {
      return this.original.CanInsert(principal);
    }

    public override bool CanRead(IPrincipal principal)
    {
      return this.original.CanRead(principal);
    }

    public override bool CanUpdate(IPrincipal principal)
    {
      return this.original.CanUpdate(principal);
    }

    public override object EvaluateForeignKey(object row, string foreignKeyName)
    {
      return this.original.EvaluateForeignKey(row, foreignKeyName);
    }

    public override IQueryable GetQuery(object context)
    {
      return this.original.GetQuery(context);
    }

    public override ICustomTypeDescriptor GetTypeDescriptor()
    {
      return this.original.GetTypeDescriptor();
    }
  }
}
```

Thanks to the power of LINQ to Objects, the `UnleashedTableProvider` constructor packs quite a bit of logic in just a few lines of code. Breaking it down into steps...the first part, shown next, uses the static `TypeDescriptor` class to obtain a list of `PropertyDescriptor` objects that represent custom properties of the entity class:

```
IEnumerable<PropertyDescriptor> customProperties = TypeDescriptor
    .GetProperties(original.EntityType).Cast<PropertyDescriptor>()
    .Where(p => !p.PropertyType.IsSubclassOf(typeof(EntityReference))
    .Where(p => this.RootEntityType.IsAssignableFrom(p.ComponentType))
    .Where(p => original.Columns.All(c => c.Name != p.Name));
```

Several `Where` calls are used to filter out inapplicable properties. The first `Where` call eliminates the "reference" properties that Entity Framework generates for every foreign key property, such as the `SupplierReference` property, which accompanies the `Supplier` property. Whereas the `Supplier` property returns an object of type Supplier, the `SupplierReference` property returns an `EntityReference<Supplier>` that for the purpose of filtering represents the same logical metadata column. The *second* `Where` call removes the properties declared in the `EntityObject` base class or higher in the inheritance hierarchy of the entity class, such as the `EntityKey` property. The last `Where` call removes all entity properties already recognized by the original table provider:

```
this.columns = original.Columns
    .Concat(customProperties.Select(p => new UnleashedColumnProvider(this, p)))
    .ToList().AsReadOnly();
```

Having obtained `PropertyDescriptor` objects, the second part of the `UnleashedTableProvider` constructor creates an `UnleashedColumnProvider` object for each custom property and "concatenates" them with the collection of `ColumnProvider` objects returned by the original `TableProvider`. Stored in the private *columns* field, this combined collection is returned by the `Columns` property overridden in this class.

To recap, the `UnleashedTableProvider` class implements the Decorator pattern and extends the list of columns returned by the original table provider to include the `UnleashedColumnProvider` objects for custom properties defined in the entity class. All other properties and methods overridden in the `UnleashedTableProvider` call the original implementation, reusing and preserving the built-in logic.

Extending the DataModelProvider to Support Custom Properties

The `UnleashedModelProvider` inherits from the built-in `DataModelProvider` and encapsulates metadata information describing one or more entity classes. Each `DataModelProvider` is responsible for creating and returning a collection of `TableProvider` objects. Just like the `MetaModel` class discussed earlier in this chapter, you must subclass the `DataModelProvider` whenever you subclass the `TableProvider`.

The `UnleashedModelProvider` also implements the Decorator pattern by wrapping an original `DataModelProvider` instance. The main purpose of this class is to change the `Tables` property so that it returns a collection of UnleashedTableProvider objects instead of the built-in TableProvider instances. All other properties and methods (thankfully there are only two) simply call the original implementation. The complete source code of the new class is shown in Listing 13.8, with important parts highlighted in bold.

LISTING 13.8 UnleashedModelProvider Implementation

```
namespace Unleashed.DynamicData
{
  using System;
  using System.Collections.ObjectModel;
  using System.Linq;
  using System.Web.DynamicData.ModelProviders;

  public sealed class UnleashedModelProvider: DataModelProvider
  {
    private readonly DataModelProvider original;
    private readonly ReadOnlyCollection<TableProvider> tables;

    public UnleashedModelProvider(DataModelProvider original)
    {
      this.original = original;
      this.tables = original.Tables
        .Select(table => new UnleashedTableProvider(this, table))
        .Cast<TableProvider>().ToList().AsReadOnly();
    }

    public override Type ContextType
    {
      get { return this.original.ContextType; }
    }

    public override ReadOnlyCollection<TableProvider> Tables
    {
      get { return this.tables; }
    }

    public override object CreateContext()
    {
      return this.original.CreateContext();
    }
  }
}
```

As you can see, the `UnleashedModelProvider` constructor receives the original `DataModelProvider` as a parameter. It takes the original `Tables` collection and creates a new `UnleashedTableProvider` object for each `TableProvider` in it. This collection of `TableProvider` decorators is stored in the private field called *tables* and returned by the overridden `Tables` property.

Replacing the Built-in DataModelProvider

Now that the `UnleashedModelProvider` that supports custom properties has been implemented, all that's left to do is replace the built-in `DataModelProvider` Dynamic Data creates by default.

Unfortunately, the built-in providers are internal to the `System.Web.DynamicData` assembly and cannot be instantiated directly. However, the `MetaTable` class defines a property called `Provider`, which returns the built-in `TableProvider` and, through its `DataModel` property, allows you to get a hold of the original `DataModelProvider`. The following code snippet illustrates how this can be done:

```
var model = new MetaModel(false);
model.RegisterContext(typeof(NorthwindEntities));
DataModelProvider provider = model.Tables[0].Provider.DataModel;
```

Notice that this code creates a new `MetaModel` instance with `false` as the `registerGlobally` argument. Because you only need the original model provider, you don't want the next call to the `RegisterContext` method to register the `NorthwindEntities` class in the global list of models used by Dynamic Data and causing an exception when you try to register it again with your custom model provider. Having a temporary `MetaModel` instance with the `NorthwindEntities` context registered, you can extract the original model provider from the first `MetaTable` object in it.

Using the original provider object, you can create a new `UnleashedModelProvider` object and register it globally and place this code directly in the `Global.asax`, next to the model registration code. However, it definitely feels like a hack, and because the `UnleashedModel` already extends the built-in `MetaModel` class, this workaround can be hidden inside of it, keeping the application code clean.

Listing 13.9 shows the source code of the `UnleashedMetaModel` class with a redefined `RegisterContext` method. Just like the built-in version, it takes `Type` and `ContextConfiguration` objects as parameters. However, instead of registering the context directly, it creates a temporary `MetaModel` to obtain the original model provided and registers the context with the `UnleashedModelProvider`.

LISTING 13.9 UnleashedMetaModel Implementation with RegisterContext Method

```
using System;
using System.Web.DynamicData;
using System.Web.DynamicData.ModelProviders;

namespace Unleashed.DynamicData
```

LISTING 13.9 Continued

```
{
  public class UnleashedMetaModel : MetaModel
  {
    public UnleashedMetaModel()
    {
      this.FilterFactory = new UnleashedFilterFactory(this);
    }

    protected override MetaTable CreateTable(TableProvider provider)
    {
      return new UnleashedMetaTable(this, provider);
    }

    public new void RegisterContext(
      Type context, ContextConfiguration configuration)
    {
      var model = new MetaModel(false);
      model.RegisterContext(context, configuration);
      DataModelProvider provider = model.Tables[0].Provider.DataModel;
      this.RegisterContext(new UnleashedModelProvider(provider), configuration);
    }
  }
}
```

If you open the metadata explorer with these changes in place, you notice that the metadata information describing entity classes now includes MetaColumn objects for custom properties. All that is left to enable support for custom properties in the dynamic page templates is to modify the EntityDataSource controls and set their EnableFlattening attributes to false.

Thanks to the default support for string properties provided by the Text field template in Dynamic Data, the Country custom property defined in the Product entity now shows up in the list of GridView columns on the Product list page and enables you to see the country of each product without having to navigate to its Supplier page. However, functionality you can get out of Dynamic Data for custom properties is not limited to simple display. You can further customize it using data annotation attributes.

Building Dynamic Pages with Custom Properties

The Parent field and filter templates developed in Chapter 12, "Building Custom Search Pages," make it easy to implement custom pages that display information from related entities using their own metadata. It is a simple matter of adding a dynamic field or filter control to a page and setting the hint and display field attributes. With custom properties now supported by Dynamic Data, you should be able to take advantage of the Parent templates without having to create custom pages. You can apply the UIHintAttribute and

FilterUIHintAttribute to the Country property of the Product entity class, as shown in the following example:

```
partial class Product
{
  [UIHint("Parent", null, "DisplayField", "Country")]
  [FilterUIHint("Parent", null, "DisplayField", "Country")]
  public string Country { get { return this.Supplier.Country; } }
}
```

From the compiler standpoint, nothing prevents you from using the Parent field and filter templates this way; however, code in these templates currently assumes that they are associated with a *foreign key* property. Although Country, the *custom* property you created, uses the Supplier foreign key property internally, this information is not immediately available to the template. You can provide the missing information by passing an additional control parameter, ForeignKeyField, with the name of the foreign key property, as shown next:

```
[UIHint("Parent", null,
  "ForeignKeyField", "Supplier",
  "DisplayField", "Country")]
[FilterUIHint("Parent", null,
  "ForeignKeyField", "Supplier",
  "DisplayField", "Country")]
public string Country { get { return this.Supplier.Country; } }
```

To take advantage of the new control parameter, the Parent templates need to be modified. The code snippet that follows shows how to extend the Parent *field* template to define a public property called ForeignKeyField, matching the name of the control parameter specified in the UIHintAttribute and replacing the ForeignKeyColumn property to locate the foreign key column based on its name. If the ForeignKeyField was not specified, the property falls back to the inherited implementation, which assumes that the template is associated with a foreign key property. The *filter* template can be extended in the same way; you can see its implementation in the source code that accompanies the book:

```
public partial class ParentFieldTemplate : UnleashedFieldTemplate
{
  private MetaForeignKeyColumn foreignKeyColumn;

  public string ForeignKeyField { get; set; }

  public new MetaForeignKeyColumn ForeignKeyColumn
  {
    get
    {
      if (this.foreignKeyColumn == null)
      {
```

```
            if (!string.IsNullOrEmpty(this.ForeignKeyField))
                this.foreignKeyColumn = (MetaForeignKeyColumn)
                    this.Column.Table.GetColumn(this.ForeignKeyField);
            else
                this.foreignKeyColumn = base.ForeignKeyColumn;
        }

        return this.foreignKeyColumn;
    }
  }
}
```

This simple enhancement of the Parent field and filter templates allows you to provide all metadata information required to generate a *dynamic* list page that displays information not only from the Product entity itself, but also from its parent entity, Supplier, without having to create a custom page template. Figure 13.6 shows a screenshot of the Product list page, which includes the Country property both as a filter control at the top of the page and as a column in the GridView. Both display and filtering of Country property values works in this dynamically generated page just as well as in the *custom* page created with the help of the Parent field and filter templates earlier.

FIGURE 13.6 Product List page with the custom Country property.

Notice that the order of columns in the grid has been modified to make both the filter and the grid column fit on the page without the user needing to scroll. This brings up an important point you might want to consider when using custom properties along with the metadata classes in your project. Here is a larger extract from the Product entity class, which shows how the DisplayAttribute was applied to the ProductName and Country properties to change their default order:

```
[MetadataType(typeof(Metadata))]
partial class Product
{
  [Display(Order = 20)]
  public string Country { get { return this.Supplier.Country; } }

  private abstract class Metadata
  {
    [Display(Name = "Product Name", Order = 10)]
    public object ProductName { get; set; }
  }
}
```

With entity classes generated automatically from the model definition by Entity Framework or LINQ to SQL, you normally use a metadata class to specify data annotations, such as the DisplayAttribute, for regular entity properties. The custom properties, on the other hand, are created manually in the partial class, and you can apply data annotations directly. Which approach is better?

In the example just given, placing the DisplayAttribute directly above the definition of the Country property allows you to have all of its annotations in a single place (the UIHint and FilterUIHint attributes are not shown to make the example shorter). However, it also splits the information about the order of properties between the metadata class and the entity class itself. Notice how the Country property appears first in the source file and second in the dynamically generated web page. Alternatively, you could also consolidate data annotations for *all* properties in the metadata class, as demonstrated in the next code sample. While this approach brings the order of properties in the metadata class in sync with their order on the dynamically generated pages, definition of the Country property is now split between two different places:

```
[MetadataType(typeof(Metadata))]
partial class Product
{
   public string Country { get { return this.Supplier.Country; } }

  private abstract class Metadata
  {
    [Display(Name = "Product Name", Order = 10)]
    public object ProductName { get; set; }
```

13

```
    [Display(Order = 20)]
    public object Country { get; set; }
  }
}
```

Both approaches become problematic as the size and complexity of your entity classes increases. You should settle on a particular one early on and use it consistently throughout the project to make maintenance easier.

Sorting of Custom Properties

At this point, the Country custom property you added to the Product entity is not sortable—the GridView column generated by Dynamic Data for this property on the Product list page appears as plain text and cannot be clicked. This is because the UnleashedColumnProvider object that the model provider creates for this property does not have its IsSortable property set to true. Simply saying that a column is sortable is not enough. Because sorting and paging are delegated by the GridView and EntityDataSource controls to the database server for a column to be sortable, it has to have a valid *sort expression*.

For regular properties, like ProductName, the sort expression matches the name of the property. However, the Entity Framework cannot infer mapping of custom properties to database tables based on their names alone and need an explicit sort expression. Inside of a custom page, you can specify it by setting the SortExpression attribute of the UnleashedField in page markup, as shown in the code snippet that follows. For pages generated dynamically, the sort expression has to come from the metadata.

```
<unl:UnleashedField DataField="Supplier" UIHint="Parent"
  DisplayField= "Country"
  SortExpression="Supplier.Country"/>
```

Specifying Sort Expression for Custom Properties in Entity Model

You can provide the sort expression metadata by applying a new data annotation attribute to the custom property in the entity model. Here is how this would look:

```
partial class Product
{
  [CustomProperty(Expression = "Supplier.Country")]
  public string Country { get { return this.Supplier.Country; } }
}
```

The source code of the CustomPropertyAttribute is shown in Listing 13.10. As you can see, it is very short. At this point, its only purpose is to store the Expression value for the entity property to which it is applied. The actual logic to take advantage of this information has to be implemented in the Dynamic Data application.

LISTING 13.10 CustomPropertyAttribute Implementation

```
using System;

namespace Unleashed.DataAnnotations
{
  [AttributeUsage(AttributeTargets.Property, AllowMultiple = false)]
  public class CustomPropertyAttribute: Attribute
  {
    public string Expression { get; set; }
  }
}
```

Extending Dynamic Data to Support Sort Expression Metadata

The first task is to let Dynamic Data know that a custom property with an expression specified is sortable. This can be done in the UnleashedColumnProvider class, by setting its IsSortable property to true. The code snippet that follows shows how this can be done (only the new code is shown; you can see the rest of the code indicated by the ellipsis back in Listing 13.6):

```
public UnleashedColumnProvider(
   UnleashedTableProvider table, PropertyDescriptor descriptor)
   : base(table)
{
   // ...
   this.IsSortable = descriptor.Attributes.OfType<CustomPropertyAttribute>()
      .Any(a => !string.IsNullOrEmpty(a.Expression));
}
```

Unfortunately, the current version of Dynamic Data does not allow you to specify the actual sort expression through the metadata. On one hand, the ColumnProvider base class does not have a SortExpression property you can set. On the other hand, although the MetaColumn class does have a SortExpression property, it is nonvirtual and cannot be overridden. MetaColumn assumes that the sort expression always matches the name of the property returned by its ColumnProvider. Although you can have the UnleashedColumnProvider use the expression of the custom property as its name, it leads to other problems and makes working with metadata more confusing.

Luckily, DataControlField (the base class used by the GridView control to represent columns) defines its SortExpression property as virtual. The DynamicField class provided by Dynamic Data actually overrides this property to get SortExpression from its MetaColumn by default. To work around the limitation in the metadata and provider APIs, this property was overridden in the UnleashedField created earlier to get the expression from the `CustomPropertyAttribute` if it is available. Listing 13.11 shows the updated source code of the class.

LISTING 13.11 UnleashedField Implementation with SortExpression Property

```
using System.Linq;
using System.Web.DynamicData;
using Unleashed.DataAnnotations;

namespace Unleashed.DynamicData
{
  public class UnleashedField : DynamicField
  {
    public override string SortExpression
    {
      get
      {
        object obj = this.ViewState["SortExpression"];
        if (obj != null) return (string)obj;

        if (this.Column != null)
        {
          CustomPropertyAttribute property = this.Column.Attributes
            .OfType<CustomPropertyAttribute>().FirstOrDefault();
          if (property != null && !string.IsNullOrEmpty(property.Expression))
            return property.Expression;

          return this.Column.SortExpression;
        }

        return string.Empty;
      }

      set { base.SortExpression = value; }
    }

    protected override DynamicControl CreateDynamicControl()
    {
      return new UnleashedControl();
    }
  }
}
```

For consistency with the built-in implementation in the DynamicField, the getter of the overridden SortExpression property is a bit more verbose than it could have been had you simply called the inherited implementation. It first checks the ViewState to determine if the value was set explicitly, such as when the SortExpression attribute was specified in page markup. Otherwise, the getter looks for the CustomPropertyAttribute applied to the property and returns its Expression property, Supplier.Country in this example. In the absence of the CustomPropertyAttribute, the getter falls back to the default sort expression supplied by the MetaColumn, which matches the name of the entity property— Country. The inherited getter implementation was not called because it wouldn't allow to distinguish between a SortExpression specified explicitly and a default value determined based on the property name.

With the CustomPropertyAttribute implemented and UnleashedField updated to support it, you enable Dynamic Data list pages to support sorting of columns based on custom properties. Figure 13.7 shows a screenshot of the Products list page that was sorted by clicking the header of the Country column. Notice that thanks to the EntityDataSource control, processing of both sorting and paging is still delegated to SQL Server. In other words, it is performed without fetching all data from the database, even when you click a column that represents a custom property.

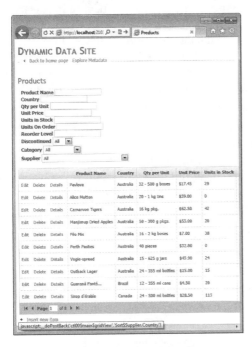

FIGURE 13.7 Product list page with custom property sorting.

Generating Metadata Attributes

Data annotations or, more correctly, the data annotation attributes, were created out of a necessity to extend the metadata information supplied by the raw entity classes of the underlying data access frameworks. Entity classes are simply not expressive enough to provide all metadata required for Dynamic Data to generate the user interface. For instance, the .NET type String does not allow you to specify maximum length, which is a pervasive requirement when storing string values in relational tables. As a result, the metadata API and the larger Dynamic Data framework in general, rely on the data annotations, such as the StringLengthAttribute, to get the additional information they need.

> **NOTE**
>
> The metadata limitation applies not only to the code generated by the Entity Framework and LINQ to SQL but also to code written by developers using the code-first approach to create the entity model as well.

In some instances, the required information, such as the maximum string length, is available in the model definitions, the .EDMX, or .DBML files, but is not publicly exposed by the data access framework through the generated entity classes. To avoid having to specify the same information twice—once in the Entity Designer and second time in the metadata classes, the Dynamic Data providers can *generate* data annotation attributes automatically. For instance, if you have an entity property, such as the ProductName in the Product class, which is mapped to a database column with a "not null" constraint, the Dynamic Data model provider will automatically add a RequiredAttribute to the list of attributes in the ColumnProvider that represents it.

A somewhat similar situation exists with the custom properties. The Country property defined in the Product class needs a UIHintAttribute and a FilterUIHintAttribute to use the right templates, but also a CustomPropertyAttribute to support sorting. As you can see in the following code sample, the required data annotations are quite verbose and, if you need a fair number of custom properties, having to specify all this information in the entity model quickly becomes less practical than creating custom pages:

```
[CustomProperty(Expression = "Supplier.Country")]
[UIHint("Parent", null,
    "ForeignKeyField", "Supplier",
    "DisplayField", "Country")]
[FilterUIHint("Parent", null,
    "ForeignKeyField", "Supplier",
    "DisplayField", "Country")]
public string Country { get { return this.Supplier.Country; } }
```

Because the UI and Filter hints can be inferred from the custom property expression, you can generate the UIHintAttribute and FilterUIHintAttribute automatically in the model provider, leaving only the need to supply the CustomPropertyAttribute, like so:

```
[CustomProperty(Expression = "Supplier.Country")]
public string Country { get { return this.Supplier.Country; } }
```

Eliminating the UIHintAttribute and FilterUIHintAttribute from the entity model not only reduces the amount of code you must write, but also changes the nature of this code. Unlike the low-level hint annotations, the CustomPropertyAttribute does not include hard-coded UI information.

13

Generating attributes is actually quite simple. If you have already created a class that extends the built-in MetaColumn, you can do it by overriding the virtual BuildAttributeCollection method, which, by default, simply returns the attributes collection of the MetaColumn.Provider object. However, because the sample solution already has an extended ColumnProvider, the easiest way to generate attributes is by overriding its Attributes property. The following snippet shows an extract from the UnleashedColumnProvider source code that demonstrates how to do this:

```
partial class UnleashedColumnProvider : ColumnProvider
{
  public override AttributeCollection Attributes
  {
    get
    {
      var attributes = base.Attributes.Cast<Attribute>().ToList();
      var customProperty = attributes.OfType<CustomPropertyAttribute>()
        .FirstOrDefault();
      if (customProperty != null &&
          customProperty.Expression.Contains('.'))
      {
        string[] fields = customProperty.Expression.Split('.');
        string foreignKeyField = fields[0];
        string displayField = fields[1];
        if (!attributes.OfType<UIHintAttribute>().Any())
        {
          attributes.Add(new UIHintAttribute("Parent", null,
            "ForeignKeyField", foreignKeyField,
            "DisplayField", displayField));
        }
        if (!attributes.OfType<FilterUIHintAttribute>().Any())
        {
          attributes.Add(new FilterUIHintAttribute("Parent", null,
            "ForeignKeyField", foreignKeyField,
            "DisplayField", displayField));
        }
```

```
        }

        return new AttributeCollection(attributes.ToArray());
      }
    }
  }
```

Notice that the overridden getter first calls the inherited `Attributes` property to obtain the initial list of attributes. This includes all default attributes already discovered by the column provider, which in the case of `UnleashedColumnProvider` includes the attributes returned by the `PropertyDescriptor` object that represents the custom entity property. If the list of attributes includes a `CustomPropertyAttribute`, the getter parses the names of the foreign key and the display fields from its `Expression` value and adds a `UIHintAttribute` and a `FilterUIHintAttribute` to the list. In the end, the combined list of attributes is used to create a new `AttributeCollection` object, which the getter returns.

Even when generating attributes, such as the `UIHintAttribute` and `FilterUIHintAttribute` in this example, it is important to still allow specifying these attribute explicitly. One one hand, you might need to specify more information than can be inferred programmatically. But more importantly, imagine trying to troubleshoot a problem caused by the model provider silently replacing the attributes you applied in code when the application runs. If you are careful, however, the automatic generation of attributes fits well in the convention-based development experience offered by Dynamic Data—out of the box, it just works, but you can change it if you want.

Summary

The approach to developing metadata-driven list pages is similar to building dynamic forms. You want to provide enough information in the entity model to generate a reasonably good UI dynamically, eliminating or postponing the need to create and maintain custom pages. You do that by specifying data annotation attributes, such as the `FilterUIHintAttribute`, for entity classes and their properties in the entity model. With the additional metadata information, you can take advantage of the built-in capabilities of Dynamic Data controls or extend the framework to eliminate its shortcomings.

One of the biggest shortcomings in the built-in support for filter templates in Dynamic Data is the simplistic algorithm used to look up filter templates. Unlike the sophisticated algorithm used for field templates, the filter template algorithm assumes the existence of only three filter templates that come with Dynamic Data out of the box. By replacing the built-in `FilterFactory` with the `UnleashedFilterFactory`, you can bring the filter lookup functionality up to the same level with field templates and eliminate the need to specify the `FilterUIHintAttribute` for every filterable property in the entity model.

The built-in model provider can be extended to enable support for custom entity proper-ties in Dynamic Data. With their help, you can define calculated entity properties and properties that return information from related entities. With the first-class support in Dynamic Data, including templating, sorting, and filtering, custom properties allow you to postpone the need to create custom pages further and reduce the time and cost of developing web applications. Custom properties are not limited to list pages; they can be used in dynamic forms just as well.

Last, you learned about automatic generation of data annotation attributes in the model provider based on existing metadata. Whenever higher-level metadata already exists, perhaps in the underlying entity model or supplied by the developer as another annota-tion, generating the low-level annotations helps you not only reduce the amount of code you have to write, but also improve the quality of the entity model.

13

Implementing Security

Dynamic Data includes an extensible security system that enables you to secure metadata-driven web applications at several different levels. At the top level, you can control whether a particular *entity*, such as Customer or Product, is accessible through the pages dynamically generated from page templates. At the next level down, you can configure any given entity type to allow or deny users to perform specific *actions*, or in other words, access the dynamically generated List, Details, Insert, and Edit pages. At the lowest level, the framework provides limited support for row-level security and allows you to limit the set of rows a user will be able to see through the dynamically generated web pages, such as allowing a customer to see only the orders they submitted and not everyone else's.

In this chapter, you learn the specifics of different approaches for implementing security in Dynamic Data applications. The simplest and most straightforward approach is to specify authorization rules in the *Web configuration* file. Based on the standard location-based configuration syntax, this approach should be already familiar to ASP.NET developers building WebForms and MVC applications. This approach supports both entity- and action-level access control.

The second option to implementing security is based on *metadata* information. Although the Web.config-based authorization rules work well to prevent unauthorized access, they are not easily accessible in the dynamic templates. Having simple programmatic access to rule definitions, dynamic templates can not only prevent unauthorized access, but also *trim* the dynamically generated web pages to hide inaccessible information and actions.

Dynamic Data has built-in support for access control only at the *entity* level. However, it also provides extension points that you can take advantage of to implement more granular access control at the *action* level.

The last option in implementing security is to do it in *code*. Entity- and action-level access rules can be stored in a custom database and loaded by the application at runtime. Code is the only option available when it comes to implementing row-level security, and you see how this can be done in the last section of this chapter.

Table Scaffolding

You can control whether or not *all* users have access to a particular table through the dynamically generated web pages by applying the ScaffoldTableAttribute to the entity class. Here is an example of explicitly disabling scaffolding for the Customer entity:

```
[ScaffoldTable(false)]
partial class Customer
{
    //...
}
```

By default, scaffolding is turned off and has to be enabled on a per-entity basis. This is a safe default; it prevents you from accidentally giving users access to all of the application data. However, you can also change the default scaffolding option during registration of the entity model. This can be useful in the early stages of a web application project when you want to collect as much feedback about the entity model from the business as possible. Listing 14.1 shows the code in Global.asax.cs that enables scaffolding of all tables.

LISTING 14.1 Scaffolding Configuration in Global.asax.cs

```
using System;
using System.Web;
using System.Web.DynamicData;
using System.Web.Routing;
using DataModel;
using Unleashed.DynamicData;

namespace WebApplication
{
  public class Global : HttpApplication
  {
    public static readonly UnleashedMetaModel DefaultModel;
    private void Application_Start(object sender, EventArgs e)
    {
      DefaultModel = new UnleashedMetaModel();
      var modelConfiguration = new ContextConfiguration {ScaffoldAllTables = true};
```

```
    DefaultModel.RegisterContext(typeof(NorthwindEntities), modelConfiguration);
    RouteTable.Routes.Add(new DynamicDataRoute("{table}/{action}.aspx"));
  }
 }
}
```

When scaffolding is turned off for a particular table, users cannot access it through the dynamically generated web pages. For example, based on the DynamicDataRoute registration in Listing 14.1, you would normally expect to be able to access the dynamic Customer web pages by navigating to a URL that looks like this:

```
http://localhost:2103/Customers/List.aspx
```

However, with scaffolding for the Customer entity disabled, Dynamic Data returns the HTTP error 404 (Resource cannot be found) when you try to access this address in a browser (see Figure 14.1).

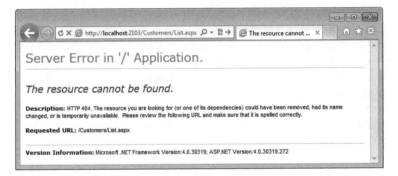

FIGURE 14.1 Resource cannot be found error page.

As a security mechanism, the table scaffolding option alone is too crude—it controls access only at the entity level and does not allow distinguishing between different users or roles. However, turning off scaffolding for a given table disables only its dynamic routing, not metadata. This allows you to create *custom* pages that use rich Dynamic Data controls to display data for entities that are not accessible through the dynamically generated web pages. With custom pages, you can use the standard authentication and authorization functionality of ASP.NET and implement security the same way you would for a traditional WebForms application.

Route Constraints

Route constraints are a more powerful and granular access control mechanism than table scaffolding options. They allow you to control access not only to *entities*, but to *actions* as well. Here is how to change the route registration code from Listing 14.1 to enable only the dynamic List pages and only for the Product and Category entities.

```
RouteTable.Routes.Add(new DynamicDataRoute("{table}/{action}.aspx") {
   Constraints = new RouteValueDictionary {
      { "table", "Products¦Categories" },
      { "action", "List" },
   }
});
```

As you might recall from a discussion in Chapter 6, "Page Templates," route constraint is specified as a RouteValueDictionary object that contains regular expressions for validating route parameters with the matching names. In this example, you have a regular expression pattern "Products¦Categories" that will be used to validate the "table" parameter, accepting only "Products" or "Categories" values, and rejecting all others. "List" is also a regular expression pattern, a very simple one; it matches only "List" values for the "action" parameter.

If the actual value of any route parameter does not match the regular expression pattern specified in the route constraint, Dynamic Data returns the HTTP error code 404 (Resource cannot be found), and the user sees an error page similar to that shown back in Figure 14.1.

Similar to scaffolding options discussed in the previous section, route constraints can be used to selectively enable or disable dynamic web pages for specific entities in your model. Route constraints can be used in combination with the default scaffolding option. For instance, having the default scaffolding turned on, you can use route constraints instead of the ScaffoldTableAttribute to allow access only to specific tables. However, like the scaffolding options, the route constraints lack the ability to implement authorization rules based on identity or roles of the application users.

Web.Config Authorization Rules

You can also specify authorization rules for dynamic pages generated by Dynamic Data in the web configuration file. As you are well aware, ASP.NET allows you to define authorization rules for a given folder of the web application by creating a Web.config file in it and placing <allow/> and <deny/> elements inside of an <authorization/> element. Here is a configuration file that prevents unauthenticated users from accessing any page:

```
<?xml version="1.0"?>
<configuration>
  <system.web>
    <authorization>
      <deny users="?"/>
    </authorization>
  </system.web>
</configuration>
```

Web configuration files are hierarchical; folders inherit authorization rules from their parents and can override them with their own `Web.config` files. So with traditional ASP.NET WebForms web applications, you would typically implement security by placing pages that can be accessed only by certain users in a separate subfolder and giving it its own `Web.config` file. For example, you could have created a subfolder called *Customers*, and placed all custom pages that display customer information in it, along with the following Web.config file, to allow access only for users in the *Manager* role:

```xml
<?xml version="1.0"?>
<configuration>
  <system.web>
    <authorization>
      <allow roles="Manager"/>
      <deny users="*"/>
    </authorization>
  </system.web>
</configuration>
```

Because Dynamic Data applications rely on URL routing, there are no physical folders that represent entities—and no *Customers* folder in the sample application. Therefore, you cannot simply create new configuration files for them. Instead, you can specify authorization rules in the main `Web.config` of the application, with the help of the `<location/>` element. Here is a configuration file that implements the same authorization rules: Only authenticated users are allowed to access the root of the application, and only users in the Manager role are allowed to access the Customers pages:

```xml
<?xml version="1.0"?>
<configuration>
  <system.web>
    <authorization>
      <deny users="?"/>
    </authorization>
  </system.web>
  <location path="Customers">
    <system.web>
      <authorization>
        <allow roles="Manager"/>
        <deny users="*"/>
      </authorization>
    </system.web>
  </location>
</configuration>
```

You can further taylor access rights for the Customer entity by creating authorization rules for specific dynamically generated pages. For instance, by adding the following configuration snippet to this `Web.config` file, you can extend the authorization rules and allow users in the `Employee` role to access the dynamic `Customers/List.aspx` page. In other words, managers will be allowed to access all dynamic pages for the Customer entity, and employees will be able to access only its List page.

```
<location path="Customers/List.aspx">
  <system.web>
    <authorization>
      <allow roles="Employee"/>
    </authorization>
  </system.web>
</location>
```

When processing authorization rules, ASP.NET starts with the `<authorization/>` section closest to the URL in question. If no matching rule is found, it continues with the next available parent configuration until it finds a matching rule. This works the same with both physical Web.config files and `<location/>` elements as well. In this particular example, when an unauthenticated user is trying to access the `Customers/List.aspx`, ASP.NET first evaluates the `<allow roles="Employee"/>` rule defined specifically for this dynamic page. Because the rule does not match the unauthenticated user, ASP.NET continues with the `<allow roles="Manager"/>` rule defined for the dynamic Customers folder. Because this rule does not match either, it then evaluates the `<deny users="*"/>` rule defined for the folder. This last rule does match, and ASP.NET denies the unauthenticated user access to the dynamic `Customers/List.aspx` page.

> **NOTE**
>
> If a matching authorization rule cannot be found all the way up to the root of the web application, ASP.NET *allows* access by default. In a dynamic web application, where new entities can be added without creating physical folders, it is easier to overlook missing authorization rules and allow access by accident. If you want to rely on Web.config files to implement security, you might want to deny access by default as a precaution. Here is an example that does that:
>
> ```
> <?xml version="1.0"?>
> <configuration>
>   <location path="Default.aspx">
>     <system.web>
>       <authorization>
>         <allow users="*"/>
>       </authorization>
>     </system.web>
>   </location>
>   <system.web>
>     <authorization>
>       <deny users="*"/>
>     </authorization>
>   </system.web>
> </configuration>
> ```

Having access denied by default forces you to modify the Web.config for every new
entity you want to access through the dynamically generated web pages. In other
words, if you decide to enable dynamic pages for the Customer entity, you have to
create authorization rules for it in the Web.config before you can test it in the browser.

Limitations of Configuration-Based Rules

Web configuration files allow you to implement a complete authorization system for
Dynamic Data applications. You can configure access rules based on *entities*, *actions*, *users*,
and *roles*. However, there are several significant drawbacks associated with this approach
as well. On one hand, configuring a set of rules for a sizable entity model is often very
verbose. You must create a separate <location/> element for every entity and potentially
for every action that needs different authorization rules. With at least seven lines of XML
configuration for every location element, the size of configuration can quickly reach
hundreds of lines.

A bigger problem with configuration-based approach is that enforcing access rules at the
page level is often not granular enough. Take a dynamic search page for the Product entity
as an example. Suppose you want all your customers and even unauthenticated users to
browse the product catalog. However, you also want to restrict access to Suppliers so that
only employees of your company can see them. To enforce these rules, you could try
implementing the following authorization rules in the Web.config file:

```
<location path="Products">
  <system.web>
    <authorization>
      <allow users="*"/>
    </authorization>
  </system.web>
</location>
<location path="Suppliers">
  <system.web>
    <authorization>
      <allow roles="Manager,Employee"/>
      <deny users="*"/>
    </authorization>
  </system.web>
</location>
```

These authorization rules prevent customers from seeing the Suppliers page itself.
However, they can still see supplier names on the dynamic Products page. The Product
entity has a navigation property, Supplier, and Dynamic Data automatically generates a
foreign key field template for it. Figure 14.2 shows an example.

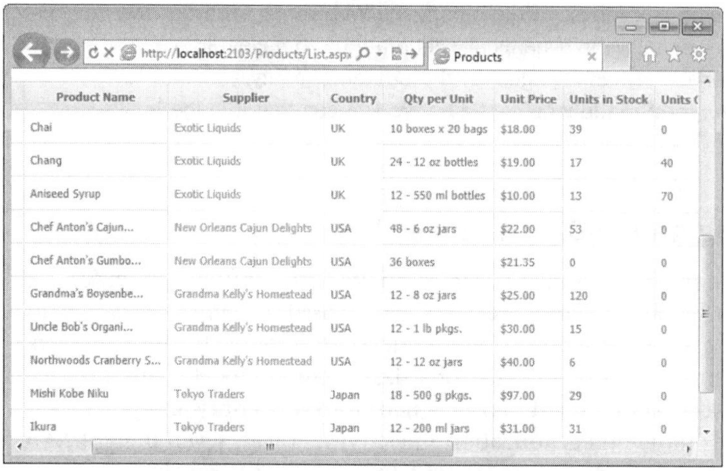

FIGURE 14.2   Products page displaying inaccessible suppliers.

To prevent inaccessible entity information from appearing in pages of related entities completely, the dynamic page templates must somehow hide it. Implementing this functionality, sometimes also referred to as *security trimming*, by reading complex authorization rules from the Web configuration is challenging. Instead, it is often more practical to simply create a custom page or page template for the entity, such as Product in this example, that requires trimming.

Metadata Security API

The metadata API provides a good foundation for implementing entity-level security with both access control and trimming. As discussed in Chapter 7, "Metadata API," the MetaTable class defines the following methods that encapsulate *action*-level authorization rules for individual *entities* based on the *identity* and *roles* of a given user:

```
public virtual bool CanDelete(IPrincipal principal);
public virtual bool CanInsert(IPrincipal principal);
public virtual bool CanRead(IPrincipal principal);
public virtual bool CanUpdate(IPrincipal principal);
```

As implemented in the built-in MetaTable class, the permission methods always return true, allowing any user to access any entity by default. However, because these methods are virtual, you can override them and implement your own authorization rules.

In simplest form, you could hard-code the authorization rules. The example that follows demonstrates implementation of the CanRead method, which allows all users to access the Product and Category entities and only users in role Employee to access the Suppliers and other tables:

```
public override bool CanRead(IPrincipal principal)
{
    if (this.Name == "Products") return true;
    if (this.Name == "Categories") return true;
    return principal.IsInRole("Employee");
}
```

Hard-coding the authorization rules in the permission methods is straightforward and helps consolidate security settings. It usually produces a much more compact definition of authorization rules than the Web.config-based approach (how much more depends on you code formatting style, of course). On the other hand, hard-coding the rules, by definition, means that they cannot be changed at run time. And perhaps the more important drawback is that the size and complexity of the permission methods also continue to grow as the size of your entity model increases.

To allow changing the authorization rules at run time, you could define much more granular, action-level roles for each entity and require a user to be in a corresponding role to perform the action. For example, the Product entity could have corresponding roles called CanDeleteProducts, CanInsertProducts, CanReadProducts, and CanUpdateProducts. With similar roles defined for all other entities, implementation of the CanRead and other methods in the MetaTable descendant could be as simple as the one shown here:

```
public override bool CanRead(IPrincipal principal)
{
    return principal.IsInRole("CanRead" + this.Name);
}
```

By defining granular, action-level roles, you can make the permission methods simpler, but only at the cost of having to manage more roles at run time. If you are using the built-in ASP.NET web configuration tool, the large number of roles required with this approach is usually too much to handle. If runtime configuration of the authorization rules is required in your application, you might want to consider using the Microsoft Authorization Manager (AzMan), which allows you to define entity actions as low-level "operations" instead of the high-level roles. AzMan provides a powerful configuration console that allows mapping operations to roles and assigning roles to individual users or groups.

Some applications have their own authentication and authorization systems, often with user information and their access permissions stored in a database. If that is the case in your application, you can also reuse your existing security system when implementing the MetaTable permission methods. Keep in mind, however, that these methods can be called multiple times for each page request. It is important to cache the authorization rules in memory and avoid hitting the database every time to make rule evaluation as fast as possible.

14

Modifying Dynamic Templates to Support the Security API

Dynamic Data offers limited support for the `MetaTable` permission methods out of the box. The `VisibleTables` property of the `MetaModel` class returns only the `MetaTable` objects whose `CanRead` method returns `true` for the current user; the Default page relies on this property to display a list of tables he is allowed to see. Figure 14.3 shows how it looks when authorization was implemented to allow unauthenticated users and customers to access only the Product and Category entities.

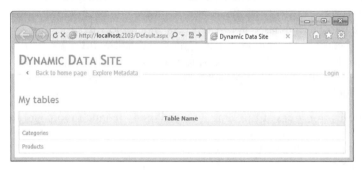

FIGURE 14.3   Default page showing only accessible tables.

The `GetScaffoldColumns` and `GetFilteredColumns` methods of the `MetaTable` class also exclude the *foreign key* columns if the current user does not have the permission to read his parent table. So if you override the `CanRead` method to allow only users in the Employee role to read the Supplier entity, the dynamic Products page no longer displays the Supplier column to unauthenticated users and looks similar to what is shown in Figure 14.4.

	ProductName	QuantityPerUnit	UnitPrice	Units in Stock	UnitsOnOrder	Reorder
Edit Delete Details	Chai	10 boxes x 20 bags	18.0000	39	0	10
Edit Delete Details	Chang	24 - 12 oz bottles	19.0000	17	40	25
Edit Delete Details	Aniseed Syrup	12 - 550 ml bottles	10.0000	13	70	25
Edit Delete Details	Chef Anton's Cajun...	48 - 6 oz jars	22.0000	53	0	0
Edit Delete Details	Chef Anton's Gumbo...	36 boxes	21.3500	0	0	0
Edit Delete Details	Grandma's Boysenbe...	12 - 8 oz jars	25.0000	120	0	25
Edit Delete Details	Uncle Bob's Organi...	12 - 1 lb pkgs.	30.0000	15	0	10
Edit Delete Details	Northwoods Cranberry S...	12 - 12 oz jars	40.0000	6	0	0
Edit Delete Details	Mishi Kobe Niku	18 - 500 g pkgs.	97.0000	29	0	0
Edit Delete Details	Ikura	12 - 200 ml jars	31.0000	31	0	0

I◄ ◄ Page 1   of 8 ► ►I

✦ Insert new item

FIGURE 14.4   Products page displaying inaccessible actions.

Aside from using `MetaTable` permission methods to hide the foreign key columns the user is not allowed to read, Dynamic Data doesn't do anything else out of the box. In other words, it *ignores* the values returned by the `CanInsert`, `CanUpdate`, and `CanDelete` methods; in fact, it never calls them. For example, if you try to prevent unauthorized users from making changes in any of the tables by implementing the three permission methods similar to this

```
public override bool CanUpdate(IPrincipal principal)
{
  return principal.IsInRole("Employee");
}
```

...the dynamic Products will still display the Edit, Delete, and Insert new item links shown in Figure 14.4. Even more importantly, if the unauthorized user actually clicks one of these links, he can access it. He can even access the dynamic Suppliers page by typing its address directly in the address bar of their web browser, even though the Products page might not display the Supplier hyperlinks for them. Luckily, with just a few changes, you can make the dynamic page templates support the permission methods completely and implement both access control and UI trimming.

Modifying Page Templates to Prevent Unauthorized Access

The *Insert* page template generates web pages that allow users to create new entity instances, or in database terms, insert new records in a particular table. To determine whether the current user is authorized to perform this action, it needs to call the `CanInsert` method of the `MetaTable` object describing the entity type. Here is a code snippet that shows how access security can be implemented in this template:

```
public partial class Insert : Page
{
  protected MetaTable table;
  protected override void OnPreInit(EventArgs e)
  {
    base.OnPreInit(e);
    this.table = DynamicDataRouteHandler.GetRequestMetaTable(this.Context);
    if (!this.table.CanInsert(this.User))
    {
      FormsAuthentication.RedirectToLoginPage();
      this.Response.End();
    }
  }
}
```

> **NOTE**
>
> This and other code snippets in this section are small extracts from the markup and code-behind files of the dynamic page templates. Please refer to the sample source code accompanying this book for complete details.

By overriding the `OnPreInit` method, you inject the code into one of the earliest stages of processing a page request. This code relies on the built-in `DynamicDataRouteHandler` helper class to get a `MetaTable` object based on the dynamic URL of the page request. This sample project uses Forms authentication, and if the `CanInsert` method returns `false`, this code redirects users to the login page specified in the application's `Web.config` file. Figure 14.5 shows how this looks. Notice the `ReturnUrl` parameter in the address bar of the web browser. This allows the authorized users to provide their credentials and get back to the page they wanted to access. Otherwise, they will not be able to get past the login page. With *Windows* authentication, you can redirect them to another page of the web application or simply return the HTTP error code 403 Forbidden and let IIS serve the error page configured for it.

FIGURE 14.5 Login page displayed instead of products Insert page.

> **NOTE**
>
> After redirecting the unauthorized user to the login page, the code calls the `End` method of page's `Response` object. This immediately terminates processing of the page request and prevents any other methods or event handlers in this page from executing. This is important from both a security and performance standpoint; when you know the user is not authorized to access a particular page, you don't want to let the request to consume any additional server resources (memory, CPU, or I/O bandwidth).

The *Edit* page template is slightly more complex. Because it generates web pages that allow users to edit existing records, it needs to verify that users have not only the *update* permission for the given entity type, but also the *read* permission as well. Otherwise, an inconsistency in authorization rules could allow someone to read entity information by manually typing URLs for the dynamic Edit pages, even if they cannot access the List and Details pages.

```
public partial class Edit : System.Web.UI.Page
{
  protected MetaTable table;
  protected override void OnPreInit(EventArgs e)
  {
    base.OnPreInit(e);
    this.table = DynamicDataRouteHandler.GetRequestMetaTable(Context);
    if (!this.table.CanRead(this.User) || !this.table.CanUpdate(this.User))
    {
      FormsAuthentication.RedirectToLoginPage();
      this.Response.End();
    }
  }
}
```

The *Delete* page template created in Chapter 6 is similar to the Edit page template in that it allows users to perform two distinct actions: "read" or "delete" existing records. Implementing authorization checks is also similar to the Edit page template—you need to call the CanRead and CanDelete methods of the MetaTable object associated with the page and redirect the user to the login page if either one of them returns false.

At first glance, the *Details* and *List* page templates are simple. They generate web pages that allow users to "read" existing records and should prevent user access when the CanRead method of the MetaTable object derived from the URL route returns false. You already know how to implement access security for page templates that perform a single action. Here is how you would do it in the code-behind of the Details page template:

```
public partial class Details : Page
{
  protected MetaTable table;
  protected override void OnPreInit(EventArgs e)
  {
    base.OnPreInit(e);
    this.table = DynamicDataRouteHandler.GetRequestMetaTable(this.Context);
    if (!this.table.CanRead(this.User))
    {
      FormsAuthentication.RedirectToLoginPage();
      this.Response.End();
    }
  }
}
```

However, unless your application has a separate Delete page template, both the Details and the List page templates also allow users to *delete* the existing records as well. You cannot simply check the delete permission in the OnPreInit method of the page because that would prevent users without the delete permission from being able to access it at all. Instead, you can handle the ItemDeleting event of the FormView control or the RowDeleting event of the GridView control and check user permissions there. Alternatively, to make implementation simpler and more consistent between the Details and List page templates, you can also handle the Deleting event of the EntityDataSource control, which works the same way with both UI controls. Here is the markup:

```
<asp:EntityDataSource ID="dataSource" runat="server" EnableDelete="true"
    OnDeleting="DataSource_Deleting" />
```

In the event handler, you simply call the CanDelete method of the MetaTable object associated with the page, redirect users without the delete permission to the login page, similar to the one shown back in Figure 14.5, and terminate further request processing:

```
protected void DataSource_Deleting(object sender, EventArgs e)
{
  if (!this.table.CanDelete(this.User))
  {
    FormsAuthentication.RedirectToLoginPage();
    this.Response.End();
  }
}
```

Modifying Page Templates to Hide Inaccessible Actions
The dynamic List page displays links that allow users to Insert, Edit, Delete, and see Details of entities. Likewise, the Details page displays the links that allow users to Edit and Delete the current entity. If you want the users of the application to see these links regardless of whether they are authorized to perform the actions, nothing else needs to be changed. The out-of-the box page templates already display them, and if the user tries to perform an unauthorized action, with the changes already put in place in the previous section, he is redirected to a login page similar to that shown in Figure 14.5. However, if you want to implement security trimming and *hide* the actions that users cannot perform, several additional changes in the page templates are required.

In the List page template, the Details link takes the user to the Details page where they can "read" a single record or entity instance of the same entity type. Like the List page itself, it requires the user to have the CanRead permission. Therefore, if the user is authorized to see the List page, she is also authorized to see the Details page, and you don't need to worry about hiding or showing the Details link dynamically. The Edit, Insert, and Delete actions, however, require the CanUpdate, CanInsert, and CanDelete permissions, respectively, and you need to hide the links if the user is not authorized to perform them.

Here is the (abbreviated) markup to recap how the List page template implements the action links:

```
<asp:GridView ID="gridView" runat="server">
  <Columns>
    <asp:TemplateField>
      <ItemTemplate>
        <asp:DynamicHyperLink runat="server" Action="Edit" Text="Edit"/>
        <asp:DynamicHyperLink runat="server" Action="Delete"
          Text= "Delete"/>
        <asp:DynamicHyperLink runat="server" Text="Details" />
      </ItemTemplate>
    </asp:TemplateField>
  </Columns>
</asp:GridView>

<asp:DynamicHyperLink ID="insertLink" runat="server">
  Insert new item
</asp:DynamicHyperLink>
```

The Edit and Delete hyperlink controls are generated dynamically, a separate instance for each row displayed in the GridView control. The best way to manipulate them in this scenario is by specifying an OnInit event handler. Here is how you need to modify markup of the Edit hyperlink:

```
<asp:DynamicHyperLink runat="server" Action="Edit" Text="Edit"
  OnInit="EditLink_Init" />
```

In the code-behind, you access the dynamically generated control through the *sender* argument the event handler receives. To determine if the user should see the Edit link, call the CanUpdate of the MetaTable object associated with the current page. Based on the boolean value it returns, you simply set link's Visible property to show or hide it:

```
protected void EditLink_Init(object sender, EventArgs e)
{
   ((DynamicHyperLink)sender).Visible = this.table.CanUpdate(this.User);
}
```

Similar changes are needed for the Delete and Insert hyperlinks in the List page template as well. In other words, in page markup, you need to specify the OnInit event handlers for both of these controls. In the code-behind, create the event handlers and implement them by calling CanDelete and CanInsert methods of the MetaTable class, respectively. Because the code is so similar to what was done for the Edit link, it is not shown here; you can find it in the sample project accompanying the book.

NOTE

Although the Insert hyperlink appears directly in the page markup and you could access it through the page field generated by Visual Studio, you still want to use control's `OnInit` event handler to set its visibility. The obvious first reason is consistency—it is nice to have security trimming implemented the same way for all action links. However, it is also important to use the `OnInit` event handler to initialize controls to prevent the unnecessary `ViewState` bloat.

By setting control's `Visible` property to `false`, you remove it from the resulting HTML that is sent to the user's web browser. With the `DynamicHyperLink` control, this means that the `<a href="…" />` element is not generated. However, unless you set the `Visible` property in the `OnInit` event handler of the control itself, the page stores its value in the `ViewState`. Because the List page does not expect visibility of the Insert links to change between post-backs of this page, this information will increase the page size unnecessarily.

The same principle applies to other control properties as well. Setting them at any point after control's own initialization ends, such as page's `Init` event or control's `Load` event, results in property values being recorded in the `ViewState`. If you don't expect control properties to change based on user actions, you can avoid the unnecessary `ViewState` overhead by setting them in the control's `Init` event handler.

Figure 14.6 shows how the Products list page looks with the completed List page template when the current user does not have permissions to update, insert, and delete Product entities. If you compare it to the previous version shown back in Figure 14.4, you will notice that it does not display the Edit and Delete links in the grid and the Insert link under it.

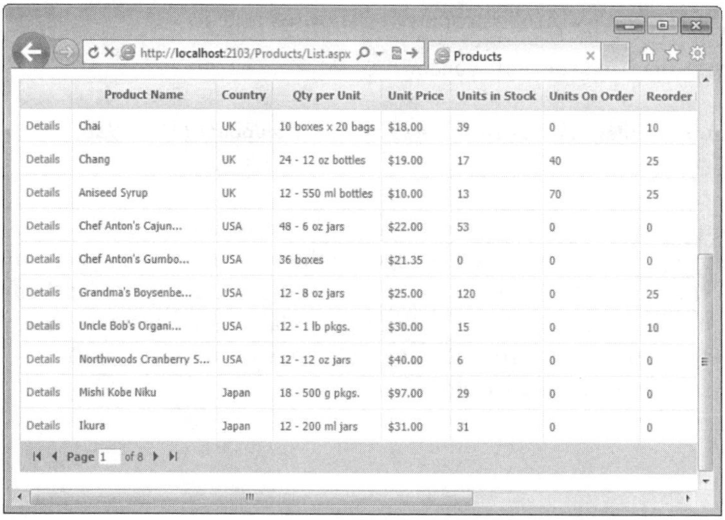

FIGURE 14.6 Products List page hiding inaccessible actions.

In the *Details* page template, the Edit and Delete links are implemented as DynamicHyperLink controls inside of the ItemTemplate of a FormView control:

```
<asp:FormView runat="server" ID="formView" DataSourceID="dataSource">
  <ItemTemplate>
    <unl:UnleashedEntity runat="server" />
    <tr>
      <td colspan="2">
        <asp:DynamicHyperLink runat="server" Action="Edit" Text="Edit" />
        <asp:DynamicHyperLink runat="server" Action="Delete" Text="Delete"/>
        <a href="<%= this.table.ListActionPath %>">Show all items</a>
      </td>
    </tr>
  </ItemTemplate>
</asp:FormView>
```

Just like with the Edit and Delete link controls in the List page template, the Details template needs to implement Init event handlers and call, respectively, the CanUpdate and CanDelete methods of the MetaTable class and set the controls' Visible property based on the values they return. The code is identical to the EditLink_Edit event handler example discussed earlier for the List page.

Figure 14.7 shows how the trimmed Details page looks when the current user does not have the update and delete permissions. Notice that the Edit and Delete links that normally appear at the bottom of the form are not displayed.

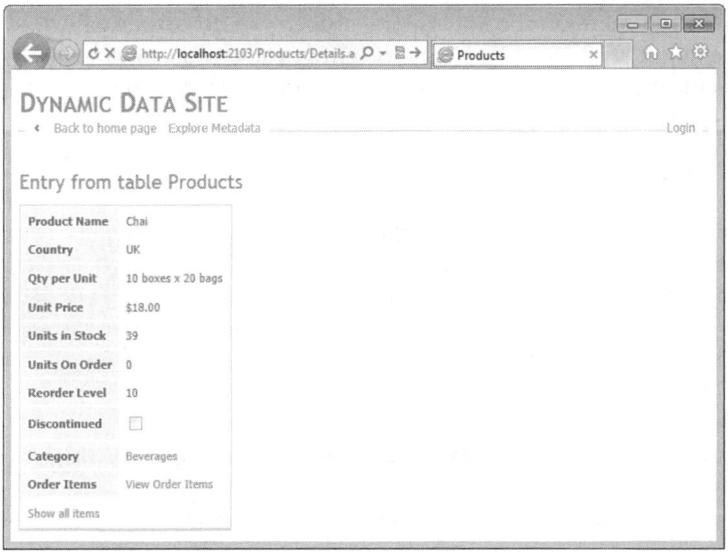

FIGURE 14.7 Product Details page hiding inaccessible actions.

Implementing Row-Level Security

In addition to the *entity-* and *action-*level authorization rules, the metadata API also has a limited provision for implementing *row-*level security. In particular, the MetaTable class defines the following virtual method you use to implement row-level security for read operations:

```
public virtual IQueryable GetQuery(object context);
```

The GetQuery method receives an instance of the ObjectContext class, such as the NorthwindEntities in this example, and returns a LINQ query object that will be used by the dynamic templates to load data of the entity for display.

> **NOTE**
>
> Because Dynamic Data supports multiple data access frameworks, Entity Framework, and LINQ to SQL out of the box, and allows third-party vendors to create their own providers, the actual context object passed to the GetQuery method varies based on the framework used by application. This is why the type of the context parameter is object instead of a more strongly typed ObjectContext. With LINQ to SQL, the argument would be of type DataContext, and the only common ancestor they have with Entity Framework's ObjectContext is object.

Similar to the permission methods, you can override the GetQuery method in the custom descendant of the MetaTable class. The next code snippet shows how you could implement this method and allow users in role Customer to access only their own customer record and orders. Notice how it relies on the EntityType property to determine which entity class the MetaTable object represents. Knowing the entity class, you can cast the untyped IQueryable object to a strongly-typed IQueryable<T> and use LINQ to filter out records that the user does not have access to:

```
public override IQueryable GetQuery(object context)
{
  IQueryable query = base.GetQuery(context);
  IPrincipal user = HttpContext.Current.User;
  if (user.IsInRole("Customer"))
  {
    if (this.EntityType == typeof(Customer))
    {
      query = query.Cast<Customer>()
        .Where(customer => customer.EmailAddress == user.Identity.Name);
    }
    else if (this.EntityType == typeof(Order))
    {
      query = query.Cast<Order>()
        .Where(order => order.Customer.EmailAddress == user.Identity.Name);
```

```
        }
    }
    return query;
}
```

Out of the box, Dynamic Data applications use the `GetQuery` method of the `MetaTable` class in the implementation of the foreign key templates (both field and filter) as well as in the many-to-many field template. So when users open the `DropDownList` generated by the ForeignKey filter template, they will only see those records from the parent table that were returned by the `GetQuery` method provided. You can see how the Customer filter control looks in Figure 14.8 when a customer, *Alfreds Futterkiste* in this example, accesses it. Notice that the drop-down list contains only one item.

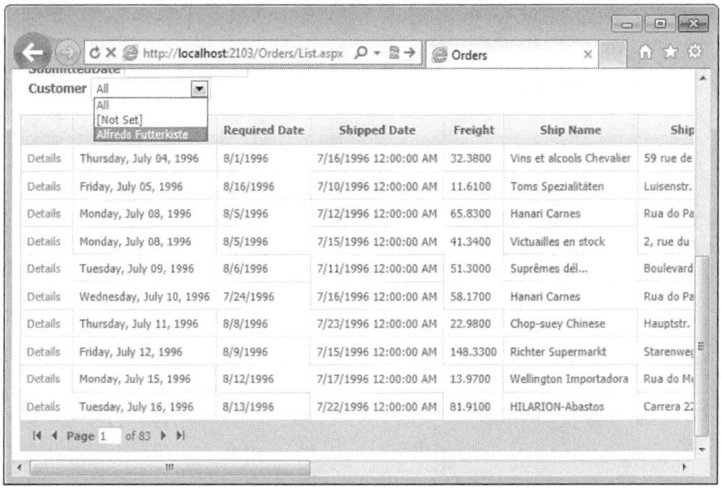

FIGURE 14.8 Orders List page with the customer filter showing GetQuery results.

Unfortunately, the page templates, such as the List template in the last screenshot, do not use the `GetQuery` method. Even though the foreign key filter list might be correct, the page itself still displays all records. If you take a closer look at the *Ship Name* column in Figure 14.8, you notice that it lists orders shipped to various customers, not just the *Alfreds Futterkiste* the `GetQuery` method returns for the current user of the application.

> **NOTE**
>
> Neither `EntityDataSource` nor `LinqDataSource` controls allow replacing the default logic for creating queries. This is a bit surprising because both of these controls define a `ContextCreating` event. The dynamic page templates handle this event to have the data source control use the context object returned by the metadata API, or more specifically, the `CreateContext` method of the `MetaTable` class. The absence of a similar `QueryCreating` event might explain why the `GetQuery` method is ignored by Dynamic Data out of the box.

You can work around this limitation with the help of the `QueryCreated`, the same event used by the `QueryExtender` control and dynamic filters. This event enables you to modify the query object already created by the data source control; you need to extract the actual row filtering logic from the `GetQuery` into a separate method. For consistency with dynamic filters and to avoid naming collisions with the main `GetQuery`, in the `UnleashedMetaTable` class that comes with this book, the new method is called `GetQueryable`,

```
public override IQueryable GetQuery(object context)
{
    IQueryable query = base.GetQuery(context);
    return this.GetQueryable(query);
}

public IQueryable GetQueryable(IQueryable query)
{
    IPrincipal user = HttpContext.Current.User;
    if (user.IsInRole("Customer"))
    {
        if (this.EntityType == typeof(Customer))
        {
            query = query.Cast<Customer>()
                .Where(customer => customer.EmailAddress == user.Identity.Name);
        }
        else if (this.EntityType == typeof(Order))
        {
            query = query.Cast<Order>()
                .Where(order => order.Customer.EmailAddress == user.Identity.Name);
        }
    }
    return query;
}
```

Notice that the main `GetQuery` still calls the new `GetQueryable`, which keeps the foreign key and other templates respecting the row-level security rules it implements. But now you can modify the dynamic page templates to also call it from the `QueryCreated` event handlers. For example, in the List page template, you need to modify markup of the `EntityDataSource` control and hook up the event handler, like so:

```
<asp:EntityDataSource ID="dataSource" runat="server"
    EnableFlattening="false"
    OnQueryCreated="DataSource_QueryCreated"/>
```

As you might recall from the discussion of filter templates in Chapter 5, "Filter Templates," the `QueryCreated` event handler receives a `QueryCreatedEventArgs` object as its second parameter. Through this object's `Query` property, you can get the original

IQueryable object created by the data source control as well as replace it with a new one you create. The following code snippet shows how to take advantage of the event argument, call the new GetQueryable method defined by the UnleashedMetaModel, and replace the original query object with the one it returns.

```
public partial class List : Page
{
  protected UnleashedMetaTable table;
  // ...
  protected void DataSource_QueryCreated(
    object sender, QueryCreatedEventArgs e)
  {
    e.Query = this.table.GetQueryable(e.Query);
  }
}
```

Figure 14.9 shows the Orders list page after making this change. You can tell that the page only shows the current user's own orders by looking at the Ship Name column, which displays the name of her company, *Alfreds Futterkiste*, which is also the only customer shown in the Customer filter drop-down.

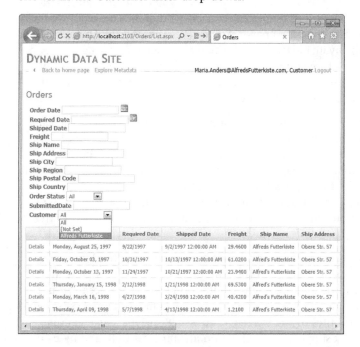

FIGURE 14.9 Orders List Page with row-level security applied.

To finish implementing the row-level security for read access, you need to implement a similar change in the Edit, Delete, and Details page templates. The process is identical—create a QueryCreated event handler for the EntityDataSource control and have it call the `GetQueryable` method of the `UnleashedMetaTable` class associated with the page. The same code samples are not repeated here; you can find the complete details in the sample project accompanying this book.

> **NOTE**
>
> The page in Figure 14.9 does not display the grid columns and filters for the Employee foreign key column of the Orders table. This is a result of the entity-level authorization rules implemented by overriding the `CanRead` method of the `MetaTable` class discussed earlier. In this example, the `CanRead` method allows reading Employee entity information only to users in the Employee *role*. Combined with the row-level filtering just implemented, the entity- and action-level authorization gives you the ability to create a search page that is both dynamic and secure at the same time.

Security Annotations

To recap what has been discussed so far in this chapter, Dynamic Data offers two major methods for implementing security. With Web configuration, you can define authorization rules on per-entity and per-action basis and reject users who do not have appropriate permissions to access dynamically generated pages. You can also extend the Dynamic Data metadata API by overriding the available `CanRead`, `CanInsert`, `CanUpdate`, `CanDelete`, and `GetQuery` methods. Unlike the web configuration alone, extending the meta model not only prevents unauthorized access, but also performs UI trimming and hides information and commands the users are not authorized to see.

Extending the metadata is clearly a superior way to implement security in Dynamic Data web applications. However, real-world applications usually have a substantial number of non-dynamic pages, implemented with ASP.NET WebForms or MVC. Any authorization rules hard-coded into the custom `CanRead`, `GetQuery`, and other methods of the `MetaTable` class are not useful to the rest of the application. On the other hand, implementing authorization with web configuration does not allow you to take full advantage of the Dynamic Data framework and pushes you to developing custom pages much earlier than you might want.

This tradeoff is not unique to security. You face a similar dilemma when implementing business rules; you can solve this problem with the help of *data annotations*—general-purpose .NET attributes that can be used by any presentation layer. As you recall from the discussion in Chapter 8, "Implementing Entity Validation," Dynamic Data makes heavy use of validation and other attributes in the `System.ComponentModel.DataAnnotations` namespace. The MVC framework supports the validation attributes as well, and by using them, you can implement business rules in a way that works with both. Moreover, by extending the Entity Framework's `ObjectContext`, NorthwindEntities class in this example, you can extend these benefits to all applications that might need to access the Northwind database.

By defining authorization rules and row-level security as data annotation attributes applied to entity classes, you can implement a security system that is independent of the specific presentation framework and equally useful in Dynamic Data as well as traditional web pages of the application. Although no built-in attributes enable you to accomplish this task, creating custom attributes is not difficult. In this section, you learn about two custom attributes from the sample solution that comes with this book—AuthorizationAttribute and CustomQueryAttribute—and how the Dynamic Data and Entity Framework can be extended to take advantage of them.

NOTE

The accompanying sample solution illustrates the security annotations discussed here to implement different levels of access to the Northwind Traders website. You might want to refer to the running application while reading this section.

The web application uses Forms authentication and defines three roles the users might have: Customer, Employee, and Manager. Visitors can log in by clicking the "Login" link in the upper-right corner of any web page. The login page lists several sample user accounts that can be used to access the application in different roles.

The *unauthenticated* site visitors can only see the "product catalog"—the dynamic web pages for the Product and Category entities. They cannot insert, update, or delete any entities. This is implemented by applying the AuthorizationAttribute to every entity class in the model and denying anonymous access to all entities with the exception of Product and Category. Only these two entity classes allow Read action for all users.

When logged in, the users in the *Customer* role can see not only the product catalog, but also their past orders and profile information—the Order and Customer entities. The CustomQueryAttribute is used with both of these entities to implement row-level security. Even though Northwind Traders application assigns an employee for each order, customers cannot access this information because they have no read access to the Employee entity. Customers cannot modify any information.

Users in the *Employee* role can read all entities in the model; however, they can only change the Customer, Order, and Order_Detail entities. Only the users in the *Manager* role can perform all actions—Read, Insert, Update, and Delete for all entities in the model.

AuthorizationAttribute

AuthorizationAttribute is a custom .NET attribute you find in the Unleashed.DataAnnotations project of the sample solution accompanying this book. It enables you to define authorization rules for a given entity class or its actions similar to how you would normally do it in the web configuration file. As you recall from the earlier discussion in this chapter, here is how to configure security to allow only users in Manager or Employee roles to access the dynamic Suppliers pages in the sample application:

14

```
<location path="SUPPLIERS">
  <system.web>
    <authorization>
      <allow roles="Manager, Employee"/>
      <deny users="*"/>
    </authorization>
  </system.web>
</location>
```

You can define the same authorization rules by applying the `AuthorizationAttribute` to the Supplier entity class, as shown here:

```
[Authorization(
  Allow.Roles, "Manager", "Employee",
  Deny.Users, "*")]
partial class Supplier  { ... }
```

The `AuthorizationAttribute` constructor takes an open array of parameters, which can be used to define one or more authorization rules. Rules start with values from one of the two enumerated types—`Allow` or `Deny`, both of which have the same two items defined, `Roles` and `Users`. In other words, the rules begin with `Allow.Users`, `Allow.Roles`, `Deny.Users`, or `Deny.Roles`, followed by one or more strings that specify names of users or roles, respectively. This allows you to mimic the web configuration rules such as `<allow roles="…"/>` with C# code that looks like this: `Allow.Roles, "…"`. Although this is not a requirement, by convention, you place different rules on different lines of code to make the rules easier to read.

> **NOTE**
>
> Only one instance of the `AuthorizationAttribute` is allowed per class. Having to define multiple authorization rules in a single attribute is not ideal. It would be much cleaner if you could define authorization rules with separate `Allow` and `Deny` attributes, similar to this:
>
> ```
> [Allow(Roles = "Manager, Employee")]
> [Deny(Users = "*")]
> partial class Supplier  { ... }
> ```
>
> Unfortunately, the .NET runtime does not guarantee that the order of attributes retrieved via reflection match the order of attributes in code. In this example, the *Deny* attribute could have been returned first, which would deny access to all users.
>
> The .NET Framework also prevents attributes from having properties of user-defined types, which rules out the possibility of defining the authorization rules as custom Allow or Deny classes and using them similar to this:

```
[Authorization(
    new Allow(Roles = "Manager, Employee"),
    new Deny(Users = "*"))]
```

Without the ability to use multiple attributes and custom types, you are left only with the primitive types, like strings and enumerations, which can be used in constant expressions.

The `AuthorizationAttribute` also enables you to define action-level permissions by including one or more `Actions` in the rule. For instance, here is how to permit employees to access suppliers in Read-only mode while still giving the managers full access:

```
[Authorization(
    Allow.Roles, "Manager",
    Allow.Roles, "Employee", Actions.Read,
    Deny.Users, "*")]
partial class Supplier  { ... }
```

`Actions` is an enumerated type shown next. Notice that it represents a bit field, which enables you to specify multiple actions in the same rule using the bitwise or operator (| in C#). For instance, you could have allowed employees to read and update Suppliers by specifying actions as `Actions.Read | Actions.Update`. Unless an `Actions` value is specified in a rule explicitly, the `AuthorizationAttribute` assumes it to be `All`, which is why the rule just described gives managers permission to perform all actions and limits customers to read only access:

```
[Flags]
public enum Actions
{
    None = 0x00,
    Read = 0x01,
    Insert = 0x02,
    Update = 0x04,
    Delete = 0x08,
    All = Read | Insert | Update | Delete
}
```

As you can see, the `AuthorizationAttribute` enables you to express entity- and action-level permissions on per-*user* or per-*role* basis. The resulting annotations closely mimic the structure of the `<authorization>` configuration section with the exception of the `Actions` parameter, which is not available in the `<allow/>` and `<deny/>` elements. Although this difference may be confusing at first, the resulting definitions of authorization rules is much more compact than the typical web configuration needed for action-level rules due to the need to create separate `<location/>` sections for each action. Attribute-based authorization rules also allow you to change routing configuration without having to update the rules in web.config.

Now take a closer look at how this attribute is implemented and how it can be used to extend the Dynamic Data meta model:

```
[AttributeUsage(AttributeTargets.Class)]
public class AuthorizationAttribute : Attribute
{
  public AuthorizationAttribute(params object[] rules);
  public ReadOnlyCollection<AuthorizationRule> Rules { get; }
  public bool IsAuthorized(IPrincipal principal, Actions actions);
}
```

The main access point of the AuthorizationAttribute is the IsAuthorized method. It takes an IPrincipal object, which represents a user of the application, one or more Actions the user needs to perform, and returns a Boolean value that indicates if he is permitted to do it. Before evaluating the rules for the first time in a given attribute, the IsAuthorized method parses the open array of objects specified in the constructor into a collection of AuthorizationRule objects, exposed by the Rules property.

```
public class AuthorizationRule
{
  public bool Authorize { get; }
  public Actions Actions { get; }
  public ReadOnlyCollection<string> Roles { get; }
  public ReadOnlyCollection<string> Users { get; }
}
```

Although the main purpose of the AuthorizationRule class is to assist in rule evaluation, you might find it useful when implementing administrative functionality in your application. For instance, the metadata explorer built into the sample application uses it to display security information about entity types.

NOTE

To mimic the default behavior of the configuration-based authorization rules, the IsAuthorized method returns true unless one or more of the requested actions are explicitly denied by a matching rule. Just as discussed earlier in this chapter, it is important to include a wild-card *deny* rule after specifying all appropriate *allow* rules to prevent unauthorized access.

Implementing MetaTable Permission Methods with AuthorizationAttribute

You can take advantage of the AuthorizationAttribute when overriding the CanRead, CanInsert, CanUpdate, and CanDelete methods in your custom MetaTable class. Here is how the CanDelete method is implemented in the UnleashedMetaTable (which you can find in the Unleashed.DynamicData project of the sample solution accompanying this book):

```
public partial class UnleashedMetaTable : MetaTable
{
  private readonly AuthorizationAttribute authorizationAttribute;

  public UnleashedMetaTable(
    UnleashedMetaModel model, TableProvider provider)
    : base(model, provider)
  {
    this.authorizationAttribute = this.Attributes
      .OfType<AuthorizationAttribute>().FirstOrDefault();
  }

  private bool IsAuthorized(IPrincipal user, Actions actions)
  {
    if (this.authorizationAttribute == null) return true;
    return this.authorizationAttribute.IsAuthorized(user, actions);
  }

  public override bool CanDelete(IPrincipal user)
  {
    return base.CanDelete(user) && this.IsAuthorized(user, Actions.Delete);
  }
}
```

14

Notice how the `UnleashedMetaTable` constructor tries to find the `AuthorizationAttribute` that might be applied to the entity class this meta table object represents and stores it in the `authorizationAttribute` field. Performing this step only once, when the meta table object is created, is important to improve performance of the application as the permission methods can be called multiple times for each page request.

The `IsAuthorized` method is responsible for determining whether a given user is allowed to perform one or more `Actions`. This method is responsible for checking whether the entity class has the `AuthorizationAttribute` applied and if so, delegating the authorization to the attribute. If the entity class does not have the `AuthorizationAttribute`, the method assumes that all users are allowed to perform all actions for the entity and returns true. Although this might not be very secure, it is consistent with the behavior of authorization rules in the Web configuration file.

The overridden `CanDelete` method simply calls the inherited implementation and the `IsAuthorized` method and returns `true` if both of them return `true`. Implementation of the `CanInsert`, `CanUpdate`, and `CanRead` methods is very similar. They only differ in the `Actions` values they pass to the `IsAuthorized` method, for instance, the `CanRead` method uses the `Actions.Read` instead of the `Actions.Delete`.

```
public override bool CanRead(IPrincipal user)
{
  return base.CanRead(principal) && this.IsAuthorized(user, Actions.Read);
}
```

Implementation of the MetaTable permission methods is much shorter with the
AuthorizationAttribute than the initial implementation with hard-coded rules for multiple entities within a single method. Compare the last code snippet with the one here,
which you saw earlier in this chapter:

```
public override bool CanRead(IPrincipal principal)
{
  if (this.Name == "Products") return true;
  if (this.Name == "Categories") return true;
  return principal.IsInRole("Employee");
}
```

Of course, the code did not disappear; it simply moved from the meta model to the individual entity classes:

```
[Authorization(
  Allow.Roles, "Manager",
  Allow.Users, "*", Actions.Read,
  Deny.Users, "*")]
partial class Product { ... }
```

Although the security system with rules applied to entities is more verbose and not as
encapsulated, it is actually easier to maintain. With the centralized, hard-coded implementation, there is always a risk of affecting rules of unrelated entities with any change you
make, and the real-world implementation of security for an entity model of decent size
would be many times bigger and more complex than what we have in this sample.
However, the more important benefit is being able to enforce it consistently across
dynamic and regular web pages as well as other applications.

Extending ObjectContext to Authorize Insert, Update, and Delete Actions

You can extend the Entity Framework ObjectContext class to take advantage of the
AuthorizationAttribute and prevent unauthorized Insert, Update, and Delete actions.
Doing so enables you to enforce the same security rules in the *custom* pages of your web
application that are already enforced by the *dynamic* pages.

Back in Chapter 8, the UnleashedObjectContext base class was introduced to perform validation at the ObjectContext level. Because authorization logic is so similar to validation,
you can use the same approach to implement it. Specifically, the authorization needs to
happen in the overridden SaveChanges method of the ObjectContext class before the
inherited implementation is called to persist the changes. Here is how this looks in the
UnleashedObjectContext class in the sample project:

```
public override int SaveChanges(SaveOptions options)
{
   IEnumerable<ObjectStateEntry> stateEntries = this.ObjectStateManager
      .GetObjectStateEntries(ChangedEntityStates)
      .Where(stateEntry => !stateEntry.IsRelationship);

   foreach (ObjectStateEntry stateEntry in stateEntries)
      this.BeforeSaveChanges(stateEntry);

   return base.SaveChanges(options);
}
```

When the SaveChanges method is called, you could have multiple entities that were added, modified, and deleted. The modifications are stored in the ObjectContext but not saved in the database yet. The BeforeSaveChanges method ensures that each of these changes is valid according to the business rules defined by the entity type. Authorization, being a specialized form of business rules, fits this pattern as well and you can extend the code to perform it. Here is a new version of this method with the changes highlighted in bold font:

```
private void BeforeSaveChanges(ObjectStateEntry stateEntry)
{
   Authorize(stateEntry.Entity.GetType(),
     EntityStateToAction(stateEntry.State));

   var savable = stateEntry.Entity as ISavableObject;
   if (savable != null)
      savable.BeforeSave(stateEntry);

   if (stateEntry.State != EntityState.Deleted)
      this.Validate(stateEntry);
}
```

For each added, modified, or deleted entity, the BeforeSaveChanges method now calls the Authorize method, passing it the type of the entity and the action performed. Notice that the State property of the ObjectStateEntry defines the action performed on an entity as a value of the built-in enum type EntityState; however, the AuthorizationAttribute relies on the custom Actions enum type instead. To translate between the two types, you need a simple function, EntityStateToAction, shown here:

```
private static Actions EntityStateToAction(EntityState state)
{
   switch(state)
   {
      case EntityState.Added:    return Actions.Insert;
      case EntityState.Modified: return Actions.Update;
      case EntityState.Deleted:  return Actions.Delete;
```

```
      default: throw new ArgumentException("state");
    }
  }
```

The `Authorize` method is responsible for throwing `SecurityException` (a built-in exception class defined in the `System.Security` namespace) if the current user is not authorized to perform a given set of actions for the specified entity type. Here is how this method is implemented in the `UnleashedObjectContext` class:

```
private static void Authorize(Type entityType, Actions action)
{
  IPrincipal user = Thread.CurrentPrincipal;
  if (!IsAuthorized(user, entityType, action))
  {
    throw new SecurityException(string.Format(
      "User '{0}' is not authorized to {1} entities of type '{2}'",
      user.Identity.Name, action, entityType.Name));
  }
}
```

To obtain the `IPrincipal` object representing the current user of the application, the `Authorize` method relies on the static property of the `Thread` class called `CurrentPrincipal`. This is different from how you implemented the authorization logic in the dynamic page templates earlier. There, you used the `User` property of the `Page` class, and although the static `User` property of the `HttpContext` class would be a closer alternative, using the `Thread.CurrentPrincipal` in the UnleashedObjectContext avoids adding dependency on the ASP.NET to the business layer.

The `Authorize` method delegates the task of evaluating the authorization rules to the `IsAuthorized` method, which takes a user, an entity type, and a set of actions as parameters and returns a boolean value, which indicates whether the user is permitted to perform them. This method tries to find the `AuthorizationAttribute` that might be applied to the entity class and, if found, calls its `IsAuthorized` method to evaluate the authorization rules. If the `AuthorizationAttribute` cannot be found, `IsAuthorized` method returns true, following the ASP.NET convention of allowing access unless it is explicitly denied.

```
private static readonly ConcurrentDictionary<Type, AuthorizationAttribute>
  authorizationAttributes = new ConcurrentDictionary<Type,
    AuthorizationAttribute>();

private static bool IsAuthorized(IPrincipal user, Type entityType,
  Actions action)
{
  var authorizationAttribute = authorizationAttributes.GetOrAdd(
    entityType,
    type => TypeDescriptor.GetAttributes(type)
      .OfType<AuthorizationAttribute>().FirstOrDefault());
```

```
    return authorizationAttribute == null
      || authorizationAttribute.IsAuthorized(user, action);
}
```

In any performance-critical method, such as IsAuthorized, it is important to minimize the amount of reflection-based code executed repeatedly. This code relies on the TypeDescriptor API to locate the AuthorizationAttribute and, to minimize the performance impact, caches the search results in the static authorizationAttributes dictionary. When the AuthorizationAttribute for a given entity type has been located, next time it is retrieved from the dictionary, resulting in a much faster execution.

The IsAuthorized method can be executed by several different threads simultaneously, especially in a web application, and has to be thread-safe. To implement thread-safe caching, this code uses the ConcurrentDictionary type from the System.Collections.Concurrent namespace, which offers a specialized method GetOrAdd for safely retrieving an existing value from the dictionary or adding it if it does not exist. As its second parameter, this method takes a *function* that is executed if the dictionary does not contain a value for the given key; the value it returns is stored in the dictionary and returned to the caller of the GetOrAdd method. It is this anonymous function (this example uses the shorter *lambda* syntax to define it) where the code calls the TypeDescriptor.GetAttributes method to find the AuthorizationAttribute.

Extending ObjectContext to Enforce Read Permission

The SaveChanges method of the ObjectContext allows you to enforce only the Insert, Update, and Delete permissions. Because this method does not have to be called by code retrieving entities from the database, you cannot enforce the Read permission here. It is actually quite challenging to authorize the Read actions properly because there are so many different ways of reading the entity information. First, there is the straightforward access through the ObjectSet properties, which can be illustrated with code like this:

```
using (var context = new NorthwindEntities())
{
    var supplierInformation = context.Suppliers;
}
```

You can implement Read authorization for the Suppliers object set by changing implementation of its property. Here is the default implementation of the Suppliers property in the NorthwindEntities class generated by the built-in Entity Framework code generator, which was modified to call the Authorize method of the UnleashedObjectContext base class:

```
public ObjectSet<Supplier> Suppliers
{
    get
    {
        Authorize(typeof(Supplier), Actions.Read);
        if (_Suppliers == null)
```

```
            _Suppliers = base.CreateObjectSet<Supplier>("Suppliers");
        return _Suppliers;
    }
}
private ObjectSet<Supplier> _Suppliers;
```

Now the code in the first snippet peforms authorization check and throws a `SecurityException` when the application tries to access the `Suppliers` property and the current user does not have the permission to read it.

> **NOTE**
>
> You cannot change implementation of the entity set properties directly in the code generated by the Entity Designer without losing the changes the next time the code is regenerated. As discussed in Chapter 8, you need to replace the built-in generator with a T4-based template provided by the ADO.NET team and modify the template logic responsible for generating these properties.

Unfortunately (from the perspective of implementing security), you could also retrieve suppliers throught the `Products` object set, with the help of the `Supplier` navigation property:

```
using (var context = new NorthwindEntities())
{
    var supplierInformation = context.Products.Select(p => p.Supplier);
}
```

And if that weren't enough, you could also use projection and return supplier information in objects of an anonymous type:

```
using (var context = new NorthwindEntities())
{
    var supplierInformation = context.Products
        .Select(p => new { p.Supplier.CompanyName, p.Supplier.Address });
}
```

Code in the last two examples is compiled into LINQ expressions. You cannot inject the authorization logic by simply changing implementation of the `Supplier` navigation property of the Product entity because the property getter will not be called during query execution. At this time, you have to leave this problem unsolved because in the current version, the Entity Framework does not provide extensibility mechanisms that would allow implementing Read authorization in all possible scenarios.

CustomQueryAttribute

CustomQueryAttribute is another attribute you can find in the Unleashed.DataAnnotations project in the sample solution accompanying this book. It enables you to implement limited row-level security at the entity class level. The code snippet that follows illustrates how to use this attribute to allow users in Customer role to see only their own Customer records:

```
[CustomQuery(typeof(Customer), "GetQueryable")]
partial class Customer
{
  public static IQueryable GetQueryable(IQueryable query)
  {
    IPrincipal user = Thread.CurrentPrincipal;
    if (user.IsInRole("Customer"))
    {
      query = query.Cast<Customer>().Where(
        customer => customer.EmailAddress == user.Identity.Name);
    }
    return query;
  }
}
```

Similar to the built-in CustomValidationAttribute discussed in detail back in Chapter 8, the CustomQueryAttribute takes two parameters—name of a static "GetQueryable" method and the type where it is implemented. This method is similar to the GetQueryable method used by the dynamic filter templates and the GetQueryable method implemented in the UnleashedMetaTable class earlier. It takes an entity query as a parameter and modifies it based on the permissions of the current user. In this example, the GetQueryable method adds a where clause, filtering out customer records that the current user should not be able to access.

Implementation of the CustomQueryAttribute is quite simple. Aside from the constructor, the main API of this attribute is the GetQueryable method, which uses reflection to invoke the actual method specified in the arguments of the attribute's constructor:

```
[AttributeUsage(AttributeTargets.Class)]
public class CustomQueryAttribute: Attribute
{
  public CustomQueryAttribute(Type type, string method);
  public IQueryable GetQueryable(IQueryable source);
}
```

Implementing MetaTable.GetQuery with CustomQueryAttribute

You can take advantage of the CustomQueryAttribute when implementing the GetQuery method of the MetaTable class. The code snippet that follows illustrates how this was

done in the UnleashedMetaTable class in the Unleashed.DynamicData project of the
sample solution accompanying this book:

```csharp
public partial class UnleashedMetaTable : MetaTable
{
  private readonly CustomQueryAttribute customQueryAttribute;

  public UnleashedMetaTable(
    UnleashedMetaModel model, TableProvider provider)
    : base(model, provider)
  {
    this.customQueryAttribute = this.Attributes
      .OfType<CustomQueryAttribute>()
      .FirstOrDefault();
    // ...
  }

  public IQueryable GetQueryable(IQueryable query)
  {
    if (this.customQueryAttribute != null)
      query = this.customQueryAttribute.GetQueryable(query);
    return query;
  }

  public override IQueryable GetQuery(object context)
  {
    IQueryable baseQuery = base.GetQuery(context);
    IQueryable customQuery = this.GetQueryable(baseQuery);
    return customQuery;
  }
}
```

The overridden GetQuery method is the same as you left it in the discussion of implementing row-level security with the metadata API earlier in this chapter. However, the
constructor now tries to find the CustomQueryAttribute that might have been applied to
the entity class this meta table object represents and stores it in the read-only
customQueryAttribute field. The GetQueryable method of the UnleashedMetaTable uses
this field to call the method specified in the attribute (if any) and replaces the original
query with the object it returns.

NOTE

The new implementation of the GetQueryable method is significantly shorter than the
following version created earlier, which hard-coded the query logic directly:

```csharp
public IQueryable GetQueryable(IQueryable query)
{
    IPrincipal user = HttpContext.Current.User;
```

```
    if (user.IsInRole("Customer"))
    {
      if (this.EntityType == typeof(Customer))
      {
        query = query.Cast<Customer>()
          .Where(customer => customer.EmailAddress == user.Identity.Name);
      }
      else if (this.EntityType == typeof(Order))
      {
        query = query.Cast<Order>()
          .Where(order => order.Customer.EmailAddress == user.Identity.Name);
      }
    }
    return query;
}
```

Similar to how the AuthorizationAttribute simplified implementation of the CanRead, CanInsert, CanUpdate, and CanDelete methods, the CustomQueryAttribute made the GetQueryable implementation shorter by pushing the entity-specific logic out of the UnleashedMetaTable class, with similar trade-offs between encapsulation of security logic and entity logic.

Extending ObjectContext to Enforce Row-Level Security

Implementing row-level security in the ObjectContext presents the same challenge as the authorization of the Read operations—there are multiple ways to query a particular table, and the Entity Framework does not offer the extensibility points to intercept them all at this time. However, you can implement *limited* support for row-level security by modifying the LINQ queries generated by the strongly typed object sets. Here is how to modify implementation of the Customers object set property in the NorthwindEntities class:

```
public IObjectSet<Customer> Customers
{
  get
  {
    Authorize(typeof(Customer), Actions.Read);
    if (_Customers == null)
    {
      var original = base.CreateObjectSet<Customer>("Customers")
      _Customers = new FilteredObjectSet<Customer>(original);
    }
    return _Customers;
  }
}
private IObjectSet<Customer> _Customers;
```

14

Notice that the type of the Customers property is now the IObjectSet<T> interface and not the concrete class, ObjectSet<T>. The property getter no longer returns the built-in object created by the CreateObjectSet method provided by the Entity Framework. Instead, it returns an instance of the FilteredObjectSet, a custom class created to modify the default Customers query. This class reimplements the IObjectSet<T> interface by wrapping an original ObjectSet<T> instance, delegating most of the properties and methods to the original and augmenting the functionality of the IQueryable properties based on the CustomQueryAttribute. In other words, the FilteredObjectSet class implements the Decorator pattern to add row-level security to the built-in ObjectSet class. Listing 14.2 shows its entire source code with important areas highlighted in bold.

LISTING 14.2 FilteredObjectSet Implementation

```
using System;
using System.Collections;
using System.Collections.Generic;
using System.ComponentModel;
using System.Data.Objects;
using System.Linq;
using System.Linq.Expressions;
using Unleashed.DataAnnotations;

namespace DataModel
{
  public class FilteredObjectSet<T> : IObjectSet<T> where T : class
  {
    private static readonly CustomQueryAttribute customQueryAttribute =
      TypeDescriptor.GetAttributes(typeof(T))
      .OfType<CustomQueryAttribute>().FirstOrDefault();

    private readonly ObjectSet<T> original;

    public FilteredObjectSet(ObjectSet<T> original)
    {
      this.original = original;
    }

    public IEnumerator<T> GetEnumerator()
    {
      return ((IEnumerable<T>)this.original).GetEnumerator();
    }

    IEnumerator IEnumerable.GetEnumerator()
    {
      return this.GetEnumerator();
    }
```

```csharp
public Expression Expression
{
  get { return this.GetQueryable().Expression; }
}

public Type ElementType
{
  get { return this.GetQueryable().ElementType; }
}

public IQueryProvider Provider
{
  get { return this.GetQueryable().Provider; }
}

public void AddObject(T entity)
{
  this.original.AddObject(entity);
}

public void Attach(T entity)
{
  this.original.Attach(entity);
}

public void DeleteObject(T entity)
{
  this.original.DeleteObject(entity);
}

public void Detach(T entity)
{
  this.original.Detach(entity);
}

private IQueryable GetQueryable()
{
  if (customQueryAttribute == null) return this.original;
  return customQueryAttribute.GetQueryable(this.original);
}
  }
}
```

492   CHAPTER 14   Implementing Security

Notice that the `FilteredObjectSet` constructor takes the original `ObjectSet` instance as a parameter and stores it in the private field. Most of the properties and methods, such as `AddObject`, simply call the same method on the original instance. However, the `Expression`, `ElementType`, and `Provider` properties that implement the `IQueryable` interface are different; they also take into account the `CustomQueryAttribute` that might be applied to the entity type. Instead of delegating their implementation directly to the *original* `ObjectSet`, these properties delegate to the object returned by the `GetQueryable` method, which returns the *original* if the entity type has no `CustomQueryAttribute` or the modified query if it does.

> **NOTE**
>
> By having `FilteredObjectSet` class reimplement the `IObjectSet` interface instead of inheriting from the built-in `ObjectSet` class, you lose the ability to access some of the additional APIs the Entity Framework provides on top of the plain LINQ, such as the `Include` method discussed in Chapter 2, "Entity Framework." Although it is usually possible to work around the loss of this particular extension and others, you might find this approach impractical if your application uses them pervasively.

With the `FilteredObjectSet` implemented and the T4 template modified to generate object set properties based on it, you now have row-level security available in any application using the `NorthwindEntities` object context. For instance, the following pseudo-code returns just *one* Customer entity when the current user of the application is in the Customer role and *all* entities when the current user is a Manager or an Employee:

```
using (var context = new NorthwindEntities())
{
   var customers = context.Customers;
}
```

The automatic filtering will work with LINQ queries as well, so the following pseudo-code will not allow a customer from New York to access records of customers in London:

```
using (var context = new NorthwindEntities())
{
   var customers = context.Customers.Where(c => c.City == "London");
}
```

However, just like authorization of Read access discussed in the previous section, this limited implementation of row-level security can be circumvented by LINQ queries that do not use the Customers object set directly. Queries that return Customer information via navigation properties or projection allow unrestricted access, and if you plan to take advantage of this functionality in your applications, keep in mind you cannot rely on it exclusively.

> **NOTE**
>
> Changing the strongly typed object set properties to implement row-level security does not remove the need to handle QueryCreated event in dynamic page templates and call the GetQueryable method of the UnleashedMetaTable class. Unfortunately, the EntityDataSource control does not rely on ObjectSet properties of the generated ObjectContext classes, such as the NorthwindEntities in this sample project. Instead, it calls the CreateObjectSet method directly, bypassing any logic you might have in the property getters. Because this method is defined in ObjectContext class as nonvirtual, you cannot override it and have to resort to the event handlers and code-behind.

Summary

Dynamic Data offers several options for implementing security. Table scaffolding enables you to specify whether all or specific entities will be accessible for all users through the dynamically generated web pages. Route constraints can be used to specify not only the entities, but also the actions (the types of dynamic pages) that will be accessible. Neither of these two options alone is robust enough to allow implementing a true role-based security system. However, they can be used in combination with custom pages where security is enforced with standard ASP.NET capabilities, such as the authorization rules in web configuration files.

Web configuration files can be used to apply standard authorization rules to the dynamically generated URLs using the <location/> element. This approach enables you to specify flexible authorization rules for entities, actions, users, and roles. However, the resulting configuration is rather verbose and quickly reaches the volume where ongoing maintenance becomes difficult.

The metadata API provided by Dynamic Data includes security-focused methods that can be overridden to implement a fully featured authorization system based on entities, actions, users, and roles, plus limited support for row-level security. A significant advantage of using the security APIs is the ability to not only prevent unauthorized access to entire web pages, but also to perform UI trimming and hide inaccessible information and actions from dynamic pages as well.

Although the metadata API is the best way to implement security in Dynamic Data web pages, it is not directly applicable to the custom WebForms and MVC pages that most real-world applications still need to get the job done. With the help of *security annotations*, custom attributes similar to data annotations, you can define security rules that can be equally accessible from web pages based on Dynamic Data and other ASP.NET frameworks. You can also take it a step further and extend the Entity Framework's ObjectContext to support these security annotations and enable reuse of the same security rules in other types of applications as well.

Index

A

How can we make this index more useful? Email us at indexes@samspublishing.com

G–H

S

W–Z

informIT.com

InformIT is a brand of Pearson and the online presence for the world's leading technology publishers. It's your source for reliable and qualified content and knowledge, providing access to the top brands, authors, and contributors from the tech community.

✦Addison-Wesley   **Cisco Press**   EXAM/**CRAM**   **IBM** Press.   QUe˙   ◈ PRENTICE HALL   **SAMS** | Safari˙ Books Online

LearnIT at InformIT

Looking for a book, eBook, or training video on a new technology? Seeking timely and relevant information and tutorials? Looking for expert opinions, advice, and tips? **InformIT has the solution.**

- Learn about new releases and special promotions by subscribing to a wide variety of newsletters.
  Visit **informit.com/newsletters**.

- Access FREE podcasts from experts at **informit.com/podcasts**.

- Read the latest author articles and sample chapters at **informit.com/articles**.

- Access thousands of books and videos in the Safari Books Online digital library at **safari.informit.com**.

- Get tips from expert blogs at **informit.com/blogs**.

Visit **informit.com/learn** to discover all the ways you can access the hottest technology content.

Are You Part of the IT Crowd?

Connect with Pearson authors and editors via RSS feeds, Facebook, Twitter, YouTube, and more! Visit **informit.com/socialconnect**.

informIT.com THE TRUSTED TECHNOLOGY LEARNING SOURCE   PEARSON

✦Addison-Wesley   **Cisco Press**   EXAM/**CRAM**   **IBM** Press.   QUe˙   ◈ PRENTICE HALL   **SAMS** | Safari˙ Books Online

UNLEASHED

Unleashed takes you beyond the basics, providing an exhaustive, technically sophisticated reference for professionals who need to exploit a technology to its fullest potential. It's the best resource for practical advice from the experts and the most in-depth coverage of the latest technologies.

informit.com/unleashed

Microsoft Visual Studio LightSwitch Unleashed
ISBN-13: 9780672335532

OTHER UNLEASHED TITLES

Microsoft Dynamics CRM 4 Integration Unleashed
ISBN-13: 9780672330544

Microsoft Exchange Server 2010 Unleashed
ISBN-13: 9780672330469

WPF Control Development Unleashed
ISBN-13: 9780672330339

Microsoft SQL Server 2008 Reporting Services Unleashed
ISBN-13: 9780672330261

ASP.NET MVC Framework Unleashed
ISBN-13: 9780672329982

SAP Implementation Unleashed
ISBN-13: 9780672330049

Microsoft XNA Game Studio 3.0 Unleashed
ISBN-13: 9780672330223

Microsoft SQL Server 2008 Integration Services Unleashed
ISBN-13: 9780672330322

WPF 4 Unleashed
ISBN-13: 9780672331190

Microsoft SQL Server 2008 Integration Services Unleashed
ISBN-13: 9780672330322

Microsoft SQL Server 2008 Analysis Services Unleashed
ISBN-13: 9780672330018

ASP.NET 3.5 AJAX Unleashed
ISBN-13: 9780672329739

Windows PowerShell Unleashed
ISBN-13: 9780672329883

Windows Small Business Server 2008 Unleashed
ISBN-13: 9780672329579

Microsoft Visual Studio 2010 Unleashed
ISBN-13: 9780672330810

Visual Basic 2010 Unleashed
ISBN-13: 9780672331008

C# 4.0 Unleashed
ISBN-13: 9780672330797

ASP.NET 4.0 Unleashed
ISBN-13: 9780672331121

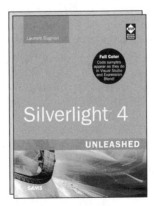

Silverlight 4 Unleashed
ISBN-13: 9780672333361

informit.com/sams

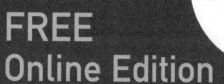

FREE
Online Edition

Your purchase of **ASP.NET Dynamic Data** includes access to a free online edition for 45 days through the **Safari Books Online** subscription service. Nearly every Sams book is available online through **Safari Books Online**, along with thousands of books and videos from publishers such as Addison-Wesley Professional, Cisco Press, Exam Cram, IBM Press, O'Reilly Media, Prentice Hall, Que, and VMware Press.

Safari Books Online is a digital library providing searchable, on-demand access to thousands of technology, digital media, and professional development books and videos from leading publishers. With one monthly or yearly subscription price, you get unlimited access to learning tools and information on topics including mobile app and software development, tips and tricks on using your favorite gadgets, networking, project management, graphic design, and much more.

Activate your FREE Online Edition at
informit.com/safarifree

STEP 1:   Enter the coupon code: IVYHEBI.

STEP 2:   New Safari users, complete the brief registration form.
           Safari subscribers, just log in.

If you have difficulty registering on Safari or accessing the online edition,
please e-mail customer-service@safaribooksonline.com